CHESS SECRETS

Great Attackers

Colin Crouch

EVERYMAN CHESS

www.everymanchess.com

First published in 2009 by Gloucester Publishers plc (formerly Everyman Publishers plc), Northburgh House, 10 Northburgh Street, London EC1V 0AT

British Library Cataloguing-in-Publication Data
A catalogue record for this book is available from the British Library.

ISBN: 978 1 85744 579 4

Distributed in North America by The Globe Pequot Press, P.O Box 480, 246 Goose Lane, Guilford, CT 06437-0480.

All other sales enquiries should be directed to Everyman Chess, Northburgh House, 10 Northburgh Street, London EC1V 0AT
tel: 020 7253 7887 fax: 020 7490 3708
email: info@everymanchess.com; website: www.everymanchess.com

EVERYMAN CHESS SERIES
Chief advisor: Byron Jacobs
Commissioning editor: John Emms
Assistant editor: Richard Palliser

Typeset and edited by First Rank Publishing, Brighton.
Cover design by Horatio Monteverde.
Printed and bound in the UK by Clays, Bungay, Suffolk.

Contents

Bibliography

Books

Best Chess Games 1970-1980, Jonathan Speelman (Allen & Unwin 1982)

Fighting Chess: My Games and Career, Garry Kasparov (Batsford 1983)

Garry Kasparov's Greatest Chess Games, Volume 1, Igor Stohl (Gambit 2005)

Gary Kasparov: My Games, edited Marvin & Klaric (Batsford 1983)

Le Tournoi International d'Échecs, Montréal 1979, Gilles Brodeur, Pierre Jodoin, Jacques Labelle, Pierre Lemyre & Kevin Spraggett (Guérin 1979)

Leonid Stein: Master of Attack, Raymond Keene (TUI Enterprises 1988)

Leonid Stein: Master of Risk Strategy, Eduard Gufeld & Efim Lazarev (Thinkers' Press 2001)

Mikhail Tal: Tactical Genius, Alexander Raetsky & Maxim Chetverik (Everyman Chess 2004)

My Great Predecessors, Part II, Garry Kasparov (Everyman Chess 2003)

My Great Predecessors: Part III, Garry Kasparov (Everyman Chess 2004)

The Art of Chess Analysis, Jan Timman (RHM 1980)

The Magic of Mikhail Tal, Joe Gallagher (Everyman Chess 2000)

The Soviet Championships, Bernard Cafferty & Mark Taimanov (Cadogan 1998)

The Test of Time, Garry Kasparov (Pergamon 1986)

The World's Greatest Chess Games, Graham Burgess, John Nunn & John Emms (Robinson 1998)

Periodicals & computers

Informator

ChessBase and *Fritz*

Preface

It has been several years since I last wrote a full-length book, on *How to Defend in Chess*, based on the games of Lasker and Petrosian. I am now writing on the attack, on games by Tal, Kasparov and Stein, and in some respects there is a similarity in format.

This is in part accidental, as a serious illness, including partial loss of sight, has made it difficult for me to contemplate until now writing a full-length book.

In my book on Lasker and Petrosian, I worked without computer analysis. I wanted to see what the great World Champions would have been able to think about over the board, and also I wanted to work on my own playing strength. In addition, I did not like the idea of an anachronistic arrogance, trying to pretend that, with a few clicks on the computer, any ordinary player can have the authority of a world champion. Naturally there were going to be mistakes, but at least they were, I hope, honest mistakes, and I felt reasonably confident that I was adding something to each game.

These days, with my mind slowing down through brain damage, I no longer quite trust my analysis with my own head. It has forced me to reconsider my thoughts about the role of the computer and the human in chess analysis. I have found that the use of computer analysis is just as time-consuming as traditional analysis, but that more variations can be covered in a given time. Probably there will be serious mistakes in my analysis, but these are now more likely to occur at move 10 in a variation rather than move 3. Most of the time, this would be beyond the horizon for practical players.

I also need to add a small point. Just after my stroke, I was close to being blind, and I could not read. It is still difficult to cover large texts. Meanwhile, the multi-volume collection by Kasparov has been published. My eyesight is gradually improving, and I hope very much to go through Kasparov's comments and analysis in detail, for pleasure and information. But this is for the future. For my own book, I have covered only two games annotated by Kasparov, on Tal versus Spassky and Velimirovic, and some of Kasparov's notes on Stein. Mostly, though, I have written this book as if it were, in effect, written in 2002. So please do not regard any comments on history as definitive.

My thanks to my mother, for her understanding and company when suddenly I encountered a life-threatening illness. Also, my club colleagues, particularly from Harrow, the Braille Chess Association, and Drunken Knights, and, at an early stage of my recovery process, the encouragement I received from Hilsmark Kingfisher.

Colin Crouch
Harrow Weald
London, 2009

Introduction

I was asked by my editor John Emms to write a book on attack, on those who inspired and influenced me. That was easy. Although Garry Kasparov was almost a decade younger than me, he was still the player I wanted to learn from in the early 1980s, when I started to make a serious attempt at playing chess, possibly somewhat belatedly in life. Kasparov's play seemed superbly original and dynamic, and I was waiting to see what sort of strength he would aspire to, and indeed how quickly.

Remembering further, Tal's performance at Montreal 1979 was a great comeback. Tal, it seemed, was revitalized, playing the sort of audacious attacking chess that we learned from the time he became a youthful World Champion, but adding to that the maturity of age. For a glorious moment, the Tal of yesteryear had returned. Ill-health had long dogged his chess-play, and he was no doubt wanting to show, proba-

bly for one last time, what he was able to achieve.

Then the 46th Soviet Championship, Tbilisi 1978, must surely be one of the momentous tournaments in recent chess history. It was the case of the king and the apprentice, both Tal and Kasparov being inspired by each other, and Tal being encouraged by the thought of the new style of chess.

But there is another great attacking player, Leonid Stein (1934-73), who died just as he was about to play for the Soviet Union in the European Team Championships. He was still competing at very high level, therefore, and he was saying that perhaps this time it was a chance to end up higher in the World Championship. It was not to be.

Stein was three-times Soviet Champion, in 1963 (after a play-off against Spassky and Kholmov), and in 1965 and 1966, a splendidly consistent result against world-class grandmasters. He also had reasonable success in the Interzonal phases of the World Championship, but he was not quite successful enough, and he was also a victim of a ruling limiting the number of players from each country who could qualify for the next Candidates' stage. In the play-off at the end of the 1962 Stockholm Interzonal, the winner of the 6= players, Stein, Benko and Gligoric, would qualify for the next stages, except that only Benko or Gligoric were eligible to qualify. Stein "won" the event, but Benko qualified, and made only a slight impact in the Candidates' at Curacao 1962.

This latter event, won by Petrosian, was notable also for Tal's first widely publicized serious illness, with kidney problems. Only four years earlier, Tal won the previous Candidates' event (Bled 1959) in great style, gaining the opportunity to play a match against the World Champion, Botvinnik. He won in 1960, at the age of 24. Then Botvinnik won the return in 1961, with Tal suffering from the early stages of his kidney illness; and in Curacao 1962, he was unable to play the last seven games.

Tal was still a great player, and in isolated games he was absolutely brilliant, but he never quite reached his potential. It was Kasparov, another World Champion in his early twenties, who showed what Tal might have achieved, had he been in better health.

Stein, too, had his health problems, in that he died young. There were perhaps some slight indications that he was making a few unforced errors in his final year, but really this would not have been noticed at the time. He was still at the top of his form, or very close to it. The one genuinely noticeable aspect of his play in the final couple of years was that he was playing much sharper chess, particularly against top level opponents. The games against Smyslov and Karpov, at the 1972 Spartakiad, were clear indications of a direct aim for an attack. Stein must clearly have wanted to become World Champion, but time was not on his side. Coming equal first with Karpov at the 1971 Alekhine Memorial in Moscow was a great achievement, but Karpov was young and still improving and, if anything, an even more solid performer. Stein had to move fast.

Maybe there is something to be said for providing a collection of Stein's attacking games from the mid-60s, but for better or worse, the author wanted to provide a collection of games from the 70s or very early 80s and Stein's final year was definitely of interest. In terms of style of play, the reader will quickly recognize that Stein was very much a sound and solid positional player, even when playing for the attack. Given the opportunity, he could, however, play extremely sharply, and if his opponent occasionally made a slight mistake in the opening, then he would hit hard.

Tal and Kasparov were much more aggressive sacrificers, but aggression in chess means the taking of further risks. Tal was the greatest exponent of piece sacrifices in chess, finding a way of opening up incalculable games from seemingly the quietest positions. If one analyses a Tal game, especially with the help of the computer, it will often be demonstrated that with accurate play, Tal should have lost, but in the meantime his opponent has lost, and Tal has moved on to the next game.

Kasparov's speciality, certainly in his earlier years, was the pawn sacrifice, and more specifically the central pawn sacrifice. He was a dauntingly heavy hitter with White, scoring around 80% throughout his career, against all recorded opponents. This indicates both excellent theoretical preparation and the ability to attack ruthlessly when he has found a weakness. Tal's score with White was around 70%, still admirably high, but considerably below Kasparov's score. Imagine Tal, with his imaginative chess ideas, alongside Kasparov's relentless preparation, and this is indeed formidable. Of course Kasparov was as talented as Tal, and he had good health on his side.

Games by three attackers
If I were to choose a favourite game by each of these players in this 1970s (or early 1980s) selection, I would probably pick:

1) Stein's win with Black against Ljubojevic. Normally readers might well skip over, what is in effect, a quick win in a dozen moves, followed by a desperate attempt to avoid resignation, on the argument that the loser's opponent must surely have made some dreadful mistake, and really it is more interesting to play through a well-matched game.

But look at it the other way round, and just try to imagine how Stein, against an almost world-class opponent, could find the ingenuity to produce a 12-move win. It takes a mixture of delicate thinking and a powerful thud to win so quickly.

2) Tal's win against Velimirovic, a magnificently wild piece sacrifice. Over the years, I suppose I have spent a month analysing this game, and still I find it almost incomprehensibly difficult to grasp. Possibly Tal's play was over-optimistic, and he could instead have gone for a slight positional edge, while Velimirovic had rejected a reasonable repetition, and later he could have played for more. But does it matter? Chess in the end is for real live games, and if the opponent cannot find the right moves over the board, then the player has every right to win.

3) Kasparov's win against Pribyl is attractive and, on closer analysis, is much deeper than it looks. Kasparov shows his ability to set up a raging attack with the white pieces, and to carry the attack through with sacrifices, if required. There are plenty of other Kasparov games, but why is this one special? If we go through all the buried subvariations, we find just about the perfect attack, starting off from gambit play in the opening, through a sharp sacrificial attack with plenty of cut and thrust, and even ending up in a delicate king and pawn endgame. It would seem, from his commentary, that Kasparov did not see all this wonderful line, but does this really count as a de-

fect? The human player is incapable of seeing everything in advance with total accuracy, and has to try to readapt with every move, every slightly unexpected variation. We can feel reasonably confident that, had Pribyl's best line been played, Kasparov would have had the flexibility to aim directly for the win.

Three games, three different ways of starting an attack. Learn and enjoy.

Before plunging into the games presented here, it is worth considering the difference between classical positional play and tactical attacking play. Positional play depends on clear and logical thought processes, which give the opportunity, if the player makes no serious error, of aiming either for safety, or, if the opponent makes a mistake, for an advantage.

If a player calculates a winning sacrifice three moves later, this is regarded as simply a positional sacrifice, not an attack. Everything is under control, and the rest is a matter of technique. For the reader, I emphasize that it is best, if possible, to play positionally. If the opponent makes any sort of mistake, then jump on it, and do not aim for pretty effects. It is only in a minority of games that sacrificial play is effective.

If we go through the three games noted above, the Stein win is not really a sacrificial attack, as if Ljubojevic were to try to take the piece, he would lose the queen, through simple calculation. Stein played it superbly, but he was not taking any sort of risk, he was simply play-

ing good and creative positional chess.

This is in contrast with the Tal-Velimirovic and Kasparov-Pribyl games, where the attacker is genuinely taking risks. In the win against Pribyl, it turns out that Kasparov's moves were good, even under close analysis, and this makes the game particularly impressive. In many of the other games in this collection, objectively Kasparov had overpressed, and likewise Tal. So why could they not cut out risky play when they were capable of sound positional chess? We will start by considering a few first principles:

Attack for beginners – and the start of positional attack

"I want to beat my opponent. I want to win this. I want to play better than anyone".

Who, as a junior starting the game, has not thought like this? If you can play better than your opponent, then you will win. Obvious, isn't it? One nine-year-old player will beat another nine-year-old player, and the winner takes the glory, but next time round, the winner of that game might well lose to a good ten-year-old, who in turn might lose to a twelve-year-old, who perhaps has played in serious events, maybe even against adults, and so on.

Sooner or later, though, the concept of scientific chess will start to kick in. The number one principle of scientific chess is that a player cannot lose if he or she makes no mistakes. Play through several of the wildest games in this selection, and quite often you will find that the most interesting lines will end up as a perpetual, or maybe a level endgame, or a draw of a different kind. This is no accident; this is to be expected, under the central principle of scientific chess. If neither player has a clear advantage, then if both players play completely accurately, the result is a draw, however fiercely the attacker may press, and however resiliently the defender grabs pawns and other concessions.

An attack, therefore, does not automatically mean a win. Indeed, if the attacker makes even the slightest mistake, the defender has the opportunity of aiming for an advantage in reply. This is especially so if the intending attacker was already no better anyway. The old positional principles still apply. Develop first, then you can think about an attack. If your opponent makes a mistake, then concentrate on exploiting that mistake. If your opponent's pawn structure is weak, then make pressure there. Most of the time, there is no real advantage on attacking a well-covered king.

What happens, though, if you feel there is a possible slight weakness in your opponent's position, but that with normal quiet play you judge that you cannot play for more than equality, or the normal slight edge, gradually ending up as a draw? Quite often the position is imbalanced, and if one were to try deep analysis, maybe with the help of the computer, it would turn out that the likely result is a draw. Even so, the player has every right to consider trying for an advantage, trying for a win. Concentrate on an incipient weakness, press

hard, and if your opponent cannot, under pressure, find the best moves, then you are on the way to an attack.

Quite often, in an asymmetrical position, your opponent can attack in return. Do not be disconcerted. It is normal for one player to attack on one side of the board, the kingside or the queenside, while the opponent attacks on the other side of the board. Quite often the natural result is a draw. Maybe the play is extremely complicated, and one cannot possibly expect that a quiet draw will be the outcome. The golden rule, however, is that a player cannot lose a game unless there is a mistake.

Nearly every game in this book is a win, either by the attacker or after sharp defence by the counter-attacker. Read closely through the notes, however, and you will find that quite often the game should end up as a draw, maybe with a perpetual check, or maybe after sacrifice and counter-sacrifice, just fizzling out to a draw. The defender will often need considerable nervous strength when under attack, and quite often the attacker wins.

So we are beginning to see an answer to the problem of how to play for a win. It is genuinely positionally acceptable to aim for a win and to create pressure. If in your attack you do not make a mistake, you will not lose.

Gambit, gamble and sacrifice
The next stage is more controversial. If a player attacks with extreme accuracy, then the defender has no chances of a win. With accurate play, often beyond

the abilities of a defender, the result will be equal. With any inaccuracy by the defender the result will be a loss.

In most of the games in this selection, however, it will be found that, with best play, the defender would have had an advantage, maybe even a winning advantage. Therefore, strictly speaking, Tal and Kasparov have made serious errors in many of these memorable games. Kasparov, in his World Championship matches against Karpov, found that his aggressive play did not work early on, so he had to limit his attacking intentions, and did so successfully.

An enterprising and entertaining attack will have an element of uncertainty. When there is a sacrifice involved, giving up pieces or pawns with the aim of setting up a big winning attack, the uncertainty is extreme. If the sacrificer does not create a successful win, he is likely to lose. Often there is no middle path.

It is doubtful that an attacker will deliberately aim for a losing position. There is the exception, the "cheapo", when a player recognizes that he has a poor position. Instead of giving up the struggle, he mixes things up, giving the opponent a small chance of missing something and making a blunder. We are dealing with something different here though.

Imagine a position is about equal, but one player sees the chance of trying for an edge. It is going to be very tactical, inevitably so if a sacrifice is involved, but the confident and optimistic player will tend to assume that after a sacrifice, a gambit, he has the better chances, maybe because he thinks his position is genuinely better, or maybe because he has the feeling that at some stage the opponent will make a mistake. If the attacker does not make the sacrifice, then the position may well dwindle to equality.

Then the gambler's instinct kicks in. He looks at his position, and then looks closely at his opponent, trying to work out whether his opponent will be disconcerted by the attack, or whether he will be rock-solid. He decides to take a punt, and if he has judged the psychological state of the game correctly, he will win. If the position over the board is inappropriate, then OK, he is unlucky, but in the long run a bold attack will often lead to success.

When writing this, I have in mind Tal, rather than the young Kasparov. Tal would genuinely gamble. Kasparov, in his younger years, would have had the confidence of youth: that all his ideas, however outrageously fanciful, are good ideas.

For the reader

We could expand these arguments further, but it is time for the reader to play through some actual chess.

The games in this book are all highly complicated, probably much more so than in strategic or positional duels. To see what is going on in a highly tactical game, thorough analysis is required. Just saying "I think Black has a little bit of compensation for his sacrifice" is not enough. The analyst must delve deeper, and must hope that the reader will be entertained and informed about what is happening.

Some readers might enjoy going through everything at Black's 12th, then play through a page on White's 13th, and then examine Black's reply, and so on. Please remember, though, that few analysts will work like this. Instead, play through the games first, perhaps noting the verbal comments in order to gain an impression of the structure of the game, and just enjoy Tal's moves, or Kasparov's moves, or Stein's moves. Then go back again, think which moves seem interesting to you, and study them in greater depth. This, after all, would be the way I go through them myself.

Enjoy the games.

Chapter One

Garry Kasparov 1975-1978:
His Early Years – Before *The Test of Time*

Kasparov's early chess autobiography, *The Test of Time*, kicks off in 1978, when he was already at grandmaster level. This section of the book comes from his earlier years. In no sense is this a biography; it is just a selection of a few games, and it is concentrated on attack and sacrifice.

Garry Kasparov was born in Baku in Azerbaijan, on 13th April 1963, on the outskirts of the Soviet Union. Effectively, this was the Soviet part of the middle east, with Iran bordering on the south, and the Caucasus mountains a barrier to the north. There were also large seas to the west and the east. Kasparov's father was Jewish, and his mother Armenian, something of an outsider in ethnic terms, both in the USSR and, more specifically, in Azerbaijan. Later on, after the break-up of the Soviet Union, he had to move his family quickly out of Baku; and much later he was heavily involved in Russian politics, in opposition to Vladimir Putin.

One cannot quite avoid the question of ethnicity in the old Soviet Union, particularly when there was a one-party state covering the northern and eastern parts of two continents. The Soviet domination of chess was such that, since the Second World War, every World Champion before Fischer was part of the USSR; but none of these was pure Russian. When the young Karpov was shown to be an extraordinarily promising player, at the end of the 60s and in the early 70s, many in officialdom were relieved that there was going to be a real Russian as World Champion. Similarly, there would have been consternation in some political quarters when Kasparov, twelve years younger, was going to be a clear threat to Karpov's domination, though Kasparov had his political sympathizers too.

Kasparov was destined to be controversial, in view of this background, and he also had and has a powerful personality. However, we can leave the political intricacies and intrigues aside, as it is his early *chess* career that we are going to consider here.

At the age of 12, Kasparov qualified for the Soviet under-18 Championship, a dauntingly strong event where it was *expected*, rather than merely hoped, that the participants would end up as very top grandmasters. He started well: a win in the first round being followed by another in round two against Andrei Sokolov, who at his peak qualified for the Candidates for the World Championship.

As so often with junior events, there can be some slightly substandard play, along with flashes of brilliance. Sacrifices on d5 in the Sicilian are almost routine with the knight, less so with the bishop, and quite rare with the rook. One can feel sure that the young Kasparov had already made his mark.

Game 1
G.Kasparov-A.Sokolov
USSR U-18 Championship,
Vilnius 1975
Sicilian Defence

---

1 e4 c5 2 ♘f3 ♘c6 3 d4 cxd4 4 ♘xd4 ♘f6 5 ♘c3 d6 6 ♗g5 e6 7 ♕d2 a6 8 0-0-0 ♗d7 9 f4 b5

Kasparov described this in *Fighting Chess* as "a popular but dubious system" for Black, when noting Kasparov-Panchenko, Daugavpils 1978. Certainly he has avoided this precise line as

Black by various means, mostly on earlier moves, preparing to castle kingside quickly.

He also experimented with 9...h6!? 10 ♗xf6 ♕xf6 11 ♘f3 ♕d8 12 g3 ♕c7 in H.Olafsson-G.Kasparov in a televised rapidplay game (won by Kasparov), Reykjavik 1995, in which Black castled queenside without weakening his pawn structure.

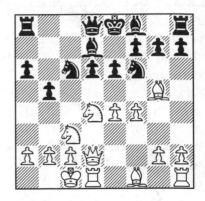

What, though, does Kasparov prefer as White?

10 a3

Kasparov found part of the answer in an even earlier game, G.Kasparov-A.Yermolinsky, Leningrad 1975, which continued 10 ♘xc6 ♗xc6 11 ♗d3 ♗e7 12 e5 dxe5 13 fxe5 ♘d7 14 ♗xe7 ♕xe7 15 ♗e4 ♕c5 16 ♖he1 ♖a7 17 ♗xc6 ♕xc6. However, he then played too passively with 18 ♕f2? ♕c5 19 ♖e3 0-0, soon losing his e-pawn without compensation. Kasparov himself gives 18 ♕g5 or 18 ♕d6 as slightly preferable for White.

If the reader is getting worried that there is starting to be a long theoretical preamble in what is supposed to be a book on attacking games, there is a reason: to introduce, briefly, another classic Kasparov brilliancy from his young years! See the supplementary game Kasparov-Panchenko, Daugavpils 1978 (Game 1.1). Kasparov had brushed up his opening between 1975 and 1978.

The future world champion was still young and was capable of making minor slips in the opening. He wants to avoid ...b5-b4, but the problem for White is that, later on, when Black has played his queen or rook to the b-file, Black will have chances of creating pressure against White's king.

Kasparov was well versed enough to avoid the positional trap 10 ♘xc6 ♗xc6 11 e5? dxe5 12 ♕xd8+ ♖xd8 13 ♖xd8+ ♚xd8 14 fxe5 h6 15 ♗h4 g5 with advantage to Black. White has fallen for this many times.

10...♗e7 11 ♗xf6 gxf6 12 f5 ♕b6 13 fxe6 fxe6 14 ♗e2 h5 15 ♘xc6 ♗xc6 16 ♖hf1

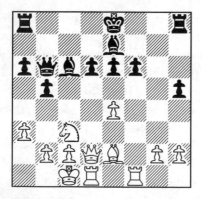

It would be over-analysing to attempt to study the last few moves in depth, given that the two players involved are juniors, and in Kasparov's case a very young junior. We know that both players will improve. Sokolov became World under-20 Champion in Copenhagen seven years later. In other words, this was a clash between two highly talented young juniors. Sokolov continued to improve, and qualified for the Candidates Matches in the late 1980s, beating Vaganian and Yusupov; but Karpov ground him down 7½-3½ in Linares 1987, and Sokolov never quite seemed to recover his confidence at the highest levels.

Back to the game, with both players very young at the time. Black has the bishop pair and, all other things being equal, should have prospects for a slight edge. Black's pawns look draughty, but provided they are well protected by pieces, and the king remains safe, he should be doing well. So far, White's attempts at attacking have led to nothing. This could change quickly if Black makes a mistake, but it is best not to rely on the opponent making a mistake.

A flick through with the computer might well give the reader the impression that 16 ♕d4 is the only good way of equalizing here, but after a queen exchange with 16...♕xd4 17 ♖xd4, Black's bishops may become even more dominant. One active plan is ...h5-h4, ...♚f7 and ...♖ag8, with obvious possibilities of pressure on the g-file.

16...0-0-0?!

This, however, is a clear positional error. Black was better; now it is only equal.

Think first of the rook. If it is

moved, where is its best back rank square? We are not saying that the rook must move immediately, but Black will need to decide on an option at some point. The rook is not doing much on d8, but there are active possibilities on either c8 or on b8. These squares would be preferable.

Now think of the king. If Black were to castle queenside, seeing as the rook's potential is not improved by going to d8, the only real justification would be to take the king from e8 to c8. The king, though, is safer in the centre than on the queenside. The pawns have formed a fortress around d6, e6 and f6, with the two bishops, in conjunction with the major pieces, helping to create a highly stable defensive structure. The king's position on c8 is less secure; if anything the king is getting in the way of the major pieces.

Instead, Black should have tried 16...b4! 17 axb4 ♛xb4 and it is White's king that is under pressure.

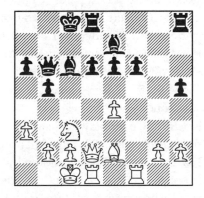

17 ♗f3 ♛c5

There is no real point in playing 17...b4 now. For the next few moves,

the players tack around, no pawn breaks being made, and no definable advantage in piece mobilization. Yet Kasparov, in a few moves time, suddenly opens up the game with a memorable sacrifice. How did this happen? We shall see.

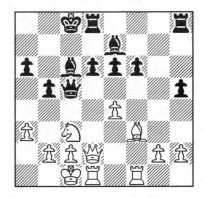

18 ♛e2

In analysing, I was at first critical of this move, on the basis that there is an obvious loss of tempo if White has then to play ♛f2. The assumption is that White could have organized his play better.

18 ♘a2 was my initially preferred option, with the idea of bringing the knight to b4, then to d3, but in retrospect simply 18...♛g5, exchanging the queens, is equal. This is presumably Kasparov wanted to avoid. After 19 ♛xg5 fxg5 20 ♘b4 ♗b7 21 e5?!, Black will take the initiative with 21...d5!.

The mysterious queen move is now explicable, but given the choice between dropping a tempo with the queen, or playing a quiet move with the king, away from any counterattacks, 18 ♔b1! looks more natural. If

Black now moves his queen to either e5 or g5, White has ♕f2, with gain of time in comparison with the main line. If instead 18...♔b7 or 18...♔b8, White keeps a slight edge with 19 ♘a2.

Tacticians may have noted that, after the white king move, if 18...b4 19 axb4 ♕xb4, White has a shot with 20 ♘d5!. It's good, but it is not an outright win: on 20...♕xd4 21 ♘xe7+ ♔d7 22 ♖xd2 ♔xe7 23 e5! ♗xf3 24 exf6+ ♔xf6 25 ♖xf3+ ♔e7 26 ♖a3 ♖a8, we have a double rook and pawn ending, with care required on both sides. White should have a slight edge, as Black has two isolated pawns, on the a- and h-flanks, and he has to be careful not to allow White to gain connected passed pawns.

As we go through this book, on attack and sacrifice, we will find many instances where sharp play suddenly ends up as a technical endgame. Be aware that all parts of the game are interconnected. In this book, I do not wish to concentrate on the endgame, but equally I do not wish to ignore it either. A century ago, a talented attacking player was reputed to have said that he was not interested in the endgame, as if he played well in the middlegame, his opponent will not last until the endgame anyway. Few now would believe that.

18...♕e5

Natural enough, but by no means the only possibility. Another thought would be to stop the white queen from taking over the g1-a7 diagonal.

There are many possibilities for Black here, and indeed for White in many of his positions. Not, though, 18...♔b7? 19 ♘d5! – a theme we have seen before, and will see again – as after 19...exd5 20 exd5 White is better. Instead, 18...♗f8!? is sensible, cutting out the idea we have just seen, and maybe equal.

19 ♕f2

With a justifiable loss of tempo. 19 g3 is an alternative, but then 19...h4 looks equal.

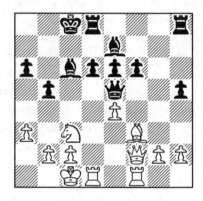

19...♔b7

Black keeps the white queen away from b6 or a7. Taking the h-pawn is foolhardy: 19...♕xh2? 20 ♕b6 ♗b7, and now there is a sacrifice in front of the barricades on a different square. After 21 e5! ♗xf3 22 ♖xf3 ♕xe5 23 ♕a7 ♗f8 24 ♘d5 exd5 25 ♖c3+ ♕xc3 26 bxc3, White should win.

Black may even have considered offering a draw with 19...♕c5, when if 20 ♕e2 ♕e5 repeats. Who would be in the position to try to play for an edge? Black's bishop pair is often more effective than bishop and knight in such positions, but only if the knight is kept quiet. Here, 20 ♘e2! ♕xf2 21 ♖xf2, followed by ♘d4, gives White an edge. Black's pawn on e6 will become weak, and if the pawn advances, the weaknesses will spread to d5 and f5.

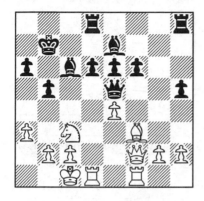

We have seen a couple of quiet, seemingly nondescript, moves, and the next couple of moves also appear to be quiet. Then suddenly there is a sensation: a rook sacrifice out of the blue. It is difficult to determine quite how far in advance Kasparov saw the sacrificial idea, other than the basic thought that sacrifices on d5 in the Sicilian are always in the air. The sacrifice does not work at the moment, but maybe in a few moves time, with constructive play, it will be a genuine option. If nothing else, the defender will have to adapt his play to cover any sacrificial attacks, and this cuts down his resources.

20 ♖fe1!

Kasparov would undoubtedly have seen the idea of the rook sacrifice by now. He was not merely overprotecting his pawn on e4, he was already looking at ideas with ♖d5. Sokolov in turn had either not seen it or, more likely, had seen it but not regarded it as significant.

It is important that ♖fe1 and g2-g3 had to be played before ♖d5, otherwise the sacrifice would not work. Which way round should Kasparov try it? 20 g3 is the more obvious move, covering the pawn on h2, and we would transpose to the main line if play continued 20...h4 21 ♖fe1 ♖c8. The critical point is that, in comparison with the actual game, Black would not play 21...♖c8 now, but would find another plan, maybe starting with 21...hxg3 22 hxg3 ♖dg8! (and not 22...♖c8? 23 ♖d5!). Black is then better, and it would be no consolation for White that he had found a fantastic sacrifice if it doesn't work.

Therefore Kasparov moves the rook first, after working out that he is not losing the pawn for nothing, and waits to see what happens.

20...♖c8

This is not yet even a mistake, and indeed it would be worrying if it were. Black merely has to be careful a little later.

20...♕xh2?!, on the other hand, would be doubtful and anti-positional. 21 ♘d5! ♗xd5 22 exd5 e5 23 ♗e4! leaves Black a pawn up, but he is worse, the white pieces being much more active. The opposite-coloured bishops help White here, as his bishop takes control of the light squares, while Black's bishop is hemmed in by his own pawns. Black's king is the more exposed, and there are chances later on with pawn breaks with a3-a4 or c2-c4. Overall, Black can do better than this.

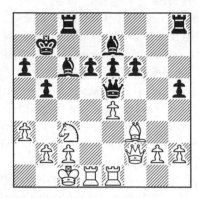

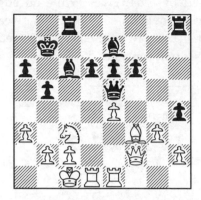

21 g3

Here, though, White must cover the pawn. The immediate 21 ♖d5? is premature, in view of 21...♕xh2!.

21...h4!?

Subjectively, this is a mistake, because it allows Sokolov to fall into positions where he is demonstrably unable to deal with Kasparov's fierce attack. Objectively, it is fine, since in the end Kasparov's imaginative sacrifice turns out not to be sound. As we go through more and more examples in this book, we find that many brilliant attacks are not quite sound, but tend to take the opponent out of his depth, and end up winning.

Fritz gives over a dozen possibilities for Black to try and equalize, and many of these seem good. Perhaps the simplest line is 21...♖h7, covering the bishop on e7, and avoiding all the tricks with sacrifices on d5. White then has to show that his last couple of moves are part of a logical process, and not merely a sophisticated cheapo. 22 ♘e2! followed by ♘f4 fits the bill, with tense equality to follow.

So far, the impression is that, by the standards of top Grandmaster play, of what both players were going to achieve in later years, the game has been worthy but not outstanding.

Here the knight sacrifice does not work, because quite simply there is no need to take it. After 22 ♘d5 ♗d8! 23 ♘b4 ♗a5 or 23 ♘f4 ♗a5, Black has the initiative and stands better. No doubt Sokolov had anticipated this, but Kasparov had prepared something much more striking.

22 ♖d5!?

Giving notice that this junior will need to be respected. Knight sacrifices on d5 are almost commonplace in the Sicilian, and in Hedgehog structures too, but a rook sacrifice is rare. Black has to take it, since the quiet preliminary 21 g3 cuts out the queen's escape square on the diagonal (compare 21 ♖d5? ♕xh2), but it's still unclear what White is planning to do after his sacrifice, given that there are two different ways to take the rook. I doubt that Sokolov would have missed the sacrifice, but he probably assumed that it would not work.

22...♗xd5

It turns out that there is only one serious way to take the rook, as after 22...exd5 23 exd5 ♕g5+ 24 ♔b1, White will win back a piece by force, with decisive compensation for the exchange. If, for example, 24...♗d7 25 ♖xe7 ♖c7 26 ♘e4! ♕xd5 27 ♘xd6+ with a winning pin, or 24...♗d8 25 dxc6+ ♔b8 26 ♖e7 ♕c5 27 ♕xc5 dxc5 28 ♖b7+ ♔a8 29 c7!, and this time it is the discovered attack on the long diagonal which wins: 29...♗e7 30 ♖xb5+ ♔b7 30 ♖b7+ ♔a8 31 ♘a4 with ♘b6 mate next move.

23 exd5 ♕g5+ 24 ♔b1 hxg3 25 hxg3 e5

Again, Black has only one sensible reply to be considered. If he were to allow White to take on e6 with the pawn, Black's position would fold sooner or later.

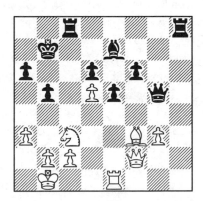

Now what? White is the exchange down, and as yet he has no significant open lines.

26 a4!!

The second wave of the attack is just as important as the first. White

needs to open up the black king's fortress, and he has to do this quickly. If Black is given any chance to return his queen to the queenside, for example with ...♕g8-d8 or ...♕f5-d7, he will have the chance to defend for victory.

Kasparov would definitely have seen this idea before sacrificing the rook, as otherwise his 22 ♖d5 would have been senseless. He would not, though, have analysed everything right through to the end. Even a superb tactician cannot see everything, the human brain having its limitations.

After you have played through and enjoyed the game, try to go through the critical sideline 26...f5, and try to do it without the help of the board. If you have good tactical vision, you will do well up to 33 ♕e2, many moves later, when White has sacrificed a second rook, Black has counter-sacrificed his exchange, White is about to queen a pawn on e8, but Black is a rook up. Is it winning for White? Or is Black winning? Or is it a draw?

Spare a thought for all Kasparov's opponents. Imagine what his opponents will have to calculate, once Kasparov finds an interesting attacking line.

26...b4!

Sokolov finds a good defence, though whether by luck or judgement, or a mixture of both, is not clear, as he blunders a move later. Instead, 26...f5! 27 axb5 a5 is the critical line, and also the best, though it is very complicated.

To avoid too much of a jungle of annotations, we give only the game

position just yet. We will come back to 26...f5! separately at the end of the game, and I promise that you will enjoy it!

27 a5

27 ♘e4? ♕g8 28 a5 ♕d8 is too slow. He has to attack.

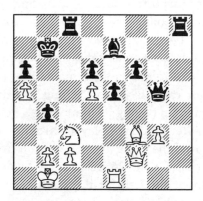

27...♖xc3??

Finally, Sokolov's nerve fails, and it was presumably at this point that he noticed a seemingly catastrophic flaw in his defence.

The difficulty for Black, when looking at this position, is that after 27...bxc3 28 ♕b6+ ♚a8 29 ♕xa6+ ♚b8, never mind that White can obviously force a draw with 30 ♕b6+, how on earth does Black defend against 30 ♖e4! with 31 ♖b4+ to follow? The rook check cannot be prevented, and attempts to escape with 30...♖c5 31 ♖b4+ ♚c7 32 ♖b7+ ♚d8 33 ♖b8+ ♚d7 34 ♕b7+ ♖c7 35 ♕b5+ or 30...♚c7 31 ♖c4+ ♚b8 (or 31...♚d7 32 ♕b7+ ♚e8 33 ♕xc8+ ♗d8 34 ♖c7) 32 ♕b6+ ♚a8 33 ♖b4 are hopeless.

Hence the text move, which seeks to give the black king some extra squares, but fails utterly.

At the risk of sounding like teaching a beginner, it is better to give up a pawn for a knight, than give up a rook for it. And so it proves here. Following 27...bxc3! 28 ♕b6+ ♚a8 29 ♕xa6+ ♚b8 30 ♖e4!, it turns out that Black can in fact hold with the hidden resource 30...cxb2!!,

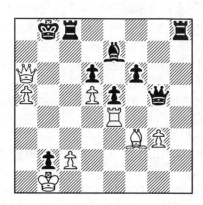

as the threat of ...♕c1+ takes away the one tempo White needs to conclude his attack. On 31 ♖b4+ ♚c7 32 ♖c4+ (there is no success to be had with 32 ♖b7+? ♚d8 33 ♕b6+ ♚e8 as the black king just slips away) 32...♚b8 33 ♕b6+ ♚a8, for example, White has no time for 34 ♖b4 or anything else, but must repeat with 34 ♕a6+ ♚b8 35 ♕b6+ etc. If he takes the disruptive pawn first with 31 ♚xb2, then 31...♕d2! prevents ♖b4+ after all, and with counter-threats on the c-file too, so again White must take the draw.

One might instinctively feel, trying to defend as Black, that White should win, but there is no checkmate after 30...cxb2!!. Instead, Black is a rook up, and is threatening a winning check of his own, so White must take the draw.

Going back, it is clear that Black needs to get rid of the knight immediately. Moves like 27...♖c5? or 27...♗d8? allow simply 28 ♘e4 with decisive threats. *Fritz* gives a little hope after 27...♔c7 28 ♘e4 ♕g6, but really White should win, being only an exchange down with excellent chances of a mating attack. Continue the line and we might see 29 ♗e2! ♔d7 30 ♗xa6 ♖c7 31 ♗b5+ ♔d8 32 a6!, when Black has no defence against the advancing a-pawn, for instance if 32...♖c5 33 ♘xc5 dxc5 34 a7 ♔c7 35 ♗c6 wins.

28 ♕b6+ ♔c8 29 bxc3

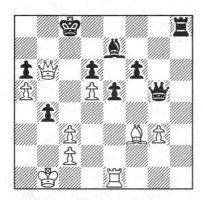

29...♗d8?!

This loses quickly. Given the time control issues coming up, 29...♕xg3 was worth trying, when surprisingly there is nothing immediately forcing resignation, and White would have to avoid perpetuals, on either side. But after 30 ♖e4 ♖h4 31 ♖xh4 ♕xh4 32 ♕xa6+ ♔d7 33 ♕c6+ ♔d8 34 a6 ♕e1+ 35 ♔a2 ♕f2 36 cxb4, White wins.

30 ♕c6+ ♗c7

If 30...♔b8 31 ♕xd6+ ♗c7 32 ♕xb4+ ♔c8 33 d6 is simple.

31 ♕a8+ ♗b8 32 ♖e4 1-0

So there was a draw if Black had been very careful, and played with great imagination and confidence. But could Black have tried for a win? Or would White have won, with even the slightest deviation from the main line? Let's return to the position after Kasparov's **26 a4!!**.

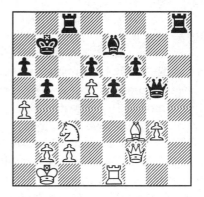

There are several possibilities here, and I tried to examine all of those that *Fritz* suggested was good or winning for Black, whether White or Black is on the move. This is quite a task, as *Fritz* gives any benefit of the doubt to Black in positions where he is the exchange up. The human player tends to be more flexible on this.

I eventually found a convincing, though extremely complicated, win for Black. This helps to cut down a number of lines where we might say that "White can play this, and it looks promising, but Black can keep compensation, and Black is equal/at-least-equal/better". Just one line that is good for Black, and we can cut down several pages!

So the line is:

26...f5!

Returning the exchange with 26...♖xc3!? is also possible, when Black has a slight edge. But why not play for a win?

27 axb5 a5!

A more cautious player might consider 27...axb5!? 28 ♘xb5 ♖c5 29 ♗e2, when Black remains the rook for knight and pawn ahead. Without full analysis the impression is that Black has an edge, but White's position should just about be tenable. It is certainly good and playable for Black, but he has something even better.

In other words, we can already say that, after Kasparov's imaginative sacrifice, Sokolov should nevertheless have gained an advantage. But could he have found an even bigger edge? Or alternatively, after some imaginative tactics, does have White new resources?

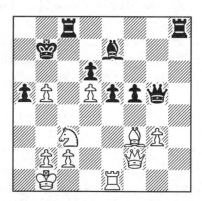

Black has done well with his last couple of pawn moves, cutting down the exposure to his king, while also ensuring that White cannot even safely

advance his pieces beyond the third rank (apart from the unimportant ♘a4, which is easily covered by ...♗d8). One can feel reasonably certain that Sokolov, a strong player, would have seen this far in advance, and then got frightened by the next move.

28 ♖xe5!

Win or lose, this is a wonderful idea, and it is a pity it did not actually get played. In fact, had he held his nerve, Sokolov could have refuted Kasparov's plan.

28...♖xc3!

This is the only way. The immediate 28...dxe5? 29 d6+ e4 30 ♘xe4! fxe4 31 ♗xe4+ leads to checkmate.

29 bxc3

It has to be tried. 29 ♖xe7+ ♕xe7 30 bxc3 ♖c8 leaves White the exchange down, with a wrecked pawn structure and no counterplay. So White has to continue the sacrifice.

29...dxe5 30 d6+ e4 31 dxe7

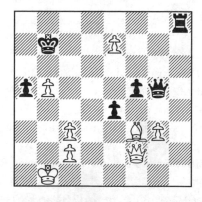

This, believe it or not, is the logical result of the play since White's first rook sacrifice with 22 ♖d5, and his second with 29 ♖xe5. Not surprisingly,

White has now run out of rooks, but his queen is still dangerous and active.

Black can swipe the bishop too, ending a full rook ahead, but this is not the best. 31...exf3?! 32 ♕xf3+ ♔b8 33 ♕e2 reaches the position mentioned in the game (in the notes to 26 a4), and it seems to be a draw.

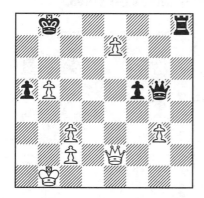

After 33...♕g8 34 c4! there is no obvious way for Black to coordinatee his pieces. If Black tries to attack with his extra rook by 33...♖h1+? (instead of 33...♕g8), an entertaining fantasy of a white king march begins: 34 ♔b2! ♕c1+ 35 ♔b3 ♕b1+ 36 ♔c4 ♕a2+ 37 ♔c5 ♕a3+ 38 ♔d5 ♖d1+ 39 ♔e6 ♕d6+ 40 ♔f7 ♕d5+ 41 ♔f8. Black has run out of checks, and the rest is straightforward, a queen sacrifice following after 41...♕d6 42 ♕xd1 ♕xd1 43 e8♕+ ♔a7 44 ♕c6, when White is gradually chewing Black up.

Play through this for enjoyment, and marvel at all the variety of chess, but remember that by showing better control, Black could have won this comfortably. We have instead:
31...♕xe7!! 32 ♗e2 ♕e5!

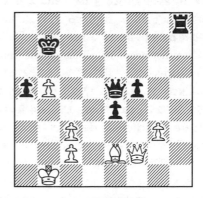

Preferring centralization, rather than an attack, as 32...♕a3? 33 ♕xf5! allows White to recover his composure. Now Black is "only" the exchange up, but he is fully in command, and will win before long. His king is safe, his queen and rook are active, and he has central control, enough for a win.

So Kasparov's attack was not quite sound after all. Nevertheless, who, on seeing a young chessplayer of such talent, could fail to be fascinated by such wild and brilliant chess, and appreciate that he was going to have the ability to play such games?

Supplementary game

Game 1.1
G.Kasparov-A.Panchenko
USSR Championship semi-final,
Daugavpils 1978
Sicilian Defence

No detailed notes, just enjoy the attack!

1 e4 c5 2 ♘f3 ♘c6 3 d4 cxd4 4 ♘xd4 ♘f6 5 ♘c3 d6 6 ♗g5 e6 7 ♕d2 a6 8 0-0-0 ♗d7 9 f4 b5 10 ♘xc6

Varying from 10 a3 as in the main game above.

10...♗xc6 11 ♗d3 ♗e7 12 e5 dxe5 13 fxe5 ♘d7 14 ♗xe7 ♕xe7 15 ♗e4 ♗xe4

Here Panchenko deviates from the game G.Kasparov-A.Yermolinsky, Leningrad 1975, in which Black played 15...♕c5. Kasparov, in *Fighting Chess*, notes that Panchenko's move was better, but gives no indication as to why he lost against Yermolinsky. It is understood that you do not have to give all your opening secrets away, for the benefit of future opponents.

16 ♘xe4 ♘xe5 17 ♕d4 f6 18 ♘d6+ ♔f8 19 ♖hf1

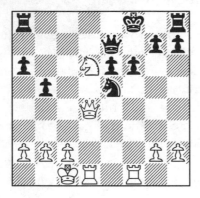

19...♔g8?

Here 19...♘f7 looks like an improvement, to expel the enemy knight or else neutralize his initiative by means of exchanges. After 20 ♕b6 ♘xd6 21 ♖xd6 ♔f7 it seems White has nothing better than to regain his pawn by 22 ♖fd1 (if 22 ♖e1 e5 23 ♕c6 then 23...♖hc8 24 ♕d5+ ♔f8 25 ♖d7 ♖d8!

defends) 22...♖a7 23 ♖xe6 ♕xe6 24 ♕xa7+ ♔g6 and the black rook emerges with equality. Any improvements for either side? The amateur chess sleuth might well concentrate on White's 20th, notably 20 ♘e4!? ♖c8 21 ♖d2.

20 g4 h6 21 h4 ♘f7 22 ♕e4 ♖f8 23 ♘f5 ♕e8 24 ♘d4 e5 25 ♘f5 h5 26 ♖g1 ♖h7 27 ♕b7 ♔h8 28 gxh5 ♕e6

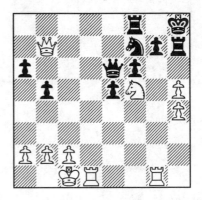

29 ♘xg7!!

If you have a realistic chance to play for an attack, then the classic method is to centralize your pieces, ram your pawns forward, open up attacking lines, and then sacrifice and go for a mating attack. This is well demonstrated in this game here.

29...♕xa2

If Black takes the knight, there is a quick checkmating attack on the g-file: 29...♖xg7 30 ♖xg7 ♔xg7 31 ♖g1+ ♔h8 32 ♕g2, forcing Black to return the piece with 32...♘g5 for a losing position.

That is simple chess. The rather more sophisticated idea is that of, believe it or not, winning by force with the queen on the f6-h8 diagonal.

Watch, then see!

30 ♕e7!

White's attack is far more impressive than Black's counter-attack, which is just a couple of queen checks leading to nothing.

30...♖g8 31 ♕xf6!

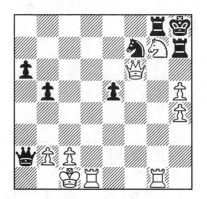

And now we can see the overturn of the f6-h8 diagonal.

31...♕a1+ 32 ♔d2 ♕a5+ 33 ♔e2 ♖gxg7 34 ♖xg7 ♖xg7 35 ♖g1 1-0

Relentless attack on the diagonal.

The year following the under-18 championship, Kasparov won another startling shoot-out against another future grandmaster. Lputian must have assumed that Kasparov had blundered, but it turned out that the younger opponent had seen things much more deeply.

This was the first genuinely famous win by Kasparov, and a few players copied his opening, possibly unwisely as the variation seems not to have quite been sound.

The "almost sound" opening was a significant repertoire in Kasparov's younger days, and indeed throughout Tal's career. Naturally, few players deliberately try unsound openings. What is more likely to happen is that the ambitious player sees something interesting, sees the chance of playing for a win, and opens up the game for dangerous chess. Quite often it is unsound, but neither player notices it at the time, and the attacker wins.

> ### Game 2
> ### S.Lputian-G.Kasparov
> ### Caucasus Youth Games,
> ### Tbilisi 1976
> ### *King's Indian Defence*

1 d4 ♘f6 2 c4 g6 3 ♘c3 ♗g7 4 e4 d6 5 f3 ♘c6 6 ♗e3 a6 7 ♕d2 ♖b8 8 ♖b1 0-0

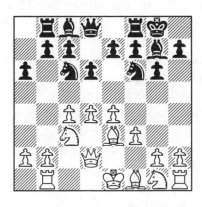

A standard enough position, although even here Kasparov was trying to test his opponent by varying his move order slightly. It is normal to castle earlier, on move 5, but he wanted to be prepared to advance quickly on the queenside. There are various technical questions for the players to consider, and in later years Kasparov was a great expert in finding the best move order. For this book, however, we concentrate on attack and sacrifice, rather than opening subtleties.

9 b4

Lputian tries out an unusual idea himself. The normal move is 9 ♘ge2, which White would generally play earlier, on move 6 or 7, but he wants to prevent Black from advancing with ...b7-b5. Lputian's move is promising, particular if Black plays passively, but Kasparov is always ready to open play up, given a chance.

The standard line is 9 ♘ge2 b5 10 cxb5 axb5 11 b4 e5, when White seems to have a slight edge after 12 d5 ♘e7 13 ♘g3 or 13 ♘c1.

A few years after the current game, Lputian tried something else. 12 dxe5 ♘xe5 13 ♘d4 ♗b7 14 ♗xb5 d5! 15 exd5 ♘xd5 16 ♘xd5 ♗xd5 was S.Lputian-Z.Lanka, Baku 1979, where Black had again sacrificed a pawn, opening up the centre before the white king had castled. Maybe 17 ♗e2, followed by ♖d1, is best here, but Lputian overlooked a simple tactic: 17 0-0? ♗c4! and Black wins material, as 18 ♗xc4? runs into 18...♘xc4 followed by ...♘xe3 and ...♗xd4. Instead, Lputian gave up the exchange with 18 a4 ♗xf1 19 ♖xf1, but Lanka won later on.

9...e5!?

Easily the most vigorous choice, and dangerous for the opponent, but it is far from clear that this is the best. Indeed, after close analysis, it seems that Black's opening leaves him as

worse, though it is very difficult to sort this out over the board.

Instead, something like 9...e6 might not give White a major advantage, but Black is likely to be uncomfortable for quite a while. The hallmark of Kasparov's play as Black, even from his early years, is that he gives no ground, but plays as if already fully equal. This is an aggressive and dynamic equality, aiming for active pressure on White, rather than the quiet and stable equality, favoured by his predecessor Karpov.

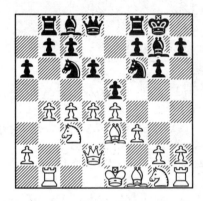

10 d5 ♘d4!

Kasparov has to play boldly here, pressing forward in the centre.

10...♘e7?!, followed possibly by ...♘h5, ...f7-f5, would be a standard enough attacking technique, but it is inappropriate here. First, and most obviously, Black's ...♖b8 and ...a7-a6 would then have been a waste of time. Second, if Black aims for an attack on the king, on the kingside, White can delay castling, and evacuate the king to the queenside at an appropriate moment.

11 ♘ge2

White cannot yet win a pawn, in view of 11 ♗xd4? exd4 12 ♕xd4?? ♘xe4 13 ♕xe4 ♖e8. But now he really does threaten to capture the knight on d4.

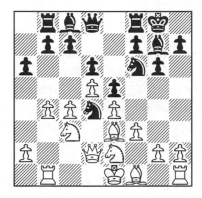

11...c5

11...♘xe2? 12 ♗xe2 would be even worse for Black, who would have no play on the kingside, while White can roll his pawns forward on the queen-side.

12 dxc6 bxc6!

If Black is worried about the loss of a pawn, then 12...♘xc6 is at least semi-respectable. White is clearly more active though, with a wide choice of possibilities. Play might start off with 13 b5 ♘a5 14 ♘g3.

However, a well-timed pawn sacrifice can be an essential component of positional chess, and Kasparov was more than happy to give the pawn away here. He was to become very much a specialist at pawn sacrifices in the centre, as we shall see in Chapter Four.

13 ♘xd4 exd4 14 ♗xd4

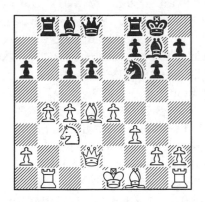

14...♖e8

Just a quiet, but active, developing move?

In fact, Kasparov, as he noted in *Fighting Chess*, had considered starting his violent attacking plan right here, but decided to wait, bringing in the rook first. An extra attacking piece is useful, particularly if the opponent's move is a less significant addition to the defence.

What Kasparov looked at was 14...c5 15 bxc5 ♘xe4 16 fxe4 ♕h4+ 17 ♔d1! ♖xb1+ 18 ♘xb1 ♕xe4 19 ♗xg7 ♕xb1+ 20 ♕c1 ♗g4+ 21 ♔d2 ♕xc1+ 22 ♔xc1 ♔xg7 23 cxd6 ♖d8 24 c5 ♖c8 25 ♗xa6 ♖xc5+ 26 ♔b2 with an edge to White. Move on a little and, after 26...♖c6 27 ♗b5 ♖xd6 27 ♔c3, it becomes clear that the outside passed pawn creates some problems for Black. An interesting line, therefore, but not as yet very practical, unless he is worried about a loss, and trying to aim for a draw. Temperamentally, Kasparov prefers playing for a win!

Going back, Stohl also suggests the crazy-looking king advance with 17

♔e2!? (rather than 17 ♔d1). The king runs into checks and pins, but somehow White seems to keep the extra piece. For example, 17...♖xb1 (17...♗g4+ 18 ♔d3 ♖xb1 19 ♗xg7! does not help for Black) 18 ♗xg7 ♔xg7 19 ♕d4+ ♔g8 20 ♘xb1 dxc5 21 ♕e3 ♖d8 22 ♘d2 should, according to Stohl, disentangle White's pieces, although he would still have to be careful.

This is effectively a side issue, as Kasparov decided to avoid the whole line. It is one of the variations that the player needs to analyse, or at least part-analyse and part-intuit. Kasparov had seen that the timing was wrong for this combination, but also that the idea itself was promising, if only he could develop a little more first.

Do not forget that Kasparov had the imagination to think of the sacrificial idea. If he had missed it, then probably he would not have seen the sacrifice a move later!

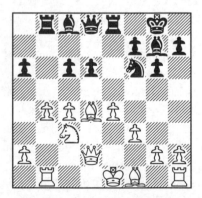

Following 14...♖e8 we reach a critical position. Can White use his extra pawn, and still successfully develop his pieces? Black, meanwhile, has two well-placed attacking rooks, while his dark-squared bishop, as so often in the King's Indian, has gained massive potential as a result of the pawn sacrifice.

The next move is vital if White is to prove that he can demonstrate any sort of edge.

15 ♗e2?!

After this move, White still has chances to hold with accurate play, but it is difficult. In *Fighting Chess*, Kasparov gives 15 ♗d3 as "probably the best decision", which is very complicated. We could use the well-known get-out clause, "with compensation for the sacrificed material", but one senses that Kasparov may have overpressed his attack.

In which case should White be trying for even more, and playing for a win? Why not! Black's counterplay depends too much on just one idea, ...c6-c5. If White can neutralize this, he should have serious chances of an edge. The bite with ...c6-c5 is that the pawn, in normal lines, will provide a serious fork on White's b4 and d4 units, and if as a result White has to play b4xc5, Black will, as we shall soon see, open up the b-file with unpleasant consequences. It is time for prophylaxis, for defending before the attack on b4 has even started. Cue 15 a3!.

The onus is now on Black to try to prove he can equalize. There seem to be no realistic prospects of an edge; but if Black can keep his pieces active, even when he may be a pawn or two pawns down, and if White cannot fully consolidate, then he still has chances.

The main priority is to prevent White from bringing the king into safety. One possibility is 15...a5!? 16 b5 cxb5 17 cxb5 d5 18 ♗xf6 ♕xf6 19 ♘xd5 ♕d6,

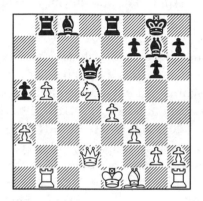

when Black has an active bishop pair, and White has extra dangers. If, for example, he tries 20 a4?! (the *Fritz* suggestion), Black has good play with 20...f5 21 ♗c4 ♔g8. Maybe the safest way for White here is 20 ♗c4, immediately shedding one of the pawns, with a queen exchange to follow after 20...♕xa3 21 ♕e3 ♕xe3 22 ♘xe3. There is little doubt that White is better, if only slightly as the extra pawn (on e4) would be difficult to promote.

Naturally, this is only one line out of numerous possibilities, but it seems to be safe for White, with good chances of a slight edge. Lputian's line is far more dangerous.

It is interesting to note that, looking through annotations by Kasparov, Stohl, and Burgess (in the *World's Greatest Chess Games*), this good defensive line has not been mentioned. Probably, though, others will have no-

ticed the improvement in White's play.

There is a lesson for the defender here. Schematically, both pieces and pawns have important roles in attack and defence. If an attacker tries to force through for a win with his pieces, then quite naturally the defender will need to defend with pieces most of the time. If, however, a pawn leads the charge, the attacker will often be trying to take over a critical defensive square, rather than trying to checkmate or win material. And if a pawn is attacking a critical square, then the defender may need to defend the same square. For instance, in this game it is important for Black to attack the white b4-pawn, in which case it makes sense for White to defend the b4 in advance with a2-a3.

15...c5!

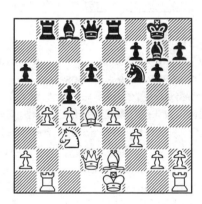

This causes problems now. White is fortunate that, with best play and with great imagination, he can hold; unfortunately he could not find the best line over the board.

16 bxc5

White has no choice but to capture here, as otherwise the b-pawn will fall.

16...♘xe4!

A knight sacrifice to open up lines for the long-range pieces. Any strong player will see this idea, but the timing has to be correct. Here, the suspicion is that Lputian may have thought that the sacrifice was seriously mistimed, but Kasparov had seen a decisive resource a few moves later.

17 fxe4 ♕h4+

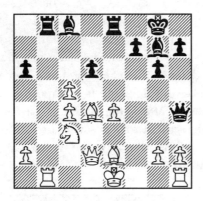

18 g3?

Playing for a quick win, but ending up instead with a slow loss.

Kasparov gives 18 ♗f2 ♗xc3 19 ♗xh4 ♖xb1+ 20 ♔f2 ♗xd2 21 ♖xb1 dxc5 "with a serious advantage for Black". White's isolated c- and e-pawns, with the bishop stuck behind them, look uncomfortable, but he should still be able to hold.

Stohl makes a similar assessment. We can try a sample continuation, with 22 ♗d3 ♗c3 23 ♔f3 h5 24 h3 f6 25 ♗f2 ♖d8 26 ♗c2 ♗b4 27 ♖d1 ♖xd1 28 ♗xd1 ♗e6 29 ♗e2 ♔f7 30 ♗d3 a5 31 a4 ♔e7 32 g4 hxg4+ 33 hxg4. Contrary to appearances, White's four isolated pawns and restricted light-squared bishop

seem safe enough, since Black's dark-squared bishop is ineffective as well. The remaining bishops on either side cannot make much progress.

Then there was a last-round game in an American tournament. Presumably the players, mid-table with nothing at stake except pride, decided that they wanted to demonstrate another drawing line in this position, one which Kasparov did not examine in his book. Play continued 18 ♔f1 ♖xb1+ 19 ♘xb1 ♕xe4 20 ♗xg7 ♕xb1+ 21 ♕d1 ♕f5+ 22 ♗f3 ♔xg7 23 cxd6 (23 ♕d4+! first is probably more accurate) 23...♗e6 24 ♕d4+ ♔g8 25 ♔f2 ♕c2+ 26 ♔g3 ♕xc4 27 ♕xc4, agreed drawn in L.Quigley-R.Henry, Chicago 1987.

Either way round, it seems to be a draw. Instead, Lputian fell into an exceptionally well-hidden trap.

18...♖xb1+ 19 ♔f2

Naturally he wasn't intending to play 19 ♘xb1?? ♕xe4 and wins. Rather, he was planning to win himself.

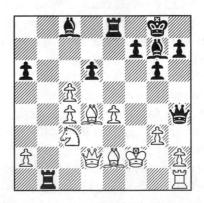

19...♖b2!!

Black has detonated a well-prepared shock. Kasparov, from his early days on, glorified in open lines, with queens, rooks, and bishops all being used here. He seemed to grasp the possibilities unusually quickly.

An interesting contrast can be made with another World Champion, Petrosian, who tended to enjoy intricate knight manoeuvres, and other short-range sorties, trying to take over positions move by move, rather than by a swift attack.

20 gxh4

What else? 20 ♕xb2? ♗xd4+ 21 ♔e1 ♗xc3+ 22 ♕xc3 ♕xe4 leads to an immediate win for Black.

20...♖xd2 21 ♗xg7 ♔xg7 22 ♔e3

If 22 cxd6, then 22...♖xd6 is simplest, with White's five isolated pawns all in danger of dropping. Yes, five. Two are doubled as well as isolated. A small curiosity. There were six isolated pawns by White just before. Any records for seven or eight isolated pawns?

22...♖c2

But not 22...♖b2? 23 cxd6, when some of these pawns start to look good. Kasparov plans to return his extra exchange in order to clarify the pawn structure.

23 ♔d3 ♖xc3+! 24 ♔xc3 dxc5

The complications are over, and material is level. There is no real excitement, however, as White's pawns are isolated and in the way of his bishop, while Black's pawns and pieces cooperate smoothly. There is not much to add for the dozen or so moves that remain. White's e-pawn eventually falls, giving Black a protected passed f-

pawn, and that is about it.

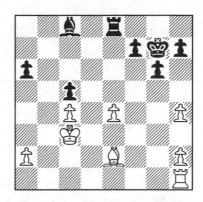

25 ♗d3 ♗b7 26 ♖e1 ♖e5 27 a4 f5 28 ♖b1 ♗xe4 29 ♖b6 f4 30 ♖xa6 f3 31 ♗f1

Or if 31 ♖a7+ ♔f6 32 ♗xe4 ♖xe4 33 ♖a8 ♔e7 34 ♖a7+ ♔e6 35 ♖a8 ♖xh4 emerging with an easily winning rook endgame.

31...♗f5 32 ♖a7+ ♔h6 33 ♔d2 f2 34 ♗e2 ♗g4 35 ♗d3 ♖e1 36 ♖f7 ♗f5 37 a5 ♗xd3 38 ♖xf2 ♖f1 0-1

Supplementary games

All this looked so brilliant and smooth that one gains the impression that Kasparov had perfect pitch for chess, even in his early teens. He still made his blunders, but far fewer than other players.

Sometimes, however, Kasparov would tend to overpress. The next supplementary game gives a brief but startling battle of back rank checkmates, with queen and rook offers accepted and declined by both sides. Enjoy the combinational cut and thrust, but note too that Kasparov could have done much better with quieter, more restrained, play.

White should be on the way for a win.

A more immediate question for White is what to do with the bishop. It is under threat, though not as yet under attack, since ...♖xc2 is met with ♕xb6, and this exchange is likely to be good for White. Therefore the white bishop is no immediate hurry.

However, Kasparov forces the pace, and soon finds himself in danger.

28 ♗xf5?

Crashing through the glass. Black can take with the rook, but it would have to leave f8, when surely, one assumes, his back rank collapses? The problem is that White's combination doesn't quite work, so that the bishop is surrendered for nothing much.

Most players, from grandmasters down, would play more quietly, centralizing and keeping the extra pawn. There are a few reasonable options, one of the most natural being 28 ♖ad1, and if 28...♖xc2 29 ♕xc4+ ♕f7 30 e6 ♕e7 31 ♖xb6 secures White's advantage. He has simplified, and has made progress with his passed e-pawn.

28...♖xf5 29 ♖e6

Game 2.1
G.Kasparov-E.Magerramov
Moscow 1976
Ruy Lopez

1 e4 e5 2 ♘f3 ♘c6 3 ♗b5 a6 4 ♗a4 ♘f6 5 0-0 ♘xe4 6 d4 b5 7 ♗b3 d5 8 dxe5 ♗e6 9 c3 ♗e7 10 ♘bd2 0-0 11 ♗c2 f5 12 ♘b3 ♕d7 13 ♘bd4 ♘xd4 14 ♘xd4 c5 15 ♘xe6 ♕xe6 16 f3 ♘g5 17 ♗xg5 ♗xg5 18 f4 ♗d8 19 ♔h1 ♗b6 20 a4 c4 21 axb5 a5 22 ♕f3 ♖ac8 23 b3 ♖c5 24 bxc4 dxc4 25 ♖fd1 ♖xb5 26 ♖d6 ♕e7 27 ♕c6 ♖b2

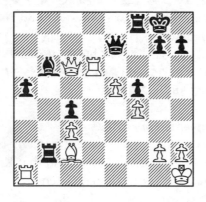

White has a passed e-pawn. His major pieces are centralized and active, his queen being more prominent than his opponent's. It is true that Black has managed to keep some counterplay on the queenside, his rook creating a problem, and he has an advanced passed pawn which might become significant later on. It is also true that White's king is potentially exposed on the back row, and will need some care. Even so, weighing up attack and counter-attack,

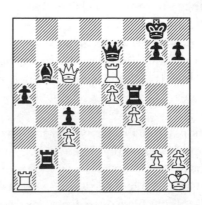

Now what?

29...♕a3!!

The black queen threatens checkmate and cannot be taken. This refutes White's piece sacrifice.

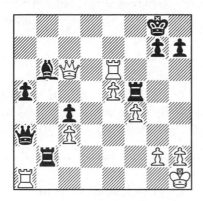

Black's queen sortie is attractive, but one cannot believe that Kasparov, even as a young teenager, will have overlooked this idea. More likely he assumed that White, with the queen and rook in threatening positions, would win quickly. After all, it does look as if White, with reasonable chess justice, should win this, but it just doesn't happen. Good chess instinct is a valuable trait, but it needs to be accompanied, as far as possible, with detailed analysis.

It may be that Kasparov got distracted by concentrating on 29...♕c7 30 ♕d5! ♔f8! 31 ♖c6, deciding to his satisfaction that White was winning after 31...♕d8 32 ♕e6 ♖xf4 33 ♖c8. This is not quite as straightforward as it might appear, as 31...♖d2! allows Black to equalize, for instance 32 ♕e4 ♕d7 33 ♖e1 ♕d3 34 g4! ♖d1 35 ♖c8+ ♗d8 36 ♖xd8+ ♕xd8 37 ♕xf5+ ♔g8 and a draw

is inevitable draw. But this is all irrelevant as the text move just wins for Black.

30 ♖d1

An admission that White's play has gone seriously wrong, but it is now too late to recover.

There is an extraordinary finish after 30 ♖e8+, and it's possible that Kasparov might have become engrossed examining 30...♖f8 31 ♕xc4+ ♔h8 32 ♕a4, and if it is beautiful it must be true.

However, Black also has the right to truth and beauty, and it is his extra bishop that decides with 32...♗c5!!, making the a3-f8 diagonal secure. There is no immediate mating attack, but Black keeps his extra bishop and wins.

30...♖xf4

There is no mind-blowing finish in the rest of this line, but Black still has to play vigorously, and here he must use the whole of the f-file for his rook.

31 ♖f6

Maybe with the assumption that something would turn up. Again 31

♖e8+ ♖f8 32 ♕xc4+ ♔h8 33 ♕a4 does not work, this time due to 33...♕c5! 34 ♖f1 ♖bf2, but not 33...♗c5?? 34 ♖xf8+ ♗xf8 35 ♕xa3 ♗xa3 36 ♖d8+ and mates.

31...gxf6 32 ♕e6+ ♔f8

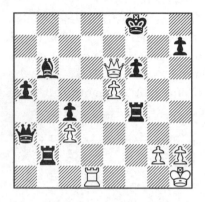

Visually, Black's king looks dangerously naked, but his queen, two rooks and bishop are all covering vital defensive squares.

33 ♕c8+ ♔g7 34 exf6+ ♖xf6 35 ♕g4+ ♔h8 0-1

Magerramov lost numerous times against the future world champion, in the Caucasus and in Russia, and some of the results looked humiliating. But here it was he who managed the brilliant finish.

Despite Kasparov's undoubted great tactical talent, he was occasionally blunder-prone. It happens to us all. We give two more games from the same period, in which Kasparov is winning, then gets careless, maybe over-confident, and then blunders. Mind-reading is notoriously difficult in chess, and most of the time only the player himself is able to say with certainty what is going wrong while thinking up a blunder. What is noticeable here, though, is that Kasparov has been attacking with vigour, then needs to calm down a little, but carries on aggressively, trying new and unnecessary ideas. Against Magerramov, for example, he had no need to sacrifice the bishop. A few days after his painful but just about excusable loss, he makes a simple blunder, completely missing a knight fork.

Game 2.2
A.Velibekov-G.Kasparov
Moscow 1976
Sicilian Defence

---

1 e4 c5 2 ♘f3 e6 3 d4 cxd4 4 ♘xd4 ♘f6 5 ♘c3 d6 6 ♗e2 a6 7 0-0 ♘bd7 8 f4 b5 9 ♗f3 ♗b7 10 a3 ♕c7 11 ♔h1 h5 12 ♗e3 ♘c5 13 e5 dxe5 14 fxe5 ♘g4 15 ♗xb7 ♕xb7 16 ♗g5 ♘xe5 17 ♕e2 ♘cd7 18 ♖ad1 ♗e7 19 ♘e4 ♕c7 20 ♗xe7 ♔xe7 21 ♘g5 ♖af8 22 ♕e1

22...♘c5??

The position is difficult for Black, but there are many reasonable tries, maybe starting off with 22...♔e8.

23 ♕xe5! 1-0

If 23...♕xe5 24 ♘c6+ ♔e8 25 ♖d8 is mate.

A pleasant enough finish to teach young juniors, but Kasparov ought to have been beyond all that. His win against Lputian was at a vastly more sophisticated level than this simple mating attack. We can feel sure that Kasparov would have seen this instantly as White, as the attacker, but sometimes blind spots can occur for the defence.

And all of us have blundered at the time control. Fortunately for Kasparov, in the next game he dropped only half a point.

Game 2.3
G.Kasparov-A.Badalian
Tbilisi 1976
Ruy Lopez

---

1 e4 e5 2 ♘f3 ♘c6 3 ♗b5 a6 4 ♗xc6 dxc6 5 0-0 ♗g4 6 h3 h5 7 d3 ♗c5 8 ♗e3 ♗xe3 9 fxe3 ♗xf3 10 ♕xf3 f6 11 ♘c3 ♕d7 12 b4 g5 13 a4 g4 14 ♕f5 gxh3 15 gxh3 ♖h6 16 b5 ♘e7 17 ♕xd7+ ♔xd7 18 bxc6+ ♔xc6 19 ♔h2 ♖g8 20 ♖f2 ♔d7 21 a5 ♖hg6 22 ♖b1 ♖b8 23 ♘a4 ♔d6 24 ♖bf1 ♖f8 25 ♘b2 ♔e6 26 ♘c4 f5 27 d4 exd4 28 exd4 ♖gf6 29 d5+ ♔d7 30 e5 ♖g6 31 e6+ ♔c8 32 ♘e5 ♖g7 33 c4 ♖fg8 34 ♖d1 ♖g3 35 c5 ♖e3 36 ♘f7 ♖gg3 37 d6 cxd6 38 cxd6 ♖xh3+ 39 ♔g1 ♘c6

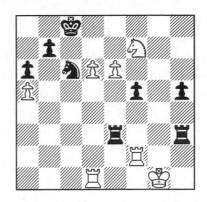

White is about to make his 40th move, the classic time to make a blunder. He cannot gain a whole queen by force, so the best plan is 40 d7+ ♔c7 41 d8♕+ ♘xd8 42 ♖d7+! followed by 43 ♘xd8 with an extra piece. This is enough to win.

Instead, he pins the black knight with **40 ♖c1??**, intending d6-d7-d8♕, but allowing simply **40...♖xe6**. It says a lot about the young Kasparov's determination that he eventually held the draw, two pawns down.

There are various possible explanations for this blunder, but the simplest is that he completely overlooked that the pawn was under attack.

For the chess psychologist, blunders are fascinating, as they often give the clearest indication of what players are thinking about. A good player will cut out bad ideas, but every so often bad ideas slip through.

Naturally, an improving player will want to note the mistakes in his or her own game, and will cut out the nonsense, and try to improve. Kasparov was probably the greatest of all at continuously improving his play. Many years later, this was essential when he played his first match against Karpov, quickly adjusting to four early losses, learning from it, and pulling the match back to 5-3 when it was finally abandoned after a further 39 games – but this is jumping ahead in the story. We are back in the late 1970s, and it is time to see what happened next.

The attack in the next game was very much a bolt from the blue. Kasparov played unusually quietly, looking as if he was happy for a quick draw, then there was a brief pawn skirmish, then an unexpected pawn sacrifice, luring the enemy queen to an only slightly vulnerable square; and then it was all over, Kengis's knight being pinned and trapped in multiple directions. The attack is not so much a checkmating attack, but rather to pick up a minor piece or two.

The one mystery of this game was why, at the beginning, Kasparov played his opening so quietly, when even at the age of 13 he could have had confidence in beating his strong opponent. Look through the databases, and the answer will soon become clear. Kasparov had five wins and a draw and, with three rounds to go, all he needed was to secure a quick and safe draw in round 7. He did that, and more. In the end he reached 8½/9 and won the event by two clear points. Quite fantastic.

Play through this game, then go through all his other games at Riga (which are widely available in databases or by download), and you will quickly see that there are other attacking gems. There would be no shortage of attacking ideas for this book.

Game 3
G.Kasparov-E.Kengis
USSR U-20 Championship,
Riga 1977
London System

---

1 d4 ♘f6 2 ♘f3 b6 3 ♗f4 ♗b7 4 e3 c5 5 ♘bd2 g6 6 c3 ♗g7 7 h3 0-0 8 ♗e2 ♘c6 9 0-0 d6 10 a4

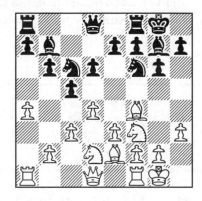

It's so quiet...

Nevertheless, with all the pieces and pawns still on the board, there is no prospect of an immediate draw, unless both players are happy with an early cessation of conflict.

10...a6

In *Fighting Chess*, Kasparov was critical of this move, regarding it as a slight weakening of the pawn on b6, and the square itself.

Kasparov himself suggested 10...♘a5 11 b4 cxb4 12 cxb4 ♘c6 13 ♕b3 e5 as equal, while others have tried more direct ways of playing for ...e7-e5, such as via 10...♖e8 and ...♕c7. Black was already better, for example, after 10...♖e8 11 ♘c4 ♕c7 12 ♖c1 ♖ad8 13 dxc5 bxc5 14 ♕c2 e5, in P.Pcola-L.Salai, Slovakian Championship, Martin 1996, although no doubt White can play slightly more accurately.

On the other hand, there must be greater mistakes in the game for Black's position to collapse by move 23.

11 ♘c4 b5

There are of course other moves, *Fritz* giving a dozen or so equal suggestions. For instance, 11...d5!? 12 ♘ce5 ♘e4 is quite direct, while Kengis also plays sharply.

12 ♘a3 b4

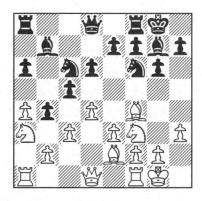

13 cxb4 ♘xb4

It's the one chance for Kengis to try to close the gap on the tournament leader, and he would presumably be reasonably happy to keep up pressure on the long dark-squared diagonal. Otherwise 13...cxb4 is equal. Not,

though, 13...cxd4? 14 b5! with advantage to White.

14 dxc5!

Kasparov decides to open up the game. This passes with comment in his own notes, but it is in fact highly committal, for good or bad. White does not have to open the long diagonal, and could simply block with one of many quiet moves, but Black would then be comfortably equal.

14...♘fd5

14...dxc5? 15 ♖c1 ♘fd5 16 ♗e5 leaves Black with weaknesses, so he must sacrifice.

15 cxd6

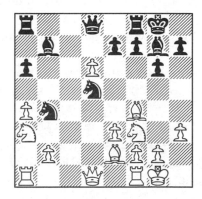

Comparing the last two diagrams, it is amazing how quickly the pawn centre has cleared. The position has not been stabilized yet, and so there are tactics likely to come up.

15...♗xb2?!

Spare a thought for Kengis. He has worked hard, played imaginatively, made pawn sacrifices as Black to open up the centre, cleared both diagonals for his fianchettoed bishops, and found two strong squares for the knights.

Now he regains one of his pawns, planning to win the exchange, and everything looks good. But everything crumbles after a hidden resource.

Black's position is still playable at this point, but he needs to cut down his ambitions. After 15...♘xf4 16 exf4 ♕xd6! 17 ♕xd6 exd6, Black is a pawn down, with the queens exchanged, but he has a good bishop pair. White's f-pawns are doubled, and cannot provide any massive edge on the kingside, while his queenside pawns are vulnerable. This gives indications that Black probably has excellent drawing chances. For example, after the continuation 18 ♘c4 ♖fe8 19 ♘xd6 ♖xe2 20 ♘xb7, play is roughly balanced. It is probably unwise for either player to try for more.

Kasparov mentions the more ambitious 16...♗xb2 for Black, but as he notes, 17 ♕b3 ♗xf3 18 ♗xf3 ♗xa1 19 dxe7 ♕xe7 20 ♗xa8 ♗d4 is somewhat better for White. Offering the queen exchange with 16...♕xd6! is preferable.

16 ♗h6!

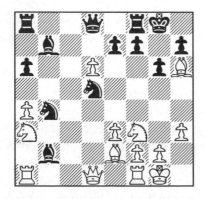

He keeps the bishop. Instead, 16

dxe7?! ♕xc7 17 ♘c4 ♘xf4 18 ♘xb2 ♖fd8 favours Black.

16...♖e8?

The younger Kasparov suggests, in *Fighting Chess*, that White has a clear edge after 16...exd6 17 ♗xf8 ♕xf8 18 ♕d2 ♕g7 19 ♘d4 ♗c3 20 ♕c1 ♖c8 21 ♘c4 ♗xa1 22 ♕xa1 ♕f6. Alas, there is a slip in this, as *Fritz* points out. After 18...♕g7?, White has 19 ♖ab1! ♗xa6 20 ♖b3, keeping the extra exchange with a winning position. However, this can easily be amended with 18...♗c3! 19 ♕c1 ♗xa1 20 ♕xa1, and no doubt Kasparov would have amended it himself had *Fritz* been around, without much change in the substance.

The more interesting question is whether Black has any problems in holding the position in view of his isolated d-pawn. If the queens stay on the board, Black is in serious trouble, as the white queen is far more active, so he has to offer a trade with 20...♕g7!. Play might continue 21 ♕xg7+ ♔xg7 22 ♖c1 ♖c8! (both sides must take care of the open c-file) 23 ♖xc8+ ♗xc8, and what saves Black here is that the white a-pawn is itself isolated and weak, after for example 24 ♘c4 ♗d7!.

Much earlier, instead of 18 ♕d2, White seems able to play more accurately with 18 ♕b3! ♗xa1 19 ♖xa1, making it more difficult for Black to exchange the queens, and consequently more difficult for him to manoeuvre his minor pieces. There is a long slow grind coming up, in which Black will have problems; but at least he is not lost by move 23.

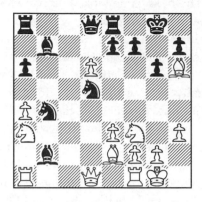

Still, it's looking good for Black so far. After all, isn't White sacrificing material?

17 d7!!

A later game in this collection, against Pribyl (Game 18), involves another unexpected pawn sacrifice, this time with d7-d8. Both moves are striking, but have different motives. Kasparov's win against Kengis is virtually inexplicable if one thinks of it in terms of an aggressive sacrifice. Precisely because of this, his move has considerable charm.

Let us look at another point of view. White is a pawn up, but two of his pieces are under attack by the bishop on b2. In addition, Black is threatening to attack the queen with ...♞c3, with all three minor pieces buzzing around the white camp. What then can White do? The answer is that he can return his extra pawn to gain time. When Black captures on d7, his knight will be pinned against the queen. This in itself gives a sufficient explanation why the pawn sacrifice is at least worth thinking about. The aggressive knight is no

longer effective. White still has the problem of dealing with the threats from Black's bishop and other knight, but this is not so great a problem. He can sacrifice the exchange! After all, Black would then have no bishop on the long dark-squared diagonal.

So:

17...♕xd7 18 ♞c4!

18 ♖b1 ♗xa3 19 ♖b3 ♕xa4 20 ♕a1 could perhaps be tried; for example, 20...e5 21 ♖xa3 ♕c2? 22 ♞xe5 f6 23 ♞g4, but the exchange sacrifice is simpler, more direct, and more effective.

18...♗xa1 19 ♕xa1

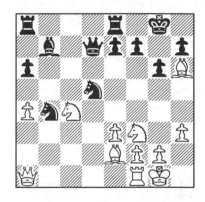

19...e5

Do you remember how Kasparov criticized Black's earlier 10...a6, weakening a queenside pawn? Suddenly this is of significance: 19...♞f6 20 ♞b6 ♕e6 21 ♞xa8 recovers the sacrificed exchange, and White's bishop pair gives a clear edge when we go towards the endgame after 21...♖xa8 22 ♕e5 ♕xe5 23 ♞xe5. Also, if 19...f6 then 20 e4 causes problems.

20 ♞cxe5

An important knight move. Now

the diagonals take centre stage.

20...♕e6?!

This leads to a quick finish. 20...♕d6!? might be tried, and if 21 ♘xf7, then not 21...♔xf7? 22 ♕g7+ ♔e6 23 ♘d4 mate, but rather 21...♕f6. It is still good for White, but at least there is a contest. This seems the best line for White, too, as after 22 ♕xf6 ♘xf6 22 ♕xf6 ♘xf6 23 ♘d6 ♖e7 24 ♘xb7 ♖xd7 25 ♗c4+ ♔h8 26 ♖b1 a6 27 ♘e5, the bishop pair and two extra pawns are far superior to Black's extra exchange.

If instead White tries the line from the main game, then 21 ♘g4 f6 22 ♗c4 ♔h8! creates a problem, as after 23 e4?, Black has simply 23...♖xe4. Kasparov would presumably find a way to win without too much difficulty, but at least he would have to work a little. 23 ♘g5 ♖e7 24 e4 ♘c2!? 25 ♕b2 ♕b4 26 ♕xc2 ♖c8 27 exd5 ♖xc4 28 ♕a2 fxg5 29 ♗f8 would be one way of finishing.

21 ♘g4 f6 22 ♗c4 ♖f8 23 e4 1-0

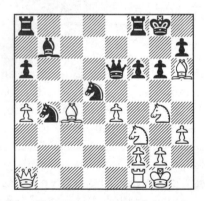

Pins wins! If 23...♕xe4 24 ♘xf6+ ♖xf6 25 ♕xf6 and mate follows. So it is time for Black to resign.

The next game looks relatively simple and straightforward, with plenty of sacrifices in front of Black's king, and no complicated cut-and-thrust, an attractive piece of attacking play. When initially writing this up, I added comments like "stage 1", "stage 2", etcetera, but as I started to study the game in greater depth, it became clearer that the play was not so simple, and that Begun could have held the game, and maybe even more than that. Could it be that Kasparov's gambit sacrifices were not quite sound?

Black's pieces were properly developed, except for one significant detail – his king was not securely defended by his other pieces, only pawns. Most of the time this does not matter too much, as the pawns in front of the king are a sufficient fortress. Sometimes, however, the king is protected only by a sandcastle.

It works like this. The pieces attack one of the pawns in front of the king, this pawn is sooner or later forced to advance; then one of the opposing pawns advances, to break open a crack in the structure; then it is time to sacrifice, to force the king into the open.

Any player who wants to become good at the game will need to learn about sacrificing to destroy the king-side pawn structure. Sometimes it works, sometimes it can be dangerous but the defender can just about hold, and sometimes the sacrifice is unsound. Experience is essential in judging the different cases.

Game 4
G.Kasparov-S.Begun
Sokolsky Memorial,
Minsk 1978
*Queen's Gambit,
Semi-Tarrasch*

1 d4 d5 2 c4 e6 3 ♘c3 ♘f6 4 ♘f3 c5 5 cxd5 ♘xd5

So far, a quiet opening. It soon gets livelier.

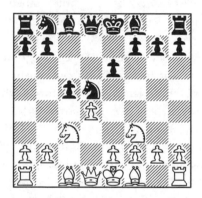

6 e3

It is interesting to note, given the similarity of the pawn structure to Kasparov's favourite 4 a3 in the Queen's Indian, that he does not try the apparently more active 6 e4 here. In his game against Gheorghiu in Chapter Four, for example, the opening moves were 1 d4 ♘f6 2 c4 e6 3 ♘f3 b6 4 a3 ♗b7 5 ♘c3 d5 6 cxd5 ♘xd5 and now 7 ♕c2 c5 8 e4 ♘xc3 9 bxc3, taking over the centre.

The difference in the current Semi-Tarrasch position is that 6 e4 would be answered by 6...♘xc3 7 bxc3 cxd4 8 cxd4 ♗b4+ 9 ♗d2, whereas in the a2-a3 Queen's Indian ...♗b4+ is clearly not possible. Kasparov usually prefers to keep the dark-squared bishops in this type of structure, and so he does not play 6 e4 here. As we shall see, the second bishop is often useful for the attacker.

6...♘c6 7 ♗d3 ♗e7 8 0-0 0-0

Kasparov noted at the time that there are several lines leading to equality, but nothing much more. He tries something out.

9 ♘xd5 ♕xd5 10 e4

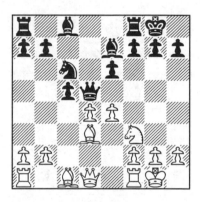

White has gained space in the centre, but his pawn structure is not yet stable.

10...♕d8

10...♕h5 is the main alternative, probably about equal. It is doubtful whether Kasparov had analysed anything in depth, he was just "trying moves".

A few years ago, Eingorn as Black managed, almost unbelievably, to win in 22 moves against a grandmaster, without there having been a simple blunder. This deserves recognition; see the supplementary game below.

11 dxc5 ♗xc5

Kasparov notes that 11...♘b4 12 ♗e2 ♗xc5 was regarded as equal by theory, but asks whether this is really so, giving White a slight edge after, for example, 13 a3 ♘c6 14 b4 ♗d4 15 ♘xd4 ♘xd4 16 ♗b2 ♘xe2+ 17 ♕xe2. White is in effect a tempo or two ahead, in an otherwise symmetrical position with opposite-coloured bishops. Black cannot win, but White can try for more. Plus over equals.

12 e5!?

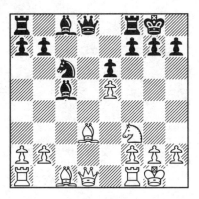

Stage 1 of the kingside attack. The pawn pushes to e5. This takes away the defensive square f6 for Black, and opens up the bishop's b1-g7 diagonal.

12...♗e7

White's play is not as quiet as it looks. Black is already threatened by 13 ♗xh7+ ♔xh7 14 ♕c2+, although this is easily contained by any normal means:

a) 12...♕d5 was tried in L.Spassov-E.Sveshnikov, Sochi 1980, when 13 ♕e2?! allowed 13...♘d4! 14 ♘xd4 ♗xd4 15 ♗f4 ♗d7 16 ♕e4 ♕xe4 17 ♗xe4 ♗c6 18 ♗xc6 bxc6 19 ♖ac1 ♗xb2 20 ♖xc6 a5,

and the noted theoretician with Black showed that he was at least equal, maybe even had a slight endgame edge; he later won.

White should prefer 13 ♕c2!, when 13...♘xe5 (or if 13...h6 14 ♗e4 ♘b4 15 ♕e2 ♕d7 16 ♗b1, planning a2-a3 and ♕e4 as in the main game) 14 ♗xh7+ ♔h8 15 ♗e4 ♘xf3+ 16 ♗xf3 ♕e5 17 ♗f4! ♕xf4 18 ♕xc5 leaves him with a strong initiative, as it is difficult for Black to complete his queenside development.

b) 12...♘b4 is playable, since 13 ♗xh7+?? ♔xh7 14 ♘g5+ ♔g8 15 ♕h5 is refuted by 15...♕d3, O.Bewersdorff-W.Schoebel, Hessen 1988. It is good to learn basic tactical ideas, but it is just as important to learn the refutations when the sacrifice is played incorrectly!

The typical retreat with 13 ♗b1 is better, and if 13...♗e7 then 14 ♕e2 transposes into the game. Note that 13...♗d7?? would then be a terrible mistake, due to 14 ♗xh7+! ♔xh7 15 ♘g5+ and wins, as there is no ...♕d3 defence this time. Instead, 13...♕xd1 14 ♖xd1 at least avoids any quick checkmates, but White's remaining pieces are the more active.

13 ♕e2

Here the question remains of whether White could, or should, cut out any ...♘b4 possibilities. 13 a3!? ♗d7 14 ♕e2 ♕c7 15 ♕e4 g6 16 ♗h6 ♖fd8 17 ♖ac1 ♗e8 18 h4 ♕b6 19 h5 ♕xb2 20 hxg6 hxg6 21 ♗c4 ♘d4 22 ♘g5 ♘f5 23 ♘xe6 fxe6 24 ♗xe6+ ♔h7 looked unimpressive in D.Cramling-T.Ernst, Swedish Championship, Karlskrona 1983,

White attempting Kasparov's attacking ideas a tempo down, and failing badly. In particular, he should not have sacrificed his b-pawn here, his timing was wrong.

Yet maybe 13 a3!? would still have been an improvement, and it was Cramling's 16th move that was a mistake, the bishop on h6 being ineffective here. Instead, 16 ♗f4!? keeps a slight edge. Cramling's innovation was therefore good, but his later implementation was incorrect. It usually takes a few attempts to work out what is going on in a new opening idea.

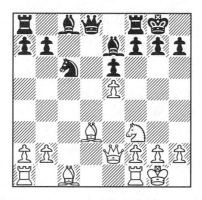

13...♘b4

Kasparov suggests 13...♘d4?!, but Black is struggling after 14 ♘xd4 ♕xd4 15 ♖d1. His queen is exposed, and it is very difficult for him to develop the rest of his pieces. For example, 15...♕a4 16 ♗e3 ♖d8? 17 ♗xh7+! ♔xh7 18 ♖xd8 ♗xd8 19 ♕d3+ wins, or 15...♕h4 16 g3 ♕h3 17 ♗e4 ♖b8 (now if 17...♖d8? 18 ♖xd8+ ♗xd8 19 ♕b5! wins) 18 ♗e3 b6 19 ♖ac1 ♗b7 20 ♗xb7 ♖xb7 21 ♕f3, and the white rooks take the seventh with a clear advantage.

14 ♗b1

The two white bishops soon jump back.

14...♗d7 15 a3 ♘d5

A good square for the knight, in general terms, but not so good in guarding the kingside fortress. If White were to have a pawn on d4, instead of on e5, a standard IQP (isolated queen's pawn) structure, Black's pieces would be fine. White could attack, but Black can defend, with ...♘f6 if necessary. The pawn on e5, however, creates a problem, as now ...♘f6 is not possible.

16 ♕e4

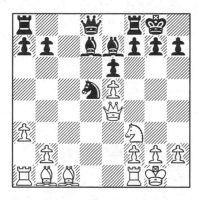

Stage 2 of the attack. White's queen and bishop threatens checkmate on the b1-h7 diagonal. Black is forced to weaken his pawn structure.

16...g6

In some positions 16...f5? 17 exf6 ♘xf6 would be acceptable. Not just here, though, as White wins a pawn with 18 ♕xb7.

17 ♗h6

A small but significant point to note: if the bishop has jumped from c1 to h6 in just one go, White has gained a tempo, when compared with ♗c1-f4-h6.

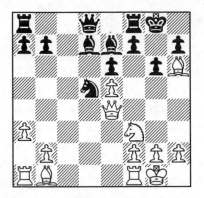

17...♖e8

17...f5 18 exf6 ♖xf6 is possible, and cuts out any quick mating attacks, but positionally Black is worse, the isolated pawn on e6 being a problem. White would also have a chance of creating outposts on e4 or e5.

18 h4

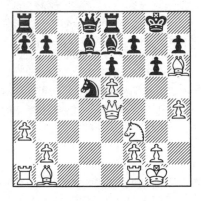

Stage 3 of the attack. White starts the h4-h5 push against the g6-pawn, with the intention of forcing an exchange, making it easier to sacrifice a minor piece and bring out Black's king into the open, totally exposed.

This plan is nothing new, it is just that here Kasparov has played the attack with brutal effectiveness.

18...♕b6?

All the same, the iron rule of chess strategy is that it is impossible to lose a game unless you have made a mistake. This move seems to be a mistake. Begun places great importance on the attack on the b-pawn, and if White tries to defend it, Black would gain a lot of time for counterplay. Kasparov shows, however, that, given the right timing, just allowing a pawn to drop, in return for accelerating an attack, can be very effective.

Surprisingly, Kasparov (in *Fighting Chess*) does not question this move, although if Black does not take the pawn at the next opportunity, he is just losing time. So what should Black try to improve his play?

The light-squared bishop is only half-developed on d7, but can easily be brought into play by 18...♗c6!, a much better diagonal, with a chance to push the white queen away. If, for example, 19 h5? ♘f6, Black wins a pawn for nothing much. Or if White makes a random developing move, Black will have ...♘c3, exchanging off White's valuable light-squared bishop. And 19 ♘d4?, trying to eliminate the black bishop, simply loses a pawn to 19...♗xh4 20 ♘xc6 bxc6, with only slight compensation.

White can still safely keep the queen for a little longer with 19 ♖d1, but after 19...♘c3 20 ♖xd8 ♘xe4 21 ♖xa8 ♖xa8 22 ♗c2 ♖d8 the late-middlegame/endgame looks fairly equal, or perhaps White has just a tiny edge. Black has other options, too, giving play for both sides, such as 19...f5.

This leaves 19 ♕g4 as the one real chance to attack, but Black seems to have adequate defensive replies.

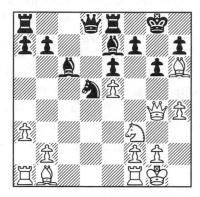

For example, 19...♘b6!? 20 h5 ♗xf3, successfully exchanges Black's previously bad bishop for a good attacking knight, and 21 ♕xf3 ♕d4 22 hxg6 hxg6 looks equal, give that Black plays with reasonable care, such as 23 ♕g3 ♔h7 24 ♕h3 ♕h4.

If White were to try for a win with 21 gxf3?!, keeping the queen on an attacking square, he would have to be careful not to overbalance. The problem is not so much the weakness of the doubled pawns, but rather the exposure of White's own king on the g- and h-files. After 21...♗f8! 22 ♗xf8 ♖xf8 23 hxg6, Black must not defend with 23...hxg6? 27 ♗xg6 fxg6 28 ♕xg6+ ♔h8 29 ♔g2 and checkmate follows soon. Instead, he should counter-attack, with 23...fxg6!, and if 24 ♗xg6 ♕e7! 25 ♗e4+ (or another discovered check) 25...♔h8

and Black is suddenly on the attack, his king being safe, whereas White's is now in grave danger.

Of course White does not have to take on g6 with the bishop and open the g-file, but he needs compensation for his damaged pawn structure. Instead, he can try 24 ♗a2 ♔h8 25 ♗xe6 but after 25...♕e7 26 ♖ae1 h5! 27 ♕h3 ♖ae8, Black should at least be equal.

Complicated for the defender? Not really. All he has to do is play his pieces to their best squares, and defend against the opponent's tactics.

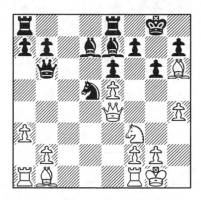

19 h5!

Kasparov gave this as an exclamation mark, usually a good sign of what is going on.

19...f5?!

As Black has spent time on 18...♕b6, he should at the very least take the b-pawn.

Kasparov, in *Fighting Chess*, gives 19...♕xb2 20 ♖a2 ♕b5 21 ♕g4 ♕a4 22 ♕g3 ♗f8 23 ♗xf8 ♖xf8. He now points out that Black is able to cover the attack after 24 hxg6 fxg6 25 ♗xe6 ♕f4!. The position is still about equal after the exchange of queens, but White was hoping for more than that. Nevertheless, it might well be that this is the best that White will achieve, despite Kasparov's question mark on 24 hxg6.

Instead, he suggests that 24 ♖d2, with an exclamation mark, is best, without giving comment. Clearly Kasparov had gone on with his analysis, and found some interesting moves, but without actually writing it up at the critical point. Let's look a bit further:

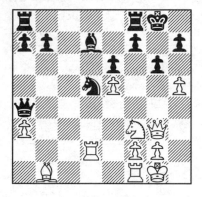

a) 24...♕xa3?! seems too dangerous, and the attacking player with White would probably be encouraged. Black has two extra passed pawns, but it will be quite some time before the pawns are at all dangerous, and meanwhile White will have plenty of opportunities to attack. One possibility, ending in a win for White, is 25 ♖d4 ♕e7 26 ♖h4 ♗b5? 27 hxg6 fxg6 28 ♗xg6 hxg6 29 ♕xg6+ ♕g7 30 ♕xe6+ ♕f7 31 ♕h3!, and Black's king is fatally exposed. It would be possible to cover a few more variations in order to find a final truth, but in practical terms, strong players would be happy enough to consider

White as being on top.

b) 24...♘f4!?, aiming for counterplay, while also covering g6, looks more interesting for Black, 25 ♗c2 being the only dangerous reply. Then the tempting 25...♘xh5? would fail to 26 ♕g5!, threatening the queen on a4, the bishop on d7, and not least the king after ♕h6 and ♘g5. However, 25...♕c4 is possible, with unresolved complications. For instance, 26 ♕h4 (26 ♕g5 is now too slow, due to 26...♗c6 and ...♗xf3) 26...♗c6 (the attempt to simplify with 26...♘e2+? just loses after 27 ♖xe2! ♕xe2 28 ♕f6 h6 29 ♗xg6! or 28...gxh5 29 ♗b1!) 27 ♗d3 (27 h6 is met simply by 27...f6) 27...♕a4 28 ♗c2 ♕c4, with repetition.

So Black's position still seems to be holding, but it requires accuracy. Begun played the game less consistently, allowing Kasparov to continue his demonstration of a clear winning plan, stage 1, stage 2, stage 3, and beyond.

20 exf6

Stage 4: The exchange of a valuable kingside pawn.

20...♘xf6

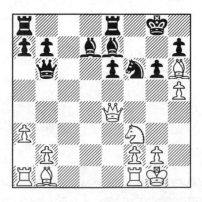

Where is the queen going to go?

21 ♕e1!

A memorable move, the only good move (21 ♕e5? ♘xh5!), and decisive. Presumably Begun had underestimated this, the longest retreat available, but the queen is now out of the way. There is also some nice geometry with the queen, ♕e4-e1-b1-g6, and Kasparov was generally extremely adept at rapid queen manoeuvring.

21...♘xh5

At least Black can capture the white h5-pawn, but is this enough? I feel sure that Begun by now appreciated he was losing.

Any attempt to win the f1-rook allows White to break through before Black can introduce pieces into play. If here 21...♗b5 22 hxg6 ♗xf1 (or 22...hxg6 23 ♕e5 ♗xf1 24 ♕g3) 23 gxh7+ ♔h8 24 ♘e5 wins for White.

22 ♘e5

Stage 5: Preparing to set up the winning sacrifice.

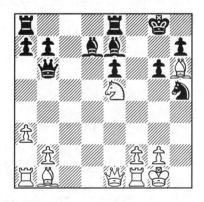

22...♗b5?

Even at this late stage, Begun had a chance to fight on. The f1-rook is an irrelevance, and his bishop is moving away from an important defending square. 22...♘f6?! 23 ♗xg6 provides little resistance either.

The best defence is 22...♖ed8!, which causes some genuine problems. Kasparov, in *Fighting Chess*, does not mention this possibility, but implies instead that Black's position is resignable. One point is that the d7-bishop can drop back to defend g6; for instance, if now 23 ♗xg6? hxg6 24 ♕b1, Black defends to victory with 24...♗e8!.

If instead 23 ♗a2, Black paradoxically replies 23...♗c8!. This is not the sort of line that one would think of over the board, but Black is not being checkmated, and is a pawn up, which is a start. There are also a few tactical resources, for example 24 ♕e4? ♘g3! 25 ♕f3 ♘f5!, or 24 ♖c1? ♕xb2! 25 ♖xc8 ♕xa2 26 ♘c4? (this looks like an attractive brilliancy, but it is an illusion) 26...♖xc8 27 ♕xe6+ ♔h8, when Black somehow covers all the main mating squares.

24 ♘g4!? seems to be the critical response, eyeing the f6- and h6-squares, while clearing the e-file and the long dark-squared diagonal. This is presumably an edge for White, which some flicks through with *Fritz* would seem to confirm; for example, 24...♗h4 25 ♗d2 a5 26 ♗c3 ♗g3 27 ♕e4 ♗c7 28 ♗e5 ♗xe5 29 ♕xe5, or 24...♖d6 25 ♖c1 ♗d7 26 ♕e5 ♕d4 27 ♖c7 ♗f6 28 ♘xf6+ ♘xf6 29 ♗f4 ♘e8 30 ♖xc7.

Nevertheless, it is unfortunate that Kasparov did not have to work harder for the win.

23 ♗xg6!

Stage 6: Sacrifice to break open the king's fortress.

If Black does not resign soon, then *Stage 7:* Checkmate.

23...♘f6

If 23...hxg6 24 ♕b1 or 24 ♕e4 wins.

24 ♗xh7+ 1-0

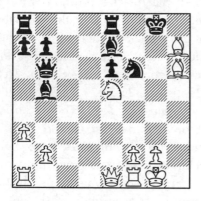

Complete destruction. Black is mated after 24...♔xh7 25 ♕b1+! ♔h8 26 ♘f7+ ♔g8 27 ♕g6, or similarly 24...♔h8 25 ♘f7+ ♔xh7 26 ♕b1+!, while if 24...♘xh7 25 ♕e4! ♘f8 26 ♕g4+, with ♕g7 mate to follow.

A crushing victory, but note that such wins can only happen if the defender defends inaccurately.

Supplementary game

> ### Game 4.1
> ### V.Tukmakov-V.Eingorn
> USSR Championship First League, Tashkent 1980
> *Queen's Gambit, Semi-Tarrasch*

1 ♘f3 ♘f6 2 c4 e6 3 ♘c3 c5 4 e3 d5 5 d4

♘c6 6 cxd5 ♘xd5 7 ♗d3 ♗e7 8 0-0 0-0 9 ♘xd5 ♕xd5 10 e4 ♕h5

Begun played 10...♕d8 in this position.

11 dxc5 ♗xc5 12 ♗f4 b6 13 e5?

White has tried alternatives, such as 13 ♕e2, with safety. It is therefore not the case that Eingorn was playing a major innovation in this game. He was simply playing good moves.

As we shall see, Tukmakov has overpressed.

13...♖d8 14 ♘g5

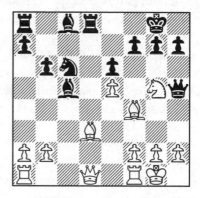

Once White has gone this far with his pawn advance, he might just as well continue. Still, his kingside attack is hardly effective. Apart from anything else, to achieve something significant, he would need to keep the queens on, which is not possible. Tukmakov actually wins a pawn, but his bishop is trapped in the process, and his other pieces will be overextended in order to save the bishop.

14...♕xd1 15 ♗xh7+ ♔h8 16 ♖fxd1 ♖xd1+ 17 ♖xd1 g6

The trapper trapped, the unicorn beats the lion.

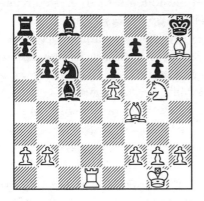

18 ♘e4

Maybe there is something more effective in 18 ♖d3, but it is unlikely that White will hold after 18...♔g7 and then:

a) 19 ♖h3 ♗b7 20 ♘e4, threatening 21 ♗h6+ ♔h8 22 ♗xg6! fxg6 23 ♘f6 and 24 ♗f8 mate, is well met by 20...♖d8!, with the counter-threat of mate on d1. Now 21 ♗h6+ ♔h8 22 ♔f1 ♗a6+ 23 ♔e1 ♘b4 24 ♗xg6 runs into 24...♘c2 mate, while if 22 ♘c3 (threatening ♗g5) 22...♗e7 23 ♗f4 ♔g7 defends successfully, with ...♖h8 to follow, picking up the bishop.

b) 19 h4 ♗e7 20 ♘xf7! (the best try, as 20 ♖h1 ♗xg5 21 hxg5 ♗b7 and 22...♖h8 wins the bishop anyway) 20...♔xh7 (if 20...♔xf7 21 ♖g3) 21 ♗g5 ♔g7 22 ♗xe7 ♔xf7 23 ♗f6 ♘b8! 24 f4 (if 24 ♖c3 ♘a6!) 24...♘d7 25 ♗g5 ♘c5 26 ♖d6 ♗a6 27 b4 ♘d3 and Black's pieces finally emerge.

18...♔g7?

An odd decision. One might even suspect a "fingerfehler", that the king slipped from Black's hand by mistake, before he could remove the bishop. Clearly 18...♔xh7 is correct, when

White has nothing for the piece, 19 ♖d3 being answered by 19...♗e7.

19 ♖d3?

Effectively gifted an extra tempo, White had the chance to create complications with 19 ♗g5!. Now 19...♔xh7? loses to 20 ♖d3, while after 19...♗d4 20 ♗f6+ ♔xh7 21 ♖d3 g5 (the only move) 22 ♘xg5+ ♔g6 23 ♘f3 ♗xb2 24 g4, the win for Black is no longer straightforward, if indeed it's there at all.

19...♗d4!

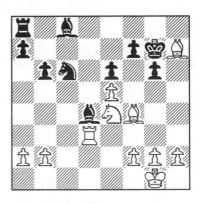

The pawn will drop first, then the bishop.

20 ♖h3 ♗xe5 21 ♗h6+ ♔xh7 22 ♗g5+ ♔g7 0-1

By 1978 Kasparov was already starting to play very, very highly theoretical games. Young players are eager to learn, and, just as importantly, can remember their analysis, even in the sharpest positions. Here we were in the spotlight of King's Indian theory of the time, and Kasparov was trying something new on move 22, in a sharp attacking variation. Stohl, in his chess biography of Kasparov, was in fact slightly critical of his innovation, but it seems no better or no worse than the previous idea, both lines ending up as equal after complications, and Kasparov had the advantage of forcing his opponent to think of something new.

Kasparov made a slip in the early middlegame, an inaccurate move order in a double knight sacrifice, and Yuferov had the opportunity of gaining an edge. He in turn let the play slip in a complicated position.

Game 5
S.Yuferov-G.Kasparov
Sokolsky Memorial, Minsk 1978
King's Indian Defence

---

1 d4 ♘f6 2 c4 g6 3 ♘c3 ♗g7 4 e4 d6 5 ♗e2 0-0 6 ♘f3 e5 7 0-0 ♘c6 8 d5 ♘e7

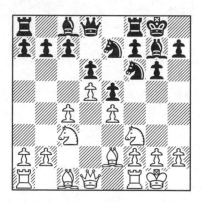

The first of many published encounters of Kasparov as Black in the Classical Variation of the King's Indian. Many full-size books have been written on this position, giving many examples of Kasparov's games. There is no need here to add in detail to the theoretical literature. Interested readers can book up on this themselves.

However, the uninitiated reader could easily gain the impression that White should be significantly better. After all, he has more space for his pieces, thanks to his pawns being more advanced. Black has a "bad bishop", his bishop on g7 being locked behind the pawns, while White has three active and manoeuvrable minor pieces, and has plenty of space to set up a broad queenside pawn advance.

All this may be true and valid, but Black has significant counterplay on the kingside. He can set up a pawn-roller with ...f7-f5-f4, followed by advances of the g- and h-pawns, and the danger for White is that his king can become stuck on the kingside. The only way for Black to exploit this is through attack, but Kasparov has no problems about that!

The reader may be wondering why White should be enticed towards castling on the kingside in the first place. Go back a few moves, for example, and White has the possibility of trying 7 ♗e3 instead of 7 0-0. Then 7...♘c6?! is a positional mistake, as after 8 d5 ♘e7 9 ♘d2, White has all his advantages on the queenside, and he can escape with his king should Black continue with his kingside pawn grind regardless. I mention this because so many of my opponents in weekend tournaments have made this mistake as Black, and I have had many relatively simple wins.

Naturally, master strength players, and of course grandmasters, tend to avoid this. Black has several other ways of handling this variation, including the straightforward 7...exd4, which leads to a different type of game altogether.

9 ♘e1

White has tried a lot of different moves here. Along with the text, the most important are: 9 b4, expanding on the queenside at once; and the alternative retreat 9 ♘d2!?, with the idea that after a later c4-c5, the knight can go to c4, putting great pressure on the pawn on d6. Black's safest response is 9...♘e8.

9...♘d7

White's knight varies, and Black's knight should also vary. There is less pressure here on the d6-square.

10 ♘d3 f5 11 ♗d2 ♘f6

This is not the only reasonable line, and in earlier years Black often opted for the quieter idea of exchanging with 11...fxe4 12 ♘xe4 ♘f6 or 12...♘f5, followed perhaps with ...c7-c6. Kasparov was very much a maximalist, though.

12 f3 f4

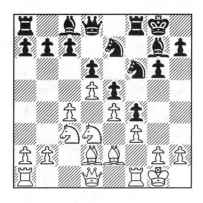

Black usually plays this here, now

that he has encouraged White to support the e4-pawn with f2-f3. Black's idea is to follow up with the g-pawn, ...g6-g5-g4, and he wants a pawn target on f3.

13 c5 g5 14 cxd6 cxd6 15 ♘f2 ♘g6

Stohl suggests that 15...h5 is slightly more flexible, forcing White to play h2-h3 if he wants to put his queen on c2. Naturally this all could easily end up with a transposition a few moves later, for instance after 16 h3 ♘g6 17 a4 ♖f7 18 ♘b5, but both players need to take account of possible interesting deviations along the way.

16 a4

White can also vary. One thought is that, if he intends to play ♕c2 and ♖fc1, he could play 16 ♕c2 immediately, and not bother with a2-a4. In fact this is now the most common approach here.

Less frequently, White argues that he wants to keep the queen on d1 for as long as possible, but still wants to play a developing move, in which case 16 ♖c1!? (and not the later ♖fc1) is a possibility.

16...♖f7 17 ♘b5

Here White could consider the relatively untried 17 ♖a3!?. In the main line, it is useful for White, perhaps, to provoke Black into playing ...a7-a6, but it costs him a couple of extra moves with his knight. So maybe White could leave the knight where it is for the moment, and quietly move the rook to the third, providing an extra defender if and when Black opens up with a later ...g5-g4.

Again, no detailed analysis. The

point to be made is that, just at the moment, this is positional chess rather than tactical chess. Both players will be aware that wild tactics might soon blow up, but at the moment the priority will be to develop their pieces as accurately as possible, anticipating the storm.

17...h5 18 h3 ♗f8

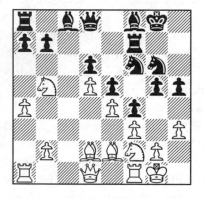

A couple of moves further on, and we are getting closer to the crunch. Looking at the position from Black's point of view, the obvious point is that his kingside pawns are pushing fast. If Black plays ...g5-g4 safely, there is a big attack coming up soon. If, as here, White has put up barricades against ...g5-g4, there may still be good attacking possibilities, maybe after a pawn sacrifice.

Even within his relatively confined space on the kingside, no pieces beyond the first three ranks, Black has made significant progress. He has set up a minimalist defence on the queenside, with the bishop on f8 adding protection to the pawn on d6, while the rook on f7 covers the weakness on c7.

The rook can also swing around on the other side, maybe later going on to g7 or h7, which will be dangerous if the kingside pawn structure is opened, or about to be opened. Meanwhile, Black's knights are well positioned. Quite often, he will need to retreat the knight again to e8, to cover the d6 and c7-squares, which slows play down a little, but it is very solid.

Black's opening has been provocative, but once he has decided on his ...f7-f5-f4 plan, he has played simply and logically. The next stage is to decide how exactly to continue the attack, and this requires a lot of thought.

19 ♕c2!?

19 ♖c1!? is still an option.

19...a6

Obviously ...g5-g4 is the key move in Black's attack, but he needs to find the right moment for it. Here 19...g4?! is premature, because of 20 fxg4 hxg4 21 hxg4 a6 22 ♘a3 ♖g7 23 ♘c4! – see the notes (to 22 ♕d1) in the supplementary game, Moiseev-Tarakanov (Game 5.1).

20 ♘a3 ♖g7

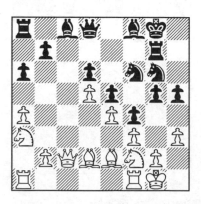

21 ♖fc1?!

We are still in 'theory', though according to *ChessBase*, the position was new at that time. The Classical Variation of the King's Indian is frightening for both sides, and both players need to have great confidence here. For my part, if I were White, I would be worried that Black is about to crash through my slender kingside pawn fortification. If I were Black, I would be worried instead that my kingside was all huff and puff, and that White is going to take over the queenside completely. Other players have more confidence, and are happy to play such lines, both as White and Black. Kasparov, of course, had plenty of confidence.

Such positions are tense, but the players can't both be wrong simultaneously. What is important, though, is that both proceed with extreme accuracy. A slight error in the manoeuvring stage can lead to a sudden collapse when play reaches the tactical stage. Kasparov proved himself at being highly adept at the King's Indian, demonstrating great understanding with the preliminary late-development stage before the storm, as well as at finding the sacrificial ideas.

Going back to the game, it would seem now that 21 ♘c4!, with ideas of ♗a5 and ♘b6, is again more accurate. Then 21...♘h4?! was tried in Moiseev-Tarakonov, Serpukhov 1999, following ideas from Yuferov-Kasparov; see the supplementary game, with some brief coverage of the theory.

21...♘h4

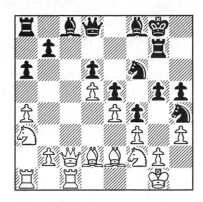

22 ♕d1

Stohl makes no comment on this move, but positionally it is critical. There are three basic questions to be answered:

First, is this a good move? And by extension, is this the best? This is central to the player at the board, deciding which move to play.

Second, is the ♕d1-c2-d1 an inspired idea, allowing White to bring a second rook to the queenside, and creating play there? Or is it an interesting or bad idea? Or something in between? This is the question for the theoreticians and analysts.

And third, is White better? Or Black? Or is it equal?

We have three slightly different points of view.

The first question is easy enough. White needs to provide extra cover on the g4-square. If he were to ignore this square, he would be heading towards disaster. For example, if now 22 ♘c4 g4 23 ♗a5 ♕e7 24 fxg4 hxg4 25 ♘b6 gxh3 26 ♘xa8 ♖xb2+ 27 ♔h1 ♕g7, and although White breaks through first on the queenside, it is Black who retaliates successfully, with checkmate. So 22 ♕d1 is essential, even if it wastes a couple of tempi.

The question in terms of opening theory is whether White could have profitably avoided ♖fc1 earlier on. There is a partial answer in the notes to the supplementary game, Moiseev-Tarakanov.

The third question is what happens next. Kasparov won the game, but with best play, including improvements by both sides, this should end up as a draw by repetition, a common theme in sharp well-played games.

22...♗d7!?

One senses that Kasparov was wholly up-to-date with this variation. He was actively improving, or attempting to improve, on games by Browne and Kavalek.

The most direct attempt of playing this position is 22...g4, but White has in reserve an exchange sacrifice with 23 hxg4 hxg4 24 fxg4 ♘xg2?! (aiming to save a tempo on Yuferov-Kasparov) and now 25 ♖xc8! ♖xc8 26 ♔xg2 ♘d7 27 b4, and White is in control. This is the basic idea behind Kasparov's 22...♗d7!?. It is not a question of finding a quiet and inoffensive development plan. Instead, he is making the bishop safe for a later raging knight sacrifice.

There are other ways for Black to try to set up a sacrificial attack, starting with 22...g4 23 hxg4 hxg4 24 fxg4 ♗xg4!? (rather than 24...♘xg2?!) 25

♘xg4 and then:

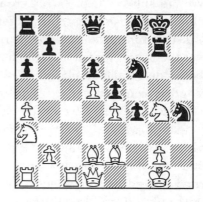

a) Black has to carry on sacrificing, it seems, as after 25...♘xe4 26 ♖c4 ♕b6+ 27 ♗e3! ♕xb2 28 ♖b1 ♕xa3 29 ♖xe4, White is in control.

b) 25...♕b6+ is similarly ineffective after 26 ♗e3!.

c) 25...♘xg4 26 ♗xg4 ♕g5 also misfires, since 27 ♗e6+ ♔h8 22 g4!, as in G.Sosonko-L.Kavalek, Wijk aan Zee 1977, suddenly blocks up Black's g-file and leaves him with no compensation for the piece. Stohl notes that 26...♘xg2 is better, but still good for White after 27 ♗e6+ ♔g8 28 ♔f1.

d) The remaining try, and the most significant, is 25...♘xg2!, and now:

d1) 26 ♔xg2? is too greedy, as after 26...♘xg4 27 ♗xg4 ♕h4 28 ♕h1 (there is nothing better; 28 ♔f1 ♖xg4 29 ♔e2 ♖g3! 30 ♕h1 comes to the same thing) 28...♖xg4+ 29 ♔f3 ♖g3+ 30 ♔e2 ♕g4+ 31 ♔f2 ♗e7!, Black has a decisive attack, with the threats of ...♗h4, or ...♔g7 and ...♖h8. For example, 32 ♖c3 ♔g7 33 ♖xg3 fxg3+ 34 ♔e3 g2 35 ♕g1 ♖h4! 36 ♖e1 ♖h1 37 ♘c2 ♗h4 38 ♖c1 ♖xg1 39 ♖xg1 ♗f2 and wins.

d2) 26 ♔f1! is a good wriggling move, unlikely though it may seem, given that the black knight is still at large, and various other pieces are starting to move in. However, White eliminates any threats on the g-file, which makes it more difficult for Black to attack. If 26...♘xg4 27 ♗xg4 ♕h4 28 ♗e6+ ♔h8 29 ♖c3! provides probably winning counterplay, though it would be natural if players without computer assistance avoided this variation.

d3) G.Carbrera-W.Browne, Las Palmas 1977, continued instead with 26 ♖c3 ♘e3 27 ♗xe3 ♘xg4 28 ♗xg4 ♕h4

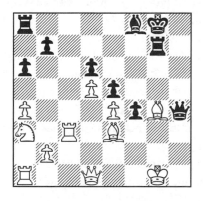

29 ♗f2 ♖xg4+ 30 ♔f1 ♕h1+ 31 ♔e2 ♕xe4+ 32 ♔f1, but now instead of taking a draw by 32...♕h1+, Black kept his initiative going, even after a queen exchange, with 32...♕g2+ 33 ♔e2 e4 34 ♕f1 ♗g7 35 ♕xg2 ♖xg2 36 ♔f1 ♖h2 37 ♖b3 ♖h1+ 38 ♗g1 f3. White has been unable to do anything so far with his extra knight, whereas Black has two big passed pawns, which proved to be decisive.

Stohl offers a possible improvement in 29 ♔f1!?, assessing 29...♖xg4 30 ♗g1

♖c6, P.Lubrano-G.Calzolari, correspondence 1987, as unclear. He doesn't give any further, probably because White appears to have made a clerical error very shortly, giving his knight away on b5. Nevertheless, while the position is absorbing, one cannot help feeling that ♔f1 would have been stronger on move 26.

All in all, Kasparov's little bishop move seems a better idea.

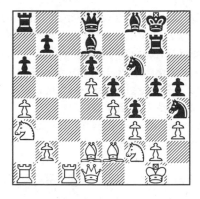

23 ♘c4

Here Stohl suggests 23 ♗e1!? as an alternative, making it more difficult for Black to open up the kingside. If, for example, he tries 23...g4 24 fxg4 hxg4 25 hxg4, there is no real attacking follow-up, as the e1-bishop is excellently placed for defence. Even so, White's extra doubled isolated pawn is not a great attacking force either, and Black could simply shuffle around with his pieces, for example 25...♘h7 26 ♘h3 ♘g6, and play continues. If White were to allow his g4-pawn to fall, he would most likely be worse, which cuts down his queenside attacking possibilities.

Black could also try keeping the

pawn structure in balance, with something like 23...♖b8. However, after 24 ♘a4! b6 (25...b5 26 axb5 axb5 26 ♘a5 favours White) 25 b4, Black is under long-term positional pressure and, although slight, this could well be uncomfortable. The pawn sacrifice seems more consistent.

23...g4!

Having prepared everything, Kasparov finally makes his pawn break.

24 hxg4

24 ♗a5 ♕e7 25 ♘b6?! is much too dangerous. After 25...♘xg2 26 fxg4 ♘e3 27 ♕d2 hxg4 28 ♘xa8 gxh3+, Black breaks through with, for example, 29 ♔h1 ♖g2 30 ♗f3 ♕g7 31 ♖g1 ♕g3 32 ♖xg2 hxg2+ 33 ♔g1 ♕xf3.

White must eliminate the pawns.

24...hxg4 25 fxg4

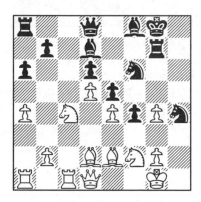

At this point White's kingside looks secure, both g-pawns being defended, and covering the space between the black rook and White's otherwise vulnerable king. There are, however, two possible knight sacrifices on the g-file. Could either of these ever be sound?

25...♘xg2

The alternative was to take on g4 before sacrificing on g2, with 25...♘xg4, and this should end up as equal:

a) 26 ♘xg4? is a mistake, due to 26...♘xg2! 27 ♔xg2 ♗xg4 28 ♗xg4 ♕h4. Have you seen this idea before? Try the analysis on Black's 22...g4 (instead of 22...♗d7). Sometimes tactical ideas repeat themselves in slightly different settings.

Here White has the extra move ♘a3-c4, which changes things a little. For instance, after 29 ♕h1 ♖xg4+ 30 ♔f3 ♖g3+ 31 ♔e2 ♕g4+! 32 ♔f2 and now 32...♗e7, White can defend with 33 ♖a3!. However, Black can play more strongly with 32...b5!, hitting the knight, while clearing the second rank for his queen's rook. If 33 axb5? ♖a7! or 33 ♘b6? ♖a7! switches over to the kingside decisively, while after 33 ♘xe5 dxe5 34 ♖c7 ♗g7 Black has regained the piece, and still has a strong attack.

b) Fortunately for White there is a superior recapture in 26 ♗xg4!.

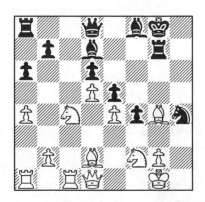

Here Stohl gives 26...♘xg2 as "similar" to 26 ♘xg4 ♘xg2, but there are various tactical differences between having the knight rather than the bishop on g4. In particular, the knight proves to be far more flexible as a short-range defender, using both light squares and dark squares, which means that White does not have to take the black knight on g2 at all.

b1) After 26...♘xg2, White can play 27 ♔f1! ♗xg4 28 ♘xg4 ♕g5 (not 28...♕h4?! 29 ♘f2, and White seems to hold out with the extra material) 29 ♘f2 ♘e3+ and then return the piece with 30 ♗xe3 fxe3 31 ♕f3! exf2 32 ♔xf2. Surprisingly, there seems to be no way for Black to exploit the fragile position of White's king and queen. White might even hope for an endgame with the superior minor piece, though it is probably just equal. I leave it to someone else to analyse the second session.

b2) If Black inserts 26...♗xg4 27 ♘xg4 before 27...♘xg2, then 28 ♔f1! is again correct, and reaches the same position. Instead, 28 ♔xg2? ♕h4 29 ♕h1 ♖xg4+ would land White in line 'a' again, but he does have an intriguing alternative in 28 ♔h1!?, when he is still a piece up, his king has escaped from the g-file, and his knight can retreat to h2, covering the h-file. However, after 28...♕h7+ 29 ♘h2 ♗e7!, Black can bring his queen's rook into the attack with ...♖f8-f6, or ...♔f7 and ...♖h8, and it is not clear how White is going to defend. 28 ♔f1 looks like the safer option.

b3) 26...♕g5 could be considered as well, but seems not fully satisfactory. After 27 ♗e1! ♗xg4 28 ♘xg4 ♕xg4 29 ♕xg4 ♖xg4 30 ♗xh4 ♖xh4 31 ♘b6 followed by ♖c7, White has a slight, but stable edge in a safe position.

Finally, and briefly, Stohl notes that 25...♗xg4?! 26 ♘xg4 ♘xg2 is bad, as White has 27 ♔f1! again. If we carry on the analysis, 27...♘xg4 28 ♗xg4 ♕h4 29 ♗e6+ ♔h8 30 ♖c3!, we see that White indeed takes over.

This is one of the hardest games in this selection to analyse, whether with or without computer help, since there are so many ways to capture or recapture, often with both players having to take with the bishop or the knight. There are also many quiet moves with the white king to consider, which sometimes break the opponent's attack, sometimes do not work, or sometimes can lead to a close struggle. No human player could be expected to analyse this in depth over the board. All that can be done is to select an interesting move, and hope for the best.

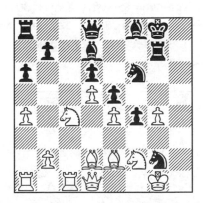

26 ♔xg2

The benefit for Black of taking on g2 first is that the knight cannot then be ignored. However, White now has a remarkable queen sacrifice coming up, which perhaps deserves much more than a zero.

It is wise, as Stohl notes, not to flick in 26 ♗a5?. After 26...♕e7! 27 ♔xg2 ♘xg4 28 ♗xg4 ♗xg4 29 ♘xg4 ♕h4 30 ♕h1 ♖xg4+ 31 ♔f3 ♖g3+ 32 ♔e2, White may have two extra moves (♘a3-c4 and ♗d2-a5) on the familiar position, but he is still in trouble after 32...♕g4+!. For instance, 33 ♔f2 ♗e7! (though not 33...b5? 34 ♘d2 ♖a7, because of 35 ♖c7!) 34 ♘d2 ♗h4 35 ♔f1 f3 (threatening ...f2 or ...♖g2) 36 ♖a3 ♖f8 wins. Or if 33 ♔d2 b5! regains the piece, while maintaining the pressure, as moving the knight loses to 34...♖g2+ 35 ♔c3 ♕f3+ 36 ♔b4 ♖xb2 mate.

"Gaining" a tempo by decentralizing is not always to be advised.

26...♘xg4 27 ♗xg4

Not 27 ♘xg4?, as this transposes to the 25...♘xg4 26 ♘xg4? ♘xg2! 27 ♔xg2 variation given earlier, where 27...♗xg4 28 ♗xg4 ♕h4 29 ♕h1 ♖xg4+ 30 ♔f3 ♖g3+ 31 ♔e2 ♕g4+ 32 ♔f2 and now 32...b5! was very strong for Black.

27...♗xg4

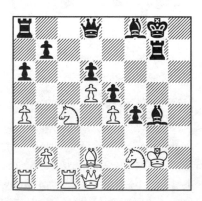

28 ♕xg4!

Desperation? Or a remarkably well-conceived counter-sacrifice? Or something in between?

Not having been in Minsk that day, it is difficult to reconstruct the thought processes of the two players. Stohl, also writing close to twenty years after the game, suggested that Yuferov was wanting to win, and to avoid the perpetual after 28 ♘xg4 ♕h4. Maybe, or maybe not.

Most players will instinctively sense that the exposure of the white king, with Black's queen and rook in strong attacking positions, offers real compensation. Many, possibly most, would consider that Black is better, and has made a brilliant sacrifice. Only very few people, perhaps, would have had the depth of thought to work the position through to its correct conclusion over the board.

The significant point for us to note here is that there is no perpetual in any case. As we've seen several times already, after 28 ♘xg4 ♕h4 29 ♕h1 ♖xg4+ 30 ♔f3 ♖g3+ 31 ♔e2, Black does not have to accede to a draw with 31...♖h3 32 ♕g2+ ♖g3 33 ♕h1 ♖h3, because 31...♕g4+! is very strong. If White instead tries to run west for the hills with 29 ♔f1!? ♖xg4 30 ♔e2, then simply 30...♖g3 keeps him in his place, when White has nothing better than 31 ♕h1 transposing.

But there is still a little comment to be made. White's queen sacrifice may genuinely be a winning attempt!

28...♖xg4+ 29 ♘xg4 ♖c8?!

Bringing the rook into the game, putting pressure on the c-file, and playing for the win; but in view of the possibility for White given in the next note, Black should probably play 29...♕h4! at once.

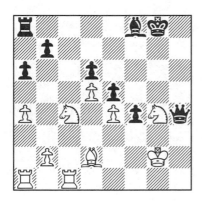

Then 30 ♖g1! ♕g3+! 31 ♔f1 ♕d3+ 32 ♔f2 leads to a host of amusing draws by perpetual check. For instance:

a) 32...♕d4+ 33 ♔f3 ♗g7 (but not 33...♕d3+? 34 ♘ge3+! ♔f7 35 ♖a3 ♕d4 36 ♖c1, and Black is in trouble) 34 ♘xd6 ♕xd2 35 ♘f6+ ♔f8 36 ♘h7+ ♔g8 (and not 36...♔e7? 37 ♘f5+! ♔d8 38 ♖xg7, with a winning attack) 37 ♘f6+ ♔f8 38 ♘h7+ etc.

b) 32...♗g7 33 ♘h6+! ♔f8 34 ♘f5 and now:

b1) 34...♕xc4 35 ♖xg7 ♕c2! 36 ♖h1 ♕xd2+ 37 ♔f3 ♕d3+ 38 ♔g4 ♕e2+ 39 ♔g5 ♕g2+ 40 ♔f6 ♕xh1 41 ♖f7+ ♔e8 42 ♘xd6+ ♔d8 43 ♘xb7+ ♔e8 44 ♘d6+ etc.

b2) 34...♖c8 35 ♗b4! ♖xc4 36 ♗xd6+ ♔e8 37 ♖xg7 ♖c2+ 38 ♔g1 ♕xe4 39 ♖g8+ ♔d7 40 ♖g7+ etc.

b3) 34...♖f6 35 ♖g6 ♗h4+! 36 ♘xh4 ♕d4+ 37 ♔f3 ♕xc4 38 ♗xf4! exf4 39 ♘f5 ♕d3+ 40 ♔xf4 ♕d2+ 41 ♔f3 ♕d3+ 42 ♔f4 ♕d2+ etc.

There are doubtless many more interesting ideas to be unearthed. Instead, we find the familiar paradox that the player – Kasparov, this time – who is trying for a win is in fact risking a loss. Sometimes the correct way for both sides is to accept that the draw is best, while perhaps secretly hoping that the opponent is about to overpress.

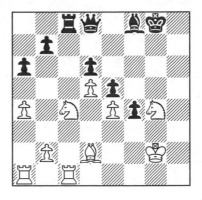

With his last move, Black has finished his development, and the initial tactics are at an end. It is time to reflect on the position.

First, material. White has a rook and two knights, versus queen and pawn. Under the normal calculations, White is, in theory, the equivalent of a pawn up. When material is strongly imbalanced, though, it is wise to think more closely about who stands better. Two knights can often be clumsy, and cannot move quickly. If the knights have to be protected by each other, they are difficult to move at all. If they are not guarded by each other, it is difficult to defend them satisfactorily, especially so if the opponent has a queen, as here.

Next, kings. Black's king is safer than White's. If necessary, Black can cover the king with the bishop. White has no countervailing defensive pieces as yet, although maybe he can try ♘h2 later.

Now pawns. Black has an extra pawn, and it is a strong passed pawn. Less immediately obvious, perhaps, is that White's e-pawn is weak. This is hardly accidental, as Black has been consistently working to break open White's kingside pawn chain in order to attack the king. If the pawn chain at the back falls apart, the reaming pawn is open to pressure.

All these considerations do not automatically mean that Black is better, as White is, after all, still nominally ahead in material. The question is how White is going to work with his pieces together.

30 ♘h2?

Yuferov has matched his opponent blow for blow in all the tactics, but now he falters when he has to make a purely positional decision. It is not easy, with *Fritz* giving a dozen alternatives as equal, but some equal lines are better than others. Summarizing what has gone before, White has more material after his queen's counter-sacrifice, but his pieces lack coordination. The problem with putting the knight on h2 is that it takes a long time to coordinate with anything in the centre. And indeed the centre is important. If pieces can work together mid-board, he can defend on the queenside, and attack on

the kingside, and make full use of his material advantage.

Sometimes the king itself is best placed in the centre. Here 30 ♔f3! ♕h4 31 ♖g1! coordinates the pieces superbly.

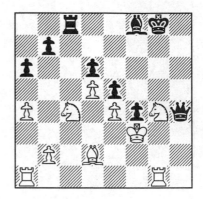

The king guards the e4-pawn and the g4-knight, both important strategic units, and White's other pieces, notably the rooks and the bishop, ensure that Black will have no dangerous attack on the white king. Indeed, it is White who can create threats against the opposing king, so that, for example, 31...♕h3+ 32 ♔e2 ♖xc4? 33 ♘xe5+ wins material for White. Alternatively, if 30...♗g7, then 31 ♖c3! ♕h4 32 ♖g1 reorganizes effectively.

This is a wonderfully elegant way of dealing with the complications of the recent moves, a good and paradoxical idea suddenly making it clear that White, Yuferov, is on top. Go back a few moves, and Yuferov's queen sacrifice was superb. Unfortunately, his mistakes came later.

When I made the selection for this book, and wanted to collect some vigorous and exciting attacking games by the young Kasparov, I did not know in advance whether the games would be sound or unsound, and in many ways this did not matter all that much. I wanted to examine the broad technique of Kasparov in the 70s, the brilliancies, the occasional blunder, and the question of whether his attacking play was generally sound, or whether he needed to consolidate to play at the strongest level.

The answer would seem to be, from the evidence of many of his games, that he was already a brilliant attacking player, but that he would often overpress. However, there was considerable excitement in Kasparov's play. If he could manage such great attacking chess in his teens, what more could he achieve as his play consolidated through his twenties or thirties? This game was "early Kasparov" rather than "mature Kasparov", but it is still exciting and, at times, brilliant.

Finally, it needs to be credited to Stohl that he was ahead of the current book in appreciating the significance of 30 ♔f3!.

30...♕h4 31 ♖c3

It may well be that Yuferov had planned 31 ♗e1, with the idea of regrouping with ♘c4-d2 and then ♘h2-f3, but had underestimated 31...f3+!. At first glance this gives up the passed pawn for not much, but if the f-pawn vanishes, the opposing e-pawn also goes, and Black's queen soon dominates. For example, 32 ♘xf3 ♕xe4 33 ♘cd2 ♕e2+ 34 ♔h1 ♖xc1 35 ♖xc1 e4,

and Black's attack is renewed.

Stohl gave 31 ♖c3 a question mark, but I suspect that White was already in deep trouble however he played it.

31...♖c7

The rook must take part in the game. The black heavy pieces on the same line will be too much to bear, so White must aim for a rook exchange on the g-file, but then the weakness on e4 emerges again.

32 ♖g1 ♖g7+ 33 ♔h1 ♖xg1+ 34 ♔xg1

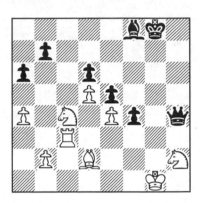

34...♕h7!

How did that happen? White cannot protect the e-pawn. A small surprise, but the geometry of moves such as ♕d8-h4-h7xe4 is part of the charm of chess. If that pawn goes, White's structure will collapse, Black will obtain advanced connected passed pawns in the centre, and the King's Indian bishop will re-emerge from behind the pawn barrier.

It is time for a hopeless sacrifice.

35 ♗xf4 exf4 36 ♘d2 ♕d7 37 ♖c4 ♗g7 38 b3 ♗d4+

More geometry. If now 39 ♖xd4? ♕g7+ picks up the rook.

39 ♔h1 ♗c5 40 ♘df3 b5 41 ♖c2 ♕e8?!

One would assume there had been a time scramble, and that the players, or at least one of the players, would have been uncertain about whether move 40 had been reached. Simply 41...bxa4 42 ♖g2+ ♔f8 43 bxa4 ♕xa4 is more convincing.

42 ♖g2+ ♔f8 43 ♘g5 ♕h5 44 ♘e6+ ♔e7 45 ♖g7+ ♔f6!

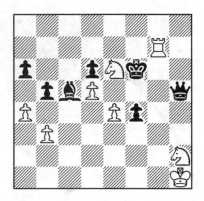

Taking advantage of White's knight on h2 being pinned, so there is no ♘g4+. The rest is relatively straight-forward, although Yuferov fights hard to the last.

46 ♖g4 bxa4 47 bxa4 ♗e3 48 ♘xf4 ♗xf4 49 ♖xf4+ ♔e7 50 ♔g2 ♕d1 51 ♘g4 ♕xa4 52 ♘e3 a5 53 ♘f5+ ♔d7 54 ♖h4 ♕c2+ 55 ♔f3 a4 56 ♖h7+ ♔d8 57 ♖a7 ♕d3+ 58 ♘e3 a3 59 ♔f4 ♕b3 60 ♘f5 ♕b2 0-1

Supplementary game

More than twenty years later, two juniors search for improvements on Yuferov-Kasparov. This is a sure sign that the next generation studied Kasparov's games with great interest, although here the player with Black could be criticized by playing on memory rather than calculation, missing a critical idea.

Game 5.1
M.Moiseev-M.Tarakanov
Russian U-16 Championship,
Serpukhov 1999
King's Indian Defence

---

1 d4 ♘f6 2 c4 g6 3 ♘c3 ♗g7 4 e4 d6 5 ♘f3 0-0 6 ♗e2 e5 7 0-0 ♘c6 8 d5 ♘e7 9 ♘e1 ♘d7 10 ♘d3 f5 11 ♗d2 ♘f6 12 f3 f4 13 c5 g5 14 cxd6 cxd6 15 ♘f2 ♘g6 16 a4 ♖f7 17 ♘b5 h5 18 h3 ♗f8 19 ♕c2 a6 20 ♘a3 ♖g7 21 ♘c4!

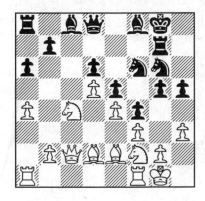

21...♘h4?!

Following Kasparov's idea, but not with great precision.

If instead 21...g4, White can choose between 22 fxg4 hxg4 23 hxg4 (transposing to the 19...g4 variation with 23 ♘c4! in the next note), and 22 ♗a5 ♕e8 23 fxg4 hxg4 24 hxg4 ♘h4 25 ♕d1, followed by ♘b6, with the advantage. For example, 25...♕g6 26 ♘b6 ♗xg4 27 ♘xg4 ♘xg4 28 ♗xg4 ♖e8 29 ♗f3! ♘xg2

30 ♔f2 ♘e3 31 ♕b3 ♖h7 32 ♔e2! ♘xf1 33 ♖xf1 ♖h3 34 ♘c4 ♖e7 35 ♘d2 ♖eh7 36 ♗b6 ♖h2+ 37 ♔d1 ♔h8 38 ♔c1, and White's king escaped to a2, after which his minor pieces dominated Black's rook and pawn, in M.Chovanec-W.Lührig, correspondence 2000.

Black could consider covering the dark squares with 21...b6, although 22 a5 b5 23 ♘b6 ♖c7 24 ♕b3 ♖aa7 25 ♖fc1 ♘d7, as in P.Scheeren-L.Hofland, Dutch Championship, Leeuwarden 1978, should be slightly better for White, for instance after 26 ♘xc8. Sadly he blundered a pawn with 26 ♘d3? ♖xc1+ 27 ♖xc1 ♘xb6 28 axb6 ♕xb6.

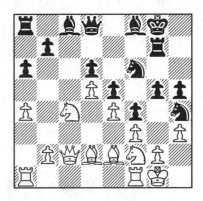

22 ♕d1?

A strange piece of chess psychology. It is possible that someone, a coach or a player, had suggested a very interesting idea, but over the board the player muddled things up. Sometimes it happens. Go back to move 19. Instead of Kasparov's 19...a6, Stohl gives 19...g4 20 fxg4 hxg4 21 hxg4 a6 22 ♘a3 ♖g7 (which was in fact the line chosen by Browne and Kavalek in the earlier games).

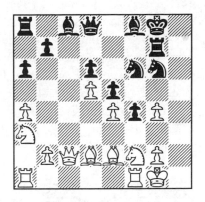

23 ♖fc1 ♘h4 24 ♕d1 now transposes into Yuferov-Kasparov, but Stohl notes that 23 ♘c4! is a possibility (which was originally suggested by Ligterink in *Informator 23*), and if 23...♘h4, White covers g4 with the familiar 24 ♕d1 (or else 24 ♗a5 followed by ♕d1). This perhaps explains why Moiseev would have remembered that ♕d1, without ♖fc1, was a good move.

Stohl then demonstrates the refutation, after 24 ♕d1, of the 24...♘xg2? idea, which is that 25 ♔xg2 ♘xg4 26 ♘xg4 ♗xg4 27 ♗xg4 ♕h4 28 ♖g1! allows White to keep the piece. He suggests instead 24...♘h5 25 ♗a5 ♕g5 26 ♘b6 ♘g3 27 ♘xa8 ♖h7 28 ♘h3, but it is clear that Black does not have enough for the sacrifice here.

Returning to the current game, Moiseev had no need to try to remember complicated lines, as he had a simple positional advantage with 22 ♗a5! ♕e8 and only then 23 ♕d1. White follows up with ♘b6, planning to exchange the critical light-squared bishop, when ...g5-g4 becomes far less dangerous.

22...g4?!

Premature. 22...♖b8 seems to equalize, as White cannot generate much pressure on the queenside without having the second rook in place. For instance, if 23 a5, then 23...g4 24 fxg4 hxg4 25 hxg4 ♘xg4! 26 ♘xg4 ♕g5, and Black will regain the piece with sufficient counterplay.

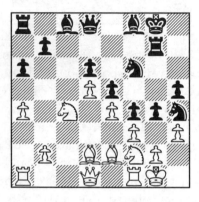

23 ♗a5?!

Mistimed, and showing that White has muddled up his move order. Instead, 23 fxg4 hxg4 24 hxg4 offered an advantage here, and if 24...♖b8, then 25 ♖a3!, when 25...♘xg4? 26 ♘xg4 ♕g5 loses to 27 ♖g3!.

23...♕e7?

Missing his chance to confuse matters with 23...♘xf3+!. For example, 24 gxf3 gxf3+ 25 ♔h1 fxe2 26 ♕xe2 ♕e8, or 24 ♗xf3 ♕e7 25 ♗e2 gxh3 26 ♗f3 hxg2 27 ♗xg2 ♗g4 28 ♕d3 f3, or 24 ♔h1 ♕e7 25 gxf3 g3! 26 ♖g1 ♘h7 27 ♕f1 ♕h4 28 ♘b6 ♘g5.

24 fxg4 hxg4 25 hxg4 ♘xg2

Tarakanov is modelling his play on Kasparov's idea in this line, but there soon appeared a slight but serious

change of set-up.

26 ♔xg2 ♘xg4 27 ♗xg4 ♗xg4 28 ♘xg4 ♕h4

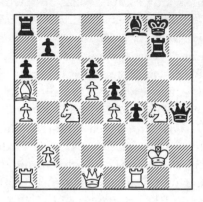

29 ♖g1!

And now we can see why White omitted the earlier ♖fc1. The rook from c1 would not be allowed to jump over the queen on d1. A brilliant inspiration? Or just a trap? It is probably a mixture of both

29...♖xg4+ 30 ♕xg4+ ♕xg4+ 31 ♔f2 ♕xg1+ 32 ♖xg1+ ♔f7 33 ♗c7

White is just a piece up, however Black struggles.

33...b5 34 ♘xd6+ ♔f6 35 ♖c1 bxa4 36 ♖c6 ♔e7 37 ♘f5+ ♔d7 38 ♗xe5 ♖e8 39 ♗d6 ♗xd6 40 ♖xd6+ ♔c7 41 ♖c6+ ♔d7 42 ♔f3 ♖b8 43 ♖xa6 1-0

Curiously, there were few completely wild attacking games by Kasparov in late 1979 and the first half of 1980. It was as if he was purposely quietening his play and consolidating, aiming to ensure becoming a Grandmaster as steadily and smoothly as possible.

If I was writing a book specifically

on Kasparov's best games in his younger years, there would be surely a couple from the Banja Luka tournament in 1979, which Kasparov won, ahead of the rest of the field by two points or more, and gaining a GM norm with great comfort. Players such as Andersson, Smejkal, and Petrosian were left a long way behind, even though Kasparov eased off, agreeing draws in the last five rounds. An awesome result, and he was still only 16.

His instinct for attack was never far behind, though, and as his play developed, he showed that he was able to find bewildering sacrificial ideas against increasingly strong opponents. The next Kasparov game in this selection, against the highly respected grandmaster, Lev Polugaevsky, was still part of his wild years.

Before we get to that, there is now a slight, natural break in this narrative, as we pay attention to the other great attackers, Mikhail Tal and Leonid Stein, to show the different ways these two great players handled their attacking games.

Chapter Two

Leonid Stein 1972-1973:
Three Times Champion of the USSR

Leonid Zakharovich Stein, born 12th November 1934, died 4th July 1973, winner of the USSR Chess Championship three times, was undoubtedly an extremely strong grandmaster. He was, as we shall see, a formidable player in terms of beating even very slightly weaker opposition. He could also hold his own against the strongest opposition. However, Stein never really gained the credit he deserved, mainly because he just missed out, on several occasions, on the chance of playing in a world championship match.

Soon after Stein died, prematurely, Raymond Keene wrote a chess biography of his career. Much of the reporting on Stein's life would have been heavily based on accounts by fellow grandmaster, Eduard Gufeld, written in Russian. Fortunately, there was a more accessible book by Gufeld and Efim Lazarev in the English language (*Leonid Stein: Master of Risk Strategy*), a few years ago, shortly before Gufeld's own death.

Handsome tribute was also paid by Garry Kasparov, in *My Greatest Predecessors* (volume 3), giving several beautiful wins over the years, concentrating on top-class opposition, and players have started to take note of his achievements. There is no doubt that Stein was of world champion class.

The recorded scores by Stein against world champions and challengers were:

Mikhail Botvinnik	+1	=2	-1
David Bronstein	+4	=11	-1
Vassily Smyslov	+1	=8	-1
Mikhail Tal	+2	=12	-0
Tigran Petrosian	+1	=7	-0
Boris Spassky	+3	=10	-0
Robert Fischer	+0	=1	-1
Anatoly Karpov	+0	=3	-2
Viktor Korchnoi	+2	=11	-2

These results are based on *Chess-Base*. Inevitably there might well be omissions.

Had Stein lived for longer, there would have been at least another decade of brilliant play. Against the World Champions of the 1960s, Tal, Botvinnik, Petrosian and Spassky, he had only one loss in 38 games, an almost unbelievable record of solidity.

The only real blot on his record was losing two games against Karpov. As we shall see, Stein played ferociously against him in his final game, trying to get back to 50%, but missed a tactic in a wild position. In the foreword to Gufeld and Lazarev's *Master of Risk Strategy*, Karpov paid tribute to the immense talent of Stein's play, but regarded him as, in effect, slightly lazy, not quite ready enough to broaden his repertoire at the very top level.

The same criticisms may also be made, and have been made by Karpov, on Stein's contemporaries such as Spassky and Petrosian. Of players of that generation, growing up during wartime, life would have been tough, and there would not have been the luxury of concentrating solely on chess from a very young age.

During Stein's childhood, his parents were evacuated during the "war of fascism", according to Gufeld and Lazarev. Stein's father died, through typhus, in 1942. The Stein family, his mother, Leonid himself, and sister, returned to Lviv in the Ukraine. He learnt chess at school, and showed considerable talent, without necessarily

demonstrating himself as a world-beater. He was tactically astute, played quickly, too quickly, and was impulsive, much like his contemporary Mikhail Tal.

Stein did not develop in chess as rapidly as Tal, later to become World Champion in his early twenties. At first Stein did not devote himself exclusively to chess, and sometimes lacked confidence in his ability at the game. He studied engineering, but then began to concentrate on chess, and his engineering studies halted. Then he was drafted into the military, went back to engineering, and started work in a factory. It was only in his mid-20s – by which age Tal had already been and gone as World Champion – that Stein started to show his abilities in the chess world, or at least in the USSR. At the age of 27, he took part in the USSR Championship, in Moscow 1961, surprising many people with wins against Bronstein, Geller, Smyslov and Spassky, in each case with blistering attacking play. Stein did not become Soviet Champion that year, but he won it three times later on, in 1963, 1965 and 1966. These were extremely strong events.

With three Soviet Championship victories, the obvious question is how come Stein did not have a chance of playing a World Championship match. One basic answer is that he was genuinely unlucky, and that had he been a citizen of any country other than the USSR, he would have had good opportunities to progress into the Candidates' and, who knows, beyond. It took time to restructure the qualification system to overcome such injustices.

This still is only a partial answer. Stein won the Soviet Championship three times, and had he finished ahead of other Soviet players in the Interzonal events, he would have had the chance to play through the Candidates' events, and then, with all good speed, play for the World Championship. Ultimately, Stein had the same opportunities as Spassky in qualifying. All he had to do was finish ahead of Spassky.

Probably the answer to the Stein question can be explained through his life biography. He started late at top level chess, too late to become World Champion. Petrosian played in the 1953 Candidates' at the age of 23, and had a decade to hone his skills before beating Botvinnik. Spassky became World under-20 Champion in 1955, and later that year played in the Interzonal, qualifying for the following years Candidates'. It still took over a decade for him to play a World Championship match, losing to Petrosian, and then three more years to win the second match. On the other side of the Atlantic, Fischer, while still a teenager, played twice in the Candidates', in 1959 and 1962, and it was only a decade later, after massive crises of confidence, that he became World Champion.

Seen in this perspective, the odds were against Stein in his quest for the World Championship. He had developed his experience sufficiently to win a national championship, indeed the strongest of all national championships, but the final step was one too far. Nevertheless, he was still a magnificent player.

Stein's sudden death in 1973 in Moscow, on the way to the European Team Championships, was a great shock to the chess world. In 1971, he tied for first in the Alekhine Memorial in Moscow, equal with Anatoly Karpov. This was an immensely strong tournament, with players such as Tal, Spassky and Korchnoi finishing well behind. Less than two years later, Stein was dead.

There has been the occasional speculation that Stein's death was not entirely clear, but there would seem to be no substance to such accusations. Stein was known to have had heart problems, and had been under medication. According to Gufeld and Lazarev, Stein had felt a pain on his chest while staying at the hotel, and the doctors could not save him. Such events, alas, sometimes happen.

It remains to note that among all Stein's chess achievements, he was also married, wedded with Lillya just after the 1962 Interzonal, and had a daughter, Alia.

Stein's style of play

My angle in this book has been to cover games from his final year, 1972/73, against world class grandmasters, through to "ordinary" master and grandmaster opposition, to provide a range of different opponents.

What becomes apparent from the games is that, while Stein may well be an attacker, his play is in some respects in contrast with the style of Tal or the young Kasparov. Play through the games in this book, and you will see that Tal would sacrifice pieces given the least opportunity, while Kasparov was more a specialist of pawn gambits. Stein makes relatively few sacrifices. Even in his wild and complicated win against Smyslov, he is creating serious imbalances in the position without giving up material.

The attacking player makes sacrifices, goes straight for the win, and if his opponent makes any sort of mistake, his position collapses. Maybe the defender makes a whole string of good moves, and can sometimes refute the attacker's imaginative ideas, but quite often he or she collapses under the psychological pressure of attack.

A favourite ploy of the attacker is the gambit, giving up material, in return for the initiative and various kinds of positional pressure. The defender often does not know whether to try to hold everything through the storm, or whether it is better to return the material, aiming maybe to equalize, maybe to show that the gambit play is positionally unsound.

We give several examples from the games of Tal and Kasparov, and of course players of all strengths like to try out for themselves sacrificial attacking chess. One senses, from his games, that Stein took a different approach. Many contradictory views of Stein's play have been voiced, and somehow we need to be able to give a rounded view.

Keene's vivid metaphor, "the Hammer of Thor", is a good starting point. Stein won many games with remarkably quick wins. A sunny day for the first few moves, then massive thunderstorms. His wins against Sigurjonsson and Ljubojevic, from his final year, are modern classics. Neither of these games start of with opening gambits, Stein just plays sensible and sound positional chess, outplays his opponent, and then lightning cracks.

Keene also gives the picture of an artist, a "master of attack", a romantic chessplayer. Maybe this is true, and then maybe it isn't.

Bernard Cafferty, working in conjunction with Mark Taimanov, gave a somewhat different perspective, noting that there were few brilliancy prizes for Stein, in view of his "pragmatic" style. However, theirs was a book on the history of the Soviet Championship, the annual event which added most to Stein's reputation. One cannot completely discount the possibility that contemporaries were irritated that Stein was winning a few games, and giving away very few losses, without doing anything obviously spectacular. This is tournament chess, and Stein showed that he was excellent at winning tournaments.

Kasparov veered towards the artistic side, and analysed several sparkling attacks against top grandmasters, but there were also many quiet "pragmatic" draws.

After playing through games by Stein, Tal and Kasparov, my view is that there were distinct playing styles between Stein and the two World Champions, and that this, if anything, adds to the interest of Stein. After all, he played blistering attacks without taking wildly over-the-top risks. This is to be encouraged.

Of the writers who knew Stein the best, Gufeld and Lazarev deserve the final word. In their book, subtitled *Master of Chess Strategy*, they noted that Stein thought hard about the subject of risk in chess, and used as his motto Tartakower's aphorism, "He who risks, may lose, but he who does not risk, loses."

The authors emphasize that Stein did not go for risk or attack on all occasions, but instead used the weapon of risk as an appropriate part of his armoury. It was always "calculated risk", a sense that, even if he is unable to calculate everything in advance, his position might well prove sound anyway, or at the very least, the opponent will make mistakes.

Stein takes calculated risks, and in every game he calculates not only whether he *should* attack and take risks, but also whether it is time *not* to take risks. Hence the large number of steady and unexciting draws, combined with many startling attacking wins. A seeming paradox of Stein's play.

Our first game is from the international tournament in Reykjavik in 1972.

There was of course a well-known event there that same year – the winner, Bobby Fischer, also spent his final years in Reykjavik, and died there recently. Rest in peace.

Iceland had, and has, a formidable reputation for chess. The game below was not played at the time of the Spassky-Fischer match, but several months earlier, in the long nights of a February winter, rather than the long summer days of the World Championship.

Game 6
G.Sigurjonsson-L.Stein
Reykjavik 1972
Sicilian Defence

---

1 e4 c5 2 ♘f3 d6 3 ♘c3 a6 4 d4 cxd4 5 ♘xd4 ♘f6 6 f4

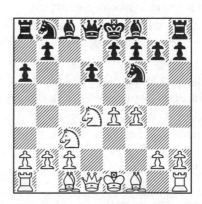

The Najdorf Sicilian was in high fashion in the early 1970s, with 6 ♗g5 being the most aggressive and complicated line. 6 ♗c4 was Fischer's line of attack, while 6 ♗e2 is a solid alternative, with Black having the choice between ...e7-e6 or ...e7-e5.

The variation with an early f2-f4, but not ♗g5, attempts a compromise between wild attack and quiet positional play. There is always a suspicion in such attempts that the attacker might fall between two stalls. Having said that, Sigurjonsson's way of handling this, rather than the opening itself, is not the best.

6...♘bd7 7 ♘f3

No detailed comments on the opening, except to say that White's play seems a bit too jerky in the next few moves. Maybe, the knight could come to b3, instead of f3, to exchange knights after ...♘c5. White could also delay retreating the knight with, for example, 7 ♕f3!? or 7 ♗d3!?.

7...e6 8 ♗d3 ♘c5 9 0-0 ♗e7 10 a4 0-0 11 ♔h1?!

Unnecessary.

11...b6

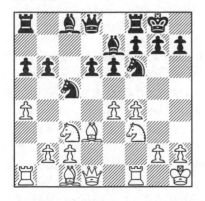

Admire the attractive play later on, by all means. After all, this is entertaining, and enjoyment in geometry is central to chess understanding. As a quick teaser, we can note that Black has a startling piece sacrifice on move 18. Can you guess which white pawn the piece sacrificed for? The answer is surprising, and helps demonstrate why we need to consider all sides of the board, the centre as well as the flanks.

But let us go back. After the standard knight recapture with 5 ♘xd4, White has only made two developing moves, 8 ♗d3 and 9 0-0, not enough. There are questions as to what White is going to do with his dark-squared bishop, lacking the opportunity to bring it to g5. His light-squared bishop is also ineffective, while Black can gain the bishop pair at any moment.

Meanwhile, Black has an easy plan of development with ...♗b7, ...♖c8, and maybe ...♘xc3 and ...d6-d5. Black is comfortable. If he can find a brilliancy, then excellent. Most of the time, though, it is just a case of good development, positional play, locating weaknesses, and grinding the opponent down.

12 b4?

White must already be careful. So far his play has just about kept his position as equal, or only very slightly worse, meaning that he has lost his advantage but should probably hold the position with reasonable accuracy. After, for example, 12 e5 dxe5 13 fxe5 ♘d5 14 ♘xd5 ♕xd5 15 ♖a3 ♗b7, *Fritz* may give this as equal, but the author's instinct would be that Black has good chances for attack, and will be able to take advantage of the bishop pair.

Probably Sigurjonsson would have been uncomfortable about this, but things turned out even worse.

12...♞xd3 13 cxd3

Sigurjonsson has had to give up the two bishops, but he would like to strengthen his pawn structure, in particular securing the e4-square.

13...♝b7 14 ♛b3

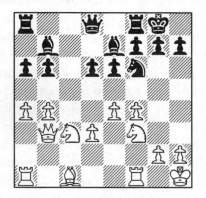

It is fascinating to see how a few slightly substandard moves as White can lead to a quick catastrophe. Black's opening manoeuvres are nothing special, they are simply natural developing ideas in a Sicilian or Hedgehog. It is White's manoeuvring that is unusual. Here the pawn on b4 is a weakness, and a surprisingly acute weakness a few moves later, even when the pawn is protected by a major piece.

Instead, 14 b5 axb5 15 ♞xb5 ♞d7 allows Black to press on the dark squares, but at least White has no immediate worries about losing a pawn.

14...♜c8

Effectively completing his development. Sometimes, as we shall soon see in spectacular fashion, the queen can jump quickly from her starting square to attack in any direction, and

so she does not need to spend a tempo to commit herself. In contrast Black needs his rook on the c-file.

15 ♝e3?

White falls into a deep combination. The fact that combinations can ever take place in chess is because of weaknesses. The white bishop on e3 is going to be attacked, and the pawn on b4 is weak. There is also a mystery weakness to be explained later on.

White could, and should, sort out the weakness of his b-pawn, and 15 b5! is still about equal.

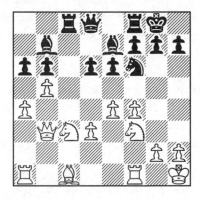

If then 15...d5 16 e5 ♞d7 17 d4 ♛c7 18 ♝b2 ♛c4 19 ♛c2, Black has some useful pressure on the c-file, but this does not seem to create an edge. Indeed, 19...axb5 20 axb5 ♛xb5?! 21 ♛xh7+ ♚xh7 22 ♞xb5, followed by exchanging bishops with ♝a3, gives White a slight edge, if anything. 18...♝b4 19 ♜fc1 is safe for White, too, and there is a danger that he will be able to exploit his extra space in the centre.

15...a5 16 ♝a3 also gives White comfortable play.

It may well be that Black should wait with the pawns, instead continuing to reorganize his pieces, which would be a familiar plan in the Sicilian or Hedgehog. White has few options of breaking through in the centre either.

15...♘d7!? keeps open the option of ...♘c5. If White counteracts with 16 d4, there is some cat and mouse play with 16...♘f6 17 d5 exd5 18 exd5 ♘d7, and the knight will finally emerge on c5.

White could try instead 16 ♗e3, with equality after 16...♘c5 17 ♕c2 d5 18 e5 f6 19 ♗d4!. However, Black might try the pawn sacrifice 18...d4!?, an interesting echo of Stein's play in the game. After 19 ♘xd4 f6, Black has an excellent open diagonal for his light-squared bishop, a secure knight, and pressure on the c- and d-files, while White has problems in activating his queen and minor pieces. Black cannot create an immediate breakthrough, but neither can White completely consolidate. Black might try for pressure with ...♕d7, ...♖f7, and possibly ...♖df8.

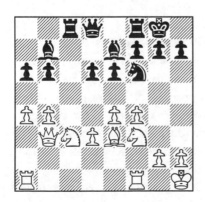

15...d5!

A classic Scheveningen-type break-

through. Black may look passive, with the pawns dormant on d6 and e6, but given the opportunity, he will be happy to break open the position, sometimes even with the f-pawn. What usually happens in such set-ups, is that Black plays ultra-solidly at first, eliminating any chances of a pawn-push behind his pieces, then aims for complete equality. Except that he can still play for more. Black often keeps open the possibility of a central breakthrough, even if postponed until quite a late stage.

16 e5?

It is unlikely that White knew what had hit him, a common result when playing against Stein, and here Sigurjonsson missed the deeply hidden tactic. 16 ♖fd1! was the best try.

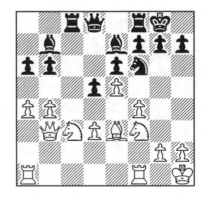

16...d4!

Black can move the knight away, and 16...♘g4 17 ♗d4 ♘h6 followed by ...♘f5 is satisfactory for equality and perhaps a little more. But Stein finds something much better, more dangerous. It all works out very well, a volcanic eruption from beneath.

In contrast with many of the games by Tal or Kasparov, Stein is playing within the rules of positional chess. There are no instances in this game where one senses that Stein has chanced his arm too much, and that if Sigurjonsson defended with 100% accuracy, he would win. We shall see, in later games, that Stein had a remarkable ability to fix an any tiny weaknesses in his opposition's play. Few could better that.

17 ♘xd4

White cannot gain by taking the knight. After 17 exf6 ♗xf6 18 ♘xd4 ♗xd4 19 ♗xd4 ♕xd4, Black has clearly the better pawn structure. 17 ♗xd4 ♗xf3 18 exf6 ♗xf6 19 ♗xf6 ♕xf6 also gives Black an edge.

17...♘g4

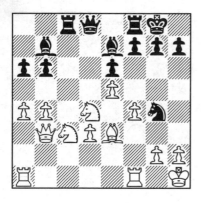

For just a single pawn sacrifice, Black has an excellent long diagonal, and lethal attacking pressure across a wide range of dark squares. The bishop on e3 is obviously attacked, the two knights, both on dark squares, are also vulnerable, and even sacrificial captures of the pawns on b4 and h2 are

being threatened.

This is a remarkable combination, and many, many people would not have noticed the well-hidden opportunity.

As the reader goes through this brief selection of Stein's games, a pattern emerges of a large number of very quick attacking wins. For a grandmaster to beat 2000-rated opponents in this fashion is nothing special. To do so time after time against GMs and IMs, that is something rather more noteworthy.

18 ♗g1 ♘xh2!!

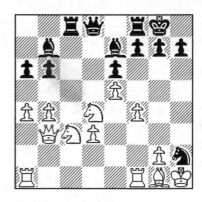

19 ♖fc1

19 ♗xh2 ♕xd4 is obvious enough, when Black immediately regains the pawn, with threats on b4, c3 and d3, and perhaps also later pressure on g2.

What is unusual is the collapse of so many dark squares after 19 ♔xh2 ♖xc3! 20 ♕xc3 ♗xb4! 21 ♕xb4 ♕h4 mate. A combination to dream of.

Stein would almost certainly have seen the idea as far back as 15...d5.

19...♘g4 20 ♘e4 ♗xb4 21 ♘g5

Sigurjonsson tries to cover all the

gaps in his structure, but it is far too late to hold. He reaches the time control without any further excitement (unless perhaps Stein's flag was close to falling), and then resigns.

21...♕d5 22 ♘gf3 ♕xb3 23 ♘xb3 ♗d5 24 ♘fd2 ♗c3 25 ♖ab1 b5 26 axb5 axb5 27 ♘e4 ♗xe4 28 dxe4 ♖c4 29 g3 h5 30 ♔g2 ♖d8

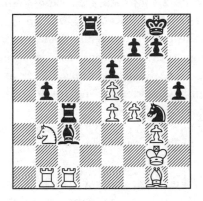

31 ♖c2 ♗xe5 32 ♖xc4 bxc4 33 ♘a5 ♖d2+ 34 ♔f3 ♗d4 35 ♗xd4 ♖d3+ 36 ♔e2 ♖xd4 37 e5 c3 38 ♖c1 ♖d2+ 39 ♔f3 ♖d3+ 40 ♔g2 ♘e3+ 41 ♔f2 ♘f5 0-1

Stein was lethal in mixed-field events. Before the big Swiss system open tournaments, there was a standard format of perhaps sixteen players, a few top grandmasters, a few mid-range grandmasters and international masters, and a few local players, some of whom occasionally felt out of depth. These days there remain several top-level tournaments with this format, and many Swiss events, but a dwindling number of other all-play-alls.

In some ways, the old-style mixed strength all-play-all was not all that different from a standard Swiss event, in which the strong players chew up lower-graded opponents, and only then, in the later rounds, battle amongst themselves for the prize money. There is, however, much less time for preparation in a Swiss. If, in a nine-round tournament, there are a hundred competitors, it is impossible to prepare against everyone.

The really successful players, and Stein was one of them, had the ability to demolish the lower half, maybe even achieving a whitewash against them, and simply taking draws in the top half, playing solidly and avoiding mistakes, only occasionally scoring a win.

For instance, at Zagreb in 1972, Stein won by 1½ points, and even then relaxed towards the end of the tournament. His main expected rival was Vlastimil Hort. There is an interesting comparison to be made:

	players on 50% or above	below 50%	Total
Leonid Stein	+1 =6 -0	+5 =1 -0	9½
Mato Damjanovic	+3 =4 -0	+1 =4 -1	8
Drazen Marovic	+2 =4 -1	+2 =4 -0	8
Vlastimil Hort	+2 =5 -0	+1 =5 -0	8

Although the three runners-up managed more wins against the stronger players, Stein's near wipeout of the weaker players gave him a decisive tournament victory. Stein was indeed the "Hammer of Thor", as Keene put it. Similar examples can be found throughout his career.

We now look through a game from Zagreb. It is another quick storming win by Stein, and one is duly impressed. But look carefully, and we can see that Stein made a big oversight. His opponent missed it, no doubt thinking he was going to resign anyway.

It is possible that health issues were starting to become a concern for Stein. He was dead only a year later, as a result of a heart attack. From my own perspective, I know that high blood pressure can make you become dizzy and lose concentration during the later parts of the game. Stein was playing creatively until his death, and was selected for the USSR team in the European Championships. Nevertheless, there are some slight hints in retrospect of an increasing number of errors.

But try to enjoy Stein's creative play, and remember that he achieved a winning position against a grandmaster in twenty moves. Again, how did he do it? Stein was not an ultra-theoretical player, although he clearly knew his openings. What seems particularly important was that his brain was working well at the beginning of the game. He was thinking from move one, while his opponents sometimes took a while to get warmed up. Some-

times he won games frighteningly quickly.

Game 7
L.Stein-M.Bertok
Zagreb 1972
Sicilian Defence

---

1 e4 c5 2 ♘f3 ♘c6 3 d4 cxd4 4 ♘xd4 ♘f6 5 ♘c3 d6 6 ♗g5 e6 7 ♕d2 a6

The pin by the white bishop is irritating, but does not as yet create threats. At various times, Black may want to consider ...h7-h6, forcing White to commit himself.

Here 7...h6 8 ♗h4? works very well for Black, as he wins a pawn with 8...♘xe4!.

8 ♗e3 ♘g4, gaining the bishop pair, should also be fine, although White is slightly ahead in development.

This leaves 8 ♗xf6 gxf6 (but not 8...♕xf6?! 9 ♘db5, winning the d-pawn), when Black is effectively a tempo down on the type of structure we have seen in Kasparov-Sokolov (Game 1). As Botvinnik and others have shown, this line is still playable, but mostly Black delays ...h7-h6, trying to avoid the tempo loss.

8 0-0-0 ♗d7

Another chance to play ...h7-h6. The alert tactician, whether as attacker or defender, will want to take note of any implications of move order.

On 9 ♗h4 Black can again safely play 9...♘xe4, as after 10 ♘xe4 ♕xh4 11 ♘xc6 ♕xe4! he keeps the extra pawn with comfort. A few players have fallen into the trap of 11 ♘xd6+? ♗xd6 12 ♘xc6, hoping to checkmate on d8, but the queen is trapped after 12...♗f4. White has occasionally tried 10 ♕f4 ♘g5 11 ♘xc6 bxc6 12 ♕a4 , but this is a rather speculative sacrifice.

The safest option for White, given that 9 ♗xf6?! ♕xf6 now does nothing, is 9 ♗e3. Then Black can just develop normally, allowing White to choose between f2-f3 or f2-f4, or else try 9...♘g4, although White probably still has a slight edge after 10 ♘xc6 bxc6 11 ♗c5. For example, 11...♗b7 12 h3 dxc5 13 ♕xd8+ ♖xd8 14 ♖xd8+ ♔xd8 15 hxg4 ♗d6 16 ♘a4 ♔c7 17 ♗c4 with the better endgame for White, due to his superior pawn structure, in V.Smyslov-M.Botvinnik, 21st matchgame, Moscow 1957, though it ended as a draw.

So 8...h6 is possible and playable, but not an improvement.

9 f3 ♗e7

Or again 9...h6, but Black's move is at least as good.

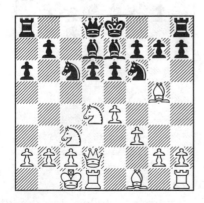

10 g4

White usually prefers 10 h4 here, not least because the bishop on g5 will be protected. It would probably be idle to speculate why Stein played one move rather than the other. We can note, though, that Black played slightly passively in reply, often bad news in a Sicilian.

There is another option in 10 ♗xf6, exploiting the fact that the bishop cannot recapture, as 10...♗xf6 11 ♘xc6 ♗xc6 12 ♕xd6 ♕a5 13 ♕d2 does not quite give Black full compensation for the sacrificed pawn. However, 10...gxf6 looks fine, and White will have lost a tempo if he tries f2-f4.

10...♕c7?!

Good news for Stein.

This is of course a natural developing move, and one can almost play such a move automatically, without needing to think. Almost, but not quite. 10...♕c7 uses up a tempo, and it is not all that clear that Black makes good progress after this move. White, meanwhile, can think about starting an attack.

Instead, 10...♘xd4!? 11 ♕xd4 could be considered, followed by ...♗c6 or ...♕a5. In supplementary game, Tarasov-Vilkov, Black in fact played both. Alternatively, he could strike back on the kingside with 10...h5!?.

11 ♗e3 h6

Strange at first. One might have expected that ...h7-h6 should come before ♗e3, rather than ♗e3 coming before ...h7-h6. Stein wanted to give room for White to play g4-g5 though, and Bertok presumably wanted to slow down White's kingside pawn push.

11...0-0 12 g5 ♘e8 13 h4 looks hazardous from the defender's point of view, though *Fritz* gives it as equal.

12 h4

Instinctively, one might feel that White has a slight edge, and if Black is not careful, he could be in trouble. Sure enough, Stein soon gives him a pounding.

12...♘e5?!

And this soon proves to be inaccurate. Black's idea is to exchange his knight for White's light-squared bishop. It is often tempting to gain the bishop pair, but try counting the tempi. Black plays ...♘c6-e5-c4, three moves. White only makes one move, ♗xc4. So Black has used up two extra tempi. Furthermore, White's bishop is not the more effective, and Black's knight is a good defender. White can be happy with all this.

12...♖c8 looks much more accurate, one point being that if 13 ♗d3, which looks natural enough, Black can try to exchange his knight for bishop with 13...♘b4!, saving a tempo.

White could try 13 ♖g1, to consolidate the threat of g4-g5, but after

13...♘xd4 14 ♗xd4 e5 15 ♗e3 ♗e6 16 g5 hxg5 17 hxg5 ♘d7 18 g6, Black seems to hold the slightly delicate balance with either 16...f6 or 16...f5.

Another interesting possibility is 12...d5!? 13 exd5 ♘xd5 14 ♘xd5 exd5, opening up the central pawn structure, although Black is not quite fully equal here. For example, 15 ♗f4 ♕b6 16 ♘xc6 bxc6 17 ♗d3 ♗e6 18 g5 hxg5 19 hxg5 0-0-0 20 ♗e5 ♖xh1 21 ♖xh1 g6 22 f4 was slightly better for White in W.Rocha-E.Limp, Sao Paulo 1998, though the game was eventually drawn after a long endgame struggle.

All in all, 12...♖c8 seems the best defensive try.

13 ♖g1

Ignoring the very minor threat. The bishop is relatively unimportant, whereas the pawn roller, when it eventually arrives, creates much more danger.

13...♘c4?!

Continuing to follow the doubtful plan, even though there is a strong argument to keep the knight of the board for a while, in view of g4-g5-g6 thrusts.

13...♘h7 keeps Black in the game, although after 14 f4 ♘c4 15 ♗xc4 ♖xc4 16 ♘f3! ♗c4 17 ♕d4 ♕xd4 18 ♘xd4 White has a space advantage on the kingside as a result of his pawn advances. Black's bishop pair is of only slight importance.

14 ♗xc4 ♕xc4 15 g5

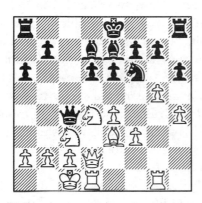

White has made real progress. Black's king is not as yet under threat, but that might well change.

15...♘h5?!

One senses that Bertok's confidence is gradually eroding, as he makes a few minor concessions without really putting up a strong fight. Instead, 15...hxg5 16 hxg5 ♘h7 17 g6 fxg6 18 ♖xg6 ♗f6 19 ♘de2 ♘f8 20 ♖g2 leaves Black's minor pieces uncoordinated, and White keeps a slight edge.

16 gxh6 g6?!

Presumably Bertok dislikes the pawn exchange, and hopes that he might have the chance of swallowing up the white pawn on h6, or at the very least that the pawn will prove harmless.

16...gxh6 17 ♗xh6 is more natural,

when Black can try to bring the king into safety by 17...0-0-0. Here a tactician might well be tempted by 18 ♘f5!? exf5 19 ♘d5 ♕xa2 20 ♘xe7+ ♔b8 21 ♕xd6+ ♔a8.

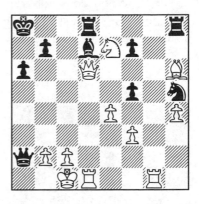

White undoubtedly has attacking chances, but Black has found some counterplay. For instance, if then 22 ♗e3 ♕a1+ 23 ♔d2 ♕xb2 24 ♗b6 ♗a4 25 ♗xd8 ♕xc2+ 26 ♔e3 f4+ 25 ♔d4 ♕b2+, and Black has at least a perpetual.

Convinced? One's chess instincts feel that White should be able to improve on this, and sure enough there is some attractive geometry earlier with 22 ♕b6! ♕a1+ 23 ♔d2 ♗b5+ 24 ♘d5 ♕xb2 25 ♖b1! ♕f6 26 ♗e3. After some drastic simplification, with 26...♕xb6 27 ♗xb6 fxe4 28 fxe4 ♖dg8 (but not 28...♖c8? 29 ♖xb5! axb5 30 ♖a1+ ♔b8 31 ♗a7+ ♔a8 32 ♘b6 mate) 29 ♖xg8+ ♖xg8 30 ♘c7+ ♔b8 31 ♘xb5 axb5 32 ♖xb5, Black receives a reminder that his knight is seriously out of place on the edge.

Alternatively, going back to move 18, a quieter player might well have been satisfied with 18 ♗g5 f6 19 ♗e3

♔b8. White is a pawn up, and has no serious disadvantages, but it would take an effort to grind the position down.

17 ♗g5 ♗f8 18 ♔b1

For safety. White does not want to allow counterplay against his king, if the position opens up during his attack.

18...b5

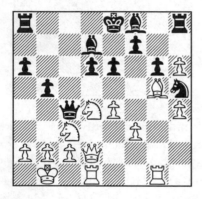

19 ♖de1!

Simple chess. Black's king is tied down by the g5-bishop, and White is eyeing up the e-file, with the aim of a ♘d5 threat, which incidentally makes Black's last move a strategic irrelevance.

The only real question here is whether the queen's rook or the king's rook should move to the e-file. The natural assumption would be that it is better, more centralized, to have the rooks on d1 and e1, rather than e1 and g1. Play through the game, however, and you will see why Stein correctly played the less obvious move.

19...♗c8

Tame. Sometimes the best practical defensive approach is to try to tempt the opponent into a crowd-pleaser which does not quite work. If, for example, Black plays 19...♗c6, White can still reply 20 ♘d5, but after 20...♗xd5 21 exd5 ♕xd5 22 ♘xe6!? ♕xd2 23 ♘c5+ ♕xe1+ 24 ♖xe1+ ♗e7 25 ♖xe7+ ♔f8 22 ♘d7+ ♔g8, White cannot quite find the winning blow, and Black holds.

There are various alternatives for White before this, some of which might give him some sort of edge, but it would be simplest not to try out the tactics at all. One way is 20 b3 ♕c5 21 ♗e3 b4 22 ♘ce2, and Black is in trouble with both the queen and bishop. Possibly this is what Bertok in the end decided to avoid.

Perhaps the best chance was to try and solidify the centre with 19...f6 20 ♗e3 b4 followed by 21...e5, even if this means giving up the g-pawn.

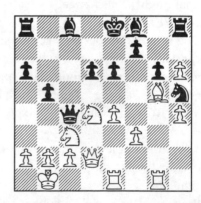

20 ♘d5!

A standard sacrifice. Black does not necessarily have to accept it, but otherwise he faces catastrophe on the dark squares. For instance, after 20...♗b7 21 ♘b6, 20...e5 21 ♕a5, or 20...♖b8 21 b3

♕c5 22 b4! ♕c4 23 ♖e3, threatening ♖c3, trapping the queen.

20...exd5 21 exd5+ ♔d7 22 ♘c6 ♗b7

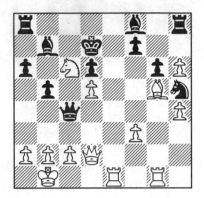

23 ♖g4?!

Just when it looks as though it is about time for Black to resign, Stein overlooks a tactic. When playing through the games against Smyslov and Grigorian in this collection, the impression is that Stein made mistakes, just when he was in a winning position. In the last year or so before his untimely death, Stein was still playing good and imaginative chess, but every so often errors were creeping in.

Here 23 ♖e4! ♕c5 24 ♗e3 wins the queen, because if Black tries 24...♗h6, White gives checkmate instead after 25 ♖e7+ ♔c8 26 ♕a5.

23...♕c5 24 ♗e3 ♗xh6!

Now Bertok is, no doubt much to his surprise, still in the game. As we have just seen, with a rook on e4 (instead of g4), White wins with ♖e7+. Unfortunately, the rook on e1 cannot jump over the bishop.

25 ♗xh6?

Stein must have been disconcerted by this chain of events, as he selects only the third best of the three main responses.

The best is 25 b4!, and if 25...♕b6? 26 ♗xb6 ♕xd2 27 ♖e7+ ♔c8 28 ♖c7 mate, while 25...♗xe3 26 ♖xe3 ♕b6 27 ♖e7+ ♔c8 28 ♘a5! still gives White a winning attack.

The second choice is 25 f4, simply avoiding the exchange of bishops, and after 25...♕c4 26 b3 ♕e4, White can clear the e-file again with 27 ♗b6, and should win.

25...♗xc6 26 dxc6+

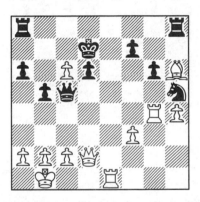

26...♔xc6??

Very difficult to understand. Kings can be fine in the middle of the board in an endgame, but not with queens and rooks in full pomp. Instead, 26...♕xc6, followed by one of the rooks to e8, gives Black chances to hold.

27 ♖e7 ♖xh6 28 b4 1-0

If the black queen goes anywhere it can't be taken (b6, d5 or f5), White forces mate with 29 ♕c3+.

Bertok clearly had one of those days when absolutely everything goes wrong.

Supplementary game

> ### Game 7.1
> ### I.Tarasov-V.Vilkov
> Kaluga 1996
> *Sicilian Defence*

1 e4 c5 2 ②f3 d6 3 d4 cxd4 4 ②xd4 ②f6 5 ②c3 ②c6 6 ♗g5 e6 7 ♕d2 a6 8 0-0-0 ♗d7 9 f3 ♗e7 10 g4 ②xd4 11 ♕xd4 ♗c6 12 h4 ♕a5

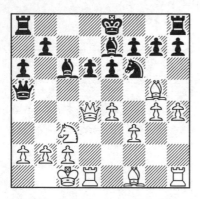

With his last few moves, Vilkov has played much more openly than Bertok, and has good chances of equalizing. White is still able to attack, but if Black defends accurately, he can hope for reasonable counterplay.

13 ♔b1 0-0 14 ♕d2 ♔h8

Black sees that ②d5 is a threat, and so moves his king away to avoid a later ②xe7+. The only danger is that the king will be exposed to tactics on the long diagonal.

15 h5 ♖fd8 16 h6 g6

White senses that there might be a quick win, maybe by a sacrificial attack, but how should he handle it?

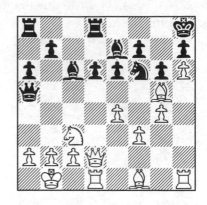

He can win a pawn with 17 ♕f4 ♕e5 18 ♖xd6!, exploiting the weaknesses on the dark squares, but Black survives after 18...♕xd6 19 ♗xf6+ ♔g8 20 ♕xd6 ♗xd6 21 ♗xd8 ♖xd8. White has no obvious way to improve his position, some of his pawns are slightly loose, and Black has the bishop pair. White can still keep playing for a win, but with accurate defence Black should be able to hold.

Naturally dissatisfied with this variation, White tried:

17 ♗b5?

Intending to follow up with ♕f4 next move, having first prevented ...♕e5, by blocking the fifth rank. It is spectacular, but should probably lose with correct play.

17...♔g8??

A complete wimp-out. There is no real excuse for this, as Black has already played ...♔g8-h8 (on move 14) to avoid the knight tactic on d5. Now he falls straight into the trap.

17...axb5! is course critical, and while Black will be unable to defend the kingside after 18 ♕f4, he has enough resources to counter-attack against his opponent's king.

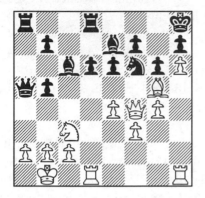

For instance, 18...b4 (18...e5! may be even better) 19 ♗xf6+ ♔g8 20 ♗xe7 bxc3 21 a3 ♕b5! (so that ♗xd8 doesn't hit the queen) 22 ♕c1 ♖xa3 23 ♖xd6 (if 23 ♗xd8 ♖a8 and ...♕a4 wins) 23...♖xd6 24 ♗xd6 ♖a6 25 ♖d1 ♗e8, when Black is ready to play ...♕a5 with a winning attack.

The reader might complain that no player could calculate all these variations over the board, from just before White's 17th move. Quite so, but this would reinforce the point that a strong player will have a good instinct of what is likely to be a good move, and what is not, without having to calculate in depth.

18 ♗xc6 bxc6 19 ♗xf6 1-0

After 19...♗xf6 20 ♘d5! ♕xd2 21 ♘xf6+ wins a piece.

In the next game Stein tried to hammer Karpov, and he came very close to succeeding, though he ultimately failed against Karpov's exemplary defence. The obvious question is

whether Stein sacrificed incorrectly. Further analysis suggests the attack was sound, but that he made a significant oversight later on.

Unlike Tal and, later on, the young Kasparov, the general conclusion is that Stein generally avoided speculative attacks. He played aggressively, and forced his opponent to work hard, but he kept within the bounds of sound positional chess.

Game 8
L.Stein-A.Karpov
USSR Spartakiad, Moscow 1972
Grünfeld Defence

---

1 c4 c5 2 ♘f3 ♘f6 3 ♘c3 d5 4 cxd5 ♘xd5 5 d4 ♘xc3 6 bxc3 g6 7 e4 ♗g7

This is so obviously a standard Grünfeld, so much so that at first it would hardly be worth placing a diagram here. However, the next diagram, a few moves later, shows that Stein is already launching a highly dangerous sacrificial attack – and that against Karpov, soon to become World Champion, and already achieving the reputation of being the most secure defensive player of the time.

Stein later lost this game, but he was clearly creating pressure, and many other Grandmasters as Black could easily have folded quickly. If anyone doubts this, just play through some of the later quick wins against strong opposition, and then go through the databases during his peak years in the 1960s and early 1970s.

We have an unusual phenomenon here: the "Hammer of Thor", as Keene once described it. I am concentrating in detail on two of Stein's games, this one against Karpov, and Stein's winning position in a dozen moves against Ljubojevic. Other games could easily have been selected.

Stein does not usually aim for gambit chess, but instead for standard attacking ideas, albeit with an unusual bite. His opponent has to think hard, as Stein is excellent at punishing even the slightest mistake. He will, if required, sacrifice with full vigour even just out of the opening, as against Karpov, but on the whole tends not to.

As for the exact move order, note that Stein started with 1 c4, rather than 1 d4, and Karpov replied with 1...c5. As a result, in the diagram position Black has played ...c7-c5 rather than ...0-0. This is often of little significance, and ...c7-c5 and ...0-0 may quickly transpose. Sometimes, however, even the slightest unusual move may quickly deviate from the expected lines.

8 &b5+

Nothing unusual yet. Indeed, this was the very oldest of Grünfeld variations, the game B.Kostic-E.Grünfeld, Teplitz-Schönau 1922, continuing 8...&d7 9 &xd7+ ♕xd7 10 0-0 cxd4 11 cxd4 ♘c6 12 &e3 0-0 13 ♖b1 ♘a5 14 d5 ♖fc8 15 &d4 &xd4 16 ♕xd4 b6 17 ♘e5 ♕d6 18 ♘g4 ♕f4 19 ♘e3, with level play and later drawn.

8...♘d7

Karpov himself enters less standard set-ups. The main line is 8...♘c6 9 0-0 cxd4 10 cxd4 0-0 11 &e3 &g4 12 &xc6 bxc6 13 ♖c1 ♕a5 14 ♕d2 with equality.

9 0-0 0-0 10 a4

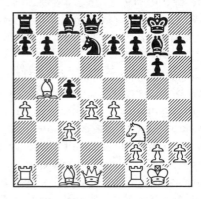

Quite a familiar idea, particularly in such positions as the Benoni. White wants to attack on the kingside and make use of his light-squared bishop, but he also wants to stabilize his pieces first and prevent Black from counter-attacking with ...a7-a6 and ...b7-b5.

A much earlier and cruder version, N.Bergqvist-L.Prins, Buenos Aires Olympiad 1939, started off with 10 e5 a6 11 &d3 b5 12 ♘g5 ♘b6, when Black was beginning to activate his pieces on the queenside. After 13 &e4 ♖a7 14 ♕f3 h6 15 ♘h3 cxd4 16 ♖d1 h5 17 ♕g3 ♖c7 18 cxd4 ♘d5 19 ♗d2 ♖c4 Black was better, and later won. White's pieces were in vaguely in the right sort of position for attack, but Black had improved his pawn structure and piece activity.

10...a6 11 ♗c4 ♕c7 12 ♕e2 b6

Black has tried out a few alternatives in the last few moves, generally with a slight edge for White. There is no obvious Black consensus.

13 e5!

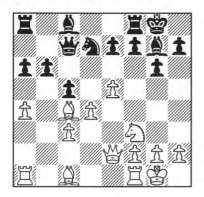

It is clear that Stein has achieved exactly what he wanted, a sharp attacking game against his young and highly talented opponent. There are a few problems on Karpov's kingside, and it is not beyond the bounds of possibility that there may be sacrifices coming up.

13...e6

Karpov wants to prevent White from pressing forward with e5-e6.

After 13...cxd4 14 e6, White is not worse, and quite likely will be significantly better. *Fritz* suggests that this is equal, but the human player, over the board, will tend to distrust this for Black. For instance, 14...♘e5 15 ♘xe5 ♗xe5 16 exf7+ ♔g7 17 cxd4 ♗xh2+ 18 ♔h1 seems better for White. If Black's queen were in front of the bishop on the b8-h2 diagonal, that would be a different matter, but this is not going to happen. If 18...♗d6 19 ♗b2 ♕d8, White sidesteps the planned queen check with ...♕h4, playing 20 ♕f3 e6 21 ♔g1!, with advantage after a few minor tactics.

Karpov avoids all this. He would have been aware that his opponent has the chance of setting off a dangerous piece sacrifice, but decided that it is best to allow the sacrifice and defend it, the position being difficult, but fully playable. Neither player gives way in the battle between attack and defence, and indeed it often happens that if either one aims for a peaceful life, the result ends up as a rout.

14 ♘g5!

With sacrificial ideas to come. Black is so reliant for defence on his pawns on the light squares that a quick knight sacrifice for a couple of them is an obvious possibility.

14...♗b7

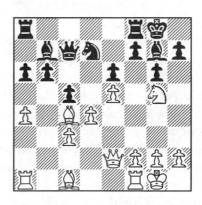

15 f4

Who would not have been tempted by this move? The pawn push is a direct plan, with all sorts of attacking ideas, and Black will have to play with considerable composure just to stay in the game. White now has the possibility of advancing with f4-f5, giving up the pawn to break open Black's kingside or, even more violent, sacrificing the knight for two pawns. Very dangerous.

Who indeed could resist? Perhaps a quiet positional player who is suspicious about unnecessary sacrifices, and would prefer a purely strategic game. One of the fascinations of chess is that, quite often, there is a clear choice between tactical and positional play, and it is very difficult to work out which plan is better in a particular position. In analysis afterwards it might be possible, for example, to pinpoint three critical lines some ten moves deep, and then decide whether each of these is good, or not. Over the board you do not know in advance whether one of these moves will prove, after some tactics, to be good, or whether any of them is playable at all.

In the end, after Karpov's sturdy defence, Stein lost this game. Had he been a quiet percentage player, it would probably have been drawn, but then Stein probably wouldn't have won so many other games either.

If we are thinking about positional as opposed to tactical chess, the natural and good reply would be 15 ♗d3!?, avoiding potential counterplay on the

c-file (...c5xd4, with pressure against c4), consolidating the d3-h7 diagonal, and providing a good retreat on e4 for the knight. White's pieces are better placed. There is no need as yet to decide on where to place the other bishop; it will become clearer after a few more moves what is going on. A slight but clear edge for White, one might possibly assume.

To this positional continuation, Black has a tactical response in 15...cxd4 16 cxd4 ♘xe5 17 dxe5 ♗xe5 18 ♖b1 ♗xh2+ with three pawns for the knight, although White looks better here. White might even improve with 17 ♗f4 f6 18 ♘xh7! ♕c6 (if 18...♔xh7? 19 ♕h5+ ♔g8 20 ♗xg6 wins) 19 ♗e4 ♕xe4 20 ♕xe4 ♗xe4 21 ♘xf8 ♖xf8 22 dxe5.

There are quieter alternatives for Black, probably not quite equalizing, though a pawn sacrifice with 15...b5!? is interesting.

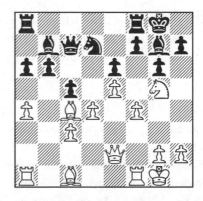

15...h6

If Stein's last move was highly characteristic of his own attacking play, then this in return is typically Karpovian. Black is not indulging in complicated manoeuvring. He is pushing away one of White's most dangerous pieces, and saying, "I don't believe your sacrifice, I'm not going to lose, and I could well win".

Such coolness of response is rare. Most of us, when we see a sacrificial attack by the opponent, see the king being pushed into the open, tend to get anxious, maybe even panicky. Quite often this is of great help to the attacker. If the critical defensive line is avoided, then there will be no refutation, and the element of bluff will quickly turn into a smooth attacking win. An excellent example involving two former World Champions is the game Spassky-Tal in Montreal 1979, where Spassky fell for the bluff. Here Karpov stayed in full control.

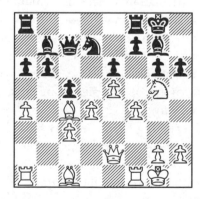

Now for the critical position. There is not much point in withdrawing the knight, 16 ♘e4? cxd4 17 cxd4? ♗xe4 being an outright blunder, so White must sacrifice. Obviously Stein has already decided on the knight sacrifice, but which one?

16 ♘xe6

Should Stein have preferred the move 16 ♘xf7 here? Or is it worse? Or about the same? In the end it would be impossible to calculate in conclusive depth over the board, time in chess being limited. The normal strategy would be to run a preliminary scan through the main candidate moves, checking if either one leads to a clear advantage or is a clear mistake. If it ends up as something in between, then who knows?

We analyse 16 ♘xf7 separately, after the main game. Instead we have 16 ♘xe6, which is probably the more natural move, though not necessarily better.

16...fxe6 17 ♗xe6+ ♔h8

17...♔h7 is also possible, but it makes sense to keep off the light squares. For instance, 18 f5!? gxf5? 19 ♗xf5+ ♔h8 20 ♗xh6! ♗xh6 21 ♕h5 ♕c6 22 d5! wins for White.

18 ♕g4

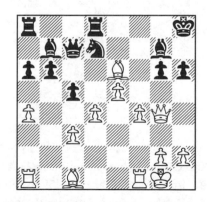

18...♖fd8!?

In a book of this type, almost all the games will necessarily show winning attacking ideas, and quite often the defence might well be slightly substandard. So this is an opportunity to have a look at aggressive defence.

Karpov, at the time of becoming World Champion, was renowned for his accurate and solid play, but this does not mean that he was a drawish player. On the contrary, given the opportunity he would grind out the most unlikely positions, taking any sort of advantage from his opponents, and aiming to win. You cannot become World Champion just by drawing every game.

So Karpov challenges Stein to do his worst, and he will also try to win himself.

Many players would want to try and simplify here, returning the material with 18...cxd4 19 ♗xd7 ♗xe5!,

when 20 fxe5 ♖xf1+ 21 ♔xf1 ♖f8+ 22 ♔g1 ♕xc3 leads to a draw after 23 ♕h4 h5 24 ♕g3 ♕xa1 25 ♕g5 ♗d5! 26 ♕h6+ ♔g8 27 ♕xg6+ and perpetual check. This would indeed be highly acceptable for Black, and is probably, objectively, the correct course of action.

The most striking point of Karpov's last move is that his rook is moving away from the king, leaving only a bishop and a couple of fragile pawns for short-range defence. One of those pawns will soon drop, or get exchanged, and Black will have little, it would seem, to hold his kingside. One could well imagine that Stein, along with most strong players confronted by this position, would feel he had excellent chances. Indeed, even the slightest hesitation by Black would lead to collapse.

However, 18...♖fd8!? is not just to defend the knight on d7, and then put pressure on the d-file. More importantly it vacates the f8-square, so that the knight can cover the light squares e6, g6 and h7, while the fianchettoed bishop, and the h6-pawn, will cover the dark squares. This is remarkable defensive minimalism, and if Black can defend with only the bishop and knight, this will create chances for counter-attack. Once he has played ...♘f8, none of his pieces are in each other's way.

Everything here is tightly balanced. The expectation, perhaps, would be that if both players find correct moves throughout, there will be a draw.

19 f5!

Neither 19 ♕xg6 nor 19 d5 would be effective, in view of 19...♘f8.

19...♘f8

It is too late now for 19...cxd4?, as White would push forward with 20 f6! in any case. Now 20...♗f8? 21 ♕xg6 is terminal for Black, while after

20...♞xe5 21 fxg7+ ♛xg7 22 ♛h3 h5 23 ♝b2, White has regained the piece and continues his attack.

20 f6 ♞xe6

21 ♛xe6!

If White were aiming for "plus over equal", he would probably consider 21 fxg7+ ♞xg7 22 ♛xg6 ♛c6, and then maybe 23 ♜f6 ♛e4 24 ♝xh6!.

In plus over equal mode, White wants to make sure first of all that he is in no danger of losing, and beyond that, he will take any chance he has of winning, but will not be totally disappointed with a draw. If anything, this line would be plus rather than equal. White has three pawns for the knight, his pawns are mobile and Black's knight is not very effective, and White's e-pawn could be dangerously advanced.

Stein instead plays all out for a win, not bothering with the drawing option, no doubt on the assumption that, if his opponent defends perfectly, he will have the draw later anyway. It looks tempting, especially with three connected passed pawns, two of them well advanced. The one disadvantage is that Black's light-squared bishop is far more effective than White's.

21...♝f8 22 ♛h3

He needs to keep his pawns working together. 22 f7?! loses some of his coordination after 22...♚h7.

22...cxd4 23 cxd4?!

An obvious and automatic recapture, but this allows the black rook to become active. It was better to play at once 23 ♝xh6! ♝xh6 24 ♛xh6+ ♛h7 25 ♛g5 ♛h5 (otherwise f6-f7 is too dangerous) 26 ♛xh5+ gxh5, and now rather than 27 cxd4 ♜xd4 transposing to the next note, White can continue his pawn push with 27 e6!.

Here Black has no time for 27...dxc3, as 28 f7 and e6-e7 picks up a rook, for instance if 28...♜f8 29 e7 c2 30 exf8♛+ ♜xf8 31 ♜f4! followed by ♜c1 wins. It seems the best he can manage is 27...♝d5 28 e7 ♜g8 29 ♜f5! ♜xg2+ 30 ♚f1 ♜g6! 31 ♜xd5 ♜xf6+ 32 ♚e2 ♜e8 33 ♜xh5+ ♚g7 34 cxd4 ♜xe7+ 35 ♚d3, when he would face a difficult endgame a pawn down.

23...♜xd4

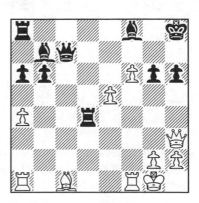

24 e6?

Probably a simple oversight.

Again 24 ♗xh6! ♗xh6 25 ♕xh6+ ♕h7 26 ♕g5! ♕h5 27 ♕xh5+ gxh5 28 e6 was correct, although Black can now solve his problems with 28...♖d2!. Then 29 ♖f5! (not 29 ♖f2? ♖xf2 30 ♔xf2 ♖f8 31 f7 ♔g7, stopping the pawns) 29...♖xg2+ 30 ♔f1 ♗e4! 31 ♖xh5+ ♔g8 should end up as a draw, Black having to concede his bishop for the two opposing pawns after 32 ♖e1 ♖g4 33 h4 ♖f4+ 34 ♔g1 ♗g6 35 ♖h6 ♖xf6 36 h5 ♔g7 37 ♖xg6+ ♖xg6+ 38 hxg6 ♔xg6 39 e7 ♔f7, followed by ...♖e8 and ...♖xe7, with a drawn king and pawn ending.

We cannot escape the iron law of chess that if players play without mistakes, the proper result is a draw. This applies whether it is a dull game, or a supremely interesting and exciting one.

Sadly Stein makes a tactical mistake, and as a result quickly loses.

24...♗c5!

Surely Black cannot abandon the defence of h6? In fact he can. The discovered attack from the rook is so strong that only an immediate check-

mate will win for White, and it simply isn't there.

25 ♔h1?

A sorry admission that he has lost a critical tempo.

25 ♕xh6+ ♕h7 26 ♕xh7+ ♔xh7 (if 27 ♔h1 ♖e4 28 e7 ♖e2 wins quickly) 27 ♗e3 ♖g4 28 ♖fe1 ♖xg2+ 29 ♔f1 ♖f8 30 f7 ♖xh2, probably followed by ...♔g7 or ...♗d5, will eventually win for Black.

White's best chance was 25 ♗e3 h5 26 ♖ac1 ♖d3 (if 26...♖g4 27 ♗xc5 bxc5 28 ♖ce1 gets the rooks behind the pawns) 27 ♖xc5! bxc5 28 f7, although after 28...♕d6 (if 28...♖f8 29 ♗d4+! ♖xd4 30 ♕e3 ♔h7 31 e7) 29 ♕g3! ♕xg3 30 f8♕+ ♖xf8 31 ♖xf8+ ♔g7 32 ♖f7+ ♔g8 33 hxg3 ♖xe3 34 ♖xb7 ♖xe6, Black is now the one with the extra pawn.

25...h5 26 ♖a2 ♗d5 27 ♖d2?!

27 ♖e2!? was the last serious try, hoping for 27...♗c4? 28 e7 ♗xe2 29 ♕e3! and wins, but Black can consolidate with 27...♖g4!, and if 28 ♗b2 ♕c6 29 e7 ♔h7.

27...♖xd2 28 ♗xd2 ♕e5

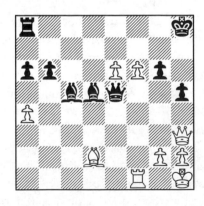

Worth a quick diagram. White's passed pawns have now lost their oomph, while Black's queen and bishops dominate.

29 ♕d3

A more entertaining finish, with a successful king escape, is 29 e7 ♕e2 30 ♖e1 ♕xd2 31 e8♕+ ♖xe8 32 ♖xe8+ ♔h7 33 ♕d7+ ♔h6 34 ♖h8+ ♔g5 35 h4+ ♔f4 36 ♕c7+ ♔g4 37 ♕d7+ ♔g3 38 ♕h3+ ♔f2, and now it is White who is going to get checkmated.

Stein would have seen all this, or at least its central outlines, and chose something quieter. It doesn't work.

29...♕xe6 30 ♕xg6 ♕g4 31 ♕h6+ ♔g8 32 f7+ ♗xf7 33 ♗c3 ♗d4

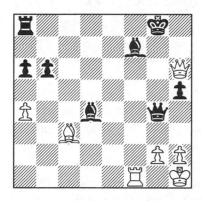

White has managed to keep some threats going for a while, but now it is all over, and once the time control is reached, he resigns.

34 h3 ♕g7 35 ♕c6 ♖d8 36 ♗xd4 ♕xd4 37 ♕b7 ♖d7 38 ♕c6 ♔g7 39 ♕c1 ♕e5 40 ♖e1 ♕f6 41 ♖f1 ♕d4 0-1

We have seen that Karpov won this game after Stein went wrong, but that with best play, it should have been drawn. However, there is still further analysis to be covered, the alternative

knight sacrifice:

16 ♘xf7!?

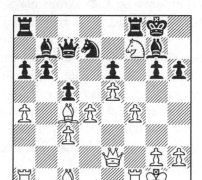

Black has two ways to take the knight. The sensible way of analysing this position, whether in an over-the-board game or through later analysis, is to look at 16...♔xf7 first, accepting the sacrifice. If it shows that Black can keep the material, essentially refuting the sacrifice, and end up with a winning game, there is no need to examine anything else in depth. Maybe a quick flick through, checking there is no obvious straightforward win with the less critical line, but basically it is best to analyse the critical line first. This is from White's point of view, trying to find a good attacking option.

Remember, though, that White has to consider three options, not two. White has 16 ♘xe6, the move actually played, as well as 16 ♘xf7 ♖xf7, and 16 ♘xf7 ♔xf7. A human will not be able to analyse everything completely, given that in any complicated line there are likely to be hidden depths later on. Even Stein missed something in the main line. What we are interested to see is whether or not Stein chose the correct sacrifice.

Now suppose that White plays 16 ♘xf7, what would Black have to think about? Should he try 16...♔xf7, aiming at a refutation? Or should he prefer 16...♖xf7 17 ♗xe6, with a nominal slight material disadvantage – losing a rook and two pawns for two minor pieces – but with much depending on the relative activity of the pawns and pieces.

Let's start off with the bang smash lines:

16...♔xf7 17 f5!

Do it immediately! 17 ♕g4?! ♕c6 18 f5 is possible, but slows White down.

The move f4-f5 is vital to White's attacking plans. He is ramming the e6- and g6-pawns, and forcing the black king into the open. He is also creating open lines for the dark-squared bishop and the rook on the f-file. This is obviously dangerous. The question is whether Black can hold.

17...gxf5

17...♘xe5 makes a return sacrifice to reduce the pressure, usually a good defensive idea, but Black's king is more vulnerable that White's after 18 fxe5 ♕xe5 19 ♗xe6+ ♔e7 20 ♖a2. Furthermore, White doesn't have to take the knight, but can play 18 ♗xe6+ ♔e7 19 ♗a3 maintaining strong threats.

18 ♕h5+ ♔e7 19 ♕g6

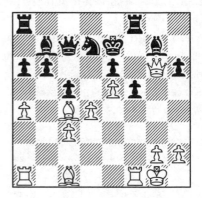

White has made some inroads into the enemy position, and one would expect that he would recover the bishop. It is impossible to know how much Stein would have looked at this position. The best guess, perhaps, is that he would have preferred the more ferocious attack actually played, with a strong passed pawn chain, and seen this alternative as only unclear.

These days anyone can try to analyse with the help of the computer, and readers might be interested in playing through this position. I leave it to you. A basic pointer, in terms of strategy, is that Black should be prepared to concede the dark-squared bishop, but will try to take advantage of the light-squared long diagonal, with the help, perhaps, of a later ...♖g8. Black's king looks awkward, but it is the white king who will face the main mating threats. Enjoy and analyse. Expect many of the lines to end up as equal. Black does not seem to be winning.

Karpov would also have considered, if only briefly:
16...罩xf7!? 17 ♗xe6 ♘f8!

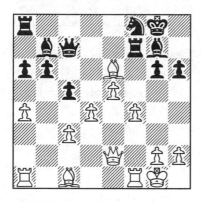

18 ♗xf7+ 豐xf7

Imaginative. Black has now sacrificed material, having bishop and knight against a rook and two pawns, leaving himself the equivalent of half a pawn down. Moreover White has two passed pawns in the centre, but these are firmly restrained, with Black aiming to blockade on the light squares.

There is just a small defect in Black's strategy. If his pawn were on a7 rather than on a6, he would have been comfortable. As it is, the pawn on b6 is a slight but serious weakness, which has the effect of distracting his pieces from enjoying firm control of the centre.

19 罩b1 cxd4 20 cxd4

White now has an edge. Black can

try to blockade, but the important point is that he does not attack anything.

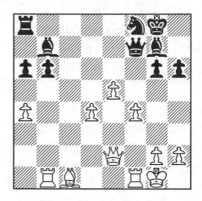

In many ways this is the closest of all the sacrifices in this book. There is no indication that White is winning. There is no indication that White's sacrifice can be refuted either, Stein's loss only coming as a result of later mistakes. Few of Stein's sacrificial attacks seem to be genuinely unsound.

The following game comes from the same event as Stein's loss against Karpov. Here Stein wins against a former World Champion, with some highly imaginative play. The game has been marred, as a result of several unforced errors by both sides, and Stein should have finished it off much earlier. But this, if anything, emphasizes the extent to which he was able to set up winning positions in twenty moves.

The opening was of considerable interest, although in later encounters White has tended to avoid the doubling of c-pawns in this line, seeing it as over-committal. Stein's h4-h5-h6 push is noteworthy, creating unusual problems for Black.

> ### Game 9
> ### L.Stein-V.Smyslov
> ### USSR Spartakiad, Moscow 1972
> ### *English Opening*

1 c4 ♘f6 2 ♘c3 e6 3 ♘f3

There is often much angling for position in the English Opening. Sometimes play will enter standard queen's pawn openings, such as the Queen's Gambit, the Nimzo-Indian or Queen's Indian, the King's Indian, or various others. Sometimes, though, White will play the English deliberately to avoid or delay particular irritating systems. Here Stein, like many others, is careful to avoid the Nimzo, 3 d4 ♗b4.

After Stein's win in this game, the line he began on move five attracted attention at the top levels, before the theoreticians gradually lost interest.

Another idea for White is 3 e4, the Flohr-Mikenas variation, when Black chooses between 3...c5, provoking the pawn advance 4 e5, or the safer 3...d5 4 e5 d4.

3...b6

Stein was happy enough to play the Queen's Gambit after 3...d5 4 d4, with either colour, but in this particular position, Smyslov, for no obvious reason, always avoided it as Black.

4 e4

Now, though, this is an irregular set-up.

4...♗b7 5 ♕e2!?

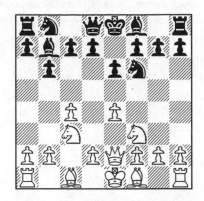

This made the players interested. 5 e5 ♘e4 looks equal or close to being equal, not least after the exchange 6 ♘xe4 ♗xe4. But delaying a move, and preventing Black's knight from emerging on e4, maybe that is interesting?

5 d3 has been tried many times, with the point that if 5...d5 6 cxd5 exd5 7 e5 ♘fd7 8 d4, White has theoretically lost a tempo, but Black's light-squared bishop is not on a good diagonal, blocked by the d-pawn.

Therefore Black usually tries 5...d6 6 g3 ♗e7 7 ♗g2 0-0 8 0-0 c5, with a Hedgehog set-up, as for example in the game V.Smyslov-S.Reshevsky, Belgrade 1970. White generally plays d3-d4 at some stage, again losing a tempo, but in a quiet manoeuvring position, such as the Hedgehog, the gain or loss of a tempo is often of little importance.

Instead, White's queen looks slightly awkward on e2, blocking his bishop, and of course Stein would have been fully aware of this, but he also has chances of active play.

5...♗b4

Stein's move was not a complete

innovation, as Portisch tried it in the 1960s, but he lost badly against Matanovic (see Game 9.1 below). When Stein beat Smyslov, other players took notice, including Korchnoi, who used it in his 1974 Candidates' matches against Petrosian and Karpov.

6 e5 ♘g8 7 d4

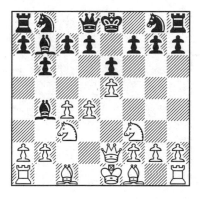

7...d6

Kasparov prefers 7...♘e7 here, keeping the option of playing ...d7-d5 in one go, seeing the position as equal. My own view is that 7...d6, challenging White's pawn phalanx in the centre, is good and provocative, the opportunity for Black to try and take the initiative.

The critical position is to be found quite a few moves later, with 13...g6!, followed by reorganizing with ...c7-c6 and ...♛c7. This appears not to have been considered by other writers. If, as I suggest, this might be good for Black, meaning at least equal and aiming for an edge, then Kasparov's assessments over the next few moves will need to be adjusted. If not, then my own adjustments would need to be readjusted. Chess is complicated, critical assess-

ments often being half-a-dozen moves deep. This explains why chess is still interesting, there being no routine drawish games if one of the players, or both, can try for advantage.

8 a3!?

Quite often the innovator goes for the sharpest variation, while subsequent players take up quieter and safer lines. Stein was presumably quite happy to gain an extra, albeit doubled, pawn in the centre. Later players have tended to prefer 8 ♗d2 (after either 7...d6 or 7...♘e7), keeping the pawn structure unbroken, or else 8 ♛d3, with the same intention, while opening up the f1-bishop. Korchnoi experimented with these ideas against Karpov, though he only managed three draws.

8...♗xc3+ 9 bxc3 ♘e7

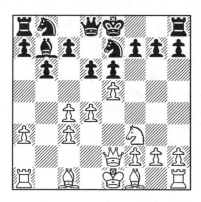

10 h4!

A very creative attacking idea, which at first glance breaks all the basic principles of positional play, but in fact is fully logical, if White plays the game sharply and dynamically. At no stage in the analysis is there any sense that White is worse, unless perhaps if

13...g6 turns out to be good. This is remarkable, considering the complexity of the idea, and to the extent to which Stein is taking risks as well as opportunities. Stein will have weighed up the position and decided, on balance, that his attacking idea is no worse, and quite possibly better for him.

The general feeling here is that if the attack falters, there is a clear danger of Black taking over, maybe opening up White's central pawns, or maybe the white king being stuck in the centre. Once White has committed himself with the h-pawn advance, there is unlikely to be a quick and stable equality. He must create weaknesses in Black's position, before Black breaks open his own set-up.

However, suppose instead that White tries fianchettoing his king's bishop with, say, 10 exd6 cxd6 11 g3 ♘d7 12 ♗g2 ♖c8 13 0-0. White has safely castled, but his queenside pawn structure is a wreck, and 13...♕c7 is better for Black. Alternatively, something like 10 ♗g5 ♘d7 11 ♖d1 0-0 12 ♗h4 ♕e8 sees White's queenside pieces now in play, but he has yet to develop his kingside, while Black is ready to seize the initiative.

Stein's approach is boldest and best. There is no safe equality in this line, so he has to attack. He makes a virtue of his kingside piece and pawn structure, rather than seeing this as a problem.

10...♘d7

Kasparov suggests 10...d5!? 11 cxd5 ♗a6 with a likely equality. This is perfectly acceptable for Black, but Smyslov

must have sensed the possibility that Stein might have been overpressing, so why should he aim for mere equality? A win with the black pieces against a world-class grandmaster is rare, and it is understandable that Smyslov would want more, when given the chance.

11 h5

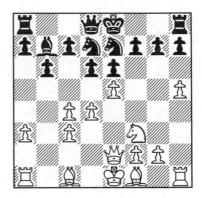

There is no good reason for half-measures. If White were to try 11 exd6 cxd6 12 ♗f4 ♘f6, he would have wasted his tenth move.

11...♗xf3

Black is planning to attack the white pawn centre, but this exchange also creates weaknesses on his own light squares, which Stein aims to exploit.

11...h6!? is a quieter option. Then 12 ♖h3 shows that White is using pieces on the kingside, as well as pawns. After 12...♗xf3 13 ♖xf3 dxe5 14 dxe5, play is unclear, though probably about equal.

12 ♕xf3!?

The last chance for White to avoid dropping a pawn. 12 gxf3 looks ugly, and White will no doubt feel the absence of the g-pawn when Black lands a knight on f5. Nevertheless, 12...dxe5 13 dxe5 ♘f5 14 ♖g1 is probably no worse for White, and if 14...♕h4 15 ♕e4 ♕xe4 16 fxe4 he might have chances of an edge, for example 16...♘xe5 17 ♗e2 ♘d6 18 ♖xg7 with active pieces.

This all seems playable for White, but Stein feels that there is something better. The point is that, while it is a problem for White that his e-pawn has fallen, the absence of Black's light-squared bishop creates a gap as well. This becomes particularly severe in Stein's gambit line.

12...dxe5 13 h6

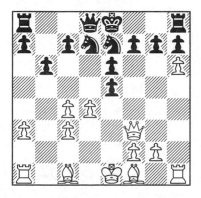

This is quite definitely gambit play. Stein wants to attack. He is not interested in maintaining the intricate balance, he wants to make a quick breakthrough.

Sometimes it feels as if the number of pawns will not matter that much, except to the extent that one might lead to promotion in a distant endgame. Meanwhile the pawns will get opened up, the kings behind will soon be exposed, with not much chance of castling, for either side.

13...gxh6

The most direct response. 13...♖g8 14 hxg7 ♖xg7 15 ♗h6 ♖g6 16 ♗e3 ♖g7 17 ♗d3 merely allows White to develop his pieces, while still keeping an attack.

However, 13...g6! may well be the best. White has spent three moves advancing the h-pawn, while Black spends only one to keep the h-file closed. This suggests a gain of two tempi for the defence, albeit at the cost of returning the gambit pawn.

The game might continue 14 dxe5 c6! 15 ♗g5 ♕c7 16 ♕e2 ♘c5, with intricate play coming up. Possibly this may end up as about equal, but I cannot help feeling that the longer that Black stays away from checkmate, the better his chances of playing for victory.

It would be tempting to describe this as classic Petrosianic defensive play, given the way in which Black abruptly changes the flow from attack to slow defence, with plenty of quiet manoeuvring with the knights, and the other pieces. Ironically, Petrosian himself, or maybe an assistant, gave this line as a big plus for White in *Informator 13*.

Chigorin would doubtless also have enjoyed this line as Black, a great pioneer of chess in the east, and a fervent advocate of the knight pair in opposition to the bishops. For the reader, analyse and learn! Black seems at the very least not to be worse, provided he plays accurately. Instinctively, the feeling must surely be that White has pressure on the dark squares, but he also needs light squares and long files to create an attack, and it seems he cannot quite break through.

Instead, Kasparov gives only 14...0-0 15 ♗g5 ♘xe5 17 ♕f6 ♘f5 18 ♕xd8 ♖axd8 19 ♗xd8 ♖xd8, sacrificing the exchange for a pawn and drawing chances, but with White being the one playing for the win.

14 ♗xh6

Here Kasparov suggests 14 ♗d3!?, bringing the light-squared bishop into play. Maybe Black can try 14...♘g8!?, and the doubled h-pawn will be something of an irritation.

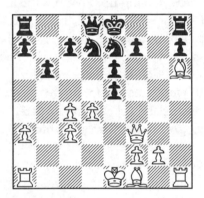

14...exd4?

A critical position. Smyslov decides that he has to chew up as much as he can in the centre, before White can force victory on the f- to h-files, and the long light-squared diagonal. After the next few moves, which are more or less forced, it turns out that Stein is on top.

This was the last real chance to consolidate in front of the king, with 14...♘f5! 15 ♗g5 f6.

Black's king looks more exposed, but his pieces and pawns now have extra energy. All the same, the human player would tend to believe that White must be better, and so Smyslov would probably have rejected this line without too much thought, whereas computer analysis suggests that Black is doing well, or reasonably well.

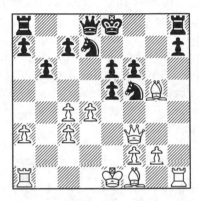

Speelman, in the days before chess computers, suggests a few apparently promising moves, and tends to assume that White is better. A quarter of a century later, it seems that his moves do not dent Black's equanimity, and that Black may be doing OK.

a) 16 d5 was Speelman's first suggestion for White. Now, *Fritz* quickly suggests 16...fxg5 17 dxe6 0-0!, and suddenly the black king is out of the box. Play might continue 18 ♕h3 ♕e7 19 ♗d3 ♘h4 20 exd7 ♖ad8, and Black is more than comfortable.

b) 16 g4 is a second Speelman idea, which looks promising after either 16...♘d6 17 ♗xf6 ♘xf6 18 dxe5, or 16...fxg5 17 gxf5 exf5 18 ♗g2, when it is difficult to believe that Black's pawn structure far in front of the king is safe.

However, there is a third possibility, 16...♘xd4!! 17 cxd4 fxg5, when Black escapes because of the g4-pawn blocking the white queen. After 18 ♖h6, *Fritz* now gives a second surprising move, 18...♔e7! with advantage.

The point is not so much the king's own safety, but rather the new coordination between Black's queen and rooks, giving him defensive and counter-attacking possibilities with ...♕f8 or ...♕g8.

After Kasparov's suggested 19 d5, intending 19...exd5?! 20 ♖d1! with active play, Black can try 19...♕f8!? 20 ♖xe6+ ♔d8. Whether or not White decides to exchange queens, Black has the chance of consolidating and playing for an edge on the dark squares. For example, 21 ♕e2 ♕f4 22 ♗g2 ♘c5 23 ♖d1 ♖e8 or 21 ♕xf8+ ♖xf8 22 ♗e2 ♖f7 23 ♖d1 ♖e7 24 ♗f3 ♖b8, followed by ...♘c5. Again this would have been an excellent demonstration of Chigorin's ideas.

c) 16 ♕h5+ looks uncomfortable for Black, with his king exposed, but 16...♔f8 17 ♗h6+ ♔e7 sees him ensconced on e7 once more, For instance,

18 ♗d3 ♕g8 19 ♗xf5 exf5 20 ♕xf5 ♕xc4 and Black is out of danger. In fact Speelman does not give this as an attempt for White.

d) This leaves Speelman's final suggestion, the "simple" 16 ♗e3. White has compensation for the pawn, but it is unlikely that he is better. Play might continue 16...♗xe3 17 fxe3 0-0!?, maybe in the end level, maybe with a slight edge for Black.

Going back a bit, the immediate 15 d5 is another attempt, without inserting ♗g5, but 15...e4!, returning the extra pawn to gain time, gives Black at least level play after 16 ♕xe4 ♕f6.

Finally, it seems the even simpler and more direct developing move, 15 ♖d1!, is best.

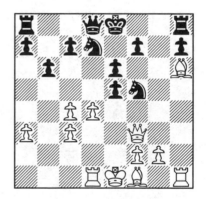

After 15...♘xh6 16 ♖xh6 exd4 17 cxd4, White has played without fuss, and has genuine compensation, and perhaps more, for the sacrificed pawn. This seems to be the only line where Black will have to work hard to equalize.

We do not know how Stein would have handled this position. One would like to think that he would have played the quiet but effective way of bringing in new attacking pieces, rather than re-developing his existing pieces.

In the game, the next few moves are semi-forced, making it easier for the players as they watch the clock. It soon turns out that Stein is making all the progress.

15 ♗g7 ♖g8 16 ♖xh7 ♘f5?

Kasparov notes that 16...♘f8 17 ♗xf8 ♖xf8 offered the best chance to put up a successful defence.

17 ♗xd4 c5

Not now 17...♘f8? because of 18 ♗f6 ♕c8 19 ♕c6+. The long diagonal, previously under Black's control, is now causing him great damage.

18 g4 cxd4 19 gxf5

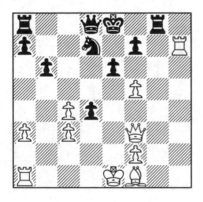

Now it starts to become more complicated again. Count the pieces and pawns, and you see they are equal. Presumably White must therefore be much better, as his pieces are more active and further developed. He has considerable pressure on the light squares, on the long diagonal (Black's queen still cannot move forward), and

the lines leading up to f7 and e6.

Black has a choice of moves, but it is not a free choice. Any bad move, and he will lose quickly. Any good move, and with luck he will stay in the game.

19...e5

This looks strange at first, surrendering control of the light squares completely, but was there any good alternative?

a) 19...exf5?! leaves White with too many open lines to be seriously considered, with Black's king stuck in the centre. Speelman suggests that 20 0-0-0 is "very strong", possibly overstating the case, but only slightly.

b) 19...♘e5 20 ♕e4 dxc3 is more testing, and indeed gives Black significant counterplay. The resulting position is wildly unclear, but Black's king is extremely close to the edge.

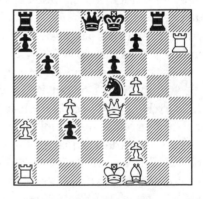

b1) 21 ♖d1?! looks like an immediate win for White, and one suspects that Smyslov did not want to calculate much further. There is a tactical resource, however, in 21...c2!, the point being that after 22 ♖xd8+ ♖xd8 23 ♕xc2, Black has a concealed knight fork with 23...♘f3+ 24 ♔e2 ♘d4+.

Speelman notes this winning line for Black, and then suggests an improvement for White in 22 ♖c1. After 22...♕d4! 23 ♕xa8+ (of course if 23 ♕xd4? ♘f3+ regains the queen) 23...♔e7 24 ♕b7+ ♔f6 25 fxe6, he gives a draw by perpetual, but in fact Black can play for more, with 25...♕c3+ 26 ♔e2 ♕xc4+ 27 ♔e3 ♕c3+ 28 ♔e2 ♕d3+ 29 ♔e1 ♕xh7 30 exf7 ♖f8, and White is in trouble. Entertaining stuff, but we must not forget that this was a case of White recovering after a tactical error.

b2) 21 ♖a2!! is much stronger, which Stein saw in advance, and Speelman analysed.

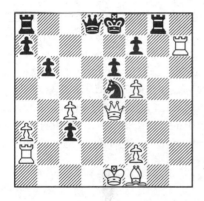

Now if 21...♕d4, Speelman notes that White wins, alongside considerable entertainment, after 22 ♕xa8+ ♔e7 23 ♕b7+ ♔d6 (23...♔f6 24 fxe6 is no better) 24 fxe6 ♖g1 25 ♕d5+ ♕xd5 26 cxd5+ ♘d3+ 27 ♔e2 ♘c1+ 28 ♔f3 fxe6 29 ♖c2.

But can Black tighten up his play? One possibility is 21...f6!? 22 fxe6 ♖c8 23 ♕b7 ♖c6, when Black's king appears absurdly fragile, but White's king is

not so far behind. If anything Black is even slightly better after, for example, 24 ♖d7 ♕c8 25 ♖e7+ ♔d8 26 ♕xc6+ ♖xc8 27 ♖xa7 ♖g1.

Trying to checkmate does not quite work, but he can hit the knight with 22 f4!, and if 22...exf5 23 ♕xf5 ♘f7 24 ♗g2 ♔f8 25 ♗d5 with probably decisive pressure. Alternatively, Kasparov gives 23 ♕h1 ♘f7 24 ♕b7 as winning.

20 ♕d5 ♖f8 21 cxd4 ♖c8

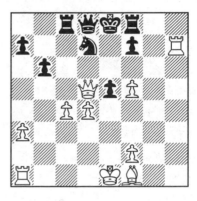

22 ♖d1?

This was a fantastic win by Stein against a former World Champion. He played a highly original opening, and found a memorable brilliancy, both of which we can admire. Unfortunately the part in between was not quite as impressive, here and a few moves later on, when both players missed an instant win.

As far as the current position is concerned, White is a pawn up, his pieces are far more active, and the black king is under pressure. All this should add up to a simple and straightforward win. Stein was unusually sharp at starting an attack, but here and in a few other places, he was slightly less confident in finishing things off. In our supplementary appendix game, against Karen Grigorian, for example, he missed a chance of a brilliant win in the same Spartakiad event. And of course he made a slip against Karpov, too.

Despite the question mark in my note, playing the rook to d1 is a good idea. He should have castled though: 22 0-0-0!.

Despite the wide-open space around the king, it's safe enough, with the queen and rooks surrounding any counter-attacks; whereas in the main game, the king gets in the way of White's pieces, slowing down his attack.

After castling, the one possible hazard is 22...♕g5+ 23 ♔b2 ♕xf5, but this is refuted by 24 ♗h3! ♕xf2+ 25 ♔b1, when Black has run out of checks, and 25...♖c7 26 dxe5 gives White a win. 22...♕e7 lasts a bit longer, but it is still only simple attacking technique. For example 23 ♖h3 (23 ♔b2 is also good) 23...f6 24 ♖e3 ♔d8 25 dxe5 fxe5 26 f6 ♖xf6 27 ♗h3 ♖c7 28 ♖g3, and Black is under too much pressure on too many

ranks, files and diagonals.

Even after the move played by Stein in the game, he still keeps a substantial edge, but less so than before.

One can imagine that both players were in considerable time pressure, as a result of the unusually complex and original chess early on, and that Stein simply wanted to play a decent move quickly, rather than thinking just here about originality. There are further identifiable mistakes later on, but the players would most likely have skimmed through at speed, and even the annotators (for example Petrosian, Keene, Speelman) ignored this part of the game.

22...♕e7

22...♕f6? fails to 23 ♕xd7+! ♔xd7 24 dxe5, winning a piece. After 22...♕c7, the best option now may well have been 23 ♖d2, threatening d4xe5 with decisive effect, and if 23...exd4 24 ♕xd4, with a winning attack. An effective line, but it also underlines the point that White's king on e1 was in the way.

23 ♗g2

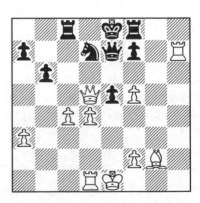

Probably in recognition that it was about time the bishop was in play. There is a secondary aspect: White does not want his king in the open for too much longer, so he needs to cover up with ♗e2, or else evacuate to g1 after a preliminary ♗g2.

Either idea looks reasonable, although 23 ♗e2 does avoid the idea of 23...♕xa3 24 dxe5 ♕c3+ and ...♕xc4, as after 23 ♗g2. See the next note.

23...♖g8

Black has two choices here, and plays probably the better move, but his next is a serious mistake.

Instead, 23...♕xa3 aims for an endgame with level pawns, after 24 dxe5 ♕c3+ 25 ♔f1 ♕xc4+ 26 ♕xc4 ♖xc4. But that is the only good news for Black. His pawns will not travel very far, while White is still creating great pressure in the centre, even without his queens, for example by 27 f6, 28 ♖h3 and 29 ♖hd3, or 29 ♖d6 and 30 ♗c6. Alternatively he might even avoid the endgame altogether by throwing in 24 c5.

24 ♕b7

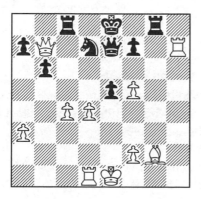

24...♖xc4?

This is a blunder which leads to the immediate loss of a rook, as a result of a back row check from the queen. One does not need computer assistance to spot the winning reply, with 25 ♕a8+, followed by a fork, but somehow the commentators missed it. Unless there was an obscure magazine at the time which spotted Stein's quick win.

Instead, 24...exd4+ 25 ♔f1 ♕c5 26 ♗d5 ♖f8 keeps the game alive. At long last, Black has some pieces active. It is enough to provide a plausible line to show that there could have been some practical chances, that it is not quite a trivial loss for Black.

We can try 27 ♕xa7 b5! 28 ♗xf7+ ♖xf7 29 ♖e1+ ♔d8 30 ♕xc5 (if 30 ♕a5+ ♖c7 is only a draw, as after 31 ♖xf7 Black has 31...♕xc4+) 30...♖xc5 31 ♖xf7 bxc4,

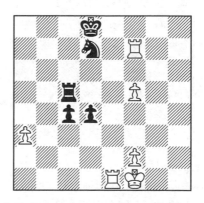

when White has rook and pawn versus knight, normally a winning endgame advantage, but Black suddenly has two dangerous connected passed pawns, which is perhaps more than he deserves, considering his bad position earlier.

The reader is encouraged to try to win this position as White. A plausible line is 32 ♖ee7 ♖d5 33 ♔e2 d3+ 34 ♔d2 ♘e5 35 ♖g7 c3+ 36 ♔xc3 d2 37 ♖a7, when it seems that White will give a back row checkmate before the pawn promotes, but Black escapes by 37...♖d3+ 38 ♔b2 ♔c4+ 39 ♔e2 ♘d6!, with a draw. The correct method is simply to trade down to a king and pawn endgame by 33 ♖xd7+! ♖xd7 34 ♖xd7 ♔xd7 35 a4, and Black cannot prevent one of the outside passed pawns going through.

But of course this would be far more difficult to calculate over the board, in the last five minutes before a time control at move 40.

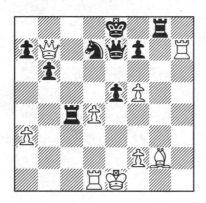

25 dxe5?

Stein misses the quick win by 25 ♕a8+! ♕d8 26 ♕d5, with a fork on c4 and f7. Move by move, it looks simple, but the backward and forward reversal can easily be overlooked, even by a strong tactician, especially when short of time.

Fortunately for us, Stein finds a

much more interesting win a few moves later on.

25...♕xe5+ 26 ♔f1 ♕b5

If 26...♕c7 27 ♕a8+ ♘b8 28 ♖e1+ ♔f8 29 ♗d5 or 27...♕c8 28 ♕d5 ♖f8 29 f6! wins for White.

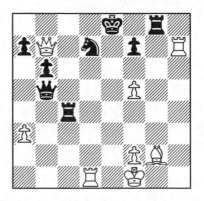

27 ♔g1

Maybe some of you have already seen this position, and remember with pleasure a series of pins and counter-pins. But have you seen the alternative winning idea?

27 a4! is also good, as after 27...♖xa4+ 28 ♔g1, the black rook has been deflected, giving White the additional threat of ♕c8+. For instance, 28...♖ag4 29 ♕c8+ ♔e7 30 ♖xd7+ ♕xd7 31 ♖xf7+ wins, or if 28...♖xg2+ 29 ♔xg2 ♖g4+, simply 30 ♔h1 and Black has no more checks.

27...♕c6 28 ♕xc6 ♖xc6

The bishop is pinned, so 29 ♗xc6??! is illegal, but White has a spectacular and memorable win:

29 ♖h8!

Such a move makes you smile. Actually 28 ♖h8! was also possible, and perhaps even more visual.

29...Rcg6 30 fxg6 Rxh8 31 Bc6 Rg8 32 Bxd7+ Ke7 33 Bf5 fxg6 34 Rd7+ Kf6 35 Bd3 1-0

This was a curious game, featuring a mixture of great imagination, especially by Stein, and mediocre play on both sides.

Many people will have focused on the unusual tactics over the last few moves. These are accidental, the result of miscalculations and omissions by both sides. What is more noteworthy was the way in which Stein, by aggressive tactical play, could force Smyslov, a great positional master, into a dismal position well before move 20.

Here is an earlier example of the same opening, which is of interest not just because of its historical value, but also because of Matanovic's knight tour. Stein was playing in this tournament, ending up equal second with Petrosian, behind Korchnoi. He would naturally have remembered this line, and against Smyslov it was time to try it again.

Supplementary games

> ### Game 9.1
> **L.Portisch-A.Matanovic**
> Yerevan 1965
> *English Opening*

1 c4 Nf6 2 Nc3 e6 3 Nf3 b6 4 e4 Bb7 5 Qe2!?

This was Portisch's innovation. It was seven years later, at least in grandmaster chess, before Stein revived the line. It has to be said that the 1965 event was not successful for White.

5...c5

Smyslov tried 5...Bb4. Both moves seem acceptable.

6 e5

The immediate 6 d4 cxd4 7 Nxd4 Bb4 leaves Black happy.

6...Ng8

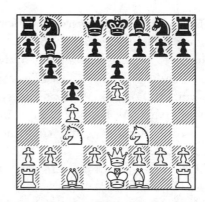

Two tempi lost, but White's pawns are arguably overextended.

7 d4 cxd4

Matanovic plays it carefully. Petrosian tried 7...Bxf3?! 8 Qxf3 Nc6 in

V.Korchnoi-T.V.Petrosian, Candidates semi-final (3rd matchgame), Odessa 1974, but after 9 d5! ♘xe5 10 ♕g3 d6 11 ♗f4 ♘g6 12 dxe6 fxe6 13 0-0-0 ♘xf4 14 ♕xf4, Black's position was under pressure, despite his extra pawn. In fact Petrosian soon lost the pawn, and then another: 14...g6?! 15 ♕e4 ♘f6 16 ♕xe6+ ♕e7 17 ♖xd6, and Korchnoi duly won after a long endgame.

8 ♘xd4 ♘c6 9 ♘xc6 ♗xc6 10 ♗d2 ♘e7 11 0-0-0 ♕c7 12 ♔b1

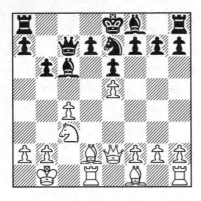

This seems unnecessary, and Black achieves a slight edge before long.

Instead, 12 ♗f4 was agreed drawn immediately in V.Neverov-V.Karpman, Podolsk 1989, and is presumably equal. 12 h4, based on Stein's idea in the previous game, could also be considered.

12...♘f5 13 ♖g1 ♖c8 14 ♗f4 ♕b7 15 ♖d3?!

No commentary over the last few moves, but White is in danger of slipping. His extravagant play makes things worse.

15...a6 16 g4 ♘h4 17 ♖h3 ♗e7

Black is already clearly better.

18 ♗c1 b5 19 f4 b4 20 ♘d1

A classic example of what can happen when White (or occasionally Black) advances the central pawns too far, leaving gaps behind. It is easy enough to see that Black can invade on the light squares, and that White may also have a weakness at d4, but can you see how Black can force victory? Where do you think the knight should manoeuvre? Obviously to f3 first, but where then?

20...♘f3 21 ♖gg3 ♗e4+ 22 ♔a1 ♘d4

Watch the squares the knight lands on in the next stage.

23 ♕d2 ♘c2+ 24 ♔b1 ♘a3+ 25 ♔a1 ♘c2+ 26 ♔b1 ♘e3+ 27 ♗d3 ♘f1!

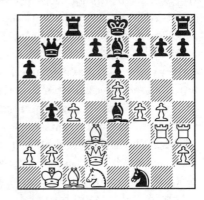

Did you see this one? Chess is geometry. The more prosaic 27...♘xc4 is also good.

28 ♕e2 ♘xg3 29 ♖xg3 ♗xd3+ 30 ♕xd3 ♕c6

And Black later won, although the remaining moves were less accurate, from both players. One suspects time pressure.

31 b3 d5 32 ♘e3 dxc4 33 ♘xc4 ♖d8 34 ♕c2 ♕d5 35 f5 f6 36 exf6 ♗xf6 37 ♖e3 0-0 38 fxe6 ♖fe8 0-1

We have already seen how powerful an attacker Stein was, in his games against Karpov (although eventually a loss) and Smyslov. Here we give a third example, only this time Stein misses the winning line, and can only manage a draw.

> ### Game 9.2
> ### L.Stein-K.Grigorian
> ### USSR Spartakiad, Moscow 1972
> ### *Sicilian Defence*
> ### *(by transposition)*

1 c4 c5 2 ♘f3 ♘c6 3 d4 cxd4 4 ♘xd4 g6 5 e4 ♗g7 6 ♗e3 ♘f6 7 ♘c3 ♘g4 8 ♕xg4 ♘xd4 9 ♕d1 ♘e6 10 ♗e2 0-0 11 0-0 d6 12 f4 ♗d7 13 f5! ♘c5 14 ♗d4 a5 15 ♘d5 ♗xd4+ 16 ♕xd4 f6 17 fxg6 hxg6 18 e5! fxe5 19 ♕h4 ♗f5 20 ♘xe7+ ♔g7

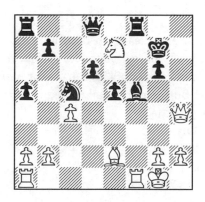

Stein has attacked vigorously in the opening, and the time to score the win is coming up.

21 g4! ♗d3 22 ♗xd3 ♘xd3 23 ♕g5 ♘f4 24 ♖xf4 ♕b6+?

Before White prevents this with

♘d5, but the queen was better where it was.

Black should play 24...♖xf4 immediately, and after 25 ♕xg6+ ♔f8 26 ♘d5, not 26...♖f7? 27 g5! ♕d7 28 ♘f6 ♖xf6 29 gxf6 ♕f7 30 ♕d3 with a winning endgame, but 26...♖f3!. Now 27 g5 ♕d7 28 ♘f6 is thwarted by 28...♕g7, or if 27 ♔g2 ♖f7 28 g5 ♕d7 29 ♘f6 then 29...♕c6+! draws. White's best try seems to be 27 ♖f1 ♖xf1+ 28 ♔xf1, though 28...b5! 29 cxb5 ♖a7 or 29 ♘f6 ♔e7 30 cxb5 ♕f8 31 g5 ♕f7 offers Black good drawing chances, due to the exposed white king.

25 ♔h1 ♖xf4 26 ♕xg6+ ♔f8

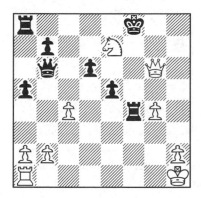

Easy to understand so far, if the reader goes slowly, move by move.

27 ♘d5?

This allows the win to slip away.

27 ♕h7! would have ended up as a fully publishable winning game. The threat is ♘g6+, and Black has no chance of any counter-threat. If 27...♖f7 28 ♘g6+ ♔e8 29 ♕g8+ ♔d7 29 ♕xf7+ wins a rook, or 27...♕d8 28 ♘g6+ ♔e8 29 ♘xf4 exf4 30 ♖e1+ ♔f8 31 ♖e6, and White wins the queen.

27...♕c6 28 ♔g2 ♖xc4 29 ♖f1+

For a couple of seconds, this might look very strong, but unfortunately the knight is pinned.

29...♖f4 30 ♖xf4+ exf4 31 ♕f5+ ♔g7 32 ♕g5+ ♔h7?!

There is no need to allow a knight check. Simply 32...♔h8 and White has nothing better than a draw.

33 ♔h3! ♖f8 34 ♘f6+ ♖xf6 35 ♕xf6

Now White is better again, but the inevitable time-pressure kicks in.

35...♕f3+ 36 ♔h4 ♕f2+

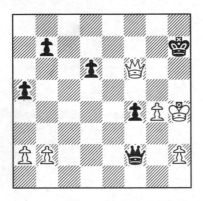

A few seconds left, what should White try?

37 ♔h5??

Stein loses a pawn for nothing. It is possible that he had a time-trouble hallucination, noticing that after 37 ♔g5! ♕c5+ 38 ♕f5+?? ♕xf5+ and 39...f3, the black pawn queens. But 38 ♔xf4! would leave him a safe pawn up, and should win.

If instead 37...♕xh2, White mops up a few pawns with something like 38 ♕e7+ ♔g8 39 ♕d8+ ♔f7 40 ♕d7+ ♔g8 41 ♕c8+ ♔f7 42 ♕xb7+ ♔e6 43 ♕e4+ ♔d7 44 ♕f5+ ♔c6 45 ♕xf4 ♕xb2 46 ♕a4+ ♔c7 47 ♕xa5+, again emerging a pawn ahead. The biggest guarantee for White is that, in almost all positions, the exchange of queens leads to an easy win, in view of his outside passed pawns.

37...♕xh2+ 38 ♔g5 f3 39 ♕f7+ ♔h8 40 ♕f8+ ♔h7 41 ♕e7+ ♔g8 42 ♕d8+ ♔f7 43 ♕c7+ ♔f8 44 ♕c8+ ♔e7 45 ♕xb7+ ♔e6 46 ♕b3+ ♔d7 47 ♕xf3 ♕xb2 48 ♕f5+ ♔e7 49 ♕xa5

After a few more inaccurate, time-pressure moves from both players, we reach an almost identical position to that after 37 ♔g5 ♕xh2 in the previous note. But here, crucially, the black king is not in check.

49...♕f6+

Black squeezes through for a draw by perpetual.

50 ♔h5 ♕h8+ ½-½

At first the next game seems like a lightweight, Stein already having a winning position by move 11, with the black pieces. Remember, though, the strength of his opposition. Ljubojevic was already a 2550-rated Grandmaster, and before long reached 2600+. Moreover, this game was played in a strong international tournament, and was not a simultaneous blitz encounter.

From which there are two main questions. First, and most obviously, how come a grandmaster went so badly wrong so quickly? Second, more fascinating and more difficult to explain, how did Stein lure his opponent into such a bad position?

Part of the art is to encourage your opponent to think that he is the one taking the initiative, and this was an important factor here. What else? Well, the author is not a mind-reader. One can only go so far in explaining the thought processes of two players. All one can do is try to find rational explanations for serious mistakes.

Game 10
L.Ljubojevic-L.Stein
Las Palmas 1973
Larsen Opening

---

1 b3

Bent Larsen tried this as a major part of his opening repertoire at the turn of the 1960s and '70s, and for a while made excellent results, scoring 30 wins in 39 games according to *Chess-Base*, although it is the disastrous 17-move loss against Spassky that most people remember.

The young grandmaster, Ljubomir Ljubojevic, was eager to carry on experimenting with this system, and also achieved good results, but by 1973 the

opposition had learnt what needed to be done against 1 b3, and his results deteriorated. Shrewdly, Larsen had already given it up the previous year.

1...e5 2 ♗b2 d6

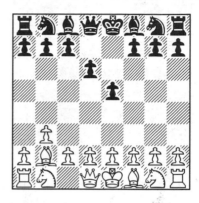

3 e3

A few months later, against Kavalek, Ljubojevic attempted an improvement, by playing 3 c4 followed by d2-d4, and omitting e2-e3, instead fianchettoing the second bishop as well. Unfortunately, this proved another disaster (see Game 10.1), and afterwards Ljubojevic played the Larsen System only very occasionally.

3...♘f6 4 c4 g6 5 d4 ♗g7 6 ♘c3

Instead, 6 dxe5 ♘fd7 7 ♘f3 ♘c6 8 ♘c3 ♘dxe5 is equal. 6 ♘f3 could be considered, and if 6...e4 7 ♘fd2 0-0 8 ♘c3 ♖e8 9 ♗e2 ♘bd7 10 ♕c2 ♕e7 11 g4 h6 12 h4 c6 13 g5 with an edge in R.McMichael-L.Williams, British League 1997. One of the few success stories for White, but Black can of course vary with, for example, 7...c6.

6...exd4 7 ♕xd4

7 exd4 0-0 gives White no advantage either.

7...0-0 8 ♞f3

8 ♞d5 ♞h5 9 ♕d2 ♝xb2 10 ♕xb2 c6 11 ♞c3 is possible, but is just equal too.

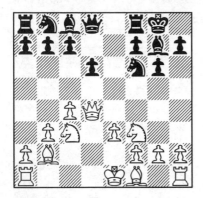

Puzzle: how can White lose this position within half a dozen moves? Black has done nothing exceptional so far, and has simply played standard developing moves.

Obviously there is no forced win for Black here, and in terms of opening theory, all we can realistically say is that the position is equal. As I type this game up, for example, six moves are given by *Fritz* as equal, three by Black's light-squared bishop, two by the undeveloped knight, and finally shifting the rook to the half-open e-file. All these are reasonable, but one, chosen by Stein, is potentially venomous.

8...♞bd7!

In practical terms, the best!

The obvious developing move is 8...♞c6, attacking the queen with gain of tempo. Then 9 ♕d2 ♝f5 10 ♝e2 ♞e4 11 ♞xe4 ♝xe4 12 0-0 a6 13 ♝xg7 ♚xg7 14 ♕b2+ ♕f6 15 ♕xf6+ ♚xf6 was just equal in T.Wall-R.Bates, Sutton 1999, and later drawn in a rook endgame.

However, Stein reasons that there is no need to attack the queen immediately, as she will sooner or later have to move anyway, the bishop fianchetto being a perennial threat. And the knight arriving on c5, rather than c6, will be positionally more difficult for White, fighting for control of e4, with no equivalent pressure against Black's central squares.

A chance, then, to play for the initiative, always welcome for the black side.

9 ♝e2 ♞c5

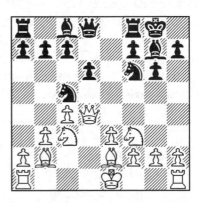

Black is already threatening ...♞fe4, winning material, an indication of how dangerous the black knights can be.

10 ♖d1?

Relying too much on one tactic, and missing the second.

There is always a tension in chess over what happens when Black has equalized, and how White should respond. A good player should be able to respond positively, whether as White or as Black. But sometimes this can go seriously wrong.

The fundamental question is

whether White is "equal, but with a tiny edge" or whether he is "equal, but with a need to defend". Misunderstand the situation, and a sudden disaster could befall. Here we have such a disaster.

If Ljubojevic were to sense that he needed to tie up the loose ends, and try to hold the position, then who knows, a quick draw might result. 10 ♕d2 doesn't give either player all that much to work on. After 10...♘fe4 11 ♘xe4 ♘xe4 12 ♕c2 ♕xb2 13 ♕xb2 ♖e8 14 ♖d1 ♗g4 15 0-0, the position is level.

Are we satisfied that Black is equal, and White, too, is equal? Maybe at the last diagram White can try for more, but with a good move, rather than a bad move. 10 b4! leads to tension, in which either player can go wrong.

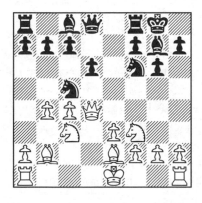

The obvious question is whether Black should accept the queen offer, after 10...♘fe4 11 ♕xg7+ ♔xg7 12 ♘xe4+ f6 13 bxc5. This is a difficult one to evaluate, not least because few of us get many opportunities to experience positions with three minor pieces versus the queen. If the minor pieces be-

come well anchored, and the queen can attack little, the lesser forces should prevail. But does White have time to consolidate?

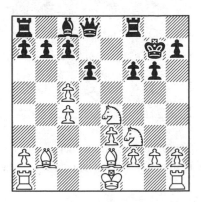

Here 13...♕e7?! 14 ♘c3 dxc5 looks like an unwise pawn snatch, as 15 ♘d5 ♕d8 16 0-0-0 or 15...♕d7 16 ♘d2 gives White a lot of pressure. 13...♕e8 seems sounder, but 14 ♘fd2! dxc5 15 ♘xc5 ♕c6 16 ♘ce4 ♗f5 17 ♘g3!? ♗e6 18 0-0 ♖ad8 19 ♖fd1 still leaves White an edge. So Black should probably not take the queen.

Another aggressive reply would be 10...♘g4 10 ♕f4 ♗e5 12 ♘xe5 dxe5 13 ♕g3 ♘d3+ 14 ♗xd3 ♕xd3, but this rebounds after simply 15 h3!.

It seems that Black cannot play sharply either. In which case 10...♘e6! 11 ♕d2 a5 12 a3 ♖e8 13 0-0 b6 is about as good as it gets for both sides. Equal, but maybe with a tiny edge.

10...♘g4!

Considerably better than 10...♘fe4? 11 ♕xg7+ ♔xg7 12 ♘xe4+ f6 13 ♘xc5 ♕e7 14 ♘d3, when this time White's minor pieces strongly outnumber the queen.

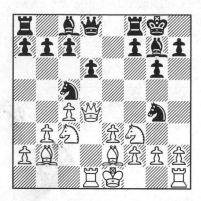

After the text move, Black, incredibly, is already winning, or very close to it.

11 ♕d2?

Presumably played without much thought, overlooking Black's reply.

11 ♕f4 was the only worthwhile try, but after 11...f5!, Black is on a full-monty squeeze. The immediate threat is illustrated by 12 h3 ♘xf2 13 ♔xf2 ♗xc3 14 ♗xc3 ♘e4+ and ...♘xc3, but how else does White improve?

a) 12 ♘d2 g5! 13 ♕f3 (or 13 ♕g3 f4 14 exf4 gxf4 15 ♕f3 ♘e5) 13...♘e5 14 ♕h5 (or 14 ♕d5+ ♗e6 15 ♕d4 ♘c6) 14...♘ed3+ also leads to a safe material advantage for Black.

b) 12 ♘d4 suffers from another tactical idea after 12...g5! (not 12...♗e5 13 ♕f3 ♘e4 14 ♘xe4 fxe4 15 ♕xe4 ♘xf2 16 ♕d5+ ♔g7, as 17 ♘c6! keeps White in the game) 13 ♕f3 ♘e4! 14 0-0 (or 14 ♘xe4 fxe4 15 ♕xe4 ♘xf2) 14...♘xh2! 15 ♔xh2 g4 16 ♕f4 ♗e5, winning the queen. Or if 13 ♕g3 f4 14 exf4 ♖xf4! 15 ♗xg4 ♗xg4 16 ♘de2 ♗xe2 17 ♘xe2 ♗xb2 18 ♘xf4 ♗e5, followed by ...♗xf4 with two pieces for the rook.

c) 12 0-0 ♘e4 13 c5! is White's remaining hope, obscure and apparently jumping straight into the lion's den.

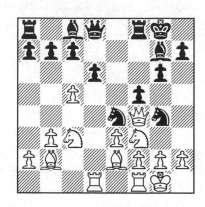

The point is that taking twice on c3 now fails to ♕c4+, regaining the piece. Instead, Black has two ways of trapping the queen, in either case with an advantage:

c1) 13...♗h6 14 ♗c4+ ♖f7 15 ♗xf7+ ♔xf7 16 ♘e5+ ♔f8 (or if 16...♔g8 17 ♘xe4! ♗xf4 18 ♘xg4) 17 ♕xg4 fxg4 18 ♘xe4 ♗f5 19 ♘g3 ♗g7 20 cxd6 cxd6 is complicated – imagine trying to calculate this over the board – and is still unclear at the end. It is probably good for Black, but he would no doubt prefer something simpler and safer, and there is a less combative line, where Black wins a minor piece for a couple of pawns:

c2) 13...g5! 14 ♘xg5 ♕xg5 15 ♗c4+ ♔h8 16 ♕xg5 ♘xg5 17 cxd6 cxd6 18 ♖xd6 is best followed up by 18...♘e4! 19 ♘xe4 ♗xb2 20 ♘g3 ♗e5 and 21...f4, and once the bishops dominate, Black's win looks assured.

It is remarkable how much trouble White can fall into as a result of a natural, but careless move in the opening: 10 ♖d1?. And a second similar move, 11 ♕d2?, now leads to catastrophe.

11...♘xf2!

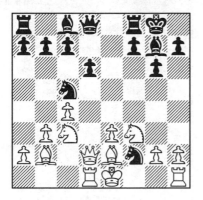

This just wins material.

12 0-0

If 12 ♔xf2 ♗xc3, and White cannot recapture due to the knight fork on e4.

12...♘xd1 13 ♗xd1 ♗g4

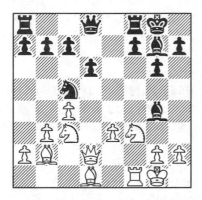

There is not much interest in the rest of the game. Stein consolidates without difficulty, the exchange and a pawn ahead.

14 h3 ♗xf3 15 ♗xf3 a5 16 ♘d5 c6 17 ♗xg7 ♔xg7 18 ♕d4+ f6 19 ♘f4 ♕e7 20 ♔h1 ♖fe8 21 ♕d2 ♕xe3 22 ♕xd6 ♕e5

23 ♕d2 ♖ad8 24 ♕xa5 ♘e4 25 ♘e6+ ♕xe6 0-1

This was Stein's last full-length tournament. He came equal first with former World Champion Tigran Petrosian, ahead of many other grandmasters, and without losing a game. Stein then played a team event in Moscow, with two wins against Evgeny Sveshnikov, and two draws against Eduard Gufeld. A few months later, he died.

Supplementary games

We have three this time, including a couple of ultra-quick wins by Stein, taken from the early 1970s. The reader will be able to find earlier examples. Before that, we show another Ljubojevic disaster in the Larsen Opening.

> ### Game 10.1
> ### L.Ljubojevic-L.Kavalek
> ### Manila 1973
> ### *Larsen Opening*

1 b3 e5 2 ♗b2 d6 3 c4 ♘f6 4 ♘c3 g6 5 d4 exd4 6 ♕xd4 ♘c6 7 ♕e3+

This was Ljubojevic's intended improvement on his game with Stein. He has deliberately avoided an early e2-e3 to leave a square for the queen.

7...♗e6 8 ♘f3 ♗g7 9 ♘g5 0-0

Stein is not the only player who has a quick eye for an initiative! Kavalek sees that he can defend the bishop with 9...♕d7, which is playable, but also that he can sacrifice a pawn or two, and accelerate his development, by not defending it.

10 ♘xe6 fxe6 11 g3

Ljubojevic decides it is too dangerous to snatch the pawn. One possibility is 11 ♕xe6+ ♔h8 12 e3 ♘d4! 13 exd4 ♖e8, with advantage to Black.

11...d5!?

Kavalek insists on gambit play. Most of us would be happy with 11...e5, taking control of the dark squares.

12 ♕xe6+

With full-blown acceptance. But otherwise the further ...d5-d4 will force White to take the pawn in any case. For instance, 12 0-0-0 d4! 13 ♕xe6+ ♔h8 14 ♗a3 ♖e8 15 ♕h3 a5, followed by ...a5-a4. Or 12 ♖d1 d4! 13 ♕xe6+ ♔h8 14 ♗a3 ♖e8 15 ♕h3 ♖e5!, followed by ...♕e8, with a strong initiative.

12...♔h8 13 ♘xd5?

Probably a miscalculation, but it is difficult to find a way for White to equalize, never mind try to refute Black's sacrifices. There is no time to castle kingside, as 13 ♗g2? ♘d4! and 13 ♕h3 ♘e4! both win for Black. And cas-

tling queenside, 13 0-0-0, transposes to the previous note after 13...d4!, where it is likely that Black keeps a slight edge.

13...♘xd5 14 ♗xg7+ ♔xg7 15 cxd5 ♖e8

Black's gambit play has been successful, as he is completely winning.

16 ♕g4

There is nothing better. On 16 ♕h3 ♕xd5 17 ♗g2, Black has 17...♖xe2+! 18 ♔xe2 (or 18 ♔f1 ♖xf2+!) 18...♕e5+ 19 ♔d2 (or 19 ♔f3 ♘d4+ 20 ♔g4 ♕f5+) 19...♖d8+ 20 ♔c2 ♘b4+ 21 ♔b1 ♖d2, with mate to follow.

16...♕xd5 17 f3 ♘e5 18 ♖d1 ♘xf3+! 19 ♔f2 ♕xd1 20 exf3 ♕d2+ 21 ♔g1 ♖e1 22 ♕c4 ♖ae8 0-1

Now back to Stein's games. The first comes from an extremely high calibre event, with, for example, Korchnoi managing only 50%, and Spassky, the then World Champion, scoring only +2. Karpov came equal first with Stein, and it was starting to look likely that Karpov was going to become the next Soviet World Champion, youth being on his side when compared with Stein.

This was always going to be serious chess, and Stein duly avoided any losses. It was noticeable, however, that he scored most of his wins against players who finished below 50% (+4 =3), and managed only one (+1 =9) against those higher up. Again, this shows both his (relative) weaknesses and his strengths – though to be fair, between the top seven players there were only two decisive games in the whole tournament.

Lengyel was having a rough time, with two draws and five losses before he played Stein. This was probably his worst moment.

Game 10.2
L.Stein-L.Lengyel
Alekhine Memorial,
Moscow 1971
Catalan Opening

1 c4 ♘f6 2 g3 e6 3 ♗g2 d5 4 ♘f3 ♗e7 5 0-0 0-0 6 d4 ♘bd7 7 ♕c2 c6 8 ♖d1 b6 9 ♘c3 ♗b7 10 b3 ♖c8 11 e4 c5

A clash of central pawns, and for a brief moment it looks complicated. Soon, three pairs of pawns are exchanged, and the player with the more active pieces will have the advantage. No detailed analysis about whether Black should equalize, or whether White is better. Leave that to opening theorists.

12 exd5

Stein is happy to trade pawns.

V.Korchnoi-J.Rubinetti, Buenos Aires 1979, saw an alternative approach:

12 e5 ♘e4 13 ♘xe4 dxe4 14 ♘d2 cxd4 15 ♗xe4 ♗xe4 16 ♕xe4 ♘c5 17 ♕e2 with a tense position. Is Black's passed d-pawn strong or weak? It is difficult to say. Eventually Korchnoi reached an endgame, exchanging his f-pawn for the passed d-pawn, and outplayed his opponent later on.

Two very strong grandmasters, two different ways of handling the same pawn structure in the opening.
12...exd5 13 ♗b2 ♕c7 14 ♘xd5 ♘xd5 15 cxd5 ♗xd5 16 dxc5

With gain of tempo, as Black's bishop is under attack.
16...♗xf3

16...♗e6 could be considered, as the c-pawn is pinned, but White can keep going with a string of minor threats, and Black ends up in trouble. After, for example, 17 c6 ♕xc6 18 ♕xc6 ♖xc6 19 ♘d4 ♖c7 20 ♘xe6 fxe6, White has the bishop pair, while Black's pawn structure has been broken up a little. All the same, it is not obvious that White has any decisive advantage, so Black can play on.
17 ♗xf3 ♘xc5 18 ♕f5

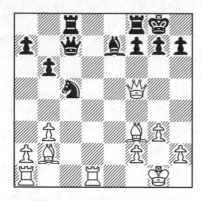

18...♖fd8??

Big blunder time. The board looks so open that the queen cannot be trapped in the middle, or so it would seem.

A quarter of a century later, Black "improved" with 18...♖cd8 (as suggested by Kotov in *Informator 12*) 19 ♗d5! ♕c8 20 ♕h5 ♘d7 21 ♗e4 g6 22 ♕f3 f6? 23 ♖ac1 ♕b8 24 ♕g4 ♘e5 25 ♕e6+ ♖f7 26 ♖xd8+ 1-0, V.Chekhov-R.Goetz, German League 1996.

18...g6 is better, but after 19 ♕g4 White is still fully in control.

19 ♗e5 1-0

If now 19...♗d6 20 ♗xd6 ♖xd6 21 ♖xd6 ♕xd6 22 ♕xc8+ wins.

It is unusual for a queen to be trapped in such an open position so early on.

Regarding the final game in this chapter, on first impression, and with the help of computer, all that seemed to happen was that play was equal throughout, until Gurgenidze made a blunder. Looking more closely, it becomes clearer that Stein was working

hard to improve his position, making full use of his adjacent bishop diagonals. There wasn't much tactical play during the game, but that was because Gurgenidze blundered just as Stein was limbering up for a full-scale attacking assault. This was, in effect, half an interesting game rather than a quick miniature.

> ### Game 10.3
> ### B.Gurgenidze-L.Stein
> Kislovodsk 1972
> *Veresov Opening*

1 d4 ♘f6 2 ♘c3 d5 3 ♗g5 c6 4 ♗xf6 exf6 5 e3 f5 6 ♗d3 g6

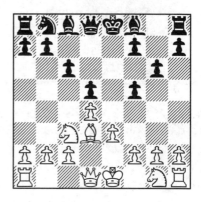

White has traded bishop for knight, and one wonders whether he has sufficient compensation for the bishop pair. In terms of minor pieces, Black's light-squared bishop is not very active at the moment, his pawns, in draughts formation, being in the way. However, sometimes bad bishops have the knack of turning into good bishops, with helpful handling, as we shall see.

White's minor pieces are unthreatening, and encourage Black to think about playing for more than equality. White's opening formation is inflexible. A better way of applying this idea is 1 d4 ♘f6 2 ♗g5, keeping back the queen's knight, and allowing the option of a well-timed c2-c4. In England, GM Julian Hodgson has played this opening with great success.

In the Veresov, which is what we have here, should Black be worried about his doubled pawns? Not really. The two f-pawns can cover two squares on the e-file and two on the g-file. The only real problem would be if, for some reason, Black no longer had an accompanying pawn on the g-file.

7 ♘ce2 ♘d7 8 ♘f3 ♗d6 9 c4 ♘f6 10 ♘c3 dxc4

Stein systematically starts a queenside initiative.

11 ♗xc4 b5 12 ♗b3 0-0 13 0-0 a6

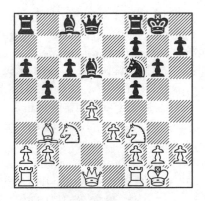

Draughts again. Black is planning to open up the long light-squared diagonal with ...c6-c5. Meanwhile, note the significance of his doubled f-pawns. The front f5-pawn covers the important

e4 central square, while the rear f7-pawn blocks the a2-g8 diagonal.

14 ♘e2 ♗b7

Black is now close to completing his development. *Fritz* gives the position as equal, but I don't believe that interpretation. Black should be better here.

15 ♖c1 ♕e7 16 ♘f4 c5 17 dxc5 ♗xc5 18 ♕e2 ♗d6 19 ♘d4 ♖fe8

Problems with the doubled f-pawns? No, more the advantages of a half-open e-file!

20 ♕d3 ♖ad8 21 ♖fd1 ♘g4

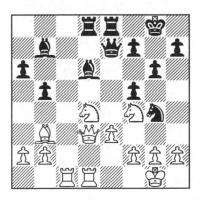

If you feel sure that you are better, first complete your development, and then attack!

22 ♕d2

White would like to get rid of the fangs on f2 and h2, but 22 h3? aggravates his suffering: 22...♘xf2! 23 ♔xf2 ♗xf4 24 exf4 ♖xd4! 25 ♕xd4 ♕e2+ 26 ♔g3 ♕xg2+ 27 ♔h4 g5+ 28 ♔h3 (or 28 fxg5 ♖e4+) 28...♕xh3+ leads to checkmate.

22...♗b8

Missing a trick: 22...♘xh2! wins a pawn, since 23 ♔xh2? loses to 23...♕g5! (threatening mate on g2) 24 g3 (or 24 f3

♖xe3!) 24...♗xf4 25 exf4 ♕h5+ 26 ♔h1 ♕h1 mate.

23 h3

Now certainly, but the kingside pawn structure is slightly weakened, and the black pieces are still strong.

23...♘e5 24 ♕e2 ♕g5 25 ♔f1 ♕f6

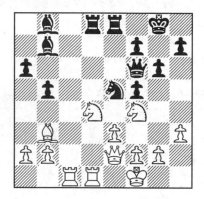

Still equal according to *Fritz*, but White has no active pieces, so Black has time to manoeuvre and then attack. Black is in fact much better.

26 ♔g1

It is too time-consuming to attempt to analyse each of the supposed equalizing moves. As a sample, with the help of *Fritz*, an attractive and effective variation would be 26 g3 h5 27 ♖c2 h4 28 ♖cd2 hxg3 29 fxg3 ♕h8! 30 h4 ♕f6 31 ♕e1 ♘g4 32 ♘c2 ♖c8 33 ♔g1 ♖xc2! 34 ♖xc2 ♖xe3 35 ♖e2 ♗a7! 36 ♖xe3 ♗xe3+ 37 ♔f1 ♘h2+ 38 ♔e2 ♕xb2+! 39 ♔xe3 ♘g4+ 40 ♔d3 ♗e4+ and wins. Very visual, and far more entertaining than the main line. Just look how every black piece had a role in the attack!

Sadly I have no knowledge of what Stein would have played in this position, but it is nice to think that he would have liked it.

26...♘c4! 27 ♕f1?

But if 27 ♗xc4 ♗xf4 28 ♗xb5 (or 28 ♗b3 ♖xd4!) 28...axb5 29 ♕xb5 ♗a6 30 ♕c6 (or 30 ♕a4 ♖xe3!) 30...♗e5 31 ♕xf6 ♗xf6 32 ♖c6 ♖e6! and Black keeps the extra piece.

27...♗xf4 0-1

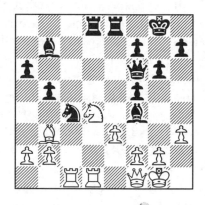

All so sudden. Black wins material.

It is now time to conclude this chapter, commemorating Stein's last full-length international tournament at Las Palmas in April 1973. He died suddenly in July, on his way to play in the European Team Championships in Bath. As his games show in his final year, he was still at the top, or close to it, in terms of playing strength.

One would like to think that, in the brief spell that he was conscious or semi-conscious before he died, he was able to recognize that he had been a great chess player.

Chapter Three

Mikhail Tal 1978-1979:
The King of Attack and his Apprentice

We are covering only a single year in the long career of Mikhail Tal, as it is unlikely that I would be able to add anything to what has already been written by others.

The simplest fact to start off with is that Mikhail Tal became World Champion in 1960 at the age of 24, which was the youngest ever at that time. Lasker was 25, also young, but Capablanca was 33, Alekhine 35, Euwe 34, Botvinnik 37, then Smyslov 36. It takes time to learn to play at the highest level.

Tal played wild and attacking chess, following the example of Alekhine, and did not bother to search for safety. He beat Botvinnik convincingly 12½-8½, but Botvinnik was extremely studious and worked out how to deal with Tal in the return match the next year. In between Tal had played like a true world champion, losing only a single game, against Jonathan Penrose at the 1960 Olympiad, but Botvinnik still won 13-8 in the spring of 1961.

Tal was a great player, that is universally agreed, but he suffered from ill health. He had, for example, to withdraw from the last seven rounds in the 1962 Curacao Candidates'. He could play brilliant chess, but never quite achieved his complete potential. In the English magazine, *Chess*, there was plenty of grumbling about Petrosian's play as World Champion, often with the viewpoint that if Tal were in good health, Petrosian would never stay as World Champion. No doubt similar comments were expressed elsewhere; understandable, if perhaps unfair to Tigran Petrosian or Boris Spassky.

The next hero was Bobby Fischer, but after winning in 1972, he completely dropped out. The author would very much have enjoyed discussing attacking games by Fischer post-1972, but there weren't any, apart from the rather meaningless 1992 match with Spassky, whereas chess life continued. RIP Robert James Fischer, 1943-2008.

Tal died in 1992, also at a relatively young age of 55. He continued to add to chess well after he was no longer World Champion. He was a coach to Anatoly Karpov for a while in the 1970s. He played more solidly, losing very few games. Then suddenly the old Tal re-emerged, attacking, taking risks, accepting that he would occasionally lose a game, but win a lot more, with great style. In the twelve years from December 1977, Tal played fabulously exciting chess. At the same time, the teenage Garry Kasparov was eager to learn from him, a great attacker learning from another great attacker.

One can only imagine what sort of creative excitement there was when Tal and Kasparov met up in Tbilisi, no doubt each wanting to outdo the other, and each learning with great respect from the other. We start off here with two wins by Tal against Mikhalchishin and Beliavsky. Then in the next chapter, we give Kasparov's game against Polugaevsky from the 1978 USSR Championship, an audacious win against one of the most respected Grandmasters in the world. In each of these games, the aim is not to play technical chess, but rather to try and beat the opponent with complete bamboozlement.

There are many books on Tal, understandably so, given that he was such an exciting player. Gallagher's *The Magic of Mikhail Tal* (2000) covers the years from 1975 to his death, concentrating mainly on detailed analysis. I have been careful not to coincide too much with Gallagher's book, and as a result a few outstandingly brilliant games from 1979 have been dropped from my selection. His wins against Velimirovic and Spassky, however, are essential reading. Also, while not actually overlapping with the current book, Raetsky and Chetverik's *Mikhail Tal, Tactical Genius* (2004) provides a collection of games and tests, asking how the reader would handle many critical positions.

The words "magic" and "genius" in these titles give an indication of the quality of Tal's play.

Now let's get straight down to business. The first game is a Botvinnik Semi-Slav, played by consenting wild tacticians, and as sharp and complicated as anything devised by Muzio, or other knights of the King's Gambit. Both players are forced to attack, both players are also forced to defend. There is no quiet variation.

Play through Tal's early games, and you will discover that he was playing this opening even at the age of 16, in 1952. Quite possibly he was trying it much earlier, too, but such games have not survived, at least not on the databases.

Game 11
M.Tal-A.Mikhalchishin
USSR Championship, Tbilisi 1978
Queen's Gambit, Semi-Slav

---

1 ♘f3 d5 2 c4 e6 3 d4 ♘f6 4 ♘c3 c6 5

♗g5 dxc4 6 e4 b5 7 a4

Tal avoids the massively theoretical main lines with 7 e5 h6 8 ♗h4 g5, etc, and elects to get his younger opponent into less familiar territory.

7...♗b4

No analysis here, except to note that this move, keeping hold of the c4-pawn for as long as he can, is the most popular choice in this position, particularly as it can also arise via the Queen's Gambit Accepted and Vienna Defence.

7...b4 and 7...♗b7 are possible, but then the extra pawn drops, and so for the addicts may be regarded as anti-theoretical.

8 axb5

8 e5 h6 9 exf6 hxg5 10 fxg7 ♖g8 is now the main line of this subsystem, but there are a few citations in *Chess-Base* before the start of the 1980s, when the Vienna had a revival.

Tal also experimented with 9 ♗h4 g5 10 ♘xg5 hxg5 11 ♗xg5 ♗xc3+ 12 bxc3 ♕a5, but now the most accurate move, 13 ♗xf6, threatening the rook, is only a draw after 13...♕xc3+ 14 ♔e2 ♕b2+ etc. In S.Loeffler-P.Heugli, Co-

penhagen 1988, White did try 15 ♕d2!? ♕xa1 16 ♕b4, but after 16...♕a2+ 17 ♔e1 ♕a1+ 18 ♔e2 ♕a2+ the draw was inevitable, as any move other than ♔e1 would allow ...♕b3+.

At most stages in his career, Tal was happy to gamble. Therefore, just to avoid the perpetual, he tried 13 exf6?! ♕xc3+ 14 ♗d2 ♕xd4 15 ♖c1 in M.Tal-Y.Yakovich, Sochi 1986.

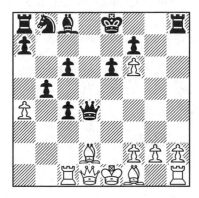

A pawn or two deficit is of course substantial, particularly if White's pieces are still on the back two ranks. Nevertheless, Black has to treat the sacrifice with some respect. His king is stuck in the middle, surrounded by some chilly dark squares, and his pawns can be nibbled at. Having said that, probably few players other than Tal could have even the slightest sniff, in advance, of a genuine attack from this position.

The game continued 15...♘d7 16 ♕f3 ♕d5 17 ♕a3 ♕c5 18 ♗b4 ♕e5+ 19 ♗e2 c5 20 ♗c3 ♕e4 21 axb5 ♕xg2, and here, probably short of time, the players agreed a draw. Tal is in a worse position, possibly even losing objectively, but his opponents had the greatest respect for his attacking talents. Even Kasparov was happy to take a draw against Tal in such positions, for example in the 1982 Moscow Interzonal.

Back to the main game, in which the players were effectively on new theoretical territory; and if one of the players might happen to slip at an early stage, this is to be expected, if even so regretted.

8...cxb5 9 e5 h6 10 ♗h4 g5 11 ♘xg5

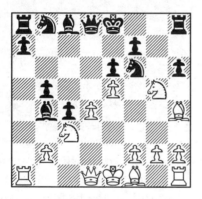

11...hxg5

Tal gives 11...♛d5 12 ♘xf7 ♘e4 as unclear in *Informator 26*, with no further explanations. Gambit a rook, or grab a rook, it is all part of the game of chess! For Tal, anyway.

Of course, few of us will be able to calculate ten moves or more perfectly, and Tal would often win after mind-blowing complications, making fewer mistakes, and finding more good moves than his opponent. For normal players, the aid of the computer will give us indications as to how play might continue, but it is only a guide, as computers can misjudge the position.

a) 13 ♘xh8, taking the rook, is the obvious move to examine first, and after 13...♘xc3, then:

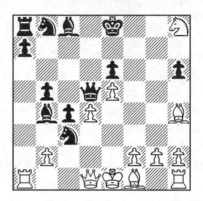

a1) 14 ♕h5+ ♚d7 15 ♕f7+ ♚c6 16 ♕f3 lets Black off the hook, as 16...♘e4+ avoids the exchange of queens, and Black can soon start attacking after ...♚c7 and ...♘c6. Instead, White can try 15 ♗e2 ♘xe2+ 16 ♚xe2, but 16...♚c7 17 ♘f7 ♘c6 is still promising, for instance 18 ♖hd1 ♕xg2 19 ♕f3 ♕xf3+ 20 ♚xf3 a5 21 ♚e3 a4 sees the queenside pawn mass rolling forward.

a2) 14 ♕g4 ♘e4+ 15 ♚e2 ♘c6 16 ♕g6+ ♚d7 17 ♕f7+ ♗e7 forces Black to retreat the bishop from its dangerous attacking square, but his queen and two knights still create problems.

Now the most straightforward plan for White is 18 ♖d1 ♘xd4+ 19 ♖xd4 ♕xd4 20 ♕xe7+ ♚f6 21 ♕e8+ ♚c7 22 ♕d8+ ♕xd8 23 ♗xd8+ ♚xd8 24 ♘f7+ ♚e7 25 ♘xh6, when he has returned his piece advantage, while keeping an extra pawn, but again Black's queenside mass is rushing forward more quickly. This should end up level.

Instead, *Fritz* suggests the unexpected king retreat 18 ♔e1!?, so that 18...♘xd4 does not come with check, and White can respond 19 ♕xe7+ ♔c6 20 ♕e8+ ♔b7 21 ♖d1. The computer initially gives this as winning, but then finds the clever resource 21...♘c3!, vacating the e4-square for the queen. Now 22 bxc3? ♕e4+ 23 ♔f2 ♘b3 is mate. Alternatively, 22 ♖xd4 ♕xe5+ 23 ♔d2 ♕xd4+ 24 ♔c2 ♕d1+ 25 ♔xc3 ♗d7! builds a mating net around the white king. For example, 26 ♕g6 b4+! 27 ♔xb4 ♕d2+ 28 ♔c4 ♖c8+ 29 ♔b3 ♕d5+ 30 ♔b4 ♕d4+ 31 ♔b3 ♕a4 mate, or if 26 ♕e7 a5! with 27...b4+ to follow.

But maybe White has an improvement? Rather than 16 ♕g6+, White might play 16 ♖d1!. Now 16...♘xd4+? would lose to 17 ♖xd4 ♕xd4 18 ♕g8+ ♔d7 19 ♕d8+ ♔c6 20 ♕xd4, while if 16...♗b7 17 f3! ♘g5 (still not 17...♘xd4+? 18 ♖xd4+ ♕xd4 19 ♕xe6+ and mates) 18 ♗e1! seems to consolidate.

b) 13 ♕h5 is also possible, following the maxim that the threat is stronger than the execution.

If Black sidesteps with 13...♔d7, then rather than 14 ♘xh8 ♘xc3 transposing to line 'a1' above, White can avoid it all with 14 ♖c1!. In turn Black might save the rook with 13...♖f8, when 14 ♘d6+ ♔d7 15 ♕xh6 ♘xc3 16 ♗xc4 bxc4 17 ♕xf8 ♘e4+ 18 ♔f1 ♗xd6 19 ♕d8+ (or 19 exd6 ♘xd6) 19...♔c6 20 ♕xc8+ ♗c7 leads to an obscure position where Black has two knights for the rook and pawns. However, White can again aim to consolidate, this time with 15 ♘dxe4! ♕xe4+ 16 ♗e2 ♗xc3+ 17 bxc3 ♕xg2 18 ♔d2 or 16...♗b7 17 ♕xh6 ♖f7 18 f3 ♕c2 19 ♕d2, keeping his extra pawns.

Entertaining chess, but consider, what would Black want to be thinking at the beginning of these lines. If White takes the rook, Black may have counterplay against the king, certainly, but it is very unclear whether it will be enough. Indeed analysis would seem to favour White. Even more significantly, would he want to take on Tal move for move in the complications? Mikhalchishin wisely decides against this.

12 ♗xg5 ♘bd7

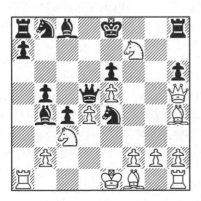

A familiar enough set-up on the kingside, but the slight variations on the queenside could well be significant in such a sharp position. White, when compared with the main line, has added a2-a4 and an exchange on b5, while Black has added ...♗b4.

Who is gaining from this? The obvious and natural answer is that Black does better, since he has developed a piece rather than spending time exchanging a pawn. Indeed, most players do not bother with the early a2-a4, but there is still room for experiment. One advantage from White's point of view is that ...♕a5, as Black played in the Tal-Yakovich game above, is not possible here.

13 ♕f3

And this is another reason why White exchanged pawns on b5, through opening up the long diagonal.

13...♖b8

14 exf6

14 ♖xa7? loses after 14...♕b6 15 ♗xf6 ♕xa7 16 ♗xh8 ♕a1+.

14...♗b7 15 ♕g3

15 ♕f4 is also to be considered, although not mentioned by Tal in his commentary. Maybe the writer would not look at it in much depth either, except that *Fritz* gives it as a better move. Black should probably start counter-attacking with 15...a5, taking advantage of White's a2-a4xb5 earlier on, and after something like 16 h4 a4 17 ♖h3 ♖a8 18 g4 ♘b6, the game is quite unclear.

15...♖g8

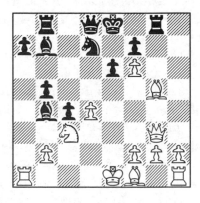

16 ♗e2?

Not the best. Tal himself regarded the position reached in the diagram as unsatisfactory, better for Black. On that sort of basis, the best he can do is to complete his development, bring the king into safety, and hope to resume the attack later on.

Tal would naturally have considered 16 h4 ♘xf6? 17 ♗xf6?, when the tactics work out for Black after 17...♖xg3 18 ♗xd8 ♖xc3 19 ♔d1 ♖b3. For example, 20 ♗a5 ♗xa5 21 ♖xa5 ♖xb2 wins. The queenside pawns supported by two rooks are far more dangerous than the h-pawn supported by one rook. However, White can do much better with 17 ♕e5!, with threats on f6 and b5. If 17...♘d7 18 ♗xd8 ♘xe5 19 ♗c7 ♘d3+ 20 ♗xd3 ♖c8 21 ♖xa7 ♖xc7 22 ♗e4, and White is on top.

What else can Black try? There is nothing particularly aggressive, once we have rejected the pawn capture. So the careful 16...a6!? looks best, preparing ...♘xf6 by defending the b5-pawn in advance, while also safeguarding the a-pawn from capture. If White continues to advance 17 h5 ♘xf6 18 h6, Black responds 18...♖xg5! 19 ♕xg5 ♕xd4 with good play for the exchange. Instead, White could consider 17 ♗e2, returning to his previous idea, although 17...♘xf6 18 ♕e5 ♗e7 or 18 ♗f3 ♕c8 is probably OK for Black. Or he might activate his rook via 17 ♖h3!? ♘xf6 18 ♕e5 ♗e7 19 ♖g3. There are other possibilities. We do not need to analyse in depth from this position, just to appreciate that 16 h4! is an improvement on Tal's 16 ♗e2, after which White could have ended up worse.

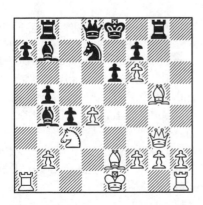

16...♕b6

Black correctly decides to crash through on the queenside, which is

great, except that White now has strong control on the empty kingside. A battle commences.

Note that 16...♘xf6? still fails to 17 ♕e5!, but 16...a6!? first is another option.

17 0-0

The logical follow-up to his previous move. His king is now safe. The only downside is that White has fewer chances to push the h-pawn forward in a promoting attack.

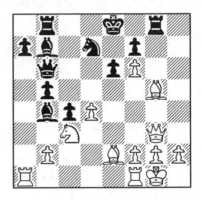

17...♗d6!

Mikhalchishin continues to play actively and, at least as importantly, to play accurately. Yet again, he does not bother about grabbing a pawn, this time with 17...♕xd4?, as unsurprisingly, there is sharp response in 18 ♘xb5!. Mikhalchishin might well have decided, just from an initial impression, that this position would be too hot to handle. Or he might even have calculated it out. Either way, he chose the correct decision.

After 18 ♘xb5, the tactics would continue 18...♕c5 19 ♘c7+ ♔d8 20 ♘xe6+ fxe6, and now rather than 21 f7+

♖xg5 22 f8♕+ ♘xf8 23 ♕xb8+ ♕c8 24 ♕xc8+ ♔xc8 25 g3, when play soon settles down to a level endgame, White can take time for 21 h4!, after which he has all the chances.

18 ♕h4 b4!

It is important for Black to try make progress, rather than simply resting on his superior pawn structure.

Tal gives 18...♘xf6? 19 g3 ♘d5 20 ♘e4 as clearly better for White. *Fritz* differs, only offering White an edge, but in terms of attacking understanding, one is more likely to prefer former World Champion Tal to the computer. For instance, if 20...♗f8, as suggested by *Fritz*, White can continue the attack with 21 ♗h5, and maybe ♖fe1, when he is starting to create real threats.

19 ♘d1 ♕b5 20 f4 ♕d5

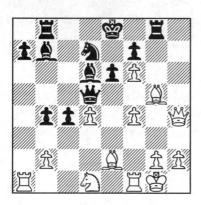

The high point of Black's early middlegame. He has clear control in the centre, and his queen and bishops are pressing on the diagonals towards the white king. Territorially, all White has in compensation are a few squares on the kingside, and some potential pawn advances, beginning with f4-f5.

At the moment, this seems merely a consolation prize. The geography of chess implies that control of the centre creates pressure on other parts of the board. White's control of the f-, g- and h- files and corners is useful, but does not have the same impact across the whole board. Therefore White has to make the mobility of this pieces work to its maximum.

There are always some surprises in the geometry of the chessboard, the ability to switch pieces around from one square to other, maybe far distant squares. Looking at this position, it is hard to believe that White can propose a winning plan involving a rush by the queen from h4, via d1 to a1, and then later a big check along the a-file, to a4, and finally a checkmate on d7. But if you find this as totally unimaginable as White, then you are missing out some useful attacking or defensive resources. As we shall see later on, Mikhalchishin was unable to focus on the a-file, and lost.

It is not being suggested that White would be able to calculate at this stage what will happen after ♕d1-a1-a4+, or even that he would give it much thought at all. It is more a case that a player needs to have the flexibility of the board.

Just now there is a more immediate question, how to defend against the mate on g2.

21 ♗f3

White has to challenge the open diagonal, otherwise his position is toast.

21...♕xd4+ 22 ♔h1

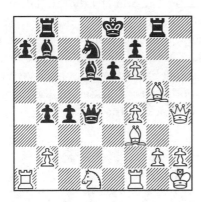

22...♘c5!

A difficult decision to make, and Tal says that this was not the best. He suggests instead 22...♗xf3 23 ♖xf3 ♗c5 as good for Black, and *Fritz* concurs, but in fact White's resources are considerable. For example, after 24 ♖f1 ♕d2 25 ♘f2 ♕xb2, everything looks to be going smoothly for Black. But play on a few moves, 26 ♘e4 a5 27 ♕h7 ♖f8 28 f5! e5 29 ♘xc5 ♘xc5 30 ♗h6 ♘d7 31 ♗xf8 ♘xf8 32 ♕h5 c3 33 ♖xa5 c2 34 ♖a7, and suddenly Black is getting mated. Alternatively, if 26...♕d4 27 f5! exf5 28 ♕h7 fxe4 29 ♕xg8+ ♘f8 30 ♖ad1 ♕c3 31 ♗h6 b3 32 ♗xf8 ♗xf8 33 ♕g4 and again White wins.

These are just a couple of variations from amongst countless others, but it seems that while Black can usually create connected passed pawns, they are not sufficiently dangerous to prove a distraction, and he has little other counterplay. Meanwhile his king remains extremely vulnerable, particularly on the light squares.

Although moving the knight from the central defensive square creates

some weaknesses, one can appreciate why Mikhalchishin felt the need to push his pieces into the attack as soon as possible.

23 ♕h7 ♖f8

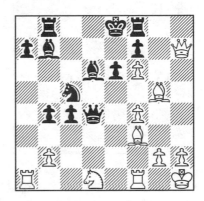

24 f5?!

Critical, and according to Tal, a mistake. Indeed, in his notes Tal regarded this as effectively losing, though as we shall see he had a deep resource he missed later on, before Mikhalchishin's time-trouble blunder.

Instead, 24 ♗xb7 ♖xb7 25 ♘f2! is given as unclear by Tal. As in the previous note with 22...♗xf3, once the white rooks and knight become fully centralized, Black will have great difficulty in maintaining his light squares. However, in his favour here, his pieces are rather better placed, in particular the rook on b7, while the knight on c5 challenges its opponent the centre.

Tal now suggests that 25...♕xb2 is weak, because of 26 ♘e4!, when White is on the attack. Indeed, 26...♘xe4? 27 ♕xe4, sees White already creating major threats on the long diagonal, while the black queen is ineffective. Therefore, 26...♕d4! makes sense, bringing the queen back into the action, and after 27 ♘xd6+ ♕xd6 28 ♗h6 ♘d7!

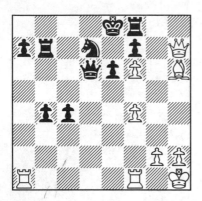

it is completely unclear whether the white heavy pieces will prevail, or Black's passed pawns, or perhaps neither. For example:

a) 29 ♗xf8 ♘xf8 30 ♕e4 ♕d5 31 ♕e2 ♘d7 32 ♖fd1 ♕b5 33 f5 c3! 34 ♕h5 c2 35 ♖xd7 ♔xd7 36 ♕xf7+ ♔d8 37 ♕xe6 ♕c5 (or 37...♖d7 38 ♕g8+ ♔c7 39 ♖xa7+ ♔b6) 38 ♖c1 b3 forces White to take the perpetual.

b) 29 f5 e5! 30 ♗xf8 ♘xf8 31 ♕h4 ♕d4 32 ♕g3 ♕c5 33 ♖fe1 ♘d7 34 ♖a6!? c3 35 ♖c6! ♕xc6 36 ♕g8+ ♘f8 37 ♖xe5+ ♔e7 38 ♖e7+ ♔d6 39 ♕xf8 ♖d7! 40 ♖e6+ ♔d5 41 ♖xc6 ♔xc6 42 h3 c2 43 ♕c8+ ♖c7 and again White must take the draw.

These are but a couple of variations to show how complicated the play can become. An objective verdict is very elusive, even to in depth analysis. It is not even easy to say which side would be easier to play over the board.

24...♗xf3 25 ♖xf3 ♘b3!

Given as a double exclamation

mark by Tal, and clearly Mikhalchishin was thinking in terms of this idea by move 22. It is formidable, exposes the lack of coordination of the white forces, and most importantly, obliges White to surrender a rook, lessening the potency of his attack a little.

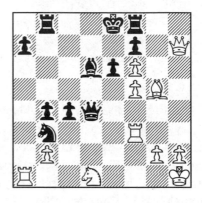

26 ♖xb3!

Tal in return gives his own move an exclamation mark, although it is effectively forced. If 26 ♖b1?, then just 26...♕e4, winning. White has to regain some of the initiative.

26...cxb3

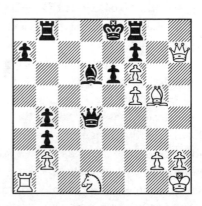

27 ♘e3?

White is the exchange down, but if

his knight reaches an effective post, and if his kingside pawns start to break open Black's kingside, then there might yet be dangerous counterplay.

After the obvious 27 fxe6! fxe6?! 28 ♘e3, White has made a vast improvement, his queen being fully activated, and with a dangerous advanced pawn, the spearhead of three kingside connected passed pawns. White is, at the very least, still in the game, and following 28...♕xb2 29 ♖d1 ♕e5 30 ♘c4 ♕xh2+ 31 ♕xh2 ♗xh2 32 ♔xh2, the pressure is on Black to hold. For example, 32...a5 33 ♖f1 ♖f7 (if 33...a4 34 f7+ ♖xf7 35 ♘d6+) 34 ♘d6+ ♔f8 35 ♗h6+ ♔g8 36 ♖f3 ♖d7 37 f7+ ♔h7 38 f8♕ ♖xf8 39 ♗xf8 b2 40 ♖b3 ♔g8 41 ♘c4 ♔xf8 42 ♘xb2, and White has the edge.

Tal rejects 27 fxe6,

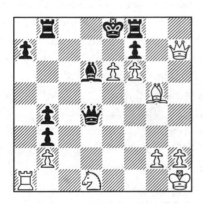

in view of 27...♕e5, which he gives as winning for Black. It looks convincing at first, with the threat of a back row mate on e1, an attack on the bishop, while gaining time to win back the e-pawn, but White can parry by nonchalantly reactivating his knight. It was, I believe, Tal's own comment that

you cannot take all your opponent's pieces at once. Here, alas, he missed a wonderful opportunity to have demonstrated his comment.

Readers, try to work out what is going on in this position. We shall return to the line after the game, which was played quickly and in time trouble.

As a further option for Black, the computer suggests 27...♖b5!?, which also seems good. After 28 e7?! ♗xe7 29 fxe7 ♖h8! 30 ♖c1! ♖xg5 31 ♕xh8+ ♕xh8 32 ♖c8+ ♔xe7 33 ♖xh8 ♖e5, Black regains the piece for a better endgame. Alternatively, if 28 exf7+ ♖xf7 29 ♕g8+ ♗f8 30 ♘e3 ♕xb2 31 ♖f1 (not 31 ♖g1? ♕d4 32 ♘g4 ♖xg1+! 33 ♔xg1 b2 34 ♕g6 ♖xg5!) 31...♕e2 32 ♗h6, Black can at worst force a draw by 32...♖f5!? 33 ♖xf5 b2 34 ♖e5+ ♔d8 35 ♖d5+ ♔e8 etc.

27...♕e4?

White's omission of f5xe6 should have been fatal. The tactical point is that after 27...♕xb2!

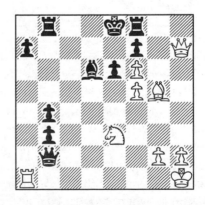

and then 28 ♖d1, Black can ignore the threat to his bishop and play 28...♖c8!, with the counter-threats of ...♖c1. As the white queen is still obstructed by the f7-pawn, 29 ♖xd6 loses to 29...♖c1+ 30 ♖d1 ♖xd1+ 31 ♘xd1 ♕e2! or 30 ♘d1 ♕e2!, with a wipeout on the back rank. It is too late now for 29 fxe6, due to 29...♖c1 30 exf7+ ♔d8 31 ♕h5 ♕d2! 32 ♖xc1 ♕xc1+ 33 ♘d1 b2!, or 31 ♕d3 ♕e5! 32 ♘f1 ♖xd1+ 33 ♕xd1 b2, with a winning position.

Against less forcing moves, such as 28 ♖g1, Black just plays 28...e5!, securing his king. For instance, 29 ♘c4 ♕d4 30 ♘xd6+ ♕xd6 31 ♗h6 ♕c5! 32 ♗xf8 ♕xg1+! 33 ♔xg1 b2 34 h4 b1♕+ 35 ♔h2 ♕b3, defending f7, and White has only tricks left.

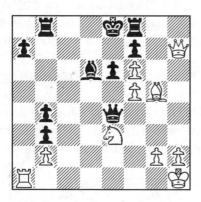

28 ♕h5 ♗c5?

A second consecutive error. Here 28...e5 would have been an improvement. It may look as if Black has already survived the worst, but after 29 fxe6 White's threats soon become overwhelming. Black should have closed the centre with 28...e5 while he still could, when 29 ♕d1 ♖d8 30 ♕xb3 ♖h8 31 ♕a4+ ♔f8 32 ♕xa7 ♔g8 sees the black king is a relatively safe position, while 29 ♘f1 ♖g8 30 ♘g3 (or 30 ♖xa7 ♖b7 31 ♖a8+ ♖b8) 30...♕c2 31 ♗e3

♕xb2 32 ♖xa7 (or 32 ♖d1 ♖d8 33 ♕f3 ♖xg3!) 32...♕b1+ 33 ♗g1 ♕xg1+! 34 ♔xg1 ♗c5+ 35 ♔f1 ♗xa7 36 ♕e2 ♗d4 37 ♕c4 b2 38 ♕c6+ is another draw.

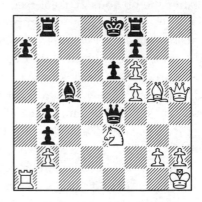

29 fxe6!

Tal has been getting battered, his opponent being the exchange and a pawn up, centralized, and even with the possibility of back row threats. And yet Tal carries on as though he was setting up a winning attack! And it turns out that he is right!

29 ♗h6 is a credible alternative, but Tal reckoned that 29...♗xe3 30 ♗xf8 ♕xf5 31 ♕h8 ♔d7 was winning. White can stay in the game with 32 ♕g7! ♕g6 33 ♖d1+ ♔c6 34 ♕xg6 fxg6 35 ♗e7, but Black has the chances in the endgame after 35...a5! 36 f7 ♗h6, his three to one pawn majority on the queenside being an important factor.

Quite how good the chances are is open to question, but it is almost zero chance of a win for White. Tal always played the opponent, as well as the board, and he would have been well aware that he had made serious mistakes earlier, but that at the moment his opponent was playing hesitantly. Maybe the win was a possibility? And if so, he would want to keep the queens.

29...♗xe3

29...♕xe6 is hopeless, as 30 ♗f4 ♗c8 31 ♘f5 creates too many threats. Instead, the text sees the dangerous knight eliminated, leaving Black a whole rook up, and... completely lost!

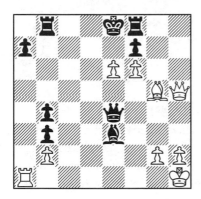

30 ♖e1?

Playing the regain the piece, but White doesn't need it!

In fact 30 ♗xe3! ♕xe3 (if 30...♕xe6 31 ♗xa7 ♖b7 32 ♗c5 opens up the a-file) 31 e7! wins for White, as the threats to the black king are too strong. After 31...♖g8 (otherwise 32 exf8♕+ ♔xf8 33 ♕h8 mate) 32 ♖d1! (threatening 33 ♕b5+! ♖xb5 34 ♖d8 mate) 32...♕g5 33 ♕f3 (threatening 34 ♕c6 mate) 33...♕b5 34 ♕e4, there is no satisfactory defence to 35 ♕d4, followed by mate on d7 or d8. Returning material doesn't help: 34...♕d7 35 ♖xd7 ♔xd7 36 ♕d5+ ♔c7 37 ♕xf7 and the kingside pawns win easily, or if 33...♕xg2+ 34 ♕xg2 ♖xg2 35 ♔xg2 and the h-pawn

advances inexorably down the board.

Also possible was 30 exf7+ ♖xf7 31 ♖e1. Black is again a rook up, but his awkward positioning on the e-file, and the pin on his rook, mean that he is the one who has to be careful. This time, though, he can escape with 31...♖b5, when 32 ♖xe3 ♕xe3 33 ♕h8+ ♖f8 34 ♕h5+ ♖f7 is a draw by perpetual check.

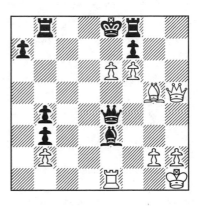

30...♖b5!

Here Tal admits, in *Informator*, that his position was losing, or at least he thought it was. Sometimes you think that it is about time to resign, but maybe there is a chance to throw the dice a couple of times...

31 ♕d1!

It was too late for 31 exf7+?, hoping for perpetual after 31...♖xf7? 32 ♖xe3 ♕xe3 33 ♕h8+, as in the line with 30 exf7+ above. Black has instead 31...♔d8!, and if 32 ♕h6 ♕xg2+ 34 ♔xg2 ♖xg5+ 35 ♔f3 ♖g3+ 36 hxg3 ♗xh6 37 ♔e4 ♖xf7 38 ♔f5 ♗g7! 39 ♔g6 ♖xf6+ 40 ♔xg7 ♖f2 with a winning rook endgame.

31 e7 is again an inviting prospect. After all, a protected passed pawn on

the seventh needs to be treated with respect. However, Black can solve his problems with 31...♖g8 32 ♕h3 ♕f5! (not 32...♖f5? 33 ♗xe3 ♕c2, when the quiet king move, 34 ♔g1!, covering f1 and threatening ♖c1, wins for White) 33 ♗xe3 ♕xh3 34 gxh3, reaching a favourable endgame.

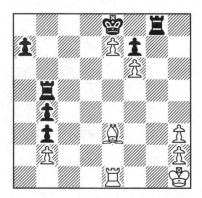

Black needs to break up the advanced pawns quickly, otherwise White would be the one playing for an edge. Therefore play might continue 34...♖g6! (not 34...♖d5?! 35 ♗h6! ♖g6 36 ♖c1 ♖xf6 37 ♗f8, and White survives) 35 ♗d4 (if 35 ♖f1?! a5 36 ♗d4 ♖g8! 37 ♖c1 ♔d7 consolidates) 35...♖f5 36 ♖a1 a6 37 h4 ♖gxf6 38 ♗xf6 ♖xf6 39 ♔g2 ♔xe7, and Black has good chances with the extra pawn, even if it's not yet a certain win.

31...♖d5

31...fxe6?! 32 ♖xe3 ♕d5 (or 32...♕f5 33 h4) 33 ♕g4 ♔d7 34 h4 leaves White with the better prospects, despite being the exchange down.

32 ♕a1!

Setting up a threat or two. He might as well try it, as 32 ♕xb3 fxe6 33 ♕a4+

♔f7 34 ♗xe3 a5 or 33 ♗xe3 ♖xf6 34 ♕a4+ ♖d7 is uninspiring for White. He can play on for a while, but what can he attack with?

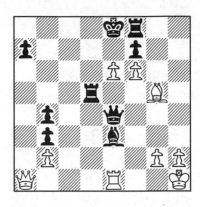

32...♖xg5??

The tragedy of time trouble. A few seconds loss of concentration, and a whole day leads to nothing, a big zero. Mikhalchishin had fought his way, punch by punch, against one of the most formidable attackers of all time, and gave away nothing. Or at least did not make more errors than Tal. But as Tartakower said, "victory goes to the player who makes the next-to-last mistake", and here Mikhalchishin makes the last one. We can only assume that in excitement, in time trouble, he overlooked that a4 could be useful.

The game concluded:

33 ♕a4+ ♔d8 34 ♕d7 mate

This wasn't a brilliancy, it was a sad blunder.

Mikhalchishin had a few good alternatives, none actually winning, but none losing either. A better move from the last diagram is:

32...fxe6!

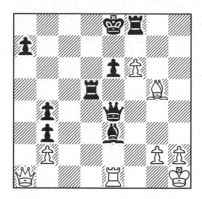

Simple and direct. Black's king is no longer under mating attack, and it is up to White to stay in the game.

32...♕c4 is also possible, when 33 ♕a4+ ♔b5 34 ♕xb5+ ♖xb5 35 ♖xe3 fxe6 (if 35...♖xg5 36 e7! regains the rook, due to the threat of ♖d3 and ♖d8 mate) 36 ♖xe6+ ♔f7 37 ♖e7+ ♔g6 38 h4 a5 leaves Black the exchange up with the better chances. White should prefer 33 e7! ♖xg5 34 exf8♕+ ♔xf8 35 ♖xe3 and if 35...♖f5 36 ♖f3! ♖xf3 37 gxf3 ♕e2 38 ♕xa7 ♕xf3+ 39 ♔g1 ♕xf6 40 ♕b8+ ♔g7 41 ♕g3+ with a probable draw.

33 ♖xe3 ♕g4

33...♕f5 34 h4 a5 35 ♕c1! is not conclusive either.

34 ♕a4+ ♔d8!

The only move. Tal gave this as winning for Black, but it has yet to be demonstrated.

Not 34...♖d7? 35 ♖d3! anyway, when in a single move by each side, White is no longer under mating threat, and Black's rook is under decisive pinning threat. After 35...♖ff7 (or similarly 35...e5 36 ♕c6) 36 ♕c6 ♔d8 37

f7+ ♕xg5 38 f8♕ mate, White wins attractively.

34...♔f7? would also be chancing his arm too much, as 35 ♕xa7+ ♔g6 36 ♕g7+ ♔c5 37 h4! keeps the black king stuck in the net, threatening the rook as well as 38 ♕h7 mate.

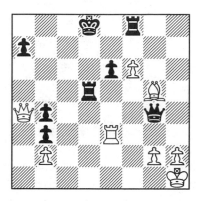

35 h4! ♖h8 36 ♕xa7

This is the most obvious direct response. White cannot give any safe check as yet, while Black does not have an immediate win either. In such positions, White should try to do some significant damage. The result is a forced draw.

36...♖d1+

36...♖xh4+ 37 ♗xh4 ♕xh4+ 38 ♖h3+ ♖d1+ 39 ♔h2 comes to the same thing, or if 36...♕xg5 37 ♕b8+ ♔d7 38 ♕b7+ ♔d8 39 ♕b8+ and White forces the draw.

37 ♔h2 ♖xh4+ 38 ♗xh4 ♕xh4+ 39 ♖h3 ♕f4+ 40 ♖g3 Drawn

The careful reader will have noted, from previous examples in this book, that much of the time even the wildest of games should end up as a draw, provided the play is accurate (and sadly only the annotator, often several years later, will have the privilege of working out in leisure what should have been played).

In the notes to follow, watch out for perpetual checks, or alternatively a level position in an endgame, after sacrifice and counter-sacrifice.

There is some even more entertaining play that we have not yet covered:

After **27 fxe6** (instead of 27 ♘e3) **27...♕e5!**,

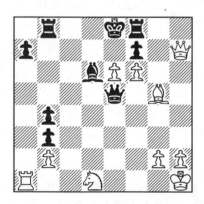

which Tal thought was winning, White in fact has two playable continuations:

a) **28 ♘f2! ♕xg5**

28...♕xb2? fails to 29 ♖c1! ♕xf2 30 e7 ♕e2 31 exf8♕+ ♗xf8 32 ♕b1! ♔d8 33 ♕xb3 and the black king is wide open, or if 29...fxe6 30 ♖c7! ♕a1+ 31 ♗c1 and Black must give up his queen.

29 ♘e4 ♕e5 30 ♘xd6+

Not 30 ♖d1? ♕xh2+! 31 ♕xh2 ♗xh2 32 ♔xh2 ♖h8+ followed by 33...fxe6 with a winning advantage.

30...♕xd6 31 e7 ♕xf6 32 exf8♕+ ♔xf8 33 ♕d3

Reaching a heavy rook endgame. Now 33...♕xb2 34 ♕d6+ ♔g7 35 ♕g3+ is an instant draw, but Black can still pile on the pressure with:

33...a5! 34 ♕xb3 ♖e8

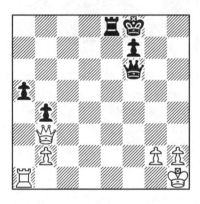

A lot has changed in the last few moves, and the good attacking player, as well as the defender, will be aware that quite often games suddenly transform themselves from crazy tactics to delicate positional play.

Pawns are level, but Black has whatever advantage is going. His queen and rook are more active than White's, and because Black's pieces are more active, his king is safer. Black also has the better pawns. Even though White has a passed pawn, it is difficult to envisage a way it could be promoted on the kingside. Black, meanwhile, has obvious pressure on the queenside, which will likely remain even if a couple of pieces are exchanged.

In practical terms this is still a good option for White, especially in time trouble, and certainly better than resigning after 27...♕e5. However, with the leisure of analysis, we discover the other knight move is even stronger:

b) **28 ♘e3!**

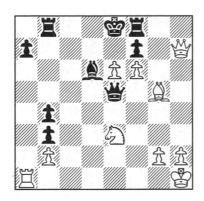

28...♕xg5

If 28...♕xb2? 29 ♖d1 wins easily.

29 ♘f5!

Better than 29 ♘c4 ♕f4 30 ♘xd6+ ♕xd6, which transposes to the 28 ♘f2 variation above.

29...♖b6!

The only move. 29...♕f4? is no good after 30 ♖d1!, as 30...♕xh2+ 31 ♕xh2 ♗xh2 32 ♘g7 is mate. Similarly if 29...♗c5? 30 ♖d1! ♕xf6 31 ♘g7+ wins, as 31...♔e7 32 ♖d7 is mate again.

30 ♘xd6+ ♖xd6 31 exf7+ ♔d7

Not 31...♖xf7? 32 ♖e1+ ♔f8 33 ♕h8+ ♕g8 34 ♕h6+ and wins.

32 ♕e4

Not 32 ♕g7? ♕h5!, hitting f7 and d1, and if 33 ♖xa7+ ♔c6 34 ♖a6+ ♔c7 35 ♖xd6 ♕e2! 36 h3 ♕e1+ 37 ♔h2 ♕e5+ picks up the rook.

After the text White is a whole rook down, but threatens catastrophic checks at e7, a7 and b7. Now Black has only one move to stay in the game:

32...♕c5!

Defending a7, while preparing to block 33 ♕b7+ with 33...♕c7.

33 ♕e7+ ♔c6 34 ♖a6+

White cannot capture 34 ♕xf8? due to the discovered attack 34...♖d1+ and wins.

34...♔d5!

Not 34...♔b5? 35 ♕e2+ ♔c4 36 ♕xc4+ ♔xc4 37 ♖xd6 and the kingside pawns are too fast.

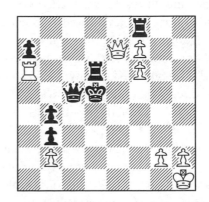

35 ♖a1!

White still cannot take the rook, due to the back rank mate on c1.

35...♔c6 36 ♖a6+ ♔d5 37 ♖a1

And the game ends in an unusual draw by repetition.

The one general point to be made is that, in a genuinely complicated chess game, there are so many ideas that no player will be able to examine everything over the board. From the negative point of view, there are bound to be mistakes. But a good player will also find good moves.

Chess is, from this respect at least, an art rather than a science. The player looks at his or her moves, and decides, through the feel of the position as well as analysis, that this choice is better than that choice. Afterwards, the critic decides, sometimes with admiration, sometimes with regret, that such-and-such a move may be seen as brilliant, good, interesting, bad or unsound.

All of these adjectives apply in different parts to the preceding game.

In the next, Beliavsky wants to attack, and to try to win. Theoretically, this is not quite as difficult against Tal as against other World Champions, as Tal is unusually willing to take risks, and if he takes risks, he will also be in a position where he might lose. However, Tal also had an unusually fine grasp of what degree of risk is acceptable, in a practical game, and what is not. He was a great chess psychologist, the best among World Champions since Emanuel Lasker. When he took risks against Grandmaster opponents, as here, he won many more games than he lost.

We have already seen his win against Mikhalchishin at Tbilisi. Here we have a second win, again in auda-cious style. In the end Tal scored 5 wins, 12 draws, no losses, and won the Championship ahead of Tseshkovsky and Polugaevsky by a clear point. Not bad for a risk-taker.

Game 12
A.Beliavsky-M.Tal
USSR Championship, Tbilisi 1978
Queen's Gambit Declined

---

1 d4 ♘f6 2 c4 e6 3 ♘f3 d5 4 ♗g5 ♗e7 5 ♘c3 0-0 6 e3 ♘bd7 7 ♖c1 a6 8 a3 dxc4 9 ♗xc4

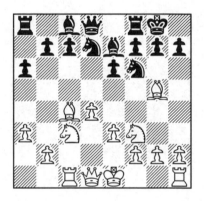

9...c5

This might even be slightly inaccurate, Black usually playing 9...b5 10 ♗a2 first, and only then 10...c5, or 10...♗b7 11 0-0 c5.

10 0-0

The point is that White could have considered 10 dxc5!? here. Black cannot reply 10...b5? because of the en passant rule, 11 cxb6, and so White has gained in flexibility. For instance, after 10...♘xc5 11 0-0 and then 11...b5, he might prefer 12 ♗e2, with a slight edge.

But Beliavsky was not interested in a quiet strategic game with a slight edge. He wanted to win! There were three rounds to go before the end of the tournament. Tal and Tseshkovsky were leading on 9/14, with four players, including Beliavsky, a point behind. He needed a win to close the gap.

10...b5 11 ♗a2 ♗b7 12 ♗b1 ♖c8 13 ♕d3!?

The first indication that something exciting was going to happen. It is not all that often that White can go for a direct attack on h7 in an Orthodox Queen's Gambit, when the black knight is still on f6.

A much earlier Soviet Championship game led to dull equality after 13 dxc5 ♘xc5 14 ♕e2 ♘ce4 15 ♘xe4 ♖xc1 16 ♖xc1 ♘xe4 17 ♖d1 ♕c7 18 ♗xe7 ♕xe7 19 ♕d3 ♕f6 20 ♕d4 ♕xd4 21 ♖xd4 ♖c8 22 ♔f1 ♘f6 23 ♔e2 ♔f8 24 e4 ♔e7 25 ♗d3 ♘d7 26 ♗b1 ½-½ N.Riumin-V.Rauzer, Leningrad 1934.

In *Informator 26*, Tal gives 13 ♕e2 as slightly better for White, but Black seems to equalize after 13...b4.

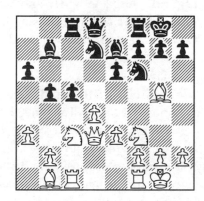

13...♗xf3!?

Tal, too, is up for the attack, or rather the counter-attack. If he has the opportunity to damage his opponent's pawn structure, then why not?

There are other ways of handling the defence, and of course the attacking player, as well as the defender, will need to be aware of the various options. Tal goes for an immediate counter-attack, with tactical play by both sides being on the cards. A much earlier World Champion, Wilhelm Steinitz, might have taken the opposite approach.

In the late 19th century, Steinitz was the first systematic thinker on defence in chess, and he was a firm advocate of not making pawn moves in front of the king, unless absolutely necessary. In positions like this, he would argue that Black could do better than the obvious 13...h6 or 13...g6, which temporarily prevent an attack on the king, but weaken the kingside pawn structure. Applying the Steinitzian principles, we might expect 13...b4!? 14 axb4 cxb4 15 ♘e2 ♕a5 16 ♗xf6 ♘xf6 17 ♘e5 ♗e4, and Black's position is secure, maybe even with thoughts of an edge.

Two different and good ways of handling the position. Perhaps a double reason why Beliavsky's approach was interesting but not effective.

14 gxf3 cxd4 15 ♘e4

Tal gives this as White's best try.

15 ♕xd4 leaves Black slightly better after 15...h6, or maybe 15...♖c4 16 ♕d1 ♘e5.

15 exd4 is possible, but not very convincing. The string of doubled and

isolated pawns are not going to be much help with the attack, and could end up just being weak themselves. 15...♖e8!? is a good reply, or else 15...g6, with ...♘h5 to follow.

15...♖xc1 16 ♖xc1

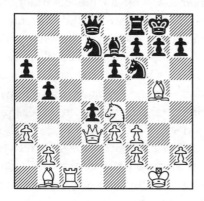

16...dxe3!?

Tal jumps from defence to attack, avoiding the intermediate attempt to equalize. He even plans to sacrifice the knight, hoping to pick up sufficient weak pawns in compensation. Not everyone would enjoy handling the game like this, especially given the option of solid defence, but the alert player will want to keep open the option of counter-attack.

White's play is arguably slightly speculative, and if so, it is within Black's rights to strike back. It is significant that White's kingside pawn structure has been compromised. For any sort of counter-attack, there has to be some sort of opposing weakness to attack. Without this, Black would have to play the position purely defensively.

Other quieter moves include 16...g6 17 ♕xd4 ♘xe4 18 ♗xe7 ♕xe7 19 ♗xe4

♘f6, which Tal gives as equal; or 16...♘d5 17 ♘c5 g6 18 ♗xe7 ♘xe7 19 ♕xd4 ♘xc5 20 ♕xc5 ♘d5, maybe even with a tiny edge for Black.

17 ♗xf6

17 fxe3? is pointless. After 17...♘xe4 18 ♕xe4 g6, Black is a pawn up, and has successfully consolidated his position.

White has to attack now, right or wrong.

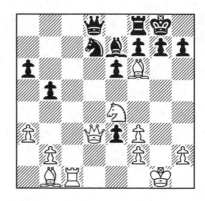

17...exf2+!?

An interesting moment. Tal gives this as a serious mistake, suggesting that the correct line is 17...♗xf6 18 ♘c5 g6 19 ♘xd7 ♗xb2 20 ♖d1, and only then 20...exf2+ 21 ♔f1, transposing into the game, as 21 ♔g2? here would allow 21...♕g5+! 22 ♔xf2 ♖d8 with strong counterplay.

In an earlier draft, I indulged in speculation as to why Tal played his early pawn check, and noted that part of his attacking technique was to find ways in complicated positions that he could play simple and direct moves, while his opponent was forced to think hard, and maybe make mistakes. A straightforward pawn check, with three possible replies, fits into this pattern of play. All this may or may not be true, but there are better examples, notably Spassky-Tal, Montreal 1979 (see Game 14).

Moreover, it turns out that 17...exf2+ wasn't really a mistake, as the position Tal is aiming for seems to be good for White in any case, so there is no need for elaborate explanations as to why Tal played it.

18 ♔f1?

Tal gives this a double question mark in *Informator*, proposing that 18 ♔g2! instead offers White a big advantage.

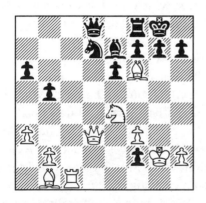

The point is that after 18...♗xf6, White can play 19 ♖d1! ♕c7 20 ♕xd7, since the king defends the h2-pawn. Black can try 20...f1♕+ 21 ♔xf1 ♕xh2, but 22 ♘xf6+ gxf6 23 ♕d4! covers everything, and keeps the extra piece.

Tal also notes 18...gxf6!? 19 ♘c5 f5 20 ♘xd7 ♗g5 21 ♖d1 ♖e8 as good for White. There seems to be a partial oversight here, because 20...♗h4! is also possible, holding on to the ad-

vanced pawn, as 21 ♘xf8?? loses at once to 21...♕g5+. However, White can consolidate his position with 21 f4 ♖e8 22 ♘e5. For example, 22...♕f6 23 ♕e3! (not 23 ♕d6? ♖d8 24 ♕xa6? ♕g7+ 25 ♔h1 ♕h6! 26 ♕xb5 ♕xf4 27 ♖f1 ♗f6, regaining the piece) 23...♖d8 24 ♘f3 ♕g7+ 25 ♔h1 ♕g4 26 ♗d3 ♗f6 27 ♗e2 ♗xb2 28 ♖f1, and White removes the annoying f2-pawn with a clear advantage.

The one line that neither player would have examined in much depth is 18 ♔xf2??, as the king is exposed to unwanted checks. After 18...gxf6! 19 ♖d1 ♕b6+, followed by 20...♖d8, Black escapes the trap and remains two pawns to the good.

18...♗xf6?

The most obvious and natural reply, but it's not the best. Surprisingly, compared with 18 ♔g2 in the previous note, the less exposed position of the white king on f1 actually improves the 18...gxf6 line for Black. The crucial difference being that after 18...gxf6! 19 ♘c5 f5 20 ♘xd7 ♗h4!, the desirable 21 f4? now loses to 21...♕a8!.

True, White can play 21 ♘xf8 here, since there is no queen check, but 21...♕g5 is still good enough for a draw: 22 ♕d1 ♕g1+ 23 ♔e2 ♕xh2 24 ♕d4 (or 24 ♕f1 ♕e5+ 25 ♔d3 ♕d5+) 24...f1♕+! and the white king cannot escape; e.g. 25 ♔xf1 ♕h3+ 26 ♔e2 ♕g2+ 27 ♔d3 ♕xf3+ 28 ♔c2 ♕c6+ 29 ♕c3 ♕e4+ etc.

White can try other moves, but Black seems to have sufficient counterplay whatever. For instance, 21 ♕d6 (or

21 ♕d2 ♖e8 22 ♕f4 ♕xd7 23 ♕xh4
♕d2) 21...♖e8 22 ♕c6 ♔g7 23 f4 (or 23
♕c3+ e5!? 24 ♘xe5 ♕g5) 23...♖g8 24
♔e2 ♔h6 and the position is quite unclear.

19 ♘c5

This wins a piece, though not the
way he would prefer to do it, as Black
gets an uncomfortable number of
pawns. White would have liked to play
19 ♖d1, but then 19...♕c7! followed by
...♕xh2 is very strong.

19...g6 20 ♘xd7

White has to do this too, as after 20
♕xd7? ♗xb2 he has too many pawns
dropping.

20...♗xb2 21 ♖d1 ♖e8

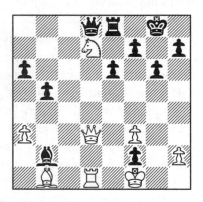

A strange set-up. White has the extra knight, in return for numerous
pawns, and it is the knight which is the
focus of play. Normally, a well-
advanced piece securely protected is a
good thing, but sometimes it is better
to be less advanced. Here the knight on
d7 is not as good as it might seem. It
cannot attack anything, it can't do anything going forward, and White can't
afford the time to retreat it either. Nev-

ertheless, it does cover a few useful
squares, notably e5, f6 and b6, so at the
moment the knight can be left where it
is.

22 ♔xf2?

Finally a definite mistake, turning
the position from more than equal to
worse. The pawn on f2 is an irritation
for White, but so too is the bishop on
b2, and this in the end tips the balance
in favour of Black.

22 ♕d2! pushes the bishop from its
attacking square, in view of the tactic
22...♗xa3 23 ♕c3! ♗e7 24 ♘f6+. After
24...♗xf6 25 ♖xd8 ♗xc3 26 ♖xe8+ ♔g7
27 ♔xf2, White is a rook up, and will
gradually sweep up the opposing
pawns, which are not close enough to
promotion squares to be dangerous.
22...♕h4 23 ♕xb2 ♕h3+ 24 ♔e2! also
wins easily, as Black's tricks vanish.

This leaves 22...♗g7, but now the
a3-pawn is safe, and after 23 ♕xf2 ♕e7
24 ♕c5 ♕h4 25 ♔g2, White's position is
to be preferred. Once he has played
♗e4, all his pieces are active, even the
knight on d7. Black could consider the
queen exchange, 24...♕xc5 25 ♘xc5 a5,
but it is clear that the height of his ambitions would be to hope for an uncomfortable draw.

Black might also deviate on his
23rd, where he has plenty of other possibilities. He could try to liquidate the
queenside pawns as quickly as possible, with 23...a5 24 ♕c5 b4, for example.
But there's nothing particularly inspiring, nor anything that alters the view
that White is just better here.

22...♕h4+ 23 ♔g2 ♖c8

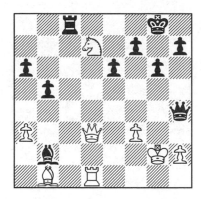

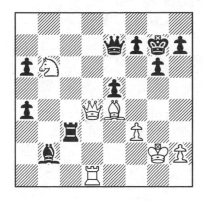

Black has gained at least a couple of tempi as a result of White's careless pawn capture on move 22. It is now easy to attack the pawn on a3, with the possibility of creating two passed pawns. Meanwhile, the white king could easily come under attack too.

24 ♕e3

Otherwise Black takes over the h6-c1 diagonal.

24...♕e7 25 ♗e4 ♔g7

Black takes time out to consolidate. Alternatively, Black could take on a3 straightaway, as the perpetual after 26 ♘f6+ ♔g7 27 ♘h5+ gxh5? 28 ♕g5+ ♔h8 29 ♖d8+ etc, can be circumvented by 27...♔h8!. But there is no need for Black to hurry.

26 a4

Possibly worried about what to do with the knight, and also aware that the a3-pawn is likely to fall, Beliavsky decides it is time to let the a-pawn drop, so that the knight can return to active play. This is sensible, but now Black has four pawns for the piece, quite a margin.

26...bxa4 27 ♘b6 ♖c3 28 ♕d4+ e5

Black continues to block up the long dark-squared diagonal. Does this mean that he is creating a "bad bishop"? Quite the opposite! The bishop is superbly supporting his pieces and pawns, and ensures that Black has a winning positional attack. Soon, for example, Black will play ...a4-a3, and this will be big trouble for White.

29 ♕d2

29 ♕xa4? leads to catastrophe on the other side of the board, after 29...♕g5+ 30 ♔h1 ♖c1+ 31 ♖xc1 ♕xc1+ 32 ♔g2 ♗d4. Then if White saves the knight, with for example 33 ♘d5, he gets checkmated as follows: 33...♕g1+ 34 ♔h3 ♕f1+ 35 ♔h4 ♗f2+ 36 ♔g5 ♕g2 mate.

Black's forces are so dominant on the dark squares he does not even have to move the bishop that far!

29...♖b3 30 ♘d5

30 ♘xa4 ♗d4 sees the white knight get stuck another way, but this could well be an improvement nevertheless. It removes the dangerous pawn on a4, while the knight prevents Black from making use of the b2-square. Black is

still better of course.

30...♕h4 31 ♗c2 ♖b7 32 ♖e1 a3

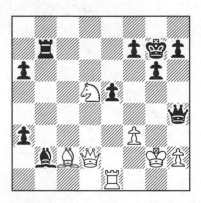

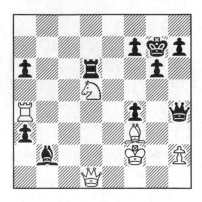

Finally Black is able to play ...a4-a3, after which he can squeeze and squeeze. Black cannot win immediately on either the queenside or the kingside, but if he can centralize his queen and rook, White will need to cover both sides of the board, and this will over-stretch his defence.

33 ♖e4 ♕d8 34 ♖a4 ♖b6

The tempting 34...♖b5 35 ♗e4 f5 36 ♖c4 fxe4? would let White escape with a draw after 37 ♖c7+ ♕xc7 (the only move) 38 ♘xc7 a2 39 ♕d7+ ♔h6 40 ♕h3+ etc.

35 ♗e4 ♖d6 36 f4

Otherwise 36...f5 wins.

36...exf4 37 ♗f3 ♕g5+ 38 ♔f1 ♕e5 39 ♔g2 ♕f5 40 ♕d1 ♕g5+ 41 ♔f2 ♕h4+ 0-1

In the days of slower time limits and adjournments after the move 40 control, this was often a convenient moment to resign. There is little doubt that Black is winning. 42 ♔g1 ♖e6 43 ♕d2 ♖e1+ 44 ♔g2 ♕g5+ 45 ♔h3 ♖f1, for instance, is simple enough.

The next game is a quick and straightforward win for Tal. There were no doubtful sacrifices this time. He was able to attack effectively, certainly, but that was because, like Stein, he rapidly found the weakness in his opponent's set-up, and exploited it mercilessly.

It is perhaps necessary to correct the false impression that players like Tal, Stein and Kasparov create magic all the time. In a selection like this, we are concentrating on the wildest and most imaginative games, but in tournament chess, quite often neither of the players will have the opportunity of extreme creativity.

In the early rounds at Montreal, for example, Tal beat Spassky in round 1, then made draws with Hort (20 moves), Ljubojevic (31), and Hübner (16) in the next three. Then came this win against Larsen, followed by more draws with Portisch (21) and Karpov (13). This was steady chess. Tal did not play for brilliancies all the time, but took his chances when they arose. He warmed up in the middle of the tournament, trying a pawn sacrifice against Kavalek, and a couple of rounds later, evidently sensed that there were weaknesses in Spassky's play, and went into gambit mode; we analyse this in Game 14.

Tal eventually finished equal first with World Champion Karpov, proving that, after a quiet few years, he could still play great chess.

Game 13
M.Tal-B.Larsen
Montreal 1979
Sicilian Defence

1 e4 c5 2 ♘f3 ♘c6 3 d4 cxd4 4 ♘xd4 ♘f6 5 ♘c3 d6 6 ♗g5 e6 7 ♕d2 ♗e7 8 0-0-0 a6 9 f4

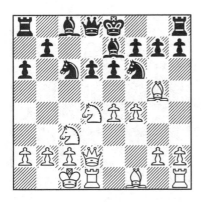

9...♕c7?!

Joe Gallagher described this as "a rather passive, half-hearted sort of move." It develops, but does not necessarily do that much. While this may well be true objectively, we should remind ourselves that back in the seven-

ties and beforehand, Larsen's move was cutting-edge main line.

It was only later that Black concentrated his resources on 9...♘xd4 10 ♕xd4 b5, the first cited example on *ChessBase* being from 1995, some sixteen years after the Tal-Larsen game.

Then the straightforward response is 11 e5 dxe5 12 ♕xd8+ (12 ♕xe5 has also been tried, but 12...♕b6 looks equal) 12...♗xd8 13 fxe5 ♘d7 14 ♗xd8 ♔xd8 15 ♗e2 ♔e7 16 ♗f3 ♖a7 17 ♖he1 ♖c7, and a draw before too long in L.Guliev-E.Guseinov, Baku 1998. If either player might have problems, it would be White with the advanced and isolated e-pawn. There is not much more on this line, indicating that theorists and players do not consider it as particularly effective for White.

Instead, 11 ♗xf6 gxf6 is regarded as critical. It was only to be expected, perhaps, that Kasparov added his own ideas, 12 e5!?, with a trademark central breakthrough, and a quick win against Zbynek Hracek at the 1996 Yerevan Olympiad. There is now considerable theory on this line.

But all this was much later on, and Larsen was playing according to the theory of the time, which makes Tal's win in 22 moves all the more impressive. It was not simply that Larsen played a known poor line. Tal was finding something new.

10 ♗e2!?

Given the context, this may be regarded as unusual, although it can transpose into, or out of, other known lines. It seems like just a quiet, natural and obvious move, but sometimes quiet lines can have a sting.

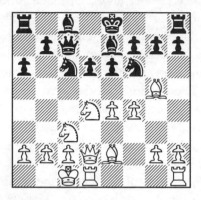

10 ♘f3 and 10 ♗xf6 were the main moves at the time.

10...♘xd4

Among the predecessors of the Tal-Larsen game, White won convincingly in O.Kinnmark-F.Petersen, Halle 1967, after 10...0-0 11 g4 ♖d8 12 f5 ♘xd4 13 ♕xd4 b5 14 ♗h4 ♖b8 15 g5 ♘e8 16 ♖hf1 b4 17 fxe6 fxe6 18 ♘d5! exd5 19 ♕xd5+ ♔h8 20 ♗c4 with a strong mating attack. Yet another example of a knight sacrifice on d5 in a Sicilian.

Another try is 10...h6, but after 11 ♗xf6 gxf6 12 ♗h5, the light-squared bishop is suddenly on an irritating square. Don't miss, either, the tactical problem of 10...b5? 11 ♘xc6! ♕xc6 12 e5, and the bishop is threatening a skewer on f3.

Tal suggested that 10...♗d7 was probably best. This transposes into a known position, with games going back at least to the 1940s. So Tal's ♗e2 offered an interesting interpretation, rather than a major novelty, transposing the ...♕c7 and ...♗d7 moves on moves 8 and 10.

11 ♕xd4 b5?

The natural follow-up to the exchange on d4, but as Tal shows, there are problems in timing.

12 e5!

In such a position, White does not need to think hard in terms of strategic chess. It is all tactics. The player needs to calculate in reasonable depth to discover whether e4-e5 is strong, or even extremely strong. If it is, then go for it. If not, it would be wiser to try something like 12 ♗f3 or maybe 12 ♗xf6.

Tal made his calculations, noticed a hidden resource, and confidently plays for a win.

12...dxe5 13 fxe5 ♘d5 14 ♗xe7 ♘xc3

Forced, as 14...♘xe7? 15 ♘xb5! axb5 16 ♗xb5+ ♔f8 17 ♕d8+ ♕xd8 18 ♖xd8 is mate.

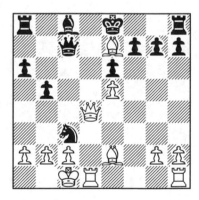

This is the position that Tal had to examine in advance. With tactics around, there is no point in finding an OK move. It has to be a good move.

15 ♗f3!!

Tal has indeed found a resource. It is difficult for White to see this over the board, there being so many threats and captures, but Tal clearly had it fully under control.

The only alternative would be to swap off pieces with 15 bxc3 ♕xe7 16 ♗f3 ♗b7 17 ♗xb7 ♕xb7 18 ♕d6 or 15 ♕xc3 ♕xc3 16 bxc3 ♔xe7 17 c4, heading for a drawn endgame.

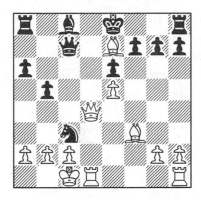

15...♘xd1?

This is clearly losing, and the rest goes quickly. White's pieces are far too strong for Black to hold his game together. The only chance for Black would be to exchange the minor pieces.

15...♗b7? does not work, in view of 16 ♗d6 ♗xf3 17 bxc3, winning a piece. So the dark-squared bishop must go.

On 15...♔xe7, it is obvious that White has at least three good moves – two checks and a capture – and it would be strange none of these turned out to be good. While thinking about 12 e5, Tal would probably not need to analyse much further. If this line actually appeared on the board, then he would start to calculate. It would be an unnecessary waste of energy to try to figure it out so far in advance, and one

senses that part of Tal's great strength was to play simple but sharp moves quickly, to force his opponent to have to work hard, and maybe in the end make mistakes. According to the tournament book Tal took only 41 minutes to achieve a winning position on move 16. Larsen was losing after an hour, and his decisive mistake on move 15 took twenty minutes of thought.

Tal later gave 16 ♕h4+ as good, while Gallagher hints that 16 bxc3 is better, leaving the queen with more options. After 16 bxc3 ♗b7?, White wins a piece with 17 ♕d6+ ♕xd6 18 exd6+ etc. So Black must try 16...♖a7, when Gallagher gives 17 ♕h4+ f6 18 exf6 gxf6 19 ♕h6, with no further analysis, but a strong implication that White should win.

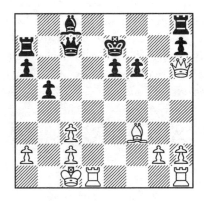

One line might continue 19...♖f8 20 ♗h5 ♖g8 21 ♖hf1 f5 22 ♕xh7+ ♔f8 23 ♕h6+ ♔e7 24 ♗g6 ♕xc3 25 ♕h4+ ♔f8 26 ♖d8+ ♔g7 27 ♕h7+ ♔f6 (a stirring king-hunt for White) 28 ♕xg8 ♕a1+ 29 ♔d2 ♕xf1 30 ♖f8+ ♔e5 31 ♕h8+! (but not 31 ♖xc8?? ♖d7+ 32 ♔c3 ♕e1+ 33 ♔b3 ♕b1+ 34 ♔a3 b4+ and Black mates)

31...♔d5 32 ♖xc8 ♕f2+ 33 ♔c3 ♕e1+ 34 ♔b3 ♕b1+ 35 ♕b2 and wins.

If this seems a bit long-winded, there are plenty of alternatives along the line, an attractive one being the rook sacrifice 24 ♖xf5 exf5 25 ♖e1+ ♔d8 26 ♕f6+ ♕e7 27 ♖xe7 ♖xe7 28 g3, with a queen and two pawns for the two uncoordinated black rooks.

As we've already noted, Tal would not have needed to analyse twenty moves ahead over the board. It is more a case of doing things step by step. While thinking at move 16, he might well decide, as in Gallagher's annotation, that 19 ♕h6 is promising, and that Black would have difficulties in holding the position. Then maybe there are a few obvious and natural moves, without White having to think in depth.

Let's go back to Black's 15th move options. The safest way, indeed the only way, to avoid a strong attack against his king is by 15...♘e2+! 16 ♗xe2 ♕xe7.

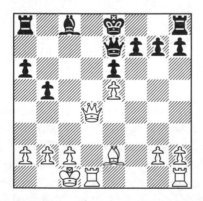

Then play might continue 17 ♗f3 ♗b7 18 ♗xb7 (or perhaps 18 ♕d6)

18...♕xb7 19 ♕d6 ♖c8 20 ♖d2 with the advantage. Again, it would have been pointless to try to analyse this in depth in advance. All Tal would have needed to do would be to confirm that White is positionally better. Here Black has problems with his queenside pawn structure, which White can attack with ♖d6 at some stage. This is difficult to confront in the longer term, leading to the danger that White will have two, or even three, united queenside passed pawns, well away from Black's king.

16 ♗d6

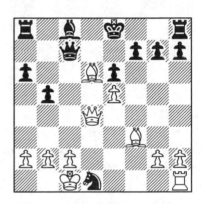

Now Black's king is stuck in the centre, and White's queen and bishop pair are lined up for a few clunking punches. And if Black gives up his rook for nothing, what will he then do with his king?

16...♕c4

If 16...♕a7 17 ♗c5 wins for White.

17 ♕b6!

Even better than regaining the rook by 17 ♕xc4 bxc4 18 ♗xa8. He is going for mate.

17...♘f2

Trying to distract White with 18

♕xf2 ♕f4+ 19 ♚b1 ♗d7, though it doesn't really achieve anything after 20 ♕b6! and if 20...♖c8 21 ♗b7 or 20...♖d8 21 ♗c7 winning. But Tal is not to be distracted in any case.

18 ♗c6+ ♗d7 19 ♗xd7+ ♚xd7 20 ♕b7+ ♚d8 21 ♕xa8+ ♕c8 22 ♕a7 1-0

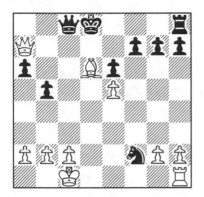

White picks up the knight as well.

I am not a poker player. Many other chessplayers have taken up the challenge of poker, after appreciating that good calculating abilities and, more specifically, the ability to find moves under pressure are useful attributes.

The following game, between two former World Champions, is as much poker as purely chess psychology, and remarkably so. A simplistic view is that you have perfect knowledge in chess. One of the central points I am making in this book is that no player has perfect knowledge over the board, since no-one would be physically able to calculate enough moves to give a clear resolution of what is going on in a complicated position. A player will of course see where the pieces are, and

will work out what he is aiming for, and what his opponent is trying to do. The uncertainty arises about what is going to happen several moves later.

In the Spassky-Tal game, Tal sees a sacrifice, and offers the sacrifice. There are, continuing the poker analogy, a couple of cards on each side that have yet to be revealed, and neither player will know in advance what they are.

What options does the defender have? He can go for broke, accepting the sacrifice, with chances perhaps of a win, but also chances of a quick loss. Or he can duck the critical decision, playing for a slight but manageable disadvantage. Spassky, it turns out, was wrong on both counts in this game. Tal's sacrifice is not winning, and with best play on both sides, it would seem to be losing. The only reason why Tal won was that Spassky's aiming for a quieter struggle left him in a bad position.

What do you think about Tal's handling of this game? Personally, I would be more inclined than most to gambit and gamble, but I doubt whether I would have played Tal's sacrifice.

There are two thoughts that need to be considered though. First, even a World Champion like Spassky can get it spectacularly wrong under the stress of attack, so much lesser players, like your opponent across the board, can easily get it wrong too. Second, if you can somehow develop a reputation as a strong and dangerous attacker, your opponent may well become frightened, and in poker terms, can sometimes bluff himself out of making the best moves.

The game itself was brief and impressive, an aggressive piece of attacking play in which Spassky's position soon crumbled. The one segment which requires detailed analysis is Tal's attempted piece sacrifice, and Spassky's declining of it. To make it easier to read, we give the main part relatively briefly, to give the flavour of the game, and then, as a supplementary, we look in detail of White's 17th move options.

Game 14
B.Spassky-M.Tal
Montreal 1979
Queen's Indian Defence

---

1 d4 ♘f6 2 c4 e6 3 ♘f3 b6 4 e3

The Queen's Indian Defence is difficult to break down. The general reputation is that 4 g3 is equal and drawish, while 4 e3 is equal but occasionally, as we shall see, lively for both sides.

Was Spassky playing for a steady game? Decidedly not. Tal notes that he sensed his opponent was in a "very aggressive" mood, presumably wanting a quick revenge for his first round loss.

In such circumstances as White against an aggressive opponent, often the most appropriate strategy is to play quietly and solidly, waiting for him to overpress. As Black, it is rather more difficult. It is still possible to play quietly, but the upshot can be a long grind

for equality, where the opponent applies long-term pressure without risk of losing.

Tal takes a different approach. At first he just develops his pieces, but then, given the slightest opportunity, starts a wild sacrificial attack. This is unwelcome for Spassky, as he would prefer to sacrifice himself. He wants to attack rather than defend, and he is not given the chance.

4...♗b7 5 ♗d3 d5 6 b3 ♗d6 7 0-0 0-0 8 ♗b2 ♘bd7 9 ♘bd2

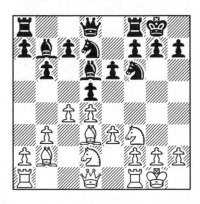

9...♕e7

Many of the games from this type of opening have ended up with White playing ♘e5 at some stage, and/or Black playing ...♘e4. As a refresher on opening tactics, we provide at the end the supplementary game, Dizdarevic-Miles, Biel 1985, a quick win for Tony Miles.

10 ♖c1 ♖ad8 11 ♕c2 c5

It's nearly symmetrical, but don't be fooled, this is unlikely to be heading for quiet equality. White now has the option of c4xd5, and Black recapturing in one of three ways; or d4xc5, also with three possible recaptures; or quietly developing, in which case Black has the option of two captures, and White recapturing in three ways, and so on. In such a situation it's almost a relief to release the tension, as Spassky elects to do here.

12 cxd5 exd5

Although in fact there is only one good way of recapturing.

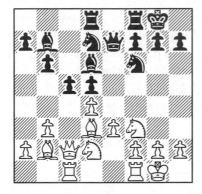

13 dxc5

Kasparov suggests that allowing the hanging pawns might have been a psychological mistake, giving Tal the chance of sharp dynamic play. Yes and no. A World Champion has fewer excuses than the rest of us in making psychological mistakes, as he is expected to find good moves whatever. If a few moves later, Tal had sacrificed a bishop without compensation, and Spassky had won, then Spassky would have been congratulated on his brilliant intuition, provoking the unsound sacrifice.

Having said that, provocation and counter-provocation is part of the chess balance. 13 ♘h4!? looks promising, and

if Black defends with 13...g6, White can quietly retreat the knight again, content with softening up the long diagonal.

However, players from Grandmaster – maybe even World Champion – to learner should consider what happens after the classic bishop sacrifice 13...♗xh2+ 14 ♔xh2 ♘g4+ 15 ♔g3. Is this good or bad? I do not know, and it would take a lot of analysis to decide. My instinct is that the sacrifice does not work here, and therefore that 13 ♘h4 is acceptable and good. But there is still some anxiety for White. Would you as a player happily allow this sacrifice over the board? Or would you avoid it on principle?

We begin so see what problems Spassky is being faced with. But there is no need for us to sympathize with him. After all, he still has the chance of a win against Tal!

13...bxc5

The position is equal. Neither player can force an edge, and if either player tries to force matters, it could collapse against him. It follows that potentially the most effective way of trying for a win can be by provoking the opponent.

14 ♕c3!?

Spassky duly provokes him, which psychologically is not such a bad idea. Indeed, one could say it's an extremely good idea. After all, in about three moves time, Spassky's position is objectively better, in the sense that if both sides play the subsequent few moves completely accurately, Spassky would be clearly ahead.

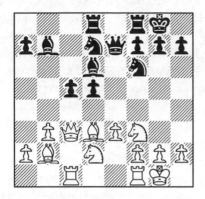

But sometimes a raging tiger in search of a good meal makes it difficult for the potential prey to be quietly objective.

If White wants to avoid facing a Tal special sacrifice, 14 ♘h4!? is still worth considering, again with the idea 14...g6 15 ♘hf3, having weakened the long diagonal. But here 14...♗e5!? 15 ♘f5 ♕e6 16 ♘f3 ♗xb2 17 ♕xb2 is about equal. In this context, the pawn exchange on c5 was mistimed.

14...♖fe8

Tal now thought for 20 minutes, already, as he noted, considering his forthcoming pawn sacrifice. On his next move, he thought for another half-hour before taking the plunge. The tournament book, *Le Tournoi International d'Échecs, Montreal 1979*, gives useful information on the clock times.

15 ♖fd1

"It would seem that Boris was betrayed by his sense of danger," wrote Tal. This is a psychological insight, not a purely analytical chess insight. What is significant here is that Spassky was about to be shocked. Obviously he would have known all about bishop sacrifices in front of the king from infant school age, but it seems he hadn't realized that one might arise in this position. If Spassky had anticipated the sacrifice well in advance, he would have had the chance of trying to refute it. Instead, in shock, he played weaker chess.

Tal notes that he had expected 15 ♖fe1, when 15...c4 was a possibility, since accepting the pawn sacrifice leaves White worse after 16 bxc4 ♗b4 17 ♕xc2 dxc4 18 ♗xc4 ♗xf3! 19 ♘xf3 (not 19 gxf3? ♗xd2 20 ♕xd2 ♘e5 21 ♕e2 ♖d2!) 19...♗xe1 20 ♖xe1 ♖c8. Kasparov suggests instead 16 ♗f5!, with sharp play, but without an obvious advantage for either side.

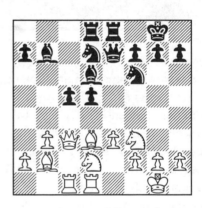

15...d4?!

A critical decision. Many would call this controversial, unsound, a purely speculative sacrifice, but the fact remains that Tal beat Spassky in 22 moves, and Spassky was World Champion for six years, and hugely experienced and competent at attack and defence. He was also an excellent chess psychologist, who could attack very hard himself, as well as defend resourcefully when under pressure. But somehow on that day he choked.

For Tal to have won this game so comprehensively, he must have done something special. That he beat Spassky in the first round might also have created that little bit of doubt in Spassky's mind. If you are worried about losing quickly, in a sacrificial attack maybe, you can tend to duck the critical line, only, as here, to fall into the same disaster you were hoping to avoid.

Tal's idea is to open up the diagonals, using the queen and bishops, assisted by the knights, for a direct attack on the white king. To do this, he jettisoned his central pawns, giving up two for one, with the intention that, if Spassky were to accept the pawn sacrifice, then Tal would immediately follow up with a bishop sacrifice to force the white king out into the open.

There were of course quieter ways to play, and *Fritz* gives a dozen or so anodyne moves, maintaining complete equality. Moves such as 15...♖a8, 15...♘b8, 15...h6, 15...a6, 15...♘f8, 15...♔h8, etc. It is hard to imagine Tal wanting to play any of these. He took the plunge, and went for the attack.

16 exd4 cxd4

Black might consider 16...♘d5 17 ♕c2 ♘b4, but only briefly, as 18 ♗xh7+ ♔h8 19 ♕f5 would see White's bishops powering up on the diagonals. The problem is not so much the loss of pawns, but the exposure of the king.

Quite simply, Black cannot attack if he is forced to defend his own king all the time.

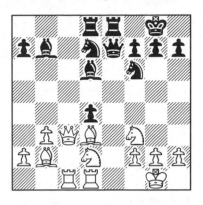

17 ♕a5?

Dare one suggest that, after his best years of chess, Spassky was starting to get lazy in calculations, and tending to avoid complicated variations? In fact, this was Kasparov's opinion. He may very well think that; I couldn't possibly comment.

All the same, this is an incredibly difficult position for White to handle. Snatching the pawn is dangerous, and it does not take long for the defender to appreciate that there is a way in which Black can sacrifice a piece to bring the king out far into the open. We are just about reaching the edge of what players are able to calculate confidently over the board, remembering that we are considering not just a one-track line reaching ten moves ahead, but rather a whole thicket of forest paths, some of which might be dangerous, while some turn out to be harmless. It all adds uncertainty to the game, and usually it is the defender who is under more pressure. The attacker has made his decision, good or bad, and all he has to do is find a few natural attacking moves. The defender is uncertain whether the attack is sound, and even if the attack is unsound, it remains extremely difficult to work out how best to defend against it. One small error, we all know, can mean a humiliating loss in a few moves time.

Even an experienced World Champion sometimes makes serious mistakes under pressure. Spassky was able to beat Kasparov twice, in wild tactics, when Kasparov was a young and fast-improving grandmaster. Here Spassky went astray. White must take the pawn, right or wrong, "good or bad", as Tal put it.

Before plunging into the main complications of the knight capture, we should consider the alternative, 17 ♕xd4.

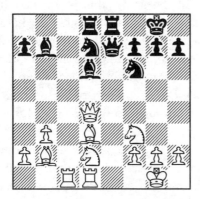

Tal's notes in *Informator 27* give simply 17...♘e5 with a clear advantage to Black, but this is presumably a misprint, since White could just take everything on e5, when he is a pawn up

for nothing. Kasparov corrects it to (17 ♕xd4?) 17...♘c5, without further comment. It is worth going on a bit, as after 18 ♔h1! ♘xd3 19 ♕xd3, the obvious discovered attacks fail to achieve anything for Black.

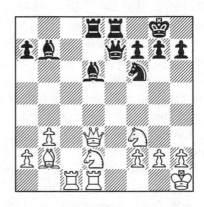

a) 19...♗xh2 20 ♕f5 ♗b8 21 ♗xf6 ♕xf6 22 ♕xf6 gxf6 23 ♘c4 ♗f4 24 ♖xd8 ♖xd8 25 ♖e1, and Black has no real advantage resulting from the bishop pair. White's knights are active, and Black has a slightly damaged pawn structure. Equal.

b) 19...♗e5 20 ♕c2 ♗xb2 21 ♕xb2 ♕e2 22 ♖e1 ♕xf2 23 ♖xe8+ ♖xe8 24 ♕d4 ♕xd4 21 ♘xd4 might be very slightly better for Black, but one would expect this to end up as equal too. Black will have to be careful not to drop the a-pawn.

c) 19...♗f4!, followed by 20...♗xf3, is the right way forward for Black, the two bishops putting pressure on the white knights. For example, 20 ♕f1 ♗xf3 21 ♘xf3 ♗xc1, winning the exchange. If White tries 20 ♕c2 ♗xf3 21 gxf3?! then 21...♕e2! wins more material, or if 20 ♗d4 ♗xf3 (20...♘e4! is also good) 21 gxf3? ♕d7! 22 ♖c4 ♕h3 23 ♘f1 ♖e5, and ...♖h5 is decisive.

So that leaves 17 ♘xd4!, inviting Tal to sacrifice a piece with 17...♗xh2+ 18 ♔xh2 ♘g4+. We shall look at this more closely at the end of the game. Almost everyone who has written up this encounter has very much wanted to prove Tal's proposed sacrifice as winning, or at least equal, but no-one has convincingly found the way, and in the end the reluctant verdict must be that it does not quite work.

17...♘e5

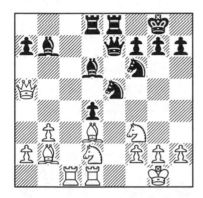

18 ♘xe5

18 ♖e1 does not help, as Black strengthens his attack with 18...♘fg4!, threatening 19...♗xf3 20 ♘xf3 ♘xf3+ 21 gxf3 ♕h4 and wins. Then 19 ♘xe5 ♗xe5 20 g3 (or 20 ♘f1 ♕h4 21 g3 ♘xf2! 22 gxh4 ♘h3 mate) 20...♕f6 21 ♖e2 ♗xg3! is crushing. If White tries 19 h3, Black switches to the queenside with 19...♗b4!, winning material.

18...♗xe5

Black is attacking, using the bishop pair as potential sacrificial forces, and White does not even have an extra pawn to offer any sort of counter-chances.

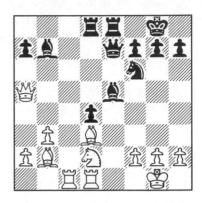

19 ♘c4?

A continuation of Spassky's ♕a5 plan, but it indicates that his sense of danger had really gone awry. Here Tal is lining up for a kingside attack and Spassky responds by moving his pieces over to the queenside. Not the recipe for a successful defence. Having said that, White is in serious trouble here, and may already be losing.

a) 19 ♘f1 ♘d5 20 ♘g3 ♘f4 21 ♗f1 at least bring some pieces into the combat zone, but then Tal intended 21...h5 with an apparently speedy kingside attack. If 22 ♖e1 h4 23 ♘f5 ♕f6! (23...♕g5 24 ♖xe5 ♘h3+ only draws, by perpetual) 24 ♘h4 ♘h3+ 25 gxh3 ♕g5+ 26 ♗g2 ♗xh2+ 27 ♔xh2 ♕xa5 28 ♖xe8+ ♖xe8 29 ♗xb7 ♕d2 and Black wins. Alternatively, 23 ♖c5 f6 24 ♘f5 ♕d7 25 ♘xh4 ♕g4 26 g3 is well met by 26...d3! 27 ♗c1 (or 27 ♗xe5 d2) 27...♘e2+ 28 ♗xe2 dxe2, winning on the light squares, 29...♗xg3! 30 hxg3 ♕h3 being just one immediate threat.

b) 19 ♖e1, with an attempted pin,

fails to 19...♘g4, as we've seen in the note with 18 ♖e1 above.

There are so many threats on h2, and so many incursions on g4, that h2-h3 comes into serious consideration, but Black has other ways to storm the fortress:

c) 19 h3 ♘h5! (intending ...♘f4) 20 g3 ♗xg3! 21 ♕xh5 ♗xf2+! 22 ♔f1 g6 23 ♕e2 (or 23 ♕g4 h5) 23...♗e3 is decisive.

d) 19 ♗a3 ♕e6 and now:

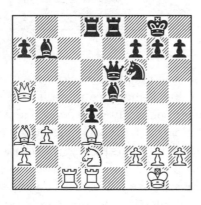

d1) 20 h3 is no better due to 20...♗xg2! 21 ♔xg2 ♘h5, again followed by ...♘f4+ with devastation. If then 22 ♗f1 ♘f4+ 23 ♔g1 ♘xh3+ 24 ♗xh3 ♕xh3 25 ♘f1 ♕g4+ 26 ♔h1 ♕f3+ 27 ♔g1 ♖d5 wins.

d2) 20 ♘f1 is suggested by Kasparov, in *My Great Predecessors*, as the only chance, and if 20...♗f4 21 ♖b1 ♕c6 22 f3 or 20...♘d5 21 ♕xa7 ♖d7 22 ♗b5 ♘c3 23 ♖xc3 ♕d5 24 f3 ♕xb5 25 ♖c5, when White is worse, but not as yet completely lost.

However, 20...♘h5 still looks strong. For example, 21 ♘g3 ♘f4 22 ♗f1 (or 22 ♗f5 ♕f6) 22...♘h3+! 23 gxh3 ♗xg3 24 hxg3 ♕e4 mates. Or if first 21

♕b5 ♖b8 22 ♕c4 ♕h6 23 ♘g3 ♘f4 24 ♗f1, then 24...d3!, with the threat of 25...♗xg2! 26 ♗xg2 ♘e2+ 27 ♔h1 ♗xg3 28 fxg3 ♘xg3+ 29 ♔g1 ♕e3 mate.

All very difficult for White, but he should not have to resign just three moves later.

19...♖d5! 20 ♕d2

A sorry retreat. The presumption is that Spassky planned 20 ♗a3, but had overlooked a tactic, and then chose something weaker.

Certainly 20 ♗a3 ♖xa5 21 ♗xe7 ♗xh2+ 22 ♔xh2 ♖h5+ 23 ♔g1 ♖xe7 24 ♘d6 would be a considerable improvement for White, who should equalize with his active pieces, despite being a pawn down at this moment.

Unfortunately there is a familiar retort in 20...♗xh2+! 21 ♔xh2 ♘g4+ 22 ♔g3 ♕f6 23 ♕d2, and now a second demolition job with 23...♘xf2!, winning.

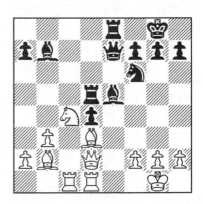

20...♗xh2+!

White has lost a couple of tempi with his ♕d2-a5-d2 manoeuvre. As a result, the bishop sacrifice is no longer "unclear", but quickly decisive.

21 ♔xh2 ♖h5+!

21...♘g4+ 22 ♔g3 ♘xf2! Also works here too, as 23 ♕xf2 is defeated by 23...♕c7+!.

22 ♔g1

Or 22 ♔g3 ♘e4+! 23 ♗xe4 ♕h4+ 24 ♔f3 ♕xe4+ 26 ♔g3 ♕h4 mate.

22...♘g4 0-1

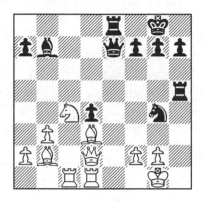

Mate is inevitable after 23 ♕f4 ♕h4 or 23 ♖e1 ♖h1+! 23 ♔xh1 ♕h4+.

And this is time to examine the more interesting and critical variation, which Spassky flunked. We go back to move 17, where Spassky played 17 ♕a5?. He should have tried:

17 ♘xd4!

Now the game becomes very complicated. We'll begin with the accepted main line, as given in the tournament book, and other authorities, and not least, Tal's own comments. If this proves unsatisfactory, we can consider other moves later.

17...♗xh2+ 18 ♔xh2 ♘g4+ 19 ♔g3 ♕e5+ 20 f4 ♕e3+

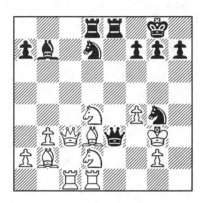

Tal's main idea. The queen and knights work closely together.

21 ♘2f3

I give this as the main line, my instincts suggesting it should be the best way to defend the position, allowing the queen or one of the rooks to cover the second rank.

In *Informator*, Tal proposed simply 21 ♘4f3 ♘df6 "unclear", but elsewhere noted 22 ♗xh7+! ♔xh7 23 ♕xe3 and White escapes with advantage. Instead, Kasparov suggests 21...♕f2+ 22 ♔h3 ♘df6 23 ♖f1 ♖xd3 24 ♕xd3 ♘h5 25 ♖xf2 ♘xf2+ 26 ♔h4 ♘xd3 27 ♔xh5 ♘xc1 28 ♗xc1 ♖e2, which seems probably drawn.

Kasparov does not mention 21 ♘2f3, but this is no real defect, as he considered 19 ♔g1 in greater depth, regarding it as a win for White. We will look at this later on.

Not, of course, 21 ♔xg4?? ♘f6+ 22 ♔h4 ♕xf4+ and soon checkmate.

21...♕f2+!

21...♗xf3 22 ♘xf3 ♘df6 23 ♗xh7+! again favours White.

22 ♔h3

There is a draw after 22 ♔xg4? ♗xf3+ 23 ♘xf3 ♕xg2+ 24 ♔h4 ♕f2+ 25 ♔h3 ♕xf3+ 26 ♔h2 ♕f2+.

22...♘df6

Not 22...♘e3? 23 ♖d2, and Black's queen gets trapped.

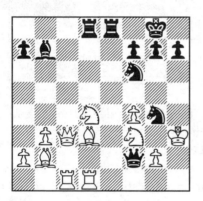

23 ♖c2!

Following Gallagher's recommendation. The alternative ways of challenging on the second rank are less effective:

a) 23 ♕d2 ♗xf3 24 gxf3 (not 24 ♘xf3? ♖xd3! 25 ♕xd3 ♘h5 and wins) 24...♖xd4 (24...♖e3!? is also possible) 25 ♕xf2 ♘xf2+ 26 ♔g3 ♖xd3 27 ♔xf2 ♖xd1 28 ♖xd1 ♘h5 is equal.

b) 23 ♕c2 ♗xf3 24 ♘xf3 ♖xd3! 25 ♖xd3 ♘h5 26 ♕xf2 ♘xf2+ 27 ♔h4 ♘xd3 28 ♔xh5 ♘xc1 29 ♗xc1 ♖e2 30 ♗d2

♖xg2 is similar to the 21 ♘4f3 line above, though White is a little better here.

c) 23 ♖d2 keeps the white rooks away from any ...♘e3 forks, but it allows Black other resources following 23...♕e3!. The critical line then runs 24 ♘f5 (not 24 ♗b5? ♕xf4, since if White continues with 25 ♗xe8?, he gets checkmated after 25...♘e4) 24...♕xf4 (and not 24...♘f2+!? 25 ♖xf2 ♕xf2, as 26 ♘h6+! gxh6 27 ♕xf6 wins for White) 25 ♕c7!, seemingly forcing the queens off, when 25...♕xc7 26 ♖xc7 ♗xf3 27 ♗xf6 gxf6 28 ♖c3! sees White finally emerging a piece up.

However, Black can in fact sacrifice the queen, playing 25...♕xd2!, and then continue the attack with the rooks and knights. After 26 ♘xd2 ♖xd3+ 27 ♘f3 ♗xf3 28 gxf3 ♖xf3+ 29 ♘g3 ♘e4 30 ♔xg4 ♖xg3+ 31 ♔f4 (or similarly, 31 ♕xg3 h5+ 32 ♔f4 ♘xg3 33 ♔xg3 ♖e2) 31...g5+ 32 ♔f5 ♖f3+ 33 ♔g4 ♖g3+, White has to return the queen with 34 ♕xg3 f5+ 35 ♔f3 ♘xg3 36 ♔xg3, when 36...♖e2 37 ♗f6 h6 offers Black reasonable drawing chances with the active rook and connected passed pawns.

23...♘d5!?

Trying to exploit the weak dark squares. 23...♕e3 is no good now after 24 ♕d2!, when the best Black can hope for is to pick up the exchange after a subsequent ♕xe3 ♘xe3, leaving him two minor pieces for a rook in arrears, and his attack at an end.

24 ♕a5!

Obviously not 24 ♖xf2?? ♘xf2+ 25 ♔g3 ♘xc3 and the knights triumph.

Instead, the queen returns to its out of the way position, daring Black to do his worst, which it turns out is not very much.

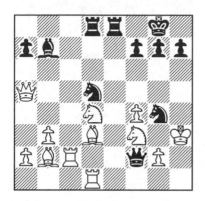

24...♘xf4+

Now 24...♕e3 25 ♗c1! ♘f2+ 26 ♖xf2 ♕xf2 27 ♖f1 traps the black queen. Or if 24...♖d6, then simply 25 ♖xf2 ♘xf2+ 26 ♔g3 ♘xd1 27 ♗a3 leaves with White a decisive material advantage.

25 ♔xg4 ♘xd3 26 ♖xf2 ♘xf2+ 27 ♔g3 ♘xd1 28 ♘f5! ♘xb2 29 ♕c3 f6 30 ♕c7

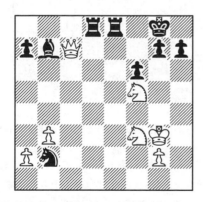

And mate follows shortly.

Let us now consider the alternative check:

19...♕d6+!? 20 f4

20...♖e3+

The most direct, forcing White to make a clear decision. But White is probably winning, either way.

The alternative is the extremely wild 20...g5!?. The annotators (Nunn, Gallagher, and others) have enjoyed this, but the general consensus is that 21 ♘e6! (both players can't be check-mated at once!) 21...♘df6 22 ♗xh7+! ♔xh7 23 ♘xg5+ ♔g6 24 ♕c2+ ♕d3+ 25 ♕xd3+ ♖xd3 26 ♘df3 ♖xd1 27 ♘h4+ ♔h5 28 ♖xd1 ♖e3+ 29 ♘hf3 is good for White, who emerges a clear two pawns up.

21 ♘2f3!

It's not immediately obvious which of the two knight interpositions is better, and such uncertainty generally favours the attacker.

After 21 ♘4f3 ♘df6! sets a dangerous trap. 22 ♘c4? allows Black a mating attack with 22...♘h5+ 23 ♔h4 ♕xf4.

Instead, White can exploit a well-hidden back row mating idea, with 22 ♕c7 ♖xd3 23 ♗xf6! (still not 23 ♕xb7? ♘h5+, winning) 23...♗xf3 24 ♘xf3 ♘xf6

25 ♕xd8+! ♕xd8 26 ♖xd3 and, in this position, the two rooks outbalance the queen.

Black can try 23...♘xf6 24 ♕xb7 ♘d5, when 25 ♔f2 ♘c3 (if 25...♘e3 26 ♖e1 ♖xd2+ 27 ♘xd2 ♕xd2+ 28 ♔g1 ♕d4 29 ♔h1 and White keeps the exchange) 26 ♖xc3 ♖xc3 27 ♕xa7 ♖d3 28 ♔g1 h6 (or 28...♕xf4 29 ♖f1) 29 ♕f2 ♕xf4 30 ♖f1 ♖xd2 31 ♘xd2 ♕xd2 32 ♕xd2 ♖xd2 reaches an endgame with equal material.

That is the good news for Black. The bad news is that White has two connected passed pawns, on the far side from the opposing king. The likelihood is that White will win.

It is amazing how many tactical and sacrificial battles end up with a level number of pieces and pawns in an endgame, but such lines are not necessarily equal.

That's incidental here though, because the other knight move is much stronger:

21 ♘2f3! ♘df6 22 ♕c7!

With the same idea, but in an even more decisive setting.

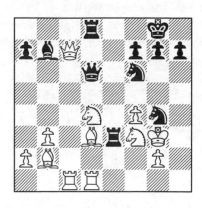

22...♖xd3

22...♗xf3 23 gxf3 also wins for White, as if 23...♘h5+, then simply 24 ♔xg4 and Black has no useful checks.

23 ♕xd6 ♖xd6 24 ♖xd3 ♘e4+ 25 ♔xg4 ♘f2+ 25 ♔xg4 ♘f2+ 26 ♔g3 ♘xd3 27 ♖c7

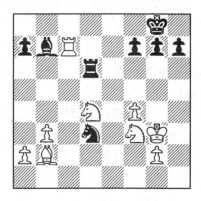

And White has kept his extra piece.

Normally, having decided that White can win with best play, we do not need to calculate other lines, unless perhaps in analysis at home. However, Kasparov proposes another variation as superior, and must be treated with respect.

19 ♔g1!?

Kasparov gives this an exclamation mark, and at the very least it has practical merit. White would much prefer his king to be stowed safely on the back rank if possible, than stuck in the open, as after 19 ♔g3. The potential drawback is that it allows Black to play:

19...♛h4!

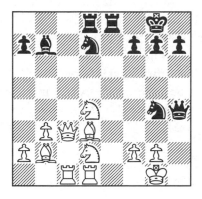

20 ♗xh7+!

The best move in the circumstances. White immediately returns the piece in order to switch his queen over to defence, and try to consolidate his extra pawn.

Gallagher follows Tal with 20 ♘4f3 ♛xf2+ 21 ♔h1, notes that Tal's 21...♖e5 22 ♗f5 ♘e3 is good for White after 23 ♗h3!, and gives an improvement in 21...♘de5!, which seems to win for Black. If now 22 ♗f5 ♘e3!, and the knights are on much stronger squares. Or 22 ♖f1 ♛b6! 23 ♗f5 ♛h6+ 24 ♔g1 ♗xf3 25 ♗xg4 ♗xg2! and Black's attack crashes through.

Instead, Kasparov suggests 20 ♘2f3 (with another exclamation mark)

20...♛xf2+ 21 ♔h1 and then if 21...♖e5?! 22 ♗f5! ♖c5 23 ♗xg4 ♖xc3 24 ♗xc3 with a lot of material for the queen. Or 21...♘df6 22 ♖f1 ♛g3 23 ♘f5 ♛b8 (if 23...♘f2+? 24 ♖xf2 ♛xf2 25 ♘h6+ wins, or 23...♛f4 24 ♛c7!) 24 ♛c2 ♗xf3 25 gxf3 ♖xd3 26 ♗xf6! gxf6 27 fxg4 ♖h3+ 28 ♔g1, "and White parries the attack, retaining a material advantage."

Oddly though, Kasparov doesn't consider what happens if Black plays in the same way as against 20 ♘4f3, with 21...♘de5!.

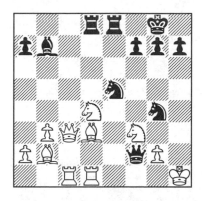

Now 22 ♖d2 ♛g3 threatens 23...♖xd4! 24 ♛xd4 ♗xf3 25 gxf3 ♛h3+ 26 ♔g1 ♘xf3 mate, and here 23 ♘f5 ♛f4 24 ♛c7? is no use, as the queen is blocked by the knight on e5, and Black wins after 24...♗xf3 25 gxf3 ♛xd2. White has to resort to 24 ♖e1, when 24...g6! 25 ♗c4 ♖xd2 26 ♛xd2 ♛xf5 regains the piece with advantage.

In fact, after 21...♘de5! White must play carefully to draw: 22 ♖d2 ♛g3 23 ♖f1! ♗xf3 24 ♘xf3 (not 24 gxf3? ♖d6 and wins) 24...♛f4 and now 25 g3! ♛h6+ 26 ♘h4 g5 27 ♖e2 gxh4 28 ♗f5 hxg3+ 29 ♔g1 ♘f3+! 30 ♛xf3 ♛b6+ 31

♔h1 (not 31 ♔g2?! ♖xe2+ 32 ♕xe2 ♘e3+ 33 ♔xg3 ♖d2!) 31...♕h6+ 32 ♔g1 ♕b6+ with perpetual check.

20...♔xh7

20...♕xh7 21 ♕h3 ♕xh3 22 gxh3 ♘ge5 is similar, but White can also play 21 ♕g3!, when there is no clear plan for Black. If instead 20...♔h8 21 ♕h3 ♕xf2+ 22 ♔h1 ♗xg2+ (the only move) 23 ♕xg2 ♕xg2+ 24 ♔xg2 ♘e3+ 25 ♔g3 ♘xd1 26 ♖xd1 ♔xh7 27 ♘c6 ♖c8 28 ♘xa7 ♖c2 29 ♘c4, and White has a clear advantage.

21 ♕h3

Now 21 ♕g3 ♕xg3 22 fxg3 ♗d5 should be fine for Black.

21...♕xh3 22 gxh3 ♘ge5 23 ♖e1

Or 23 ♖c7 ♘c5! 24 ♖xc5 ♘d3 25 ♗a3 ♖xd4 26 ♖c7 ♗d5 and if 27 ♖xa7 ♘e1 or 27 ♘c4 ♗f3 28 ♖f1 ♖h4.

23...♖c8

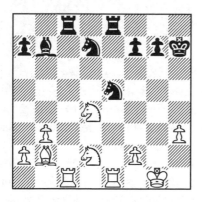

White is certainly better here, with an extra pawn and the initiative. Nevertheless, his structure is compromised, and there is the possible drawing influence of opposite-coloured bishops, or if White relinquishes his own bishop for a knight, he will leave his opponent

with the superior minor piece. White has definite winning chances, but this is far less ambitious than the 19 ♔g3 line.

Black has so many interesting resources following the bishop sacrifice, that many players, myself included, have worked hard to demonstrate that Tal could indeed have won, or at least drawn, after 17...♗xh2+. It just doesn't quite seem to be there. Black comes very close, but ultimately "close" isn't good enough.

It is important to note that Tal did have an emergency exit in mind if required, because it does appear to be required.

But first, another attempt: **17...♗e5!?**

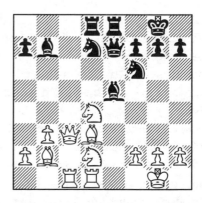

The attacking idea is that after the obvious reply **18 ♘c4**, and then **18...♗xh2+!? 19 ♔xh2 ♘g4+ 20 ♔g3 ♘df6**, White can no longer use his queen on the open c-file (as for example in the 19...♕d6+!? line above).

Can White's active and centralized

knight really be merely an obstruction? It looks unlikely, and **21 ♗a3!** puts White in control.

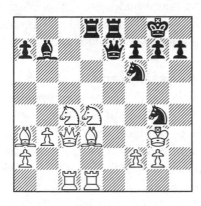

If 21...♕c7+ 21 ♘d6 wins, or 21...♘h5+ 22 ♔xg4 and there is no satisfactory follow-up to the second knight sacrifice.

Black can create a few problems with 21...♕d7!?, but the simplest way for White would seem to be to surround his king with pieces, such as by 22 ♘f5!? ♗e4 23 ♘cd6 ♗xd3 24 ♕xd3 ♘e4+ 25 ♕xe4 ♖xe4 26 ♘xe4 ♕xd1 27 ♖xd1 ♖xd1 28 ♔xg4, with three minor pieces for the rook. Of course "simplest" is a relative term. Most average players would find it difficult to calculate this with accuracy over the board.

Nevertheless, if Tal were to decide to aim for safety, he would need to abandon the tempting bishop sacrifice. Instead, he might try **18...♗xd4!?** 19 ♕xd4 ♘c5, and if 20 ♘d6?! ♖xd6 21 ♗xh7+ ♔xh7 22 ♕xd6 ♕xd6 23 ♖xd6 ♘d5! secures his position, as the c5-knight is immune from capture. White does better with 20 ♕c3!, and remains a clear pawn up, even if Black might

hope to resist for a long time after 20...♘xd3 21 ♖xd3 ♖xd3 22 ♕xd3 ♘d5.

Another possibility is **17...♕e5 18 ♘4f3 ♕h5**

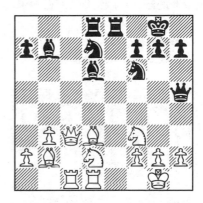

This was the line Tal was keeping in reserve, in case he had cold feet about the bishop sacrifice. Black's pieces are slightly more active, but White has the extra pawn, and if he can gradually neutralize his opponent's counterplay, White will therefore hold the edge.

19 ♖e1

The most direct way of activating his pieces.

a) 19 ♘e4? loses material after 19...♗xe4 20 ♗xe4 ♗f4, and 19...♘e5! may be even stronger.

b) 19 ♕c4 gives White less chance of an edge, as 19...♘g4! 20 h3 ♘ge5 21 ♘xe5 ♘xe5 22 ♗xe5 ♗xe5 sees Black very active, with two strong bishops.

c) 19 ♗e4!? is a better option, as 19...♘xe4?? allows 20 ♕xg7 mate, while 19...♗xe4 20 ♘xe4 ♗xh2+ 21 ♘xh2 ♖xe4 22 ♕f3 ♕xf3 23 ♘xf3 ♖de8 24 ♖c7 takes the initiative in the endgame.

19...♕h6

Otherwise his knight cannot move.

Black can also try 19...♘c5, but 20 ♖xe8+ ♖xe8 21 h3 takes care of White's defences. For example, 21...♘xd3 22 ♕xd3 ♘d5 23 ♕d4, or 21...♘e6 22 ♖e1 ♘f4 23 ♖xe8+ ♘xe8 24 ♗f1, still with the extra pawn.

20 ♖xe8+ ♖xe8 21 ♗b5 ♗f4 22 ♖d1 a6 23 ♗xd7 ♘xd7 24 ♕b4 ♗c6

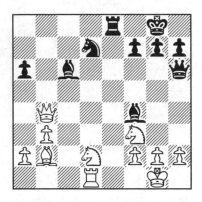

We have slightly rushed through the last few moves, for illustrative purposes. In a non-forcing position, it is to be expected that there will be alternatives at various times, but the last few moves seem reasonable. White is a pawn up, but Black has the more active pieces, and it is difficult to see how White can make complete consolidation, rather than just partial consolidation. The best guess is that it will end as a draw. How, after all, is White going to force a significant advance of his extra pawn?

This may be about as good as it gets for Black. We do not know what would have happened if Spassky had accepted the challenge with 17 ♘xd4!, nor how Tal would have responded.

Twenty minutes of intense thought, but what would Tal have played? Would he have sacrificed the bishop? Or decided that it had been a great bluff, but it was now time for less committal methods? We do not know.

Supplementary game

This is from the same opening as Spassky-Tal, and features another bishop sacrifice on h2, but a more straightforward one. Every strong player will over the years have learned many, many sacrifices of this type.

Tony Miles was for a while the most successful player in Britain, and indeed beat Spassky twice from the White side of the Queen's Indian, the year before Montreal. He also famously won against Karpov, having begun the game with 1 e4 a6!?. As well as his playing exploits, Miles was a good and entertaining writer.

Game 14.1
E.Dizdarevic-A.Miles
Biel 1985
Queen's Indian Defence

---

1 c4 b6 2 d4 e6 3 ♘f3 ♘f6 4 e3 ♗b7 5 ♗d3 d5 6 b3 ♗d6 7 0-0 0-0 8 ♗b2 ♘bd7 9 ♘bd2 ♘e4

Tal tried 9...♕e7 here.

10 ♕c2

Perhaps 10 ♘e5.

10...f5 11 ♖ad1?

Or maybe 11 ♘e5 now. Instead, White falls for a snap mating attack, nothing particularly original, just good technique. Dizdarevic is a strong player, he just makes a big slip-up.

11...♘xd2 12 ♘xd2 dxc4 13 ♘xc4?

Dizdarevic sees the double bishop sacrifice, and aims to play f2-f3 or f2-f4 at the appropriate moment, to bring the queen into the defence.

The only move was 13 ♗xc4, and after 13...♗xh2+ 14 ♔xh2 ♛h4+ 15 ♔g1 ♗xg2! 16 ♗xe6+ ♔h8 17 f3 ♗h3, then 18 ♘e4!, although 18...♗xf1 19 ♗xd7 (not 19 ♖xf1? fxe4 20 ♗xd7 ♖f6) 19...♗a6 20 ♔g2 (not 20 ♘f2? ♛g3+ 21 ♔h1 ♖f6) 20...fxe4 21 ♕xe4 ♛g5+ 22 ♔f2 ♖ad8 leaves White the exchange down and probably losing.

The knight recapture is much worse.

13...♗xh2+ 14 ♔xh2 ♛h4+ 15 ♔g1 ♗f3!!

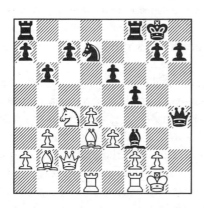

This makes it memorable. Here 15...♗xg2? would allow White to defend with 16 f3 or 16 f4. Instead, Miles wins quickly, as White is prevented from switching his queen to the kingside.

16 ♘d2

16 ♗e2 ♗xg2 17 f3 ♛g3 also wins

for Black, as the white queen is blocked by the bishop on e2.

16...♗xg2! 17 f3 ♖f6

Very simple, as now the knight on d2 is in the way of the queen. Not, however, 17...♛g3? 18 ♘e4!, and White survives.

18 ♘c4 ♗h3 0-1

Many years ago, back in the late 1980s, I became fascinated by the next game, and by its depth and complexity. I tried hard to analyse it, and could work out what was happening, move by move, during various phases, but I was completely baffled by what was going through Tal's mind. The preparation of his piece sacrifice, and then the sacrifice itself, felt so far beyond my understanding that I was awe-struck.

I was writing the game up for inclusion in a book of miniatures (30 moves or less), selected from the "ten best" list in each volume of *Informator*, and with a serious attempt to analyse each game. (Possibly it is time for the book to be reprinted?) None of the others was anything like as complicated as the Tal-Velimirovic encounter. Some were attractive but straightforward, one player making a plausible but incorrect move in the opening. But Tal enjoyed sharp games, and had an incredible ability to make things complicated.

It is easy enough for a reader to go through a game in which a player gambits a pawn or even a piece, gets an attack moving, then makes a second sacrifice, then checkmates. It is much more difficult to grasp what is happening when a player gives up a piece, and then there is close to twenty moves of unclear play, maybe with a few sensible possibilities on every turn, and eventually, with no obvious reason why, one player suddenly wins.

Tal was perhaps the greatest ever exponent of such an approach. Even Kasparov did not gambit so frequently, and was always aiming for a definite end-point in his sacrificing. Quite simply, Tal sacrificed because something looked interesting or entertaining. While professionals tend to be suspicious of playing in this fashion, scared of scoring a zero after some frivolous chess, amateurs can often enjoy playing with total freedom. Of course, Tal was vastly better than the average skittles-monger, but people still like his type of chess.

Game 15
M.Tal-D.Velimirovic
Yugoslavia-USSR match,
Teslic 1979
English Opening

---

1 c4 c5 2 b3

"To get the opponent out of the books. White does not attempt to force the pace in the centre (with for example 2 ♘f3 ♘f6 3 d4), but simply continues to develop quietly, placing his bishop on a good diagonal. If, as in the present game, Black attempts to build up a big centre, then White will have his pieces well placed."

So said I almost a decade earlier,

and I am quoting many of my original comments, in inverted commas, below. Much, though, needed to be updated, with the help of computer analysis, and taking into account later notes by Gallagher and Kasparov.

2...♘c6 3 ♗b2 e5 4 g3 d6 5 ♗g2

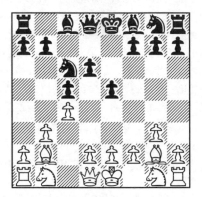

5...♗e6?!

One cannot help feeling that Black should somehow be able to equalize after White's quiet double fianchetto. White has obviously covered the d5-square well, but Black has other central squares he could use to his advantage.

When writing up my notes many years ago, I did not feel that this move was accurate. Gallagher thought so too, and went further in suggesting that Tal would already have congratulated himself in the use of his unusual opening set-up, actively provoking Velimirovic into an early charge on the light squares, slightly too early than should be justified. Gallagher also has the advantage of having played both Tal and Velimirovic. I haven't.

Gallagher did not propose any alternatives, but then Black has lots of playable continuations. I liked the idea of 5...f5!?, followed perhaps by ...♞f6, ...♝e7, in the style of Nimzowitsch. At the very least, Black would have developed his kingside pieces.

6 ♞c3 ♛d7 7 ♞f3 ♝h3

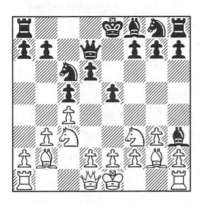

I made no comments on this position in my earlier notes, assuming, rightly or wrongly, that it was natural given Velimirovic's previous moves, even if his plan itself was not necessarily the best.

Gallagher suggested 7...h6, to prevent White from attacking the bishop with ♞g5, though this looks like a slight loss of tempo. 7...♞f6 could be better, as White does not gain all that much with ♞g5. For example, 8 0-0 ♝e7 9 ♞g5 ♝f5 10 e4 ♝g6, and Black is equal.

8 ♝xh3 ♛xh3 9 ♞d5 ♛d7

I see that some twenty years or so ago, I described this as "a sorry retreat", with the implication that White has the advantage here.

Now, I am not so sure. There is plenty of to-ing and fro-ing by both players, and the pieces need to be ma-noeuvred around, and not just developed. The queen is better, more centralized, on d7 than on h3, and neither 9...♜c8, nor 9...0-0-0, are convincing rook moves.

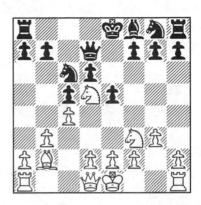

10 e3 ♞ce7

White's knight on d5 is valuable, and Black would like to exchange it off. After a later c4xd5, he would prefer not to have a knight attacked on the c6-square. Hence the ...♞ce7 move.

On the alternative, 10...♞ge7, Tal gives 11 d4 cxd4 12 exd4 e4 13 ♞d2 ♞xd5 14 cxd5 ♞b4 15 ♞xe4 ♞xd5 16 0-0 as slightly better for White.

If instead 11...exd4 12 exd4 ♞xd5 13 cxd5 ♞b4 14 0-0 ♞xd5?! (14...0-0-0 first is more prudent) 15 ♜e1+ ♝e7 16 dxc5 dxc5, and now there is the first real tactic of the game: 17 ♞e5! ♛e6 (or if 17...♛d6 18 ♛f3 0-0 19 ♜ad1 ♜ad8 20 ♞c4 ♛c6 21 ♞a5) 18 ♞g4 ♛c6 19 ♝xg7 ♜g8 20 ♛xd5! ♛xd5 21 ♞f6+ ♚d8 22 ♞xd5, winning a piece.

Notice how in all this White manages to open up the centre before Black has fully developed. This was always a Tal specialty. Here the important point arises from move 10, where Tal had played e2-e3 rather than 0-0.

To counter this Kasparov suggests 11...e4 12 ♘d2 ♘xd5 13 cxd5 ♘b4 14 ♘xe4 ♕f5, although White still seems better after 15 f3 ♘xd5 16 dxc5 or 15...0-0-0 16 0-0 ♘xd5 17 ♕d3.

11 ♘c3 ♘f6

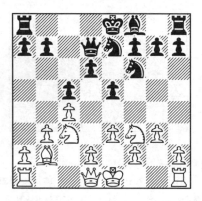

12 0-0!

I overplayed my commentary back in the early 90s, seeing this as a brilliant and more or less forced sacrifice, worth two exclamation marks. It is still a good and imaginative move, making the point that ...e5-e4 is not to be feared – provided that Tal is ready to sacrifice, in return for a couple of pawns, a piece! In compensation, Black's forces will be underdeveloped, and his king slightly exposed, but it is a slow-burning attack, with few open lines initially, and it will take time before any direct mating threats occur. Probably few players would even consider the knight sacrifice.

Instead, 12 d3 is a perfectly respectable move, with the idea of a later e3-e4, blocking the pawn structure, and trying eventually to exploit the good bishop versus bad bishop. Spassky used this idea highly effectively in a Candidates' match against Byrne (6th game, San Juan 1974). Such a line cuts out any loss, certainly, but Tal was playing for a win, rather than a win-draw option. He undoubtedly thought out the extraordinarily creative plan a few moves on, though as Gallagher noted, there were simpler and possibly stronger ways at move 13.

12 d4 is another option, opening up the centre. White seems to have at least an edge, with the better structure and development after, for instance, 12...exd4 13 exd4 cxd4 14 ♘xd4 d5 15 0-0, or 12...e4 13 ♘d2 cxd4 14 exd4 d5 15 0-0.

12...e4

12...♘g6 13 d4 again gives White a slight edge.

13 ♘g5!?

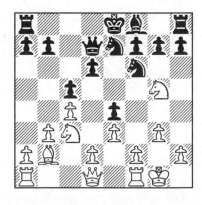

The next critical move. Tal intends to sacrifice a knight for two pawns. Is it objectively correct? Who knows, and "objectively correct" can only be established by long detailed analysis after the game. What is important, for the attacking player, is whether it works over the board.

Gallagher says that most grandmasters would prefer 13 ♘h4, without risk and maybe still with an advantage. In my own, much earlier, analysis, I suggested that 13...♕h3 14 f3 ♘g6

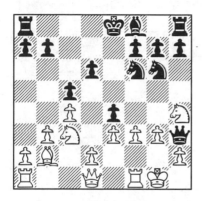

"gives White no edge" in view of 15 ♘g2? exf3 16 ♕xf3 ♘g4! 17 ♕xf7+ ♔d8 winning for Black.

Clearly this was an underestimation of White's chances. After 15 ♘xg6 hxg6 16 ♖f2, analysed by Gallagher, White is better. For example, 16...exf3 17 ♕xf3 0-0-0 (not 17...♘g4? 18 ♕xf7+ ♔d8 19 ♘d5 ♘xf2 20 ♗f6+! gxf6 21 ♕c7+ ♔e8 22 ♘f6 mate) 18 ♘d5 ♘xf5 19 ♕xd5 ♖d7 20 ♖af1, when Black has a little pressure on the h-file, but not very much, and White is superior everywhere else. Or if 16...d5 17 ♘xd5 ♘xd5 18 cxd5 ♗d6, trying to improve his development, then 19 ♖g2! consolidates the kingside, and White will be better in the centre after 19...♕f5 20 fxe4 ♕xe4 21 ♕e2 ♕xd5, and indeed can snatch a pawn with 22 ♗xg7.

White can even ignore the black knight, and simply capture with 15 fxe4!, when after 15...♘xh4 16 gxh4 ♕xh4 (if 16...♘g4 17 ♕e2) 17 ♖f4! ♕g5+ (or 17...♕h6 18 ♘b5) 18 ♔h1 0-0-0 19 ♕f3, White dominates both the centre and the kingside.

But this is still not the whole story. Gallagher concentrates his analysis on Black's attempts down the h-file, and this too was my intention earlier. It is always worth considering a threat of checkmate. If, however, the opponent can defend the threat comfortably, and the attacking piece is not all that well placed after the defence, then quieter positional play should be considered. Black captured on h3 with the queen after the bishop exchange, and then recentralized it with ...♕d7. It is, perhaps, positionally illogical to return the queen to h3 yet again, unless there is something to be directly gained.

13...♘g6!, developing with threats, looks better.

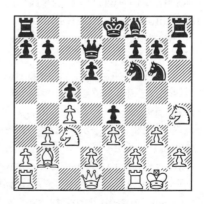

If then 14 ♘xg6 hxg6 15 f3 exf3 16 ♕xf3 ♘g4, Black has a hit on the h-file with rather more subtlety. Play is about equal, maybe a fractional edge for White after 17 ♕e4+ ♗e7 18 ♘d5 f5 19 ♕xe7+ ♔xe7 20 ♘xe7 ♔xe7 21 h4.

That is the technical analysis, but what is the psychology? We have seen that the quieter line is, in the end, about equal, with White clearly not being worse. Instead, given the choice, Tal went for the attacking option, un-clear with chances for both sides, and sacrificing a piece. He might have con-tinued more quietly at different phases of his life, but in 1979 he was playing with ambition and confidence.

Surprisingly, *Fritz* actually prefers Tal's move, and plans to follow it up with a piece sacrifice too!

13...d5

Black has to keep fighting for the initiative, otherwise he will just lose his e-pawn. If he tries 13...♕f5?, then 14 ♘b5 ♕xg5 15 ♘xd6+ and 16 ♘xf7 is winning for White.

14 cxd5!?

Here *Fritz* proposes 14 f3 and if 14...h6, then 15 ♘xf7! ♔xf7 16 fxe4. This could well be an improvement on the game, Black having wasted a move on ...h7-h6.

Now 16...dxe4? is no good, due to 17 ♘xe4 ♘eg8 18 ♕h5+ ♔e6 (or 18...♔e7 19 ♕xc5+) 19 ♘xf6 gxf6 20 ♗xf6 ♘xf6 21 ♕f5+, winning. Instead, 16...♔g8 17 cxd5 sees White already with three strong pawns for the knight. Or if 16...d4!? 17 e5! dxc3 18 ♗xc3, and White will regain one piece, while keeping a strong attack after, for ex-ample, 18...♔g8 19 exf6 gxf6 20 ♕h5, or 18...♘f5 19 ♕f3, or 18...♘eg8 19 e4.

The one drawback from Tal's per-spective is that Black might go for 14...exf3. True, White has good pros-pects for an advantage after 15 d4, opening up the centre again, with Black behind in development. But in this case Tal hasn't managed to sacri-fice.

14...♕f5

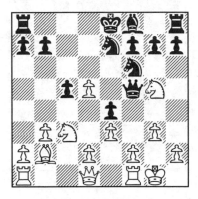

Velimirovic is playing actively, as is his wont. Do not in any sense take the impression that Tal was beating a much weaker opponent. Later in this four-game match between the then So-viet Union and the then Yugoslavia, always a prestigious event, Velimirovic got some revenge, with a kingside at-tack as Black in a sharp Benoni. Over-all, Tal won 2½-1½. There was a 16-move draw in one of the games, but even this was a sharp theoretical en-counter with pieces flying off the board. Velimirovic had in fact won from the final position, against an IM a few years earlier, but perhaps even he had decided that he wanted a quiet day against Tal.

Looking at the position in the diagram, one senses that Velimirovic would be eager for a win, and would not be interested in a draw offer here. White's knight seems ridiculously exposed. But Tal, too, had his ideas...

15 ♘xf7?!

...like, for example, this sacrifice.

15 ♕e2? ♕xg5 16 ♕b5+ is a much quicker way of starting the attack, but it fizzles more quickly as well: 16...♘d7! 17 d6 (or 17 ♕xb7 ♖b8 18 ♕xa7 ♘xd5) 17...♘c8 18 ♕xb7 ♖b8 19 ♕xe4+ ♕e5, and White has not brought his pieces into play, whereas Black is close to consolidating.

Strangely, I did not analyse any alternatives, assuming that 15 ♘xf7 was clearly Tal's intention (probably correct), and also that it was the best (very much open to debate). In fact there are several lines worth investigating:

a) 15 f4 h6 16 g4 ♕g6 17 ♘gxe4 ♘xe4 18 f5 ♘xc3 is given by Tal as clearly better for Black. Dvoretsky carries on, though, with 19 fxg6 ♘xd1 20 gxf7+ ♔d7 21 ♖axd1 ♘xd5 22 ♖f5, and White has reasonable compensation for his piece sacrifice.

Black can play more quietly with 15...♘exd5, aiming for equality after, for instance, 16 ♘cxe4 ♘xe4 17 ♕b1! ♘xg3! 18 hxg3 ♕xb1 19 ♖axb1 h6. If instead 16 ♘xd5 ♕xd5 17 ♕c2?!, White would be in danger of overpressing. 17...h6 18 ♗xf6 hxg5 19 ♗xg5 f6 20 ♗h4, and then 20...g5? 21 fxg5 fxg5 22 ♗xg5 ♕xg5 23 ♕xe4+ gives White a strong attack for the bishop, but the careful 20...♖d8! leaves the bishop out of play.

b) 15 d6!? is another option,

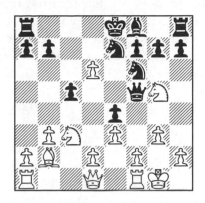

when Kasparov notes 15...♘c6 16 f4 h6 17 d7+ ♔e7 18 h4! "with the initiative", as 18...hxg5? 19 fxg5 is not a good idea for Black. He proposes that "there are more chances of equalizing" with 15...♕xg5 16 dxe7 ♗xe7 17 f3 exf3 18 ♕xf3 0-0-0. Note the precise use of language. He is not suggesting that Black is completely equal yet. After 19 ♘e4 ♘xe4 20 ♕xe4 ♖xd2 21 ♖xf7 White is slightly ahead with his attacking threats (if 21...♕h6 22 h4). If instead 18...♖d8!? 19 ♖ad1 ♖d7, then 20 d4 cxd4 21 exd4 0-0 22 d5 ♗c5+ 23 ♔h1, with a slight edge for White, his isolated d-pawn being an irritation rather than a weakness.

Black might consider 15...♘ed5, as 16 f4?! can then be met by 16...♘xc3 17 ♗xc3 h6!. However, White improves with 16 d7+!, disrupting the opposing pieces, and if 16...♔e7 17 ♘xd5 ♘xd5 18 ♕c2 ♕xg5 19 ♕xe4+ ♔xd7 20 h4 ♕h5 21 g4 ♕xh4 22 ♕xd5+ regains the piece with advantage. Or if 17...♕xd5 18 ♘h3 ♕xd7 19 ♘f4 with a pleasant edge for White. Note the tactic 19...♖d8

20 ♗xf6 ♔xf6 21 f3! ♕xd2 22 ♘d5+! ♖xd5 23 fxe4+, winning the exchange.

To complete the analysis, *Fritz* comes up with yet another sacrifice:

c) 15 f3!? ♕xg5 16 ♘xe4 with very interesting play.

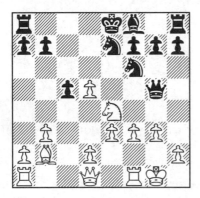

For example, if 16...♕g6 17 ♘d6+ ♔d7 18 ♘c4 ♕h5 19 e4 ♘g6 20 b4! b5 21 bxc5! bxc4 22 ♕a4+ ♔d8 23 ♕xc4, and White has a huge pawn mass heading for the black king. Alternatively, 16...♘xe4 17 fxe4 ♕g6 18 b4! ♕xe4 19 ♕a4+ ♔d8 20 ♖xf7 ♕xd5 (or 20...♕xb4 21 ♕c2) 21 ♖af1 ♘g6 22 bxc5 ♗e7 (or 22...♗xc5 23 ♖7f5 ♕d6 24 ♕b3) 23 ♗xg7 ♖e8 24 d4 again sees Black in serious difficulties. A better try may be 17...♘c8!? 18 ♕f3 ♕g6, though after 19 e5 Black is yet to find a way to mobilize his pieces, which are nearly all on the back rank. White has a great deal of play for a relatively small material investment.

After a quarter of a century, there is perhaps a chance of saying what is going on after 14...♕f5. Tal's knight sacrifice is brilliant, but as we shall see, Velimirovic had chances both of setting

up a draw, and of playing for a win. Instead, 15 d6!? aims only for a modest advantage, but objectively this is better than a clear draw for the opponent. While if White really wants to sacrifice, then *Fritz*'s second approach with 15 f3!? may well be more promising.

Of course it's all somewhat academic, because as far as I know, no one has come close to reaching this position again.

15...♔xf7 16 f3

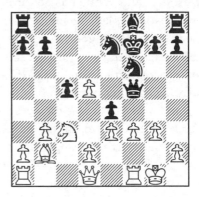

The only move that makes sense, but even so one must suspend disbelief. At the moment Tal has two pawns for the knight, and soon loses one of them, and apart from a bit of pressure on the f-file, and a slight lead in development, he has nothing concrete to show for his sacrifice.

Gallagher, when writing on this position, said that "one of the great things about Tal was that he never had any problems with sacrificing a piece and then continuing as if nothing had happened." If we look through this selection, we see wins by Tal against Mikhalchishin (a rook down, and on thin ice), Beliavsky (a knight down), Nei (a knight down), and the current game. Against Spassky, he only sacrificed a pawn, but the threat was stronger than the execution, Spassky avoided Tal's attacking idea, and went for a much inferior defensive plan. Only against Larsen was the piece sacrifice clear and decisive.

Whereas other players might sacrifice occasionally, Tal sacrificed almost routinely, on the basis that "it looks interesting, let's play it". Naturally, later players studied and learned from Tal's games, Kasparov not least. But sometimes it really was the case that "only Tal could have thought of that".

16...♘exd5

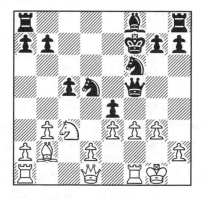

The most natural move. In my much earlier analysis, I did not bother going through any other idea. Black brings his knight into play, opens the diagonal for his bishop, grabs a pawn, and exchanges a pair of knights, all without immediate tactical redress. Positionally, what else needs to be considered?

Gallagher examines 16...exf3 17 e4,

but probably without any serious expectation that it would be a good defence for Black.

17 fxe4 ♘xc3 18 ♗xc3 ♕xe4

Now White has only one pawn for the piece.

19 ♕h5+

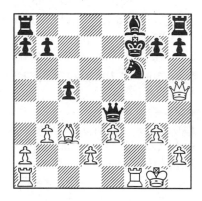

19...♔e6

A critical position for the defence, although as so often, it happens that the defence is unclear, and the attack is also unclear. This does not help Black at all to make a correct decision while the clock is ticking. It is so much easier if one of the candidate moves is clearly wrong, and can be rejected, so that the other move can be played with confidence, knowing that good or bad, this is the best.

Velimirovic, as a noted attacker himself, keeps play open, trying to find counter-attacks, even though it means leaving the king exposed. This cannot be said to be wrong.

In contrast, 19...♔g8?, trying to hide in the burrow, would have been quickly snuffed out by 20 ♗xf6 gxf6 21 ♖xf6 with checkmate to follow, for example after 21...♕e8 22 ♕g4+ ♗g7 23 ♕c4+. And while 19...♔e7?! has no immediate refutation, there's no reason at all to allow White to take the pawn on c5 with check.

This leaves 19...♕g6, decentralizing perhaps, but at least avoiding checkmate. In my handwritten notes many years ago, I used three A4 pages trying to work out what was going on. And this would still only be part of the picture, given that the play is phenomenally unclear. I quote much of my earlier notes and analysis.

Tal gives 19...♕g6 20 ♕d5+ as an outright win for White, but only, I suspect, because he missed Black's critical defence, 20...♔e8! 21 ♕xb7 ♕e4!!.

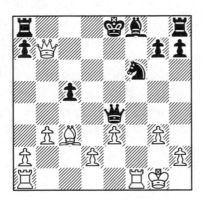

Such a move is extremely difficult to visualize in advance, even for a Tal. Black defends his rook by moving the queen back to a square it has just vacated, where it is supported by a knight that is attacked twice and was previously pinned against the king. The queen is also defending backwards down a diagonal, notoriously difficult to see, especially if the defending piece

has only just moved away.

It looks as though White's attack comes to a standstill after 22 ♕b5+ (now the queen is out of position) 22...♔f7 23 ♖f4 ♕e6!. Black is ready to develop his bishop, and if he manages to connect his rooks, he can look forward to winning. Note that 24 e4? fails to 24...♗d6 25 e5 ♗xe5 26 ♖e1 ♗d4+.

I then argued that after 22 ♕c7!? ♕e6! 23 ♖f4 ♕b6! "Black has again beaten off the attack." This now seems, with the intervention of *Fritz*, premature. After 24 ♕e5+ ♗e7, the bishop has left its starting square, at long last, but Black's defensive problems are not yet solved. 25 ♕g5! shows the white queen being remarkably nimble. If then 25...♔f7, there are numerous possibilities, such as 26 ♖af1 ♖d8, when the simplest and quietest way of finishing would be a perpetual, for example by 27 ♕h5+ ♔g8 28 ♕f5 ♖d5 29 ♕c8+ ♖d8 30 ♕f5.

Tal addicts, with the aid of the computer, might want to try for more, perhaps after 26 ♕h5+ (omitting 26 ♖af1) 26...♔f8 27 e4 c4+ 28 ♔h1 cxb3 29 axb3 ♕c6. Quite often, as the reader will by now have appreciated, the chance of taking a perpetual check is a sensible option. If everything is finely balanced, and the natural move is a draw, then a slightly unnatural move might change the balance in the wrong direction.

There are several less critical alternatives earlier on, but a main try is 21 ♗xf6 (eliminating the knight and preventing ...♕e4) 21...gxf6 22 ♕xb7 ♖d8.

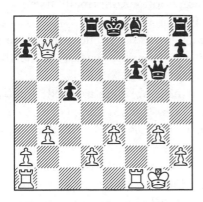

In my own notes I suggested that this position "is critical for the soundness of Tal's 12 0-0", while Gallagher, more restrainedly, merely gave it as possible. Looking closer I considered 23 ♖f4 ♗e7 24 ♖e4 ♖d7 25 ♕c8+ ♔f7 26 ♕xh8 ♕xe4, but clearly Black is winning. I noted also that more obvious alternatives, such as 23 ♕xa7, 23 ♕c6+, 23 ♕b5+, 23 d4 and 23 ♖ac1 do not look convincing. It looked like a dead end.

I then borrowed a suggestion by Tal, his inspired idea on move 21 in the game. So I examined, and was excited by, 23 b4!?.

Unfortunately, my main line was unsound, as I see only now with the help of *Fritz*. After 23...cxb4 24 ♖ac1 ♗d6 25 ♖c8 ♗xg3 26 ♖xd8+ ♔xd8 27 ♖c1, Black has 27...♗d6+! 28 ♔h1 ♕f5! 29 ♕a8+ ♔e7 30 ♕xh8 ♕d5+ 31 e4 (or if 31 ♔g1 ♗xh2+!) 31...♕xe4+ 32 ♔g1 ♗c5+ 33 ♖xc5 ♕e1+ 34 ♔g2 ♕xd2+, and Black eventually picks up the rook, with a likely win, a pawn up in a queen endgame.

However, White can improve on this line by 26 ♔h1!, and if 26...♕h5 27 ♕c6+ ♔e7 28 ♕xf6+ ♔d7 29 ♕c6+ or 26...♕h6 27 ♕c6+ ♔e7 28 ♕b7+ ♖d7 29 ♕e4+ ♗e5 30 ♕xb4+ ♔f7 31 ♕c4+ draws. Black can try 26...♗d6, but then 27 ♖xd8+ ♔xd8 28 ♕a8+ ♔d7 29 ♕xh8 forces him to take the draw himself with 29...♕e4+ 30 ♔g1 ♕g4+.

Going back a bit, Black might ignore the b-pawn, but then he would have to reckon with it advancing further. For example, 23...♗e7 24 bxc5 ♖xd2 25 ♖ad1 ♖xd1 (or 25...♕d3 26 ♖xd2 ♕xd2 27 ♕e4) 26 ♖xd1 ♔f7 27 ♖d7 ♖e8 28 ♕d5+ ♔f8 29 c6 and White seems to hold on.

Nevertheless, it is not so difficult to see that White will at least have to struggle for equality in this variation. In such complicated games, the annotator does not need to cover everything, but should only concentrate on the more relevant. If there is a better line, this should be preferred. Therefore, 21 ♕xb7! ♕e4! 22 ♕b5+ ♔f7 23 ♖f4 ♕e6, and now 24 ♕b7+ ♗e7 25 ♗xf6 gxf6 26 ♖af1 ♖he8 27 ♖xf6+! ♕xf6 28 ♖xf6+ ♔xf6 29 ♕f3+ with a probable draw.

20 ♕h3+

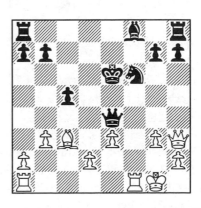

Only one move further on, and so many extra complications. Everything is so finely balanced.

20...♔d6

"Still with ideas of refuting White's play. 20...♔f7 in effect offers a draw (21 ♕h5+), although Tal notes that he could play for more with 21 ♖f5. Is this a convincing assessment, bearing in mind that White has only one pawn for the piece? Natural play for both sides would be 21...♗e7 22 ♖af1, leading to another critical position."

This is what I wrote many years ago. I then analysed several possibilities.

In case you are wondering why there is so much of my own analysis in this book, and not much from Tal himself, generally Tal did not write in-depth analysis, but concentrated on the general feel of the positions. It is up to plodders like myself who try to make sense of the game.

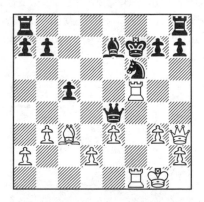

I concentrated first on 22...♕e6 23 ♕h5+ (23 g4? ♔e8 24 g5 ♘e4! 25 ♗xg7 ♖g8 26 ♕xh7 is tempting, but Black has 26...♘xg5), when Black has three rea-

sonable options. Normally a check is a relief for the attacker, as it usually means a forced or near-forced reply, but here there are several choices to be considered.

a) 23...g6? 24 ♖xf6+ ♗xf6 25 ♕g5! (25 ♖xf6+? ♕xf6 26 ♕d5+ ♕e6 27 ♕xb7+ ♕e7 28 ♕d5+ ♕e6 only draws) 25...♔e8 26 ♖xf6, "and White has a vicious attack at negligible loss of material." In fact he is winning by force.

b) 23...♔f8 wastes a move, allowing White to proceed with 24 g4. Then after 24...♔g8 25 ♗xf6 ♗xf6 26 g5! g6! 27 ♖xf6 ♕xf6 28 ♕g4 ♕e7 29 ♕c4+ ♔g7 30 ♕c3+, the game ends in perpetual check.

c) 23...♔g8! is much better.

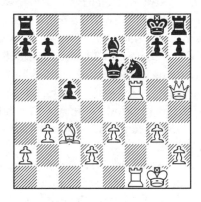

In my previous analysis, I gave 24 ♕f3 ♕c6 (not 24...♕e4?? 25 ♖xf6) 25 ♕f4, with the cop-out that "White is gradually pushing Black back." These days, the standard way of avoiding further analysis, whether through tiredness, laziness or time constraints, is to turn on the computer and find out what *Fritz*, or another analysis engine, suggests.

Here the machine proposes 25...b5! as good for Black, eliminating ♕c4+. If White tries 26 ♕g5!?, hoping for 26...♖f8 27 ♗xf6 ♗xf6 28 ♖xf6 ♖xf6 29 ♖xf6 ♕xf6 30 ♕d5+ and a draw after 30...♕f7 31 ♕a8+ or 30...♔f8!? 31 ♕a8+ ♔f7 32 ♕xh8 ♕a1+ 33 ♔f2! ♕xa2 34 ♕d8 ♕xb3 35 ♕d7+, Black throws in 26...h6! 27 ♖xf6 ♗xf6 28 ♖xf6 ♕xf6 29 ♕d5+ ♕f7 30 ♕xa8+ ♔h7 31 ♕e4+ ♕g6, and remains the exchange up.

Instead of 22...♕e6, 22...♖ad8!? is also promising. Kasparov gives 23 ♖e5 ♕c6 24 ♕h5+ ♔g8 25 ♕g5 ♖d5 with a simple material advantage for Black, but there is an alternative: 23 ♕h5+!, when I noted that Black is under strong pressure after 23...g6? 24 ♖xf6+ ♗xf6 25 ♖xf6+ ♔e8 26 ♕xc5.

Again, 23...♔g8! is more accurate. While analysing with set and boards, I assumed that White was winning, and showed the attractive thematic sacrifice with 24 ♕g5! ♘e8? 25 ♖f7! ♗xg5 26 ♖f8 mate. However, Black improves once more with 24...h6!, and if 25 ♕g6 ♖d6!,

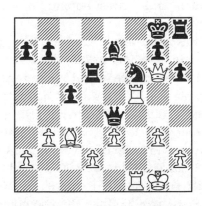

the hidden point being the x-ray after 26 ♗xf6? ♗xf6 27 ♖xf6? ♕xg6.

White does better with 26 ♖1f4! ♕c6 (not 26...♕b1+? 27 ♔g2 ♕xa2 28 ♗xf6 ♗xf6 29 ♖xf6 ♕xd2+ 30 ♔h3 ♖xf6 31 ♖xf6 ♕d7+ 32 ♔g2 ♕d5+, which is just a draw) 27 ♖e5 ♕d7 (and not 27...♕c7? 28 ♖ee4) 28 ♖xc5, picking up a second pawn. But after 28...♘e8! White's initiative is fading, and Black looks set to consolidate eventually. For instance, 29 ♕e4 ♖e6 30 ♖e5 ♖xe5 31 ♗xe5 ♕e6 32 d4 ♗g5 33 ♖f3 ♘d6 34 ♗b8 ♗f6 35 ♗xa7 ♘g5 36 ♖f5 ♔f7, when Black's rook finally emerges, and his knight is stronger than the white pawns here.

Now for the next twist in the analysis. My notes were written about a decade earlier than Gallagher's book. While studying two more alternatives, Gallagher, without knowledge of my own work, suggested that "Black has other moves, such as 22...♔e8 or 22...♕e6, which are no doubt just as complicated and unclear". If we add, too, that *Fritz* urges 22...♖ad8, we reach at least five possibilities for Black. No human player, neither Tal nor Kasparov, could calculate all this over the board.

Five complicated variations are more than enough to consider. If we were to cut down to the bare essentials, we could summarize that 20...♔f7 is possible, but that it allows White to repeat with 21 ♕h5+, which is probably why Velimirovic rejected it. Tal might well have tried for more with 21 ♖f5?!, but this would seem to be risky, as with accurate play Black has good chances of a win.

21 b4!!

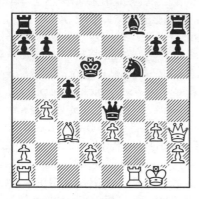

"Again Tal times his attack to perfection, forcing the opening of a new front. The three basic possibilities are either that White will open up the c-file and thus further expose the king after ...c5xb4; or that White will gain the d4-square after ...c5-c4; or that the white pawn will itself become an attacking piece if b4xc5 is allowed. This all places extra unwelcome pressure on the defence. The reader will remember also that the move b3-b4 was a critical strengthening of the attack in the variation after 19 ♕h5+ ♕g6. Flanking blows against the opposing pawn centre can be strategically important in even the most unstrategic positions.

"21 ♗xf6? would be *bad* timing. After 21...gxf6 22 ♖xf6+ ♔c7, Black has a victorious defence, whether on 23 ♖f7+ ♗e7, or on 23 ♖e6 ♕d5 24 ♖f1 ♖d8! 25 ♖f7+ ♖d7 (variations by Tal)."

The three possible plans for Black to defend (and maybe try to refute the attack?) imply at least three different variations coming up. Do the arithmetic, and you will see how complicated a chess game can be.

21...♔c7!

"The flight to the queenside continues. 21...cxb4 is obviously too risky, though finding the right move is often not as easy as stating the obvious. I am not sure whether White has an outright win after 22 ♗xf6 gxf6 23 ♖xf6+; I have not been able to find anything particularly clear."

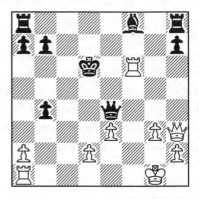

That was my (pre-computer) comment in the early 1990s. My crossed-out notes add the line 23...♔c7 24 ♖c1+ ♔d8 25 ♖f4 ♕e5 26 ♖d4+ ♗d6 27 ♕h4+ ♔d7 28 ♕g4+ ♔d8, with a draw by perpetual, and I was hoping to prove more.

Kasparov later found an improvement in 26 ♕h4+! ♗e7 27 ♖d4+ ♔e8 28 ♖e4 ♗xh4 29 ♖xe5+, and White regains the piece with substantial advantage, since if 29...♗e7 30 ♖c7 wins. *Fritz* goes further with 28 ♕g4!, which it number-crunches to a win in all variations, such as 28...♖d8 29 ♖e4 ♕d5 30 ♖c7 ♖d7 31 ♖xd7 ♕xd7 32 ♕h5+ ♔d8 33 ♕e5 ♖f8 34 ♕b8+ ♕c8 35 ♖d4+ etc. The point is that White is taking full advantage of the open lines for his queen and rooks, rather than attempting to exploit the pin on the bishop. Black has no way of solving his problems.

Instead, I concentrated on the "simple" variation 22 ♖f4, "which virtually compels Black to sacrifice his queen. Black has an outside chance of saving his game with either 22...♕xf4 23 gxf4 bxc3, or 22...bxc3 23 ♖xe4 ♘xe4, but really White should win, provided he remembers first to take charge of the open lines, and second to keep his pawn structure intact."

Actually this is very difficult to prove. In the 22...bxc3 23 ♖xe4 ♘xe4 line, Kasparov quotes Dvoretsky in assessing it as equal. After something like 24 d3 ♘f6 25 ♖c1 ♗e7 26 ♖xc3 ♘d5 27 ♖c4 (if 27 ♖b3 ♖ac8! 28 ♖xb7 ♖c1+) 27...♗f6 28 e4 ♘b6 29 ♖b4 ♖ac8 30 ♕f5, White should have enough to draw, but there's no obvious advantage.

But this was relatively a sideline. "Tal in his notes pays no attention to all this, doubtless assuming that 21...cxb4 is self-evidently bad. He gives instead a line where Black defends aggressively with 21...♘d5!?,

noting that at worst, White can keep a slight edge with 22 bxc5+ ♔c6 23 ♗d4.

"Tal also gives 22 ♖f7 ♘xc3 23 ♕xd7+ ♔e5, and now he suggests that 24 ♖e1 (idea, d4+) 24...♗d6! is unclear."

In fact 25 dxc3! seems to win for White, or similarly if 24...c4! 25 dxc3! ♕d3 26 ♕xb7 ♖d8 27 ♖f4. And Gallagher improves on this by simply playing 24 dxc3! immediately, there being no checking continuation for Black after 24...♕xe3+ 25 ♔f1, while his own king is hopelessly exposed.

It's complicated, often with positional, as well as tactical, factors needing to be considered. Velimirovic is still playing excellent moves though, and he is trying for a win. Putting it the other way round, any other moves are likely to end up in danger.

22 ♖ac1

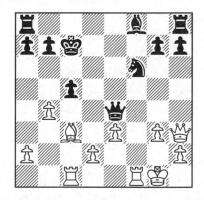

22...♖c8

"With ideas of castling by hand. Since this is perhaps Black's last chance of putting up a reasonable defence, we ought to look at alternatives." So I wrote many years ago.

Having examined the game anew, I do not like this second comment. Velimirovic is playing for a win! He had rejected the possibility of a draw by repetition a few moves ago, preferring the adventurous 20...♚d6. He has handled the middlegame well so far, and is aiming to consolidate his king, in order to be able to go for the win with his extra piece. Velimirovic is fully entitled to say that Tal's play in this game has been unsound. Velimirovic, as a renowned attacker himself, will know as well as anyone that the attacker is always on the edge of soundness and unsoundness.

Going back to my previous comments, I noted that "the basic plan Black has to oppose is the White capture on c5, followed, in the absence of a recapture, by ♗d4. White would then have two pawns for the piece, but all the pieces, and indeed his central pawns, would be extremely well connected, while Black's pieces remain undeveloped and uncoordinated." So Black has to complete his development.

There are of course alternative plans. One thought is to offer the exchange of queens with 22...♛g4, but after 23 ♗e5+ ♚c8 (not 23...♗d6?? 24 ♗xd6+ ♚xd6 25 ♖xf6+), we cannot discount the possibility of a draw by repetition with 24 ♛g2 ♛e4 25 ♛h3 ♛g4.

Or Black could try 22...♖e8!?, which creates important additional cover on the e5- and e6-squares. Gallagher suggests that White has compensation for the material after 23 bxc5. Another possibility is 23 ♖f5!?, the point being

that if 23...♛g4 24 ♛f1, White's queen is activated, while 23...♛d3!? 24 bxc5 ♖xe3!? 25 ♖e5 ♖f3 26 ♗a5+ ♚b8 27 ♛e6 b6 28 ♗xb6 axb6 29 ♛xb6+ ♚c8 ends in perpetual check by one side or the other.

23 ♖f5!

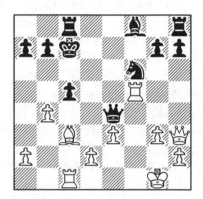

A double-exclamation mark by Tal, preparing ♗e5+, so that 23...♚b8? fails to 24 ♗e5+ ♚a8 25 ♖xf6!. But was Velimirovic's reply the best?

23...♛g4?

By this point, I had given up the analysis of the last few moves – it was fascinating, but I had taken up so much time, and I never really reached any real conclusion as to where Velimirovic could be regarded as clearly worse, or whether Tal was on top, or at least equal. This was an exceptionally dense game.

Is it just coincidence that I was running out of steam in my analysis of this game? Probably not. I was trying so hard to demonstrate that Tal's position was at the very least equal, and most likely better, that I was forgetting that this may not have been possible. It wasn't a case that, if I had the dedication, I could solve the task I had set myself. The task, it seems, was basically impossible. And Velimirovic had played it brilliantly, right up to the final few moves.

Here 23...♞d7! covers the sensitive c5- and e5-squares, and more generally activates his knight. Black also needs to develop his bishop, and take his king into safety. He is a piece up for, at the moment, a single pawn, so he can easily jettison a pawn or two in order to mobilize his pieces. Pawns matter little, provided his pieces remain active.

If White responds with 24 bxc5, Black completes his plan of redeployment with 24...♚b8 25 ♖cf1 ♝xc5 and can expect to win. 24 ♖f7! is more challenging,

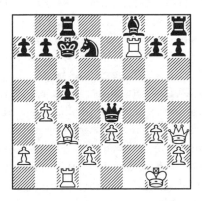

but 24...♝e7, bringing a piece into play, and then 25 ♝xg7 ♖he8 26 bxc5 ♛d5 27 ♖f2 ♚b8 sees Black more secure and ready to play for a win, while 25 bxc5 ♖hf8 26 ♖xg7 ♖ce8 27 ♛xh7 allows him at least a draw after 27...♛f3. Black might consider 24...♛d5!? 25 ♖af1 (if 25 ♝e5+ ♚d8 26 ♛f5 ♚e8! 27

♖f1 ♖d8) 25...♖e8 26 bxc5 ♖e7 as well.

Other readers and writers are welcome to examine this further, and the use of computers helps in speeding, and hence deepening, the analysis. Back in the 70s, one could write something like "23...♞d7!? is unclear". These days it is possible to look a lot deeper.

On the other hand, Kasparov was satisfied, without giving detailed analysis, that "after 23...♞d7! 24 bxc5 ♚b8 the black king would have been assured of escaping from all dangers, and the extra knight would have told." In which case, Tal's piece sacrifice was slightly unsound – it is difficult to refute it over the board, but with extremely accurate play by the defender, the attacker will end up worse. Kasparov was effectively saying, great imaginative idea by Tal, but what would have happened if Korchnoi had handled the defence?

24 ♝e5+ ♚d7 25 ♛f1!

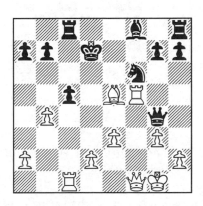

Good use of the baulk cushion. The queen can now give a check on b5, while also defending the rook on f5.

25...♛e4?!

Running short of time, Velimirovic's defence breaks down.

Not 25...cxb4? 26 ♖xc8 ♔xc8 27 ♕c1+ ♔d7 28 ♕c7+ ♔e6 29 ♖xf6+ gxf6 30 ♕c8+, and some geometry from the other side of the board.

25...c4! keeps the struggle alive, with play probably heading for a draw after 26 ♖f4 ♕e6 27 ♗xf6 gxf6 28 ♖xf6. Kasparov suggests that Black might have a slight edge with 28...♕d5, but this seems unlikely. At worst White can just chase the black queen about with his rook.

26 ♖c4

Black has managed to cover the check to b5, which is useful, but in return White gains a tempo with the rook.

26...♕c6 27 ♕h3

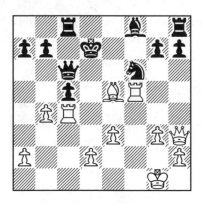

The manoeuvring of White's queen on the light squares is wonderful to see.

Fritz prefers Tal's 27 ♗xf6 gxf6 28 ♖xf6 alternative, to be followed by 28...♕d5 29 bxc5! ♗xc5 30 ♖c3! ♔e7 31 ♖f5! ♕d6 32 ♕f3!, which it calculates to a win. But this sort of precise play with

the heavy pieces is extremely difficult for a human to work out over the board. And ultimately Tal's move in the game is just as effective.

27...♕e6

If 27...♔e8? 28 ♗xf6 gxf6 29 ♖fxc5! ♗xc5 30 ♖xc5 skewers the queen and rook.

Gallagher notes that the attack is more difficult after 27...♔d8 28 bxc5 ♘d7, but White should still be winning. The critical tactical point is 29 ♖d4 ♗xc5 30 ♗f6+!, and if 30...gxf6 31 ♖xc5 wins.

He therefore continues with the alternative variation 30...♔e8 31 ♖xd7+! ♗xe3+ (or if 31...♕xd7 32 ♖e5+ ♗e7 33 ♖xe7+ ♕xe7 34 ♗xe7 ♔xe7 35 ♕h4+ and the queen is boss) 32 dxe3 ♕c1, when the strongest and most attractive line is 33 ♖d1! ♕xd1+ 34 ♖f1 with a decisive attack. Since 34...♕d7 fails to 35 ♕h5+ ♕f7 36 ♕e5+, Black has to try 34...♕xf1+ 35 ♔xf1 ♖c1+ 36 ♔e2 gxf6, but then 37 ♕e6+ ♔f8 38 ♕xf6+ ♔g8 39 ♕d8+ ♔g7 40 ♕e7+ wins for White, who arranges in turn ♕e5+, ♕b8+, ♕xb7+, and in the end, depending on where the black king chooses to run, either ♕b2+ or ♕e5+ will pick up a rook.

28 ♗xf6!

At first this looks like an ordinary way to finish the game, the bishop removing the defending knight, and White forcing the black queen out to allow a winning discovered check. But what happens if Black takes the rook rather than the bishop? Surely it cannot be playable?

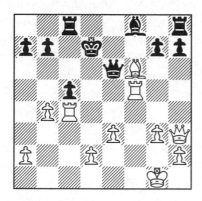

28...gxf6?!

Black had to try 28...♕xc4, when immediate discovered checks achieve nothing. 29 ♖d5+ ♔c7 30 ♕d7+ ♔b6 31 ♗d8+ ♖xd8 32 ♕xd8+ ♔b5 33 ♕d7+ ♔b6 is a perpetual for White, but there is nothing more than that to squeeze. Whereas 29 ♖xc5+? ♕e6 30 ♕xe6+ ♔xe6 31 ♖xc8 gxf6 leaves Black with his extra piece in the endgame.

It is the bishop, rather than the queen or rook, that plays the crucial role for White. The winning move is 29 ♗xg7!!,

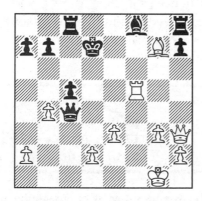

attacking the black rook, threatening to give White a material advantage

for the first time, while clearing the f-file to allow a discovered check on f7 or maybe on f8. If 29...♗xg7, White has a decisive attack, therefore, with 30 ♖f7+ ♔d6 31 ♕d7+ ♔e5 32 ♖f5+ ♔e4 33 ♖f4+. Don't miss the point that if Black had had time for ...c5xb4, he would be safe after 30...♔c6. But with the pawn on b4, White has 31 ♕d7+ ♔b6 32 ♕xb7 mate.

Black can struggle on with 29...♕e6 30 ♗xh8 h6, but if nothing else White can now swap off for a winning endgame. For example, 31 ♕h5 cxb4 (if 31...♕xa2 32 ♕f3 ♗d6 33 ♕xb7+) 32 ♖f7+ ♗e7 33 ♗f6 ♖e8 34 ♕b5+ ♔d8 35 ♗xe7+ ♖xe7 36 ♖f8+ ♖e8 (or 36...♔c7 37 ♕c5+ ♔d7 38 ♕xb4) 37 ♖xe8+ ♕xe8 38 ♕xe8+ ♔xe8 39 ♔f1 a5 40 ♔e1 a4 41 ♔d1 etc.

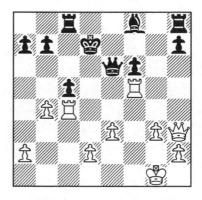

29 ♖e4

In terms of a top ten list, this is an anticlimax. Any average club player could spot this move quickly, the rook sacrifice, intending 29...♕xe4 30 ♖e5+, is straightforward. Had Velimirovic played 28...♕xc4 instead of 28...gxf6, this could easily have been remembered as one of Tal's greatest attacks.

Life is fickle.

If anyone tries to go through in depth the whole of Tal's play in this remarkable game, though, they will be mightily impressed. Concentrate on moves 1 to 28, and not just the last two.

29...♕xa2 30 ♖xc5+ 1-0

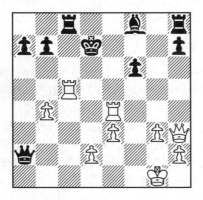

Mate follows with 30...♔d6 31 ♖d4+ ♔e7 32 ♕d7.

A strange and wonderful game. One could argue that Tal's 15 ♘xf7 was in fact inaccurate, and that White could have obtained an edge with more orthodox play. Instead, there were chances for Velimirovic to gain the advantage, but while he defended well for a long time, he did not play with total accuracy in such an unusual set-up.

There is always the danger, for the attacker, that a line might turn out to be incorrect, often because of a slight nuance a dozen moves later. It is difficult to avoid this, as over the board you cannot analyse so deeply. Ultimately, if a player is worried about slight unsoundness in sacrifices, the obvious answer is that he should not sacrifice.

On the other hand, if a player decides to take the plunge with a well-judged gambit, the likelihood is that the opponent will not defend perfectly for the next twenty moves, not least because of time pressure, so the gambiteer always has good chances of a win. It is often easier to attack than to defend, and as we saw earlier, Tal took excellent psychological advantage of this in his game against Spassky.

The final game in this section features another piece sacrifice by Tal. Of his lesser-known games from 1979, this is an obvious one to wish to annotate. It opens the usual questions of whether this is another brilliant sacrifice, or unsound, or something in the middle. Also, whether Tal could have played something quieter, maybe with a slight edge, while avoiding any possibility of a loss.

Nei's opening was undoubtedly a little too tentative, and one feels that Tal noticed the smell of fear, and this encouraged him to play even more aggressively. Tal was enjoying himself that year!

Game 16
I.Nei-M.Tal
USSR Spartakiad, Moscow 1979
English Opening

---

1 c4 e5 2 ♘c3 ♘f6 3 ♘f3 ♘c6 4 e3 ♗e7 5 ♗e2 0-0 6 0-0 d5 7 cxd5 ♘xd5 8 d3 ♗e6 9 ♕c2 f5 10 a3 a5

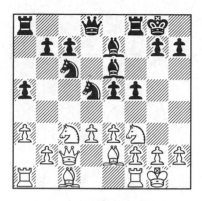

A reversed Sicilian, from the English Opening. Clearly White's position is not worse, as the Scheveningen System is highly durable. It is unlikely, though, that White's position could be substantially better.

11 ♘a4

This would seem to be the best chance for an edge, with ideas of gaining the bishop pair. Tal gives this as a slight edge for White in Informator 28, and it is the next move that turns out to be passive.

11...♕e8

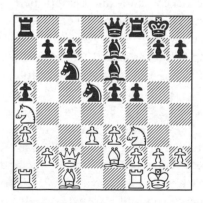

12 ♗d2

The obvious alternative is 12 ♘c5,

and if 12...♗xc5 13 ♕xc5 ♕g6, then White does not have to transpose into the game with 14 ♗d2, but can try to improve.

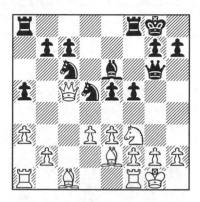

White has to be careful though. If, for example, 14 b3, then 14...e4! and Black is better. 15 ♘d4 ♘xd4 16 exd4 c6 gives Black the more secure central structure, while 15 dxe4? fxe4 16 ♘d4 ♘xd4 17 ♕xd4 ♖ad8!, threatening ...♘f4 or ...♗h3, sees White in big trouble. After 18 ♕c5 Black has a methodical plan of attack with 18...♖f5! 19 ♕d4 (not 19 ♕xe4? ♘c3 20 ♕c2 ♖g5! 21 ♕xg6 ♘xe2+, winning a piece) 19...♖d7 20 ♕b2 ♖g5 21 g3 ♗h3 22 ♖d1 h5 23 ♗d2 h4 24 ♗e1 hxg3 25 hxg3 ♗g4 26 ♗xg4 ♖xg4 27 ♖ac1 ♖g5, followed by ...♖h5 and ...♕h6.

Instead, 14 ♖e1!? might hold the balance. Then 14...e4 could be met by 15 ♘d4 ♘xd4 16 exd4, as 16...f4? 17 dxe4 f3 fails to 18 ♗f1 (compare this with 15 ♘d4 in the game), while other moves, such as 16...exd3 17 ♗xd3 or 16...a4 17 ♗d2 c6 18 ♗f1, look OK for White, with the two bishops.

If Black delays the pawn push,

White might prevent it once and for all by playing e3-e4 himself. For example 14...♖ad8 15 e4! fxe4 16 dxe4 ♕xe4 (or 16...♘f4 17 ♗xf4 ♖xf4 18 ♘xe5) 17 ♗b5 ♕g6 18 ♗xc6 ♖xf3 19 ♗xb7 ♖d3 20 ♔h1 ♕f5 (or 20...a4 21 ♗e3) 21 ♕xa5 ♕xf2 22 ♗g5 ♖b8 (or 22...♖f8 23 ♗a6) 23 ♖xe5 ♕xb2 24 ♖ae1 ♕xb7 25 ♖xe6, with a roughly equal position.

On the other hand, it is possible that Nei did not like the immediate 12 ♘c5 in view of 12...♗c8!?.

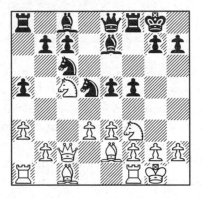

It's a loss of two tempi, yes, but the white knight on c5 is not necessarily better than on c3, which neutralizes the loss of time.

Black may even be slightly better. White has a tempting target on the vulnerable g8-a2 diagonal, but there are tactical resources for the defender. After 13 d4 e4! 14 ♕b3 (or 14 ♗c4 ♕f7 15 ♕b3) 14...♕f7 15 ♗c4 a4!, Black has magnificently turned the tables, through the white queen being exposed. If 16 ♕a2 ♖d8 17 ♘d2 b6!, and the knight is trapped – the white knight on c5 that is, rather than the black knight on d5!.

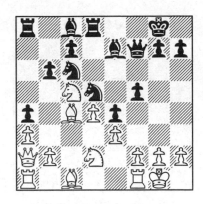

It is not to be unexpected if play continues sharply following the win of the knight, and after 18 f3! White is tactically still in the game. Nevertheless, there are some weaknesses in White's pieces, his rook, knight and bishop on the queenside all seriously underperforming. The indication is that Black should be on top. So with confidence, Black can play 18...exf3 (much better than 18...bxc5? 19 fxe4) 19 ♘xf3 (not yet 19 e4? ♘xd4!) 19...bxc5 20 e4! ♗a6 (not 20...fxe4? 21 ♘g5) 21 ♗xd5 ♖xd5 22 ♕xd5 ♕xd5 23 exd5 ♗xf1 24 dxc6 ♗b5, and his bishop pair will dominate the rest of the game.

Inserting 18 ♘cxe4 fxe4 does not help White, as after 19 f3! exf3 20 ♘xf3, Black has time for 20...♕e6!, followed by ...♘a5. For example, 21 ♖e1 ♘a5 22 e4 ♘xc4 23 exd5 ♕xd5 24 ♖xe7 ♗g4 25 ♖xc7 ♖ac8, with a clear advantage. Alternatively, 20 e4 ♘xd4 21 ♘xf3 ♘b3! shuts White's pieces out of play, and 22 ♗e3 ♗e6 23 exd5 ♗xd5 24 ♗xd5 ♕xd5 leaves Black with an extra pawn, or if 22 exd5?! ♗a6 23 ♘d2 ♕h5 24 ♗xa6 ♗c5+ 25 ♔h1 ♗d6 26 h3 ♖f8 and Black is winning. As well as having numerous pieces en prise, White is threatened with ...♕e5.

It is sometimes tempting, in the English and many other lines, to feel that White can play successfully with colours reversed, and hope for the advantage. It does not always work. The Sicilian is a good and sound opening, and if he plays carefully, Black has excellent chances of equality, and quite often the possibility of taking over if White makes even a slightest slip in a tense middlegame. With colours reversed, the Sicilian player (in this case, White) still has to proceed carefully, and defend before he can attack. To play at once for an attack with White in a reversed Sicilian is simply to open up attacking chances for Black.

12...♕g6 13 ♘c5 ♗xc5

13...♗c8!? can still be considered, but the text move looks good. Tal is not worried about the bishop exchange here, if he is gaining time to start an attack.

14 ♕xc5 e4

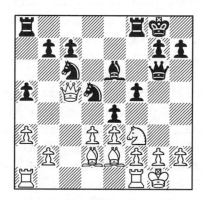

Tal gives this as equal.

15 ♘e1

Again White has to be careful.

15 ♘d4?! ♘xd4 16 ♕xd4 ♖ad8 17 ♕e5 exd3 18 ♗xd3 ♘b6 19 ♕c3 ♖d7 is good for Black, while 16 exd4? walks into 16...f4! 17 dxe4 f3 18 ♗xf3 ♖xf3 19 exd5 ♗h3 20 g3 ♕e4! 21 ♕xc7 ♖xa3! and mates.

15 dxe4 fxe4 16 ♘d4 is a bit better, though after 16...♘xd4 17 ♕xd4 ♖ad8 (threatening ...♘f4 or ....♗h3) 18 ♕e5 ♘f4!? 19 exf4 ♖xd2 20 ♖fe1 ♗d5, White still has to work hard for equality.

15...♘e5

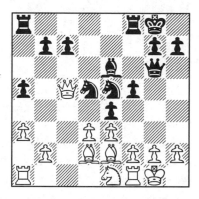

16 f4?!

A slightly unusual and negative decision. White eliminates the attacking thrust ...f5-f4, but at the cost of permanent kingside weaknesses, while leaving himself with very little counterplay.

Players with experience of French type structures might consider 16 d4?!, but this is quite passive too, and would give Tal a free hand on both sides of the board. For instance, 16...♘d7 17 ♕c2 c5! 18 dxc5 ♖fc8 takes the initiative on the queenside. If instead 17 ♕b5

Black can begin with 17...♖fb8 followed by ...c7-c6, or he might attack on the kingside after 17...♘5b6!? (threatening ...c7-c6) 18 ♗xa5 c6 19 ♕b4 ♘d5 20 ♕d2 f4 21 exf4 ♘xf4 22 ♗c7 ♘h3+, and Black has at least a draw

Rather than advancing to the fourth rank, it might be better to play 16 f3!?,

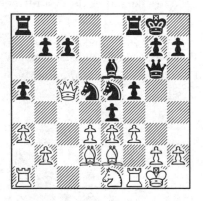

when 16...f4? is just bad after 17 dxe4 ♘d7 18 ♕c1. If Black tries 16...exd3 17 ♘xd3 ♘c4, then 18 ♕xc4!? ♘xe3 19 ♗xe3 ♗xc4 20 ♘e5 ♗xe2 (not 20...♕e8?! 21 ♗xc4+ ♔h8 22 f4 and the three pieces are better than the queen) 21 ♘xg6 hxg6 22 ♖fe1 should be a draw, with the opposite-coloured bishops.

White seems to defend against slower play as well, such as 16...b6 17 ♕d4! exd3 18 ♘xd3 ♘xd3 19 ♕xd3 and if 19...♖ad8 20 ♕c2 ♕g5 (or 20...♕h6 21 e4! ♘e3 22 ♕c3) 21 ♗c4, or 16...♘d7 17 ♕c2 ♘7g6 18 g3!? followed by ♘g2.

That said, Nei's move is understandable. When you're facing one of the greatest attackers in the history of chess, it is natural to want to block things off, to restrict his attacking op-

tions. The drawback is that your own options will be restricted too, and often more so, meaning that the attacker can simply proceed with leisure.

16...♘d7

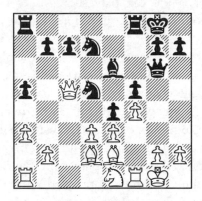

Every so often, Tal retreats! And occasionally, this may even be an unforced retreat.

Of course, don't take that comment too literally, but Tal is very much a player of the attack.

In his notes in *Informator*, Tal gives 16...♘g4 17 ♗xg4 ♕xg4 18 dxe4 fxe4 19 h3 with an edge for White. This is hard to believe, and *Fritz* and the author both see it as an edge for Black, although, admittedly, it's not easy to find a way into White's position.

Going back a move, *Fritz* suggests the unlikely-looking pawn snatch 18 ♗xa5!?, given as equal after 18...exd3 (18...b6 19 ♕c6 is the tactical point) 19 ♘xd3 ♕e2 20 ♘e5 ♕xb2 (or 20...♕xe3+ 21 ♕xe3 ♘xe3 22 ♗b4) 21 ♖ad1 ♘xe3 22 ♕xe3 ♖xa5 23 ♘c6! bxc6 24 ♕xe6+ ♔h8 25 ♕xc6 ♖xa3 26 ♕xc7. Readers are invited to search for possible improvements.

In terms of style, *Fritz* is almost the complete antithesis to Tal. Whereas *Fritz* tries to grab anything that moves, Tal loves to throw anything that jumps.

17 ♕c2

Not 17 ♕b5? ♘5b6!, threatening ...c7-c6, when White's queen is in danger. After 18 ♗xa5 c6 19 ♕b4 ♘d5 20 ♕d2 ♘c5! 21 ♗d1 exd3, Black is clearly better. The knight retreat had its points.

17...♘7f6

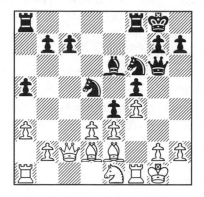

18 dxe4 fxe4

With more bite than 18...♘xe4 19 ♘f3.

19 ♗c4 c6 20 a4

This looks strange, but White wants to add an extra guard to e3, while preventing any ideas with ...a5-a4 or ...b7-b5. It also fixes the a5-pawn as a potential weakness.

20...♘g4 21 ♖a3 ♘b4?!

Tal was critical of this move in *Informator*, and indeed it is difficult to justify it. Maybe he wants to eliminate the white bishop pair, but does that really matter here? His knights are good, and his bishop is well placed,

whereas White's dark-squared bishop is not really a fully effective partner. Perhaps it was simply that, seeing White might at some point take on d5 anyway, Tal preferred to exchange his 'bad' bishop, rather than the knight. While this makes some sense positionally, the time it takes allows White to arrange his pieces much more effectively.

Instead, Tal suggests 21...♖f7!?, which is safe and maintains a slight edge for Black.

He can also gain some more terrain with 21...♖f5!,

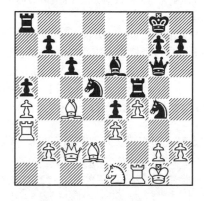

the tactical point being that if 22 ♕xe4, Black has 22...♘xh2! 23 ♖f2 (not 23 ♔xh2? ♖h5+ 24 ♔g1 ♕xe4 25 ♗d3 ♕b4! 26 ♗xb4 axb4, winning a pawn, if not the queen!) 23...♘g4, followed by ...♖e8, with excellent control of the light squares.

Alternatively, 22 h3 ♘gf6 sees Black's rook on the right side of the knight, in terms of starting an attack. If White tries to push the attackers away too crudely, there are combinations such as 23 ♖b3 ♖h5 24 ♗e2 ♖xh3 25 f5

♕g3! 26 fxe6 ♕h2+ 27 ♔f2, and rather than take the perpetual, Black can force a win with 27...♖f8! 28 ♗c4 ♕g3+ (but not 28...♘h5+? 29 ♔e2 ♖xf1 30 ♔d1!) 29 ♔e2 ♕g4+ 30 ♔f2 ♖h2!, followed by ...♕h5 and ...♘g4+.

Going back, White might consider trying 23 g4, by analogy with Nei's idea in the game, but then 23...♖h5! 24 f5 (or 24 ♘g2 ♖xh3 25 f5 ♕xg4 26 fxe6 ♕g3) 24...♗xf5 25 ♘g2 ♖xh3! 26 ♖xf5 ♕h6 27 g5 ♖h1+ 28 ♔f2 ♕g6! 29 ♖f4 ♕xg5 gives Black a decisive attack. White may have entertained the crowd with a few pawn squibs, but the black knights and heavy pieces provide the main action.

While all this does not prove conclusively that Black is winning after 21...♖f5, certainly White would have to play well to have a chance of holding.

22 ♕b3 ♗xc4 23 ♕xc4+ ♘d5

So the light-squared bishops have been exchanged, but it is unlikely that Black has gained from it. On the contrary, White's forces are now better coordinated, with the queen on a more active post, the rook coming to b3, and the knight to c2 and d4.

24 ♖b3 ♖f7 25 h3!?

Nei decides to take the initiative, and at the very least he provokes Tal into making an unclear knight sacrifice.

Otherwise he could have tried the Steinitz style, resolutely avoiding pawn moves. Tal gives the brief note 25 ♘c2!? ♘h6. So perhaps his plan was to play ...♘f5, trade off the white knight if it arrives on d4, and aim for a good knight versus bad bishop position, though even then the weakness at a5 would offer White counterplay.

Nei's next move keeps the black knight out of f5, and seems correct, but against Tal he will need good nerves.

25...♘h6

Played in an optimistic frame of mind. Instead, 25...♘gf6 26 ♘c2 is probably about level. Tal pushes for more, and does not mind sacrificing.

26 g4

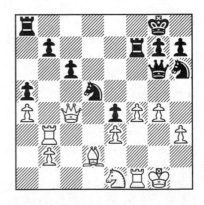

He could have opted for 26 ♘c2 here too. Nei was an old adversary over many years, and one cannot help feeling that he was positively encouraging a speculative sacrifice, as the only way to score a win from the former World Champion.

26...♘xg4?!

Once again, we see a remarkable ability by Tal not to feel constrained by the loss of a minor piece for a couple of pawns.

In the quiet of my room, I can tell myself that Black's attack is not really that impressive, and that his play can be beaten back. Over the board though, vintage Tal in sacrificial mood must be terrifying, particularly if, as was the case here, White was already in time trouble.

The position was roughly equal before the piece sacrifice. The only way for Black to try and win was to gamble. Justifiable? Or just a hack?

27 hxg4 ♕xg4+ 28 ♘g2 ♖e8 29 ♖f2?

If you are a piece up and defending, often a good idea is to use the extra piece actively. Here 29 ♗xa5! is simple and straightforward, asking the opponent to justify his sacrifice.

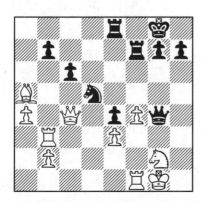

There is no immediate mating attack, so White can take the pawn. Bishop versus pawn is a much bigger material advantage than bishop versus two pawns, and other things being equal, much easier for the defender. It might, for example, be useful if White were to advance the pawn to a5 and a6, to break open the b-file and create back rank checks. Or, more immediately, the bishop can wander around, covering various important dark squares.

For instance, after 29...♖e6 30 ♗b6 h5 31 ♗d8! h4 32 ♗xh4 ♖h6 33 ♗g5 ♖h3 34 ♕xe4 wins for White. If instead 30...♕h3 31 ♗d8! (but not 31 ♗d4? ♖h6 32 ♕c2 ♕h2+ 33 ♔f2 ♖e7 34 ♗e5 ♖h3 35 ♕xe4 ♕g3+ and draws) 31...♖f8 32 ♗h4, and now 32...b6 33 a5!? bxa5 34 f5! ♖xf5 35 ♖b8+ ♔f7 36 ♖xf5+ ♕xf5 37 ♕c5 ♔g6 38 ♖c8 ♔h5 39 ♖xc6 ♖xc6 40 ♕xc6 sees Black running out of pieces.

Or maybe the bishop arrives the other way, after 29...h5 30 ♗e1 g5!? 31 fxg5 ♖xf1+ 32 ♕xf1 ♖f8 33 ♕c4 ♖f5 34 ♗h4.

In these lines the white bishop has covered enormous ground, starting at d2, and passing through a5, d8, h4 and g5, or alternatively e1 and h4. This is a "super-bishop", and such unusually active pieces need to be utilized. How might this be done? One answer is that most normal pieces are constrained by having clear attacking and/or defensive roles, and so cannot go flitting around the board. Here, because of Tal's sacrifice, White's bishop is an extra piece and is therefore free to do what it likes.

Nei makes very little use of the bishop during the rest of the game, and does not move it until he is already losing.

29...♖e6

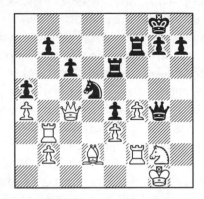

30 ♕e2?

This is, alas, more poor defensive play, doubtless affected by time trouble. Nei reacts nervously, trying to offer an exchange of queens, but Tal's queen nips away, after which he has just gained some time.

As we have so often seen in this collection, Tal plays with vigour in attack, and this creates pressure on his opponents. Under long sustained force, the defender often crumbles.

In defence as well as in attack, it is generally best for the pieces to be spread out, while still coordinated. It is not usually a good idea to have them all squashed together. After 30 ♕e2, White is only a small blunder away from playing ♔f1, and getting checkmated with ...♕h1 or ...♖h1. Unlikely? Suppose Black organizes ...♕h3 and ...♖h6, then the problem can be seen.

A better plan is to create space with 30 ♗xa5 again, and if 30...♖h6 31 ♖d2. This time, though, Black's attack is sufficient to draw after 31...♕h3 32 ♕xe4 ♖e7 33 ♕c4 ♕h2+ 34 ♔f2 ♖g6 (not

34...♖h3? 35 e4!) 35 ♕f1 ♖e4! 36 ♖xb7 (or 36 ♔e1 b6!) 36...♖xa4 37 ♗c3 ♖a1!, when White has to take the perpetual with 38 ♖b8+ ♔f7 39 ♖b7+ etc. Note that the black king cannot escape the checks, since 39...♔e8 (or 39...♔e6? 40 f5+!) 40 ♖b8+ ♔e7 (or 40...♔d7? 41 ♖xd5+!) 41 ♖b7+ ♔d8 42 ♖b8+ ♔c7? 43 ♗e5+ would all win for White.

30...♕h3 31 ♘e1

Part of his plan, but Tal has a tactic. By this stage, however, White cannot save the game, no matter what he plays. For example, it is too late now for 31 ♗xa5, in view of 31...♖h6 32 ♖f1 ♕h2+ 33 ♔f2 ♖g6 34 ♖g1 ♕g3+ 35 ♔f1 ♘xf4!, winning. Or if 31 ♖a3, to keep the rook protected, Black plays 31...♖h6 32 ♖f1 ♘f6 33 ♔f2 ♖g6 34 ♖g1 ♕g3+ 35 ♔f1 ♘g4, and ...♘h2+ is decisive.

31...♘xf4!

Demolition.

32 exf4

Inserting 32 ♖xf4 ♖xf4 33 exf4 ♕xb3 is no improvement for White. Nei hopes he can try to survive if he keeps his rook on the board, but obviously he will have appreciated that he is losing.

32...♕xb3 33 ♗c3 ♖g6+ 34 ♘g2 ♕d5 35 ♔f1 ♖g3 36 ♘e3 ♕e6 37 f5?

This speeds things up. 37 ♔e1 would keep the game alive until the time control, and perhaps a few more moves afterwards.

37...♕h6 0-1

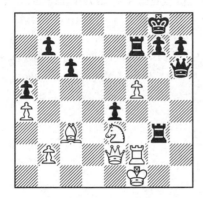

White loses the knight or gets mated on h1.

This was recognizably Tal with the black pieces, but Tal slightly off form. His bishop exchange was unnecessary, and slowed down his attack. His later sacrifice should have been inadequate, but his opponent missed the critical defensive plan. In short, this was a far from perfect game, and there are lessons to be learned from both attack and defence.

To play sharp attacking tactical chess, a player must be on a knife edge, at the peak of his form. Tal was not able to continue at that level indefinitely after his year of magic, and he slowed down, though still playing good chess.

Maybe there is an interesting article to be written about Tal in 1981, a year in which he played lots of chess, and did not lose a single game. Many draws, but no losses. We have seen some incredible games by Tal from 1979, but this could not last. He played vigorous chess in 1981, and was certainly not aiming for quick and solid draws, but there were no signs of the piece sacrifices, in 1979 style. The one really striking win was against Janos Flesch at Lvov. This game is certainly well worth studying as part of the current theme.

Tal's play gradually declined in the years before his death, though this of course is only relative. The vast majority of chess players could only dream of anything close to a 2525 Elo rating. In his final tournament, Barcelona 1992, he did well as White, with three wins and no losses, and his attacking win against Vladimir Akopian was vintage Tal. He suffered badly as Black though.

In Tal's best days, he often went very close to the edge. The big paradox was that he made more mistakes when he was playing creative chess, but won more games than when he played more classical chess. Tal, like Kasparov later on, aimed for sharp positions, and almost inevitably not everything was completely under control. That is not the fault of the players; it is the virtue of the incredible variety of chess.

Something very strange and complicated, and yet also very simple, was involved in Tal's play. Imagine your-

yourself in a friendly game at the local club. The chances are that either you or your opponent will want to try something interesting. It is not so important whether the line chosen is analytically the best, since it's "just a game". In five-minute chess, you will not have the time to calculate anyway. And if you're playing without clocks, it would be impolite to think about a move for half an hour. In such encounters you play your move, you hope for the best, and hope too that you will come out on top. And if one of your sacrifices happens to be unsound, so what? If you win, it's a job well done.

Few strong players can afford to think like this during a serious game. You have to work hard to improve; you are terrified of the thought of making a frivolous or unsound move; you have to play serious chess, not artistic chess. But Tal, at his best and in good health, he could try anything.

Chapter Four

Garry Kasparov: 1978-1982
Sacrificing Pawns, Becoming a Strong Grandmaster

There are many ways for a writer to tackle the complicated question of examining an extremely strong, up-and-coming grandmaster. Already I have decided that the theme, in agreement with the publisher, is of attack and sacrifice. But there are several subthemes to be considered.

When playing through the games in this section, I wanted first to show Kasparov showing his paces against recognized grandmaster opposition. There are plenty of examples to consider, even when he was a teenager. Then I came to appreciate that there was a definite "Kasparov theme" emerging, the pawn sacrifice in the centre. It was also a Tal specialty, as in the Spassky-Tal game at Montreal 1979 (Game 14), and later against Flesch, at Lvov 1982.

Central pawns are valuable, especially in the middlegame or endgame, and you would not want to give such a pawn away lightly. Sometimes it is a case of sacrificing one so that another has the chance to become stronger, maybe an advanced passed pawn. Kasparov-Pribyl (Game 18) is an excellent example. More commonly, though, it is a case of increasing piece mobility: maybe opening up the centre before the opponent has completed his development, and starting the attack quickly; or opening up lines in order to put pressure on a castled king; or trying to obstruct, with a pawn, the opponent's pieces; or maybe a mixture of several ideas.

A different perspective, shown by Garcia Martinez-Kasparov (Game 19), is the passive pawn sacrifice, where Kasparov decides to jettison a couple of pawns, with the thought that, while the opponent is grabbing pawns on one side of the board, he himself will gain much time for his attack on the other side.

Before examining the main games in this chapter, we look at a couple of other Kasparov examples from 1978, one highly dispiriting for him. And to start with, a famous Ljubojevic win from earlier in the 1970s. This is a extremely complicated game, which undoubtedly Kasparov and others will have learnt a lot from.

Preliminary games

Game 17.1
L.Ljubojevic-U.Andersson
Wijk aan Zee 1976
Sicilian Defence

1 e4 c5 2 ⊘f3 e6 3 d4 cxd4 4 ⊘xd4 ⊘c6 5 ⊘c3 ♕c7 6 ♗e2 a6 7 0-0 ⊘f6 8 ♗e3 ♗e7 9 f4 d6 10 ♕e1 0-0 11 ♕g3 ♗d7 12 e5!?

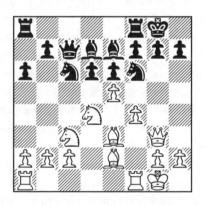

Just as extraordinary a concept as the sacrifice a few years later in Spassky-Tal at Montreal (Game 14), and one that created a deep impression on the chess community. Kasparov, as we have already seen, used this idea

more than once.

Ljubojevic's plan was extremely audacious, not least because his king was still on g1, allowing Black counter-pressure on the a7-g1 diagonal. Compared with this, Kasparov's interpretation against Korsunsky in the next game seems almost subdued.

12...dxe5 13 fxe5 ⊘xe5 14 ♗f4 ♗d6 15 ♖ad1 ♕b8

Routinely given an exclamation mark in the notes, to enable Black to withdraw the bishop to c7.

In *Informator 21*, Srdjan Cvetkovic suggests an alternative in 15...♖ad8!?, when 16 ⊘b3 ⊘d5 17 ⊘xd5 exd5 18 ♖xd5 f6 19 ⊘d4 ♖fe8 would be roughly equal. 15...♖fe8!? is also possible, and if 16 ⊘b3 ⊘d5 17 ⊘xd5 exd5 18 ♖xd5 ♗c6!, with a level position.

Andersson's move is objectively stronger, as with best play he is aiming for a win. Unfortunately, the game is difficult, and he ends up losing. Had he played one of the lesser moves, he could probably have drawn without difficulty.

16 ♖d3

16...♘e8?!

And Andersson could not find a convincing answer to Ljubojevic's somewhat speculative, if brilliant pawn sacrifice, as this move seems to be a mistake – probably! Annotating this game in *The Art of Chess Analysis*, Timman notes that White is threatening 17 ♖e3, and as he doesn't suggest an alternative for Black, implies that the move played is the best response.

In the 1970s, even the strongest players, when writing up games, would have to rely on guesswork and intuition in such complicated positions. Detailed analysis would still have been extremely important, but often a writer can only focus on a relatively small proportion of all the reasonable ideas.

These days, a quick flick on the computer, while eliminating a few poor suggestions, will give 16...♖c8! as advantageous for Black. As 16...♗c7? would now lose to the threatened 17 ♖e3, Black prepares the bishop retreat by defending c7 in advance, after which the pinned knight on e5 will be free to move. For instance, if 17 ♖fd1 ♗c7 18 ♖e3 ♘g6 escapes with the extra pawn.

If White continues with 17 ♖e3, Black has the resource 17...♘c4! 18 ♗xd6 (not 18 ♗xc4?! ♗xf4 20 ♕xf4 ♕xf4 21 ♖xf4 ♖xc4) 18...♕xd6 19 ♗xc4 ♕xg3 20 ♖xg3 ♖xc4 21 ♘xe6 ♗xe6 22 ♖xf6 ♖d8, reaching a favourable endgame. If White tries 18 ♘e4 ♘xe4 19 ♖xe4, then 19...e5! sees Black standing better, for example 20 ♗h6 ♗f8 21 ♘f3 ♘d6! 22 ♖xe5 ♘f5 23 ♕g4 ♕d6! and if

24 ♖d1 ♘xh6 25 ♕xd7 ♕xd7 26 ♖xd7 ♖xc2 27 ♖xb7 ♖c1+ 28 ♗f1 ♘g4 29 ♖e1 ♗c5+ 30 ♔h1 ♘f2+ wins.

Nunn suggests 17 ♘xe6! as a considerable improvement,

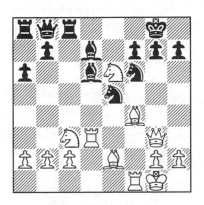

and then gives as the main line 17...♗xe6! 18 ♖xd6 ♕xd6 19 ♗xe5 ♕b6+ 20 ♔h1 ♘e8, with various continuations after 21 ♗d3 or 21 ♘e4, probably leading to draws.

What is slightly strange in Nunn's analysis is that he examines 19...♕b6+, but not the other queen check, 19...♕c5+!, which adds pressure to the bishop on e5. After 20 ♔h1 ♘e8, there are again two possibilities:

a) 21 ♗d3 f6, and now White cannot play 22 ♕h4?, (which would have been an appropriate response with the black queen on b6), because of 22...♕xe5. Neither is 22 ♘e4? satisfactory, in view of 22...♕xe5 23 ♘xf6+ ♕xf6 24 ♖xf6 ♘xf6 and Black has more than enough for the queen.

White could play 22 ♗xf6 ♘xf6 23 ♖xf6, but after 23...♖e8 Black remains the exchange for a pawn up. Note that 24 ♗xh7+? is no good, because of

24...♔xh7 25 ♕g6+ ♔g8 26 ♖xe6 ♕c6!, which is undoubtedly attractive for the viewer, and after 27 ♖xe8+ ♖xe8 28 ♕g3 Black can continue making back row mate threats with 28...♕g6 29 ♕h4 (or 29 ♕f2 ♕xc2) 29...♕g4 30 ♕f2 ♕f4 31 ♕g1 ♕d2, winning.

b) 21 ♘e4! is a better try, without a preparatory ♗d3. Black might well have a long and grinding defence the exchange up after 21...♕f8, but most players would prefer 21...♕xc2!, grabbing a pawn, opening the c-file, and using the queen in both attack and defence. 22 ♗d3 is the natural reply, but Black switches his queen to the fourth rank with 22...♕a4!, and then:

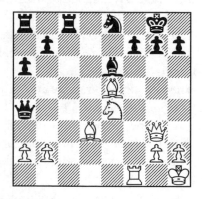

b1) 23 ♘f6+? ♘xf6 24 ♗xf6 ♕g4! covers all attacks, retaining the exchange.

b2) 23 ♗xg7? ♘xg7 24 ♘f6+ fails to 24...♔h8!, because the white queen cannot go to h4, and 25 ♗xh7 ♖c5! 26 ♗e4 ♕b5 27 ♗d3 (or 27 ♕h4+ ♘h5) 27...♖g5! 28 ♕h4+ ♖h5 29 ♕g3 ♕g5 30 ♘xh5 ♕xh5 leaves Black a piece up.

b3) 23 ♘d6 ♕g4 24 ♘xc8 ♖xc8 recovers the exchange, but Black still has his extra pawn.

b4) 23 ♘g5 ♕g4 24 ♗xh7+ ♔h8 25 ♕xg4 (25 ♘xe6 ♕xg3 26 hxg3 ♔xh7 27 ♖xf7 ♖c1+ 28 ♔h2 ♖e1 strongly favours Black) 25...♗xg4 26 ♗e4 (or 26 h3 ♗e6 27 ♗e4 ♗c4!) 26...f6 27 ♗xb7 ♗h5! (but not 27...fxg5?? 28 ♖f8+ ♔h7 28 ♗e4+ g6 29 ♖h8 mate) 28 ♗xa8 ♖xa8 leaves the two white pieces forked, since there is no mate without the light-squared bishop. Or if 28 ♗e4 ♖a7 and Black untangles, keeping his extra exchange.

b5) 23 b3 improves the previous line for White, as after 23...♕b4 24 ♘g5 ♕g4 25 ♕xg4 ♗xg4 26 ♗xh7+ ♔h8 27 h3 ♗e6 28 ♗e4, Black cannot play ...♗c4 here. Nevertheless, 28...♖c5! 29 ♗f4 (or 29 ♘xf7+ ♗xf7 30 ♖xf7 ♔g8 31 ♖f5 ♘f6) 29...♖b5 30 ♘xe6 fxe6 31 ♗d3 ♖d5 32 ♗c4 ♖d7 33 ♗xe6 ♖e7, followed by ...♘f6, still leaves Black the exchange for a pawn ahead, and it is doubtful whether White's bishops provide him with full compensation.

There is no doubt much more to be said, but time is limited, and the intention is to concentrate on the games by Kasparov, Tal and Stein. The point being made is not just that the computer finds omissions and errors in previous notes. The help of the computer extends new ideas, rather than reducing them.

No detailed analysis of the remaining moves, as this game has been covered many times. In particular, Nunn provides definitive annotations in *The World's Greatest Chess Games*. We'll just note three critical junctures.

17 ♘e4 ♗c7 18 ♖c3 ♘c6 19 ♗xc7 ♘xd4

20 ♗d3 ♛a7 21 ♘c5 ♗b5 22 ♗e5 ♘c6
23 ♗xh7+ ♔xh7

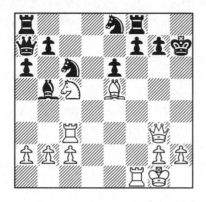

24 ♖f4

Very adventurous, but also very risky. Objectively the correct move was 24 ♗xg7! ♘xg7 25 ♛xg7+ ♔xg7 26 ♖g3+ with a draw, as given by Kavalek.

24...f6

24...f5! would have shown Ljubojevic's avoidance of the perpetual as too risky. Andersson was of course being forced to take risks himself, which is not necessarily to his liking.

Many of the contemporary writers, including Timman, have suggested 25 ♖h4+ ♔g8 26 ♛g6 ♘xe5 27 ♛xe6+ ♖f7 28 ♛xe5 ♖d8 29 ♖ch3. Play was seen as unclear after 29...♖f6 (Gligoric), but after 29...Re7!! (Nunn, much later, and assisted by computer), Black is clearly winning. The tactical point is that 30 ♛xe7 ♖d1+ 31 ♔f2 ♖f1+ 32 ♔g3 (32 ♔e3 ♖e1+) 32...♛b8+! leads to checkmate. If top grandmasters such as Timman and Gligoric overlooked this in analysis, it is understandable that the players missed this very difficult tactic.

There are many ways in which White could have avoided the decisive rook sacrifice, but without the play being convincing for White. Most lines lead to something like a pawn or two in return for the knight, and unconvincing attacking compensation. For example 25 a4 ♘xe5 26 ♖h4+ ♔g8 27 ♛xe5 ♗d7 28 ♔h1 (a safer square for the king, perhaps, than Nunn's suggested 28 ♔f1) 28...♗d7 29 ♘xe6 ♛f2 30 ♖f4 ♛d2 31 ♖cf3 ♗xe6 32 ♛xe6+ ♖f7 33 ♖xf5 ♘f6.

25 ♖h4+ ♔g8 26 ♛h3 ♘d8 27 ♗d4 b6 28 ♘xe6 ♘xe6 29 ♛xe6+ ♛f7 30 ♛e4

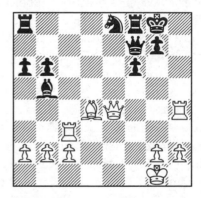

30...g5?

This is where, by general consensus, Black makes the decisive mistake. 30...♛xa2!, given by Timman, is regarded as best. Andersson's move is much too tentative, when a bold attacking counterplay is required.

Timman suggests that, in reply, White's best is to take the perpetual with 31 ♛h7+ ♔f7 32 ♛h5+ ♔g8 etc. For Black, 32...g6? would be too dangerous, due to 33 ♛h7+ ♘g7 34 ♖c7+ ♔e6 35 ♖e4+! ♔d5 36 ♖e1 ♖ae8 37 ♖d1 ♗e2 38 c4+! and wins.

Instead, Ljubojevic might have been tempted to take the rook, but this would have been risky, since as Nunn points out 31 ♕xa8? ♕b1+! 32 ♔f2 ♕f1+ 33 ♔g3 ♕e1+ 34 ♗f2 ♕e5+ 35 ♔h3 ♕e6+! 36 ♔g3 (or 36 ♖g4 f5) 36...♘d6! leads to a debacle.

31 ♖h6 ♖a7 32 ♖ch3 ♕g7 33 ♖g6 ♖ff7 34 c4 1-0

Along with numerous other lines, if 34...♗d7 then 35 ♖xg7+ ♖xg7 36 ♗xb6 wins.

Maybe it is a generous rhetorical flourish by Timman, in *The Art of Chess Analysis* (1980), to describe Ljubojevic's win as "the best game of the last twenty years", or maybe it has something much deeper to it. If we were to describe this win as something new in chess development, the start of new thoughts in attacking chess, then maybe there is a very serious point to Timman's comment. Play through the main games by Kasparov, play through the games by Tal, and decide what you think.

Game 17.2
G.Kasparov-R.Korsunsky
USSR Championship semi-final,
Daugavpils 1978
Sicilian Defence

---

1 e4 c5 2 ♘f3 e6 3 d4 cxd4 4 ♘xd4 ♘c6 5 ♘c3 d6 6 ♗e2 ♗e7 7 0-0 ♘f6 8 ♗e3 a6 9 f4 ♗d7 10 ♕e1 b5 11 a3 0-0 12 ♕g3 ♕c7 13 ♔h1 ♖ab8 14 e5!? dxe5?!

Very dangerous. In an earlier encounter, Karpov declined the sacrifice, but had to defend hard to hold the position together. W.Hartston-A.Karpov, Nice Olympiad 1974, continued 14...♘e8 15 ♗d3 b4 16 ♘e4 bxa3 17 bxa3 g6 18 ♘f3 ♘a5 19 ♗d4 ♗b5 20 exd6 ♘xd6 21 ♘f6+ ♗xf6 22 ♗xf6 ♗xd3 23 cxd3 ♖b5 24 ♖ae1, with a slight edge for White, which was still there when the game was later drawn by repetition. Other players have also refused the pawn.

15 fxe5 ♘xe5

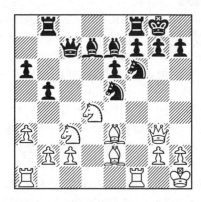

16 ♖xf6!

Kasparov demonstrates a new interpretation of Ljubojevic's idea from a few years earlier (see Game 17.1 above). In comparison with the Ljubojevic-Andersson game, Black has the extra moves ...b7-b5 and ...♖ab8, while White has a2-a3 and ♔h1. These inclusions favour White, most obviously because his king is no longer exposed to checks and pins down the a7-g1 diagonal, while Black's rook on b8 is vulnerable to a skewer behind the queen.

The alternative was to copy Ljubojevic with 16 ♗f4 ♗d6 17 ♖ad1,

and at first sight this looks promising. Black cannot respond with ...♛b8, as that square is occupied by the rook, while 17...♖fe8? loses material after 18 ♘c6! ♗xc6 (or 18...♘g6 19 ♖xc6! ♛xc6 20 ♗xb8) 19 ♖xd6 ♛xd6 20 ♗xe5, followed by ♗xf6 or ♗xb8.

However, 17...♖bd8 remains sound, despite the loss of time in having stopped at b8 on the way from a8, and 18 ♘b3 ♘d5 19 ♘xd5 exd5 20 ♖xd5 f6, or 18 ♘dxb5!? ♗xb5 19 ♖xd6 ♗xe2! 20 ♖xdf8 ♛xd8 21 ♘xe2 ♘g6, or 18 ♘xe6!? fxe6 19 ♖xd6 ♘h5! 20 ♗xh5 ♛xd6 21 ♖d1 ♖xf4! 22 ♛xf4 ♛xd1+! 23 ♘xd1 ♖f8 are all more or less OK for Black

Furthermore, the insertion of ...b7-b5 offers Black two additional defences: 17...♘c4!? 18 ♘xe6 (or 18 ♗xd6 ♛xd6!, now possible because the knight on c4 is defended) 18...fxe6 (not 18...♗xe6? 19 ♖xd6!) 19 ♗xd6 ♘xd6 20 ♛xd6 ♛xd6 21 ♖xd6 ♗c8. Or 17...b4!? 18 axb4 (not 18 ♘xe6? fxe6 19 ♖xd6 ♛xd6 20 ♗xe5 ♘h5! and wins) 18...♖xb4 19 ♘b3 ♔h8! 20 ♖xd6 ♖xf4 21

♛xf4 ♛xd6, and the best White can do is to regain his sacrificed pawn.

We can regard it as certain that Kasparov was familiar with Ljubojevic-Andersson, and 99% sure that Kasparov had analysed it at home, and probably the Hartston-Karpov game as well. We can be reasonably confident, then, that Kasparov will have appreciated the defensive resources after 16 ♗f4, and that it offered White little chance of more than a draw. It is quite likely Korsunsky was aware of this too, but if so, he failed to recognize the important differences, which Kasparov was now able to exploit.

16...♗xf6 17 ♗f4

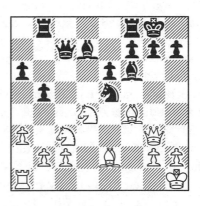

At first, Kasparov's sacrifice might seem less than impressive, Black being the exchange up, with his minor pieces well centralized. When one takes a second look, Black's pieces on the dark squares are under extreme pressure. White threatens to win the pinned knight after ♘d4-f3, and also to attack the bishop with ♘c3-e4, while Black's queen and rook are uncomfortably lined up on the h2-b8 diagonal.

17...♛b6?!

Black takes the least resistance option. Instead, 17...b4 18 ♞e4 ♚h8 would force White to find some good moves, but he seems to come out on top after 19 ♞xf6! gxf6 20 ♞f3!,

and if 20...♖g8 21 ♞xe5! ♖xg3 22 ♞xf7+ ♚g8 23 ♗xc7 leaves the two rooks forked, and White emerges a piece ahead.

So Black has to try 20...♛d8, when the immediate 21 ♞xe5? fxe5 22 ♗xe5+ f6 23 ♗xb8 ♛xb8 24 ♛xb8 ♖xb8 25 ♗xa6 bxa3 26 bxa3 ♖b2 offers him reasonable counterplay. However, White can strengthen his hand by playing 21 ♖d1! first, and if 21...♖b7, trying to hang on to everything, then 22 ♞xe5 fxe5 23 ♛f3!, with threats of ♛xb7, ♗xe5+ and ♗h6, leaves him clearly better. For example 23...♛b8 24 ♗h6 f5 25 ♗xf8 e4 26 ♛e3 ♛xf8 27 ♗xa6 ♖c7 28 ♛d4+ ♚g8 29 axb4 sees White finally a pawn up.

Black might therefore prefer to return the material, and try to survive in a worse position after 21...♞c6 22 ♗xb8 ♞xb8 23 axb4. Unfortunately, White

has no need to cash in so soon, and can continue his attack with 22 ♗c7! ♛c8 23 ♛f4 ♚g7 24 ♗d3 (threatening 25 ♛g4+ ♚h8 26 ♛h4) 24...♖g8 (not 24...f5? 25 ♛g5+ ♚h8 26 ♛f6+ ♚g8 27 ♞g5, followed by ♛h6 and mates) 25 ♖f1! (threatening ♞e5 and ♛xf6+) 25...f5 26 ♞e5 ♛xc7 27 ♛g3+, and a discovery with a knight check wins the black queen.

Ultimately, this variation turns out to be good, perhaps just winning, for White, but at least it is fairly complicated. Whereas after the move played, Kasparov will have two knights for a rook and pawn, and he gradually takes over, seemingly without undue exertion. We give the rest of the game without analysis.

18 ♗xe5 ♗xe5 19 ♛xe5

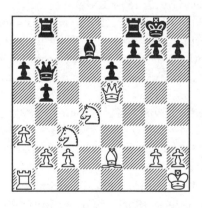

There is some interesting play subsequently, an endgame duel with a rook and two knights facing two rooks and an extra pawn, but really the main battle has come and gone.

19...b4 20 axb4 f6 21 ♛c5 ♛xb4 22 ♛xb4 ♖xb4 23 ♞b3 ♗b5 24 ♚g1 ♗e2 25 ♞xe2 ♖c8 26 ♞c3 ♖c6 27 ♚f2 ♚f7

28 ♖a2 g5 29 ♘c1 ♖f4+ 30 ♔e2 ♖g4 31 g3 h5 32 ♘d3 ♖gc4 33 ♔e3 h4 34 ♘e4 hxg3 35 hxg3 ♖b6 36 c3 ♖c8 37 ♘dc5 f5 38 ♘xg5+ ♔g6 39 ♘d7 ♖xb2 40 ♖xb2 ♖xc3+ 41 ♔d4 ♖xg3 42 ♘xe6 f4 43 ♘xf4+ ♔f5 44 ♘d3 a5 45 ♖b5+ ♔e6 46 ♘7c5+ ♔f7 47 ♖b7+ ♔g8 48 ♘e6 a4 49 ♘df4 a3 50 ♖a7 a2 51 ♖xa2 ♖g1 52 ♔e5 1-0

And just to show that the sacrifice with e4-e5 in the Sicilian is not confined to a select few, the final example before we get to the main games sees Kasparov himself on the losing side. There is a distinct impression here that, in his early years, Kasparov's defence was not as confident as his attack.

Game 17.3
Y.Razuvaev-G.Kasparov
USSR Championship,
Tbilisi 1978
Sicilian Defence

---

1 e4 c5 2 ♘f3 d6 3 d4 cxd4 4 ♘xd4 ♘f6 5 ♘c3 a6 6 a4 ♘c6 7 ♗e2 e6 8 0-0 ♗e7 9 ♗e3 0-0 10 f4 ♕c7 11 ♔h1 ♖e8 12 ♗f3 ♖b8 13 ♗f2 ♗f8 14 ♖e1 ♘d7 15 ♕e2 ♘xd4 16 ♗xd4 b6 17 e5

No in-depth theoretical analysis here. We quickly jump to the main point.

In contrast to the other examples, White has built up relatively leisurely, meaning that e4-e5 has involved no tactical risk. More specifically, with his rook on e1 and queen on e2, White's isolated e-pawn is safe, and that pawn

helps his attack.

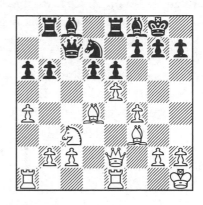

17...dxe5?!

17...d5 is still about equal.

18 fxe5 ♗b4

This looks slightly unnatural, as the pin on the knight doesn't hold and Kasparov's planned defence fails. However, 18...♗c5 19 ♖ad1 is not fully satisfactory either, since the exchange of bishops would leave a weakness on d6.

19 ♖ad1 ♘f8 20 ♖f1

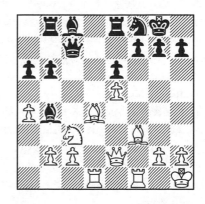

20...♘g6

Black could capture the white knight before it moves away, but after 20...♗xc3 21 ♗xc3 ♗b7 (not 21...♘g6?!

22 ♗b4!) 22 ♗h5! ♘g6 23 ♗xg6 fxg6 (if 23...hxg6 24 ♖d4!) 24 ♗b4, the bishop will be untouchable on d6, allowing White to attack at leisure.

21 ♘e4!

White is already doing quite well, but sacrificing the e5-pawn helps him to accelerate his attack. If Black does not accept, then White will have the chance of playing either ♘d6 or ♘g5, and still keep his pawn.

21...♘xe5 22 ♗h5!

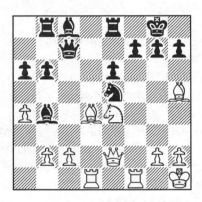

A pin-prick, but a nasty one. Strangely, this ♗h5 idea cropped up in an earlier round, with Kasparov playing White against Polugaevsky (see Game 17 below).

22...♘g6

The alternative, 22...♖f8 23 ♘g5 f6, looks attractive at first, White having only a minimal edge in the endgame after 24 ♗xe5 ♕xe5 25 ♕xe5 fxe5 26 ♗f7+ ♔h8 27 ♗xe6 ♖xf1+ 28 ♖xf1 ♗xe6 29 ♘xe6 ♔g8.

However, White can improve with 24 ♕e4!, and if 24...♘g6 25 ♘xh7! f5 26 ♕e3 (or even 26 ♘xf8!? fxe4 27 ♘xg6, threatening ♗e5) 26...♔xh7 27 ♗xg6+

♔xg6 28 ♗e5 ♕b7 29 ♕g3+ ♔f7 30 ♗xb8 recovers all the material and more, so that White is now the exchange up. 24...g6 is no better, as 25 ♖xf6! ♖xf6 26 ♗xe5 ♕e7 27 ♗xf6! ♕xf6 28 ♕xb4 sees Black defenceless after 28...gxh5 29 ♘e4 ♕f8 30 ♕c3, or 28...♕xg5 29 ♗f3, threatening ♕d6.

23 ♘g5

When attacking the king, throw all your pieces into the fray! And be prepared to sacrifice in order to force him into the open.

23...e5

Kasparov chooses a slow and painful defeat. As so often, the big sacrifices get hidden in the notes, the defending player foreseeing the sacrifices, and trying to avoid them.

If instead 23...f6, then 24 ♘xh7! ♔xh7 25 ♗xg6+ ♔xg6 26 ♕g4+ ♔f7 27 ♕h5+,

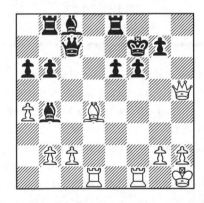

and White breaks through with a second sacrifice after 27...♔f8 28 ♕h8+ ♔f7 29 ♖xf6+! gxf6 30 ♕xf6+ ♔g8 31 ♕h8+ ♔f7 32 ♕g7 mate, or 27...♔e7 28 ♗xf6+! gxf6 29 ♕h7+ and mates, or finally 27...♔g8 28 ♕xe8+ ♗f8 29 ♗xf6!

gxf6 30 ♖xf6 ♕e7 31 ♕g6+ ♗g7 32 ♖df1 (threatening ♖f7) 32...♖b7 33 ♖6f3! (threatening ♖h3) 33...e5 34 ♖f8+! ♕xf8 35 ♖xf8+ ♔xf8 36 ♕c6! with an easy win.

One of the reasons why you should use as many pieces as possible in an attack on the king is that you will probably need to sacrifice some of them to force a way in.

24 ♗xg6! hxg6

This looks strange. Surely he doesn't want to give away the f-pawn for nothing? Then we notice another sacrifice, and a chance to give away the queen: 24...fxg6 25 ♗xe5!,

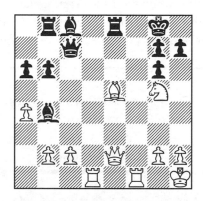

and if 25...♖xe5 26 ♕c4+!.

Black can survive a little longer with 25...♗b7, but 26 ♕d3 ♖xe5 27 ♕b3+ ♗d5 28 ♖xd5 ♕xd5 29 ♕xd5+ ♔h8 30 ♘f7+ ♔g8 31 ♘d8+ ♔h8 32 ♖f8+! ♗xf8 33 ♘f7+ ♕xf7 (otherwise 33...♔g8 34 ♘h6+ ♔h8 35 ♕g8 mate) 34 ♕xf7 gives White a straightforward win in the endgame. Alternatively, he could just play 31 c3 ♗c5 32 b4, winning the bishop, since if Black moves it away, he gets mated by 32...♗e7 33 ♘h6+ ♔h8 34 ♕g8+ or 32...♗e3 33

♘d8+.

25 ♖xf7 ♕c6 26 ♗xe5

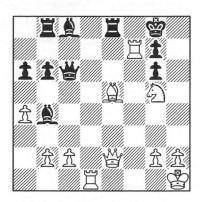

The rest is not too difficult. There are no more sacrifices that need to be considered.

26...♖b7 27 ♕f2 ♗g4 28 ♖xb7 ♕xb7 29 ♕h4 ♗h5 30 ♕c4+ ♔h8 31 ♖f1 ♗c5 32 b4 ♗f8 33 ♖f7 ♕c8 34 ♕f4 a5 35 h4 1-0

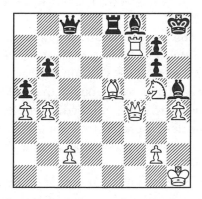

Black has no defence to 36 ♖xg7! ♗xg7 37 ♗xg7+ ♔xg7 38 ♕f7+ ♔h8 39 ♕h7 mate.

As the old chestnut goes, this is a wonderful attack, and from Kasparov's praxis. But most people would naturally assume that Kasparov would have been the winner, not the loser.

Now we return to the main games. I had considered dropping the first one for a much fresher Kasparov example. Looking through my books at home, I have this game annotated by Timman, Speelman and Stohl, and of course Kasparov himself, and no doubt others have gone through it too, so there is a sense that, fresh though it was at the time, less familiar games might be even fresher.

Kasparov, then aged 15, took on Polugaevsky in an almost absurdly sharp battle, and beat him. To beat Polugaevsky, you have to be a strong player indeed; but it was not just that Kasparov won, he went straight for the jugular, in a way not seen since Tal was a teenager. And Tal became world champion when he was in the early 20s; was this record about to be broken?

The main reason I thought about omitting this game was that I felt Kasparov's sacrifice was almost certainly flawed, and that I ought therefore to consider a more polished example. As a student, I played through this game, written up by Robert Bellin in a short-lived magazine, and was awed that Kasparov could win this, but then I quickly noticed that, at a critical point, the attack was quite simply unsound. Or, as one of the lecturers used to say, "Interesting, but is it correct?"

However, as I went through more and more games, to see which I might include in this book, it became clear that most of them were, shall we say, "interesting". There is no doubt now in my mind that if you want to play attacking chess, you will need to go beyond the bounds of what is positionally reasonable. If your opponent plays a dozen or so perfect moves, you will lose, but what is the likelihood that your opponent will play to perfection?

With Kasparov, attacking chess is now back in fashion, and sacrificial play is, if not exactly normal, at least no longer the exception. All the games in this section are based on pawn sacrifices in the centre, in effect gambit play. Kasparov, of course, had many dozens of wins with less spectacular plans, but when a theme has been isolated, it seems appropriate to examine it more thoroughly.

Game 17
G.Kasparov-L.Polugaevsky
USSR Championship,
Tbilisi 1978
Sicilian Defence

---

1 e4 c5 2 ♘f3 e6 3 d4 cxd4 4 ♘xd4 a6 5 ♘c3 ♛c7

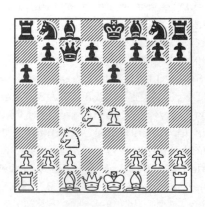

6 ♗e2

A cautious start so far, perhaps understandably. Polugaevsky was a great player, and a great theorist, and in terms of the Sicilian he could be seen as knowing everything and understanding everything. He was, after all, the instigator of one of the sharpest lines in the Sicilian, 1 e4 c5 2 ♘f3 d6 3 d4 cxd4 4 ♘xd4 ♘f6 5 ♘c3 a6 6 ♗g5 e6 7 f4 b5 8 e5 dxe5 9 fxe5 ♕c7, the renowned Polugaevsky Variation. It is extremely complicated, and Polugaevsky tested it against the strongest available opposition. He also wrote about it in depth in his 1981 book, *Grandmaster Preparation*.

Even Kasparov in his mid-teens could feel anxious, and he played a slightly passive line. The bishop deployment to e2 in the Scheveningen, with an early ...e7-e6 and ...d7-d6, is standard and very much main line, but Polugaevsky has held back ...d7-d6 in favour of a set-up enabling a quick ...b7-b5-b4 and pressure on the white e-pawn. Basically, he wanted to test his young opponent's preparation.

If White wants to develop the bishop quickly, he needs to provide extra cover for the e4-square. 6 g3, followed by ♗g2, is sensible, when the bishop is not obstructing White's f-pawn. 6 ♗d3 is also possible, though in that case White might have played it a move earlier, that is 5 ♗d3, rather than 5 ♘c3. He would then have more flexibility, in particular the possibility of seizing space against a Hedgehog with c2-c4.

6...b5 7 ♗f3

This is immediately a concession, although Kasparov soon bounces back.

White's opening was later refined to 7 0-0 ♗b7 8 ♖e1,

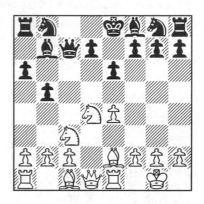

when 8...b4 can be met by 9 ♘d5!? exd5 10 exd5 with a dangerous initiative for the piece. If Black plays as in the game, 8...♘c6 9 ♘xc6 dxc6, then 10 e5! is no longer risky, as 10...♕xe5?! 11 ♗xb5 regains the pawn immediately, while 11 ♗h5 may be even stronger, effectively gaining a tempo. Black has therefore preferred 10...♖d8, 10...♗b4 or 10...♘e7, each of which leads to interesting play, but that is beyond the scope of this book.

7...♗b7 8 0-0 ♘c6 9 ♘xc6 dxc6

On 9...♗xc6, the familiar knight sacrifice 10 ♘d5!? is well worth considering, the point being that if 10...exd5 11 exd5 ♗b7, White regains the piece after 12 ♖e1+ ♔d8 13 d6! ♗xd6 14 ♗xb7 ♗xh2+ 15 ♔h1 ♕xb7 16 ♔xh2, and has good play for the pawn..

Black does not have to accept the piece, but there is a suspicion, especially if the queen retreats, that White is slightly better, whereas Black would prefer to have claimed that he is already equal.

In D.Barua-K.Bischoff, Calcutta 1997, Black opted for 10...♗xd5 11 exd5 ♖c8 12 c3 ♘f6, which should be about equal, though White's bishop pair will perhaps have an easier time. Barua eventually won the game, just after the time control.

10 ♖e1 is in fact the more common move, maybe with ♘d5 to follow later.

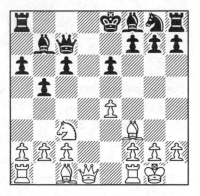

10 e5!?

This move made Kasparov famous. Or, more accurately, he showed that he could win with this move against Polugaevsky.

Kasparov is giving away a central pawn for almost nothing. The pawn is just an obstruction, he wants to get rid of it, he wants the e-file, he wants the long diagonal, and he can make use of the e4-square with the knight. All this adds up to freedom for the pieces, but is it enough? White has no realistic chances of any mating threats, if Black plays reasonably sensibly, but he is gaining time, and Black still has to develop his pieces. The outlook is that

White should have fair prospects of regaining the pawn, so long as he plays actively, but even this would only be restoring the material balance.

So this isn't a wild attempt to play for a mating attack. Kasparov is sacrificing a pawn just to keep the positional balance. He loses a pawn, but gains other advantages, and is hoping he will at least be able to maintain some sort of parity, and, if all goes well, has chances of playing for more.

It is important to recognize that White's position was starting to go wrong, and that if he just plays normal, natural chess, he would be in danger of standing worse. Black may play ...e6-e5 himself, or else 10...♗d6, and then develop his kingside pieces without trouble. An earlier game of Polugaevsky's had seen 10 a4 ♗d6 11 axb5 cxb5 12 e5 ♗xe5 13 ♘xb5 axb5 14 ♖xa8+ ♗xa8 15 ♗xa8 ♗xh2+ 16 ♔h1 ♗d6 17 ♕d3 b4 18 ♖d1 ♔e7 19 ♗e3 ♘f6 20 ♖a1 ♗c5 21 ♕c4 ♖c8 and Black consolidated in Y.Estrin-L.Polugaevsky, Moscow 1964.

10...♕xe5 11 ♖e1 ♕c7

A few players have been interested in trying out Kasparov's sacrifice, but really this should probably have been a one-off attempt to escape from a sticky opening. Some theory has developed, and it is not surprising that 11...♕d6 turns out to be one of the safest moves, offering the exchange of queens. We include a supplementary game, Arzumanian-Moroz, where Black demonstrated a comfortable equality, and went on to win, although White played seriously anti-positionally later on.

12 ♗h5

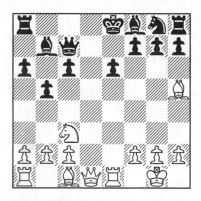

Only a gentle pin-prick this time, but White would still like to regain the pawn.

12...♗e7

A natural developing move, returning the material to try and complete development quickly. Stohl gives other lines with similar ideas, White being either equal or better, but suggests that Polugaevsky's move offers Black the best chance of playing for an edge.

Stohl's main alternative is 12...♘f6 13 ♖xe6+ ♗e7, which transposes to 12...♗e7 13 ♖xe6 ♘f6, and we will examine it there.

What is interesting and noteworthy is that neither Stohl, nor other annotators, examine 12...♗c8!?. This would be the late 19th century Steinitzian approach to defence: grab a pawn if you can, keep everything, including and especially the pawns, well-guarded, and aim slowly to consolidate. These days, players are much more aware of active defence, and are fully capable of finding good counterplay.

If White tries 13 ♕g4, the simplest

approach, perhaps, is to force the opponent's attack with 13...♘f6!? 14 ♖xe6+ ♗xe6 15 ♕xe6+ ♔d8 16 ♗xf7 ♕e7 17 ♗g5 ♕xe6 18 ♗xe6 ♗b4, when Black remains the exchange for a pawn up.

13 ♕f3 allows a possible drawing option after 13...♘f6 14 ♗f4 ♕b6 15 ♗e3 ♕c7 16 ♗f4. I leave it to the readers to decide whether either player could try for more after 14...♕b6. Instead, 14...♕b7 is possible, but leaves the queen possibly slightly misplaced. An entertaining tactical disaster follows 15 ♖ad1 c5?? 16 ♖xe6+!, winning. There are other moves for Black, such as 15...♗e7, with White having compensation for the pawn, but probably not more than that.

The interesting point to 12...♗c8!? is not so much the variation itself, but rather that the commentators do not consider it.

Another possibility, uncovered by *Fritz*, is 12...♘e7!?. If then 13 ♕f3 ♘g6 14 ♕h3 ♗c8! 15 ♗xg6 fxg6, and Black is comfortable. The critical line is 13 ♖xe6 g6 14 ♘e4!, and seems to lead to a draw.

14...fxe6 15 ♘d6+ ♔d8 16 ♘f7+ ♔e8 17 ♘d6+ is an immediate perpetual check. If White tries for more with 16 ♘xb7+?! ♔c8 17 ♘d6+ ♔b8 18 ♘e8 ♕e5 19 ♗e3, Black comes out better after, for example, 19...♘d5 20 ♗d4 ♕xh5 21 ♕xh5 gxh5 22 ♗xh8 ♔b7 23 ♘f6 ♗c5 24 ♗g7 ♘xf6 25 ♗xf6 ♖f8 26 ♗h4 ♖f4 27 ♗g3 ♖b4 28 b3 h4 29 ♗e5 ♖e4, followed by ...♖e2.

If 14...♗g7 15 ♗h6 ♗xh6 16 ♘f6+ ♔f8 17 ♘d7+ is another perpetual, but in this line White is more justified in having greater ambition. 15 ♘d6+ ♔f8 16 ♕f3 ♘c5 17 ♘xf5 fxe6 18 ♗f4 forces Black to find some good moves to survive. If *Fritz* is to be believed, best play might run 18...e5! 19 ♗g5 e4 20 ♕a3+ c5! 21 ♘xg7 ♔xg7 22 ♕c3+ ♔g8 23 ♗g4 h5! 24 ♗e6+ ♔h7 25 ♖d1 ♗c8 26 ♗d5 ♗b7 27 ♗e6 ♗c8 with a draw by repetition

Having said all that, Polugaevsky's move is not so bad either.

13 ♖xe6

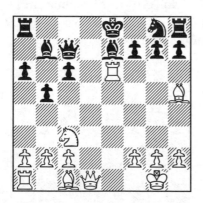

13...g6

So White sacrifices a pawn, then Black returns it, and both players hope

for the best in the tactics.

The alternative, 13...♘f6, is given by Timman as "about balanced" after 14 ♗g5 0-0 15 ♖e1 ♖fe8 16 ♗f3 ♖ad8 17 ♕c1.

He further notes that Kasparov's suggestion, 14 ♘e4 ♘xh5 15 ♕xh5 0-0 16 ♗f4, narrowly scrapes through to equality, as Black responds with 16...♕d7!, when 17 ♖e5 f6 18 ♖d1 ♕e8 19 ♘d6! ♕xh5 20 ♖xh5 reaches a level position. But not 17...♖af8? 18 ♖e1 ♗b4? 19 ♘f6+! gxf6 20 ♖g5+!, and Black had to resign in Gild.Garcia-A.Zapata, Medellin 1992, since if 20...fxg5 (or 20...♔h8 21 ♕h6) 21 ♕xg5+ ♔h8 22 ♕f6+ ♔g8 23 ♗e5 mates.

White can also try 17 ♘g5!?, with the idea that 17...h6?? 18 ♖d1! ♕e8 19 ♖xh6! wins after 19...gxh6 20 ♕xh6 ♗xg5 21 ♕xg5+ ♔h7, and then 22 ♕h4+ ♔g8 23 ♕g3+! ♔h7 24 ♗e5 f6 25 ♖d4. But the simple 17...♗xg5 18 ♖d6 ♕f5 19 ♕xg5 ♕xg5 20 ♗xg5 is just equal.

14 ♖e1

14 ♕d4? fxe6 15 ♕xh8 0-0-0 is winning for Black, who threatens 16...gxh5, as well as 16...♗f6, trapping the queen.

14...罝d8!?

This game is baffling even now, with the aid of computer technology; it was even more baffling in the 1970s and early 1980s. Many improvements, or attempted improvements, have been found in the next stage of the middle-game, but they all seem to end up as equal, or thereabouts, after complicated play. In effect, there may have been more ways for Black to equalize than previously suspected.

It turns out that the move played by Polugaevsky here, long regarded as a mistake, seems quite reasonable, and in practical terms is much simpler that the commonly accepted refutation with 14...gxh5.

White now has to play carefully. His initiative runs out after either 15 ♘e4?! 罝d8 16 豐xh5 c5!, or 15 ♗g5?! c5!. So he must make threats. After 15 豐d4 f6, it is difficult at first to believe that White can make progress.

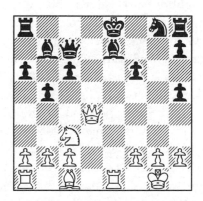

a) 16 ♘e4? 罝d8 17 ♘xf6+? fails to 17...♔f7! 18 ♘d5 cxd5 19 ♗f4 豐d7 20 豐xh8 ♘f6, trapping the queen.

b) 16 ♗f4? c5! leaves Black a piece

up. For instance, 17 豐e3 豐c6 18 豐h3 ♔f8! 19 罝e6 (or 19 罝ad1 罝d8) 19...豐e8 20 罝ae1 (or 20 罝b6 ♗c8) 20...♗c8 21 ♘d5 豐f7 22 豐f3 ♗xe6 23 ♘c7 ♗d5! 24 ♘xd5 罝c8, and Black is consolidating.

c) 16 豐c5? or 16 豐h4? both threaten 豐xh5+, but 16...0-0-0! is legal, and wins easily.

d) This leaves 16 豐d1!,

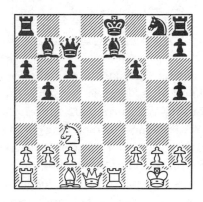

the same idea, but here Black is prevented from castling, as the king would pass through check. In his analysis Kasparov admitted that, although this was the best move, he would still have been worse. Timman carried the analysis on with 16...b4 17 豐xh5+ ♔f8, giving two possibilities:

d1) 18 ♘e4, and now rather than 18...豐e5? 19 ♗h6+ ♘xh6 20 豐xh6+ ♔f7, which after 21 罝ad1 (not yet 21 h4?! 罝ag8 22 ♘g5+ 罝xg5!) 21...罝ad8 (or 21...罝ag8 22 ♘g3 or 21...♗c8 22 罝d3!) 22 罝xd8 ♗xd8 23 h4! remains extremely unclear, Black should play 18...罝d8!, followed by ...♗c8, or if 19 ♗h6+ ♘xh6 20 豐xh6+ ♔f7 21 豐h5+ ♔g7 22 罝e3 罝d5 and the danger has passed.

d2) 18 ♗h6+ ♘xh6 19 ♕xh6+,

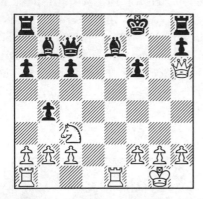

when Timman originally commented that there is no safe way of avoiding the perpetual, with 19...♔f7 20 ♕h5+ being a draw if Black wants it. In a later edition, however, he changed his mind; and Stohl, too, regards White's compensation as "nebulous". Which assessment is the more convincing?

Let us say that Black can accept a draw as a minimum. The question is whether he can win. On this basis 20...♔g8 is not the most promising option, due to 21 ♖e3! bxc3 22 ♖g3+ ♔f8 23 ♕h6+ ♔e8 24 ♖d1 ♖f8 25 ♕xh7 with perpetual check to follow. Other ideas, such as 22...♕xg3 23 hxg3 cxb2 24 ♖e1 ♔f8 25 ♕h6+, or 21...♗d6 22 ♘e4 ♗e5 23 ♖d1 ♖d8 24 ♘xf6+ ♗xf6 25 ♖xd8+ ♕xd8 26 ♖e8+ ♔g7 27 ♕g4+, seem to draw as well.

Instead, 20...♔g7! is better, as if 21 ♕g4+ ♔f8, and the queen has no check, while 21 ♘e4 ♖hg8 allows the king to hide in the corner. So White must try 21 ♖e3! again, when 21...♗d6?! 22 ♘e4 ♗e5 23 ♘xf6! ♗xf6 24 ♖g3+ ♔f8 25

♕h6+ ♔f7 26 ♕h5+ ♔e7 27 ♖d1 leads to another draw, after 27...♖ad8 28 ♖e1+ or 27...c5 28 ♕f5 or 27...♗c8 28 ♕c5+. However, 21...bxc3 22 ♖g3+ ♕xg3! 23 hxg3 cxb2 is stronger now, as with the king on g7 defending the h7-pawn, 24 ♖e1?! is met simply by 24...♖he8, while if 24 ♕g4+ ♔f8 25 ♖b1 ♖d8 26 ♖xb2 ♗c8, and the rooks and bishops can snuggle round as required.

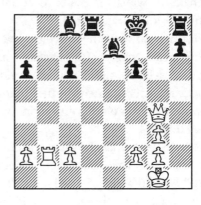

Black is certainly for preference here, though winning would not be straightforward, given his wrecked pawn structure and exposed king.

Going back, Black might also consider 19...♔g8!?. Then the rook lift to the g-file is thwarted by 20 ♖e4 ♗c8! or 20 ♖e3 ♗f8!, as if 21 ♖g3+? ♕xg3! wins. But the inferior position of the black king gives White time for 20 ♘e4!, and if 20...♕e5? 21 ♖ad1 ♖d8 22 ♖xd8+ ♗xd8 23 ♖e3 ♔f7 24 h4!, followed by ♘g5+ wins. Black has nothing better than the tempo-losing 20...♔f7, with an unclear position. For example, 21 ♕h5+ ♔g7 22 ♖e3 ♖hg8 23 ♖h3 ♕e5 24 ♕xh7+ ♔f8, or 21 ♖ad1!? ♖ag8 22 ♕h5+ ♖g6 23 f4 ♗c8 24 f5 ♔g7 25 fxg6 hxg6

26 ♕f3 ♕xh2+ 27 ♔f1. This seems inferior to the previous variation with 19...♔f7 20 ♕h5+ ♔g7!, where Black has the advantage.

But as we have already noted, the move played in the game is reasonable too, and Polugaevsky soon reaches an ending with two minor pieces for rook and pawn, which he should not really lose.

15 ♕f3 c5

In one of the earlier analyses of this game, Speelman (*Best Chess Games 1970-1980*) notes that 15...gxh5 is now bad, in view of 16 ♗f4 followed by 17 ♗e5. Timman made essentially the same point, while Kasparov and Shakarov do not mention the move. But now with computer assistance, and later ideas by Stohl, 15...gxh5!? 16 ♗f4 seems perfectly feasible for Black.

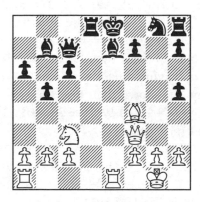

Stohl looks at 16...♕d7 17 ♗e5 f6!?, and 17 ♘e4 ♕g4 18 ♘d6+ ♖xd6, and decides that Black is doing well. He suggests instead 17 ♕xh5, cutting out any exchange with ...♕g4, while reinforcing the threat of ♗e5, which would win material. The obvious response for

Black is 17...c5 (but not 17...h6?, intending 18 ♗e5 ♖h7, as 18 ♖ad1! ♕c8 19 ♖xd8+ ♕xd8 20 ♗e5 ♖h7 21 ♕f5 just wins the rook) 18 ♗e5 ♕c6 19 f3 ♘f6 20 ♕h6 and then 20...♖g8? 21 ♗xf6 ♖xg2+, but as Stohl notes, 22 ♔h1! ♖e2 23 ♘e4! wins for White.

Stohl gives an improvement in 20...♔d7!

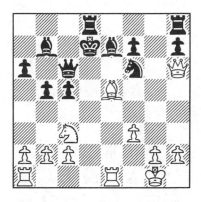

21 ♕h3+ ♔e8, suggesting that White can either repeat the position by 22 ♕h6, or try for more with the risky 22 ♘e4!? ♘xe4 23 ♗xh8, though in the latter, 23...♘g5 probably favours Black, for example after 24 ♕g3 ♕g6 25 ♖ad1 ♘e6, blocking the e-file.

However, White can improve too with 21 ♗g3!, threatening 22 ♖xe7+! ♔xe7 23 ♖e1+ ♔d7 24 ♕h3+ and wins. Or if 21...♖hg8 22 ♖ad1+ ♔e8 23 ♖xe7+! ♔xe7 24 ♕e3+ forces Black to return the piece by 24...♘e4. The critical move, according to *Fritz*, is 21...♘d5, but then White can surprisingly exchange queens by 22 ♕xc6+, since he regains the piece after 22...♔xc6 23 ♘xd5 ♖xd5 24 ♖xe7 or 22...♗xc6 23 ♖xd1 ♔e8 24 ♗h4, while remaining a pawn up.

Earlier, Black might refine Stohl's defence by playing 16...♕b6, the move Polugaevsky opts for in the game. Then after 17 ♕xh5 (or 17 ♗e5 c5 18 ♕xh5) 17...c5 18 ♗e5 ♘f6 19 ♕h6 ♔d7!, White looks to have nothing better than to take the draw with 20 ♕h3+ ♔e8 21 ♕h6. The slight difference in position (black queen on b6, white f-pawn on f2) makes 20 ♗g3?! ineffective after 20...♖hg8! 21 ♖ad1+ ♔e8, since if 22 ♖xe7+ ♔xe7 23 ♖e1+ (or 23 ♕e3+ ♔f8) 23...♔d7 24 ♕h3+ ♘g4! defends, or 22 ♕e3 ♕e6 23 ♖xd8+ ♔xd8 24 ♕d2+ ♕d7 25 ♕f4 ♕c6 consolidates.

16 ♗f4

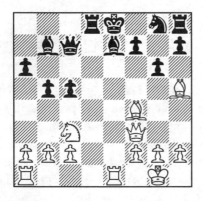

16...♕b6

On the simplifying 16...♗xf3? 17 ♗xc7 ♗xh5 18 ♗xd8 ♔xd8, Kasparov planned 19 f3! and the white forces will cause a lot of damage, while Black's are undeveloped and disorganized. For example, 19...g5 20 ♖ad1+ ♔e8 21 ♖d6 (Timman) or 19...f5 20 ♖ad1+ ♔c8 21 ♘d5 ♗h4 22 ♖e8+ ♔b7 23 ♘f4. There is a picturesque contrast between White's complete attacking development, and Black's total lack of development, in-

deed his negative development.

However, 16...♕d7!? was also playable. Indeed, if one has gone through the previous analysis, on 15...gxh5 16 ♗f4 ♕d7 17 ♕xh5, there is an obvious attraction here. If White responds with, say, 17 ♕e2?! gxh5 18 ♕xh5, Black has gained the move ...c6-c5. Or if 17 ♕g3 gxh5 18 ♕g7 ♕g4! 19 ♗e5 ♗xg2! 20 ♕xg4 hxg4 21 ♗xh8 ♗f3 and the light-squared bishop is well worth the second rook.

The best reply is 17 ♗g4 ♗xf3 18 ♗xd7+ ♔xd7 19 gxf3 ♔c6, with material equality as we approach the endgame. After 20 ♗e5 ♗f6 21 f4 ♗xe5 22 fxe5 f5 or 20 ♘e4 h5, Black will finally be able to develop his pieces. Maybe equal.

17 ♕g3 gxh5 18 ♗c7

Not 18 ♕g7? ♕g6 19 ♖xe7+, because of Kasparov's 19...♘xe7! 20 ♕xh8+ ♔d7 21 ♖d1+ ♗d5, and White must surrender the queen for not enough.

Nor 18 ♗e5? (hoping for 18...f6? 19 ♗c7!, having ruled out ...♕g6), when Timman shows that 18...♘f6! 19 ♗c7 (or 19 ♕f4 ♔d7!) 19...♕c6 20 ♗xd8 ♖g8! wins for Black.

18...♕g6

He has to exchange queens. White would win after 18...♕c6? 19 ♗xd8 ♔xd8 20 ♖ad1+ ♔f8 21 ♘d5, since there is no way to deal with the twin threats of ♖xe7 and ♕g7.

19 ♗xd8 ♕xg3 20 hxg3 ♔xd8 21 ♖ad1+ ♔c7 22 ♘d5+ ♗xd5 23 ♖xd5

The end of the long series of tactics and sacrifices, and then exchanges, and now we reach the positional phase. The rest of the game, however, shows that neither player is content to end up with a steady draw, both are eager to put the opponent under pressure. A strong player tends to have the psychology that "I'm not going to make a mistake, but my opponent will". One of them indeed overpressed, and it was not Kasparov.

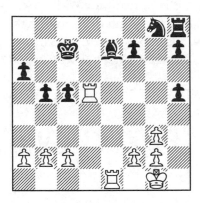

Polugaevsky still has to play actively here, as his pieces are undeveloped, and he needs to bring them into the game. The question is whether he should be happy with a draw, or whether he should try for more. If all Black's pieces are fully active, then the assumption is that, with two minor pieces against the rook, he will prevail. The trouble is that his minor pieces only become semi-active over the next few moves, which makes it difficult to establish precisely what is going on.

23...h6

He cannot move the bishop; he cannot move the knight; so somehow Black must bring the rook into play.

24 ℤxh5 ℤh7

Slow, but this is genuine progress.

He would like to exchange the rook with one of its white counterparts, though this is difficult to arrange.

25 ℤhe5 ♔d7 26 ℤ5e3 ℤg7

The escape continues. The next stage is either to try and trade rooks, or to find a way to develop the knight.

27 ℤd3+ ♔c7 28 ℤa3 ℤg6 29 ℤf3

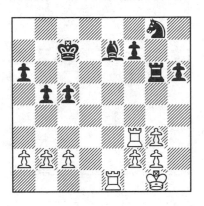

29...♗f6!?

Black is currently tied down by the repeated threats to a6, e7 and f7. The text shields the f-pawn, and in encouraging c2-c3, seeks to eliminate one avenue of attack, the third rank to a3. On the downside, the e-file is now open for the white rooks, but this was inevitable in any case if Black is ever to develop.

The alternative was to defend the f-pawn with 29...ℤg7. Kasparov notes a possible repetition with 30 ℤa3 ℤg6, but Black might prefer 30...♔b6, and follow with ...♗d6, or if 31 ℤd3 c4. Then a position arises similar to that after 32...♗e7 below, and a version favourable to Black if anything.

30 c3 ♔d7 31 ℤd3+ ♔c7 32 ℤe8

White could again try to repeat with

32 ♖f3, but here Black can respond with 32...♔g7, and if 33 ♖e8, return the bishop to e7, as with 32...♗e7 in the next note. Black could have played 30...♔g7 immediately, but presumably he wanted to gain a couple of moves towards the time control at move 40.

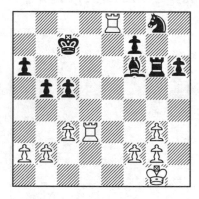

32...♘e7?

But this is still too hasty. The knight is well coordinated for defence on g8, and its first developing move proves to be a mistake.

Kasparov gives 32...♗e7 as an improvement, though his youthful assessment of a slight advantage for White looks optimistic. After ...♗d6, the bishop escapes to freedom, and will soon take an active part in the game. In other words, Black is no longer restricted to defending, he could now legitimately try for an edge.

Play might continue, in time-scramble mode, 33 ♖f3 (or 33 ♖a8 c4 34 ♖a7+ ♔b6 35 ♖dd7 ♖e6 36 b4 ♗d6 37 ♖db7+ ♔c6 38 ♖xf7 ♘f6 39 ♖xa6+ ♔d5, followed by ...♘e4) 33...♔g7 34 ♖e3 ♗d6 35 ♖a8 ♔b6 36 ♖d8 ♗c7, and if White is not careful, the two minor

pieces will start to work well together. For instance, 37 ♖f8 h5!? (37...♗d6 38 Rd9 ♗c7 is another possible draw) 38 ♖f3 ♘h6 39 ♖f6 ♖h7 40 ♖e8 ♘g4 41 ♖f5 f6, when 42 ♖xc5?! ♖d7 43 ♔f1 ♘e5 44 f4 ♗b6 45 ♖cc8 ♘c6 46 ♖f8 ♗d8 has landed White in trouble.

Stohl suggests that Black can just about hold the position after 32...♗e7, since it is difficult for White to invade, but it would seem that White is the one who has to play carefully to draw.

33 ♖ed8 ♘c6 34 ♖8d7+ ♔b6 35 ♖xf7

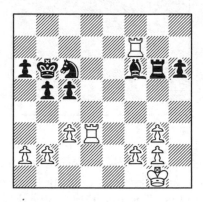

Black's pieces have been mobilized, but White now has two extra pawns.

35...♗e7 36 ♖e3 ♗d6 37 f4

A loosening of the g1-a7 diagonal, but preventing Black from using the e5-square is a gain. One problem is that there is now no obvious way for *White* to exchange a rook, as the minor pieces cover too many entry squares.

37...c4 38 ♔h2 ♗c5 39 ♖e2 b4 40 ♖e4 bxc3 41 bxc3 ♗f2 42 ♖xc4 ♗xg3+ 43 ♔h3 ♗e1

There is usually little point writing in detail about moves played in time pressure, unless they were blunders, which is not the case here. Black could well have avoided ...♗c5, or it might have been the correct move. Who knows? The players would have made moves by instinct, rather than close analysis.

Polugaevsky has kept his position active, and has caused some problems on the kingside. Nevertheless, the expectation is that he would not have enough to hold the game.

44 a4

To prevent ...♚b5.

44...♘a5 45 ♖b4+

45...♚c5??

It is worth reminding ourselves that this game, while highly intense, could have been a longer and even more gruelling battle, had Polugaevsky not blundered here. 45...♚c6! would have prolonged the battle, when it is not so easy for White to win.

In *Informator 26*, Kasparov and Shakarov give just 46 ♖f5 ♗xc3 47 ♖xa5, envisaging 47...♗b4 48 ♖xa6+ and a decisive skewer on the sixth rank. However, 46...♗xc3? is another blunder, and in fact 46 ♖f5? is too, as

Stohl shows by 46...♖g3+ 47 ♚h2 ♖xc3! 48 ♖xa5 ♗g3+ 49 ♚h3 ♗xe1+ 50 ♚g4 ♖g3+, with a draw after 51 ♚f4 ♗xb4 52 ♖xa6+ ♚d5 53 ♖xh6 ♖xg2.

So White has to improve, to which end Stohl offers 46 ♖b1 ♖g3+ 47 ♚h2 ♖e3,

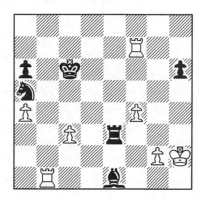

and now 48 g4!?, with the suggestion that White should gradually triumph.

This is a long game for the analyst as well as the players, so it is perhaps unsurprising that a few short cuts are occasionally taken in the endgame. After 48 g4, Black's natural response is 48...♘c4 49 ♖f6+ ♚f7, and if 50 ♖xh6 ♗g3+ 51 ♚g2 ♗xf4 52 ♖xa6 ♖g3+ 53 ♚f2 ♘e5, when his pieces are so well centralized that there is no problem of dealing with the pawns. So, draw. *Fritz* tries the exchange sacrifice 50 ♖xe1 ♖xe1 51 ♖xa6, ending up with several pawns for the knight, but White has little chance of promoting one of them. Play might continue 51...♖e2+ 52 ♚h3 ♖e3+ 53 ♚h4 ♖e4 64 ♖xh6 ♖xf4 55 ♚g5 ♖f3, followed by ...♖xc3, and again a draw is inevitable.

If White wants to play for a win, he must accept some positional risk by allowing his king to be stuck in the corner. As long as his defending rook is covering the back rank, he is not going to get checkmated. After 48 ♖f6+ ♔c7 49 f5!, we finally see a plan emerging, to push the f-pawn as far as it can go, with ♖f1 behind it as required. At the very least Black's forces will be tied down to preventing its advance, allowing White then to bring up his g-pawn. For example, 49...♗xc3 50 ♖xh6 ♘c6 51 f6 ♗e5+ 52 ♔h1 ♘d8 53 ♖f1 ♘e6 54 g4, or 49...♗g3+ 50 ♔h1 ♗d6 51 ♖xh6 ♘c5 51 f6 ♘d2 52 f7!, and if 52...♘xb1 53 ♖xd6 ♖e1+ 54 ♔h2 ♖f1 55 ♖d1! ♖xf7 56 ♖xb1 with a winning rook endgame.

46 ♖f5+ 1-0

A remarkable game, especially considering Kasparov's youth. Normally when an annotator examines a game in depth, more and more mistakes are found, the natural result of players having limited time to work everything out over the board. What is happening here is the reverse. The closer one analyses, the more one gains the impression that throughout the middlegame, Kasparov and Polugaevsky both played with great accuracy, making no mistakes. It was only when time pressure stepped in, when the queens had vanished and the players were negotiating their endgame possibilities, that the errors crept in.

Our final supplementary game, from the same opening, was not quite so well handled.

Supplementary game

Suppose Black snatches the pawn and offers an exchange of queens? This, after all, is classic defensive strategy.

Game 17.4
G.Arzumanian-A.Moroz
Marganets 1999
Sicilian Defence

1 e4 c5 2 ♘f3 e6 3 d4 cxd4 4 ♘xd4 a6 5 ♘c3 ♕c7 6 ♗e2 b5 7 0-0 ♗b7 8 ♗f3 ♘c6 9 ♘xc6 dxc6 10 e5 ♕xe5 11 ♖e1 ♕d6!?

Playing to exchange the queens, and why not? White can avoid it with 12 ♕e2, but then 12...♘f6 should be fine for Black.

12 ♗g5 ♕xd1 13 ♖axd1 ♗e7 14 ♗xe7 ♔xe7 15 ♘e4 ♘f6 16 ♘c5 ♖ab8

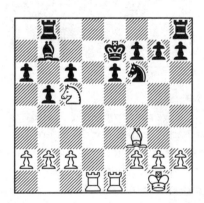

This is about as much as White can squeeze out of the position, and it is clear that at best he is only equal. White has strong enough pieces to regain the pawn, but this will involve exchanges, which only increases the likelihood of a draw. **17 c3 ♖hd8 18**

♖xd8 ♔xd8 19 ♘xb7 ♖xb7 20 ♗xc6, for example, is a level endgame.

But Arzumanian decides he wants to play for more, which is dangerous when the position is finely balanced. It is a case of "who dares, loses".

17 ♖e3

Still playable, but his subsequent plan is horrendously anti-positional.

17...♘d5 18 ♖a3?

The a-pawn is not worth chasing. If White wants to regain the pawn, he should take the one in the centre. 18 ♗xd5 cxd5 19 ♘xb7 ♖xb7 20 ♖xd5 is a drawn rook ending.

18...♗c8 19 ♘xa6 ♖a8 20 ♘c5 ♖xa3 21 bxa3

Not exactly the pawn structure White would have wanted, and it will get worse. Have a look at what happens with Black's king.

21...f5 22 ♗xd5?

Unnecessary and suicidal. The knight is not doing any damage to White, and he could have kept his options open. Maybe he had vague notions of a good knight vs bad bishop position, but for that he would need to

control the dark squares, whereas it is the black king who rules there. Put the a3-pawn on b4 and White might have a chance. As it is...

22...exd5 23 ♖e1+ ♔d6 24 ♘d3 ♗d7 25 ♘e5 ♖a8 26 ♘f7+ ♔c5 27 ♖e7 ♖e8 28 ♖xe8 ♗xe8 29 ♘g5 ♔c4 30 ♘f3 ♔c3 31 ♘e1 ♔b2 0-1

We can assume that Kasparov would have played it immeasurably better as White, but up to move 15 this could easily have been the continuation had Polugaevsky made a slight adjustment to his queen retreat, and the likelihood would have been a draw. Still an interesting game perhaps, but it would not have made the headlines.

The following year, in 1979, Kasparov was playing good attacking chess, if not quite the spectacular, and speculative, type of moves he ventured against Polugaevsky. It is as if Kasparov was consolidating, while still improving his game, coming first, for example, at Banja Luka 1979, two points ahead of Ulf Andersson and Jan Smejkal.

The games from Banja Luka are well worth studying, but it has to be said there are more exciting Kasparov encounters available. So I have included none between the win against Polugaevsky in 1978 and the win against Pribyl in 1980, and Stohl has left a similar gap in his collection.

Kasparov started off in 1980 by scoring heavily in the European Team Championship, at Skara, on the bottom board for the USSR. He racked up 5½/6, at the age of 16, against an average opposition of over 2450 Elo. This performance was at stratospheric levels, well over 2800, and suggested that maybe, just maybe, he could reach an all-time record if he could achieve this level on a consistent basis.

As we now know, he indeed gained the record, reaching 2800 in 1989, staying over 2800 for most of the time, and even going over 2850. This was phenomenal. Karpov was safely above 2700, but 2800 would have been regarded as more or less impossible, until Kasparov improved, so that his aspiring rivals had to play at a much higher level to try and keep up with him.

Going back to Skara, it was noticeable that Kasparov won games with vigorous but solid chess. He had continued to cut down his wild, if impressive, play from earlier years, but given the opportunity, he could attack and sacrifice along with the best. For the most part, however, he did not try to bamboozle his 2400+ opponents, he just wanted to play good games – and win.

The following game against Pribyl is far deeper than it appears at first, and I would regard it as the best of Kasparov's wins in this early selection. It has the standard Kasparov pawn sacrifice in the centre, and an attractively paradoxical further pawn sacrifice on the seventh rank, but there is so much more. In many ways the real high point is the manner in which, after considerable complications, the analysis suddenly ends up in a delicate king and pawn ending. This is examined further in the supplementary material at the end of the game.

Kasparov would not have seen any of this over the board, but it hardly matters. What is much more important is his sense of the initiative, the sense that once he has started the attack, maybe in conjunction with a pawn sacrifice, he would be able to carry it through to a satisfactory conclusion.

Game 18
G.Kasparov-J.Pribyl
European Team Championship,
Skara 1980
Grünfeld Defence

---

1 d4 ♞f6 2 c4 g6 3 ♞c3 d5 4 cxd5 ♞xd5 5 e4 ♞xc3 6 bxc3 ♝g7 7 ♞f3 b6

Unusual, but reasonable enough. 7...0-0 or 7...c5 are the standard moves. Kasparov notes that 7...b6 had not been played before, to the best of his knowledge. In fact, *ChessBase* gives one precedent up to that time, V.Vaisman-M.Ghinda, Bucharest 1978, which continued 8 ♗c4 0-0 9 0-0 ♗b7 10 e5 ♘c6 11 e6 f6 12 ♖e1, with White having a slight edge, though the game was later drawn.

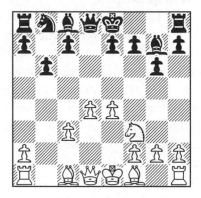

There was no particular reason why Kasparov would have known about this, but it demonstrates that he was playing off his own bat in this game, and not relying on detailed theoretical knowledge – as was quite likely Pribyl's intention, to take his young opponent out of the book.

8 ♗b5+

8 ♕a4+ ♗d7 9 ♕c4 is also worth considering, but people have remembered Kasparov's move, and have followed it.

8...c6

The tempo loss with ♗b5+ has been used by Kasparov in several lines of the Queen's Indian. We shall see later on an example against Najdorf at Bugojno 1982 (Game 21). Black's c-pawn is now in the way, blocking the long diagonal, and this will create a few small irritations. Quite often, as in Najdorf's game, Black will play ...c6-c5, to open the diagonal again, and put

pressure on White's centre, but then the tempo loss will have vanished.

More than a decade later, Pribyl tried 8...♗d7, although the bishop was then itself slightly in the way after 9 ♗e2 c5 10 ♖b1 ♘c6 11 0-0 0-0 12 d5 ♘a5 13 c4, again with a slight edge for White, later drawn in S.Chloupek-J.Pribyl, Mlada Boleslav 1993.

9 ♗c4 0-0 10 0-0

In his notes, Kasparov says that 10 ♕e2 "should possibly have been considered" to prevent ...♗a6 next move, but the bishop exchange is not that effective, so White has no real need to prevent it.

The queen does not necessarily belong on e2 in any case, and is more flexible staying on its opening square. For instance, after 10 ♕e2 b5 11 ♗b3 a5 12 0-0 b4!?, Black is beginning to put pressure on the centre, and the white queen may well be misplaced.

Kasparov's initial instincts, over the board, seem better.

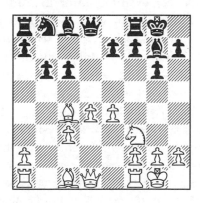

10...♗a6

Black is perhaps starting to feel uncomfortable about his position from the opening. After the exchange of the bishops, his knight is slightly out of play.

The problem is that it's unclear how Black should develop his pieces, or generate counterplay. Who knows, he might even have been worried about a snap attack against his king, Kasparov's reputation already being formidable. 10...♘d7 11 ♘g5!? h6 (or with 11...b5 12 ♗b3 inserted) 12 ♘h3 could easily lead to a direct attack with f4-f5. Comparisons might be made with Stein-Karpov (Game 8).

11 ♗xa6 ♘xa6 12 ♕a4!?

With commendable honesty, Kasparov criticizes, if only mildly, this move, arguing that 12 ♗g5 ♕d7 13 ♕d2 gives White a slight edge. It's a good story, centralization generally being preferable to putting the queen on the edge, but is it totally accurate?

With the benefit of technology, these days an amateur can easily find several possible equalizing tries for Black. For example, after 13...♖fd8 14 ♗h6 (and not 14 ♕f4? f6 15 ♗h6 g5), the calm 14...♗h8 would seem to be level. The black king might look slightly exposed, with a queen, knight and bishop threatening to attack, but White is unable to break in, while Black, in typical Grünfeld fashion, puts pressure on the white centre with the c-pawn and the major pieces. For instance, if 15 ♕f4 c5 16 ♕h4 cxd4 17 cxd4 ♖ac8 18 ♗g5 ♖e8 holds Black's position together.

Kasparov's plan in the game was more original and probably stronger. If

in this analysis we are critical of Kasparov's comments over the last few moves, our criticism is of his own criticisms of his own play, which in fact seems more accurate.

12...♕c8 13 ♗g5

If there is any slight criticism to be made of Kasparov's opening play, it is on this routine developing move. Instead, 13 ♖e1, covering the e-pawn, makes it more difficult for Black to generate counterplay. White can decide where the bishop should go at a later stage. In particular, it might prefer to go to f4.

13...♕b7 14 ♖fe1 e6

Kasparov notes 14...♖fe8!? as a possible alternative. Black might then consider rerouting the knight to c7 and e6, though White keeps a slight positional edge.

15 ♖ab1

An interesting moment. Kasparov would clearly feel that he has an advantage, but what can he do to develop it further?

An obvious response is to consolidate in the centre with 15 ♖ad1!?. After

15...c5 16 ♕b3 (if 16 d5 ♗xc3 17 ♖e2 ♗g7 18 dxe6 fxe6 19 ♖d7, Stohl notes 19...b5! "with approximate equality") 16...cxd4 17 cxd4 ♖ac8 18 d5 ♖c3 19 ♕b1 ♖fc8 20 d6 ♕d7 21 e5 ♘c5, visually White is doing well, with his protected passed pawn, but Black has succeeded in coordinating his pieces. Instead, 18 ♖e3 might be considered, when White undoubtedly is slightly better, with more space in the centre.

Kasparov was looking for more, and places Pribyl under tactical pressure. Yes, there were some opportunities for Black to draw later on, as we shall see, but only if he defends with great accuracy.

15...c5

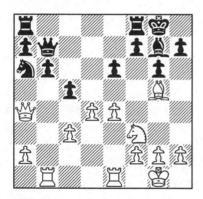

16 d5!

White can still continue quietly, in various possible ways. The assumption then would be that Black has to play reasonably accurately, but that the game would eventually end up as a draw. For the attacking player, quite happy to gambit, the preference is for the defender to have to play with *extreme* accuracy, to find a whole string

of correct moves, which is far more demanding, even if the rewards for managing to do so are potentially greater.

We have already considered pawn sacrifices with e4-e5 in the Sicilian. Sacrifices with d4-d5 have been relatively less common – unless the d-pawn is isolated – and Kasparov must be regarded as an innovator. See also his later victories against Najdorf and Gheorghiu (Games 21 and 22).

In the current game, Black will now have a three vs one pawn majority on the queenside, but it will be difficult to activate it. White in return has a massive advanced d-pawn.

16...♗xc3

He might as well take it. 16...f6 17 ♗f4 e5 keeps the bishop away from the passed d-pawn, but Black has no extra pawn, and no real counterplay.

17 ♖ed1

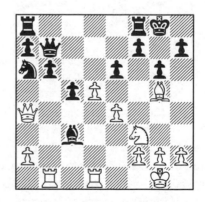

17...exd5

Black could also play 17...♗g7 at once, without the preliminary pawn exchange. Stohl gives 18 dxe6 fxe6 19 ♖d7 ♕c8 20 ♖bd1 c4 21 ♖d8 ♘c5 as being close to equality. After 22 ♕xc4 ♕b7 23 ♖xa8 ♖xa8, White can try to apply some pressure with 24 e5, but 24...♕e4! 25 ♕xe4 ♘xe4 is level. Stohl also notes 18 d6 f6 19 ♗e3 ♖ac8 20 ♕c4 ♘b8 21 ♕xe6+ ♕f7 as being unclear, and by implication equal.

Pribyl's response is not worse, only different

18 exd5 ♗g7

Retreating to safety. The alternative is to try and bring the knight into the game, but if it retreats, White can at worst play 19 ♕c4 ♗g7 20 ♕xc5, regaining the pawn with an edge. The exception is if the knight comes forward.

In *Informator 29*, Kasparov gave 18...♘b4

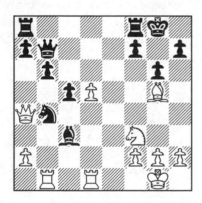

and then 19 a3 ♘xd5 20 ♕c4 as winning for White, but that's not so clear after 20...♗d4 21 ♘xd4 cxd4 22 ♖xd4 ♘e7. Although active pieces and Black's dark square weaknesses should give White enough play for the pawn, it is not clear that he has more.

Instead, the obvious continuation is 19 ♕b3 ♗g7 20 a3 ♘a6 21 d6, when

White has gained two moves on the game (♕b3 and a2-a3), and Black cannot respond with ...f7-f6, as the pawn is pinned. On the other hand, 21...♕d7 is now possible, and while the queen is not the best blockader, it cannot be easily dislodged as Black reorganizes his forces.

White might try to play around it with 22 ♕c4 ♘b8 23 ♗e7, and if 23...♖c8 24 ♘g5! ♕e8 25 ♕g4 ♘d7 26 ♘xf7! ♕xf7 (not 26...♔xf7?? 27 ♕c4 mate!) 27 ♕xd7 with a clear advantage. However, Black does better to give up the exchange by 23...♘c6! 24 ♗xf8 ♖xf8, and it is not clear how White can make progress, especially if he loses the d6-pawn.

Perhaps the best option is to continue as planned with 19 d6!, when the attempted exchange sacrifice with 19...♘c6? 20 d7 ♘d4 21 ♘xd4 ♗xd4, anticipating 22 d8♕ ♖axd8 23 ♗xd8 ♖xd8 with two strong pawns, fails to 22 ♖xd4! cxd4 23 ♕xd4, followed by ♗h6 and wins. Otherwise 19...♗g7 20 d7 f6 (or if 20...♖ad8 21 ♗xd8 ♖xd8 22 ♖d6) 21 ♕b3+ ♔h8 22 ♗f4 ♖ad8 23 ♕e6 offers White a powerful position for the pawn. No in-depth analysis here, and an attacking player would probably feel that it is good without studying it to the end. One possibility would be 23...♘a6 24 ♖b3 ♘c7 25 ♕d6 ♘a6 26 ♖e3 ♘b8 27 ♖e7, and White is slowly improving his position, whereas Black can do nothing much.

19 d6 f6

Not surprisingly, 19...h6?! 20 ♗e7 ♖fe8 leaves White in control. Black might be content after 21 d7?! ♖xe7 22 d8♕+ ♖xd8 23 ♖xd8+ ♗f8, with two pawns and a relatively solid position for the exchange. But White does not have to hurry, and 21 ♖fe1, followed shortly by d6-d7, is clearly better.

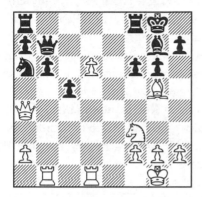

20 d7!

Demonstrating excellent attacking instincts. The bishop can go, because the passed pawn on the seventh provides ample compensation. White's queen, two rooks and knight are dangerous attackers. It is certainly not the case that the pawn on the seventh does it by itself.

At the time Kasparov suggested that 20 ♗f4 gives "undoubtedly (...) sufficient compensation for the pawn", but one senses that he did not believe this in his heart. 20...♘b4, followed by moves such as ...♘c6, ...♖ad8, ...♖f7, ...♕d7, sees Black coordinating his pieces, with a probable edge. If White pushes the d-pawn further, it is likely just to drop off, for example after 21 d7 ♖ad8 22 ♖d2 ♖f7 23 ♖bd1 b5 24 ♕b3 ♗f8 and 25...c4.

Kasparov himself notes at this point

that, "The piece sacrifice he offers might be considered debatable, but even now, after serious and calm analysis, it appears correct to me. And how much more difficult it must have been for Black to work things out over the board." Which is exactly the central point of my argument in this book – except perhaps that, in this precise position, refusing the sacrifice might well be debatable.

20...fxg5

Questioned by Stohl, but it is best to reserve judgement. Black has, in practical terms, an extremely difficult task to hold, though there are some improvements, both on this move, and later on.

In *The Test of Time*, Kasparov gives as one of his main lines 20...♖ad8 21 ♕c4+ ♔h8 22 ♘e5!! fxe5 23 ♗xd8 ♖xd8 24 ♕e6

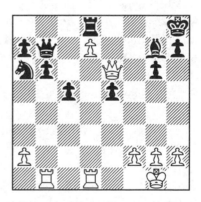

and then stops after 24...♘c7 25 ♕e7 ♕b8 26 ♖b3, with the clear implication that White will win. As is undoubtedly the case, for example 26...e4 (otherwise ♖f3-f7) 27 ♖d6 ♔g8 28 ♖h3 ♘b5 29 ♖e6 ♘c7 30 ♖c6! ♕xc6 31 ♕xd8+ ♗f8 (or 31...♔f7 32 ♕c8) 32 ♕xf8+ ♔xf8 33 d8♕+ ♘e8 34 ♖xh7 with a winning position. But 24 ♕e6 is the starting point of analysis, not the end point!

The line Kasparov gives, a knight retreat with 24...♘c7?!, is unnecessary, and wastes time. Instead, there are three queen moves to consider, delaying for a while where his knight will go. Which one, 24...♕c7, 24...♕a8 or 24...♕b8 should Black play?

a) 24...♕c7 looks the most natural, keeping close to the passed pawn, while leaving b8 for the knight. If now 25 ♖b3, then 25...e4! 26 ♖h3 ♕e5 (we will look at this via 24...♕b8 below) or 26 ♕xe4 ♗f6 27 ♕c4 ♗d4! 28 ♕xa6 ♕xd7 should be fine for Black. Unfortunately the queen is required to cover e8, as can be seen after 25 ♖d6!, with the threat of 26 ♕e8+ ♗f8 27 ♖f6. Then 25...♕b8 has lost a crucial tempo, so that 26 ♖b3 wins easily, or if 25...♗f8 26 ♕xe5+ ♔g8 27 ♕e6+ ♔g7 28 ♖bd1! ♗xd6 29 ♖xd6 c4 (or 29...♘b8 30 ♕e5+ ♔h6 31 ♖xg6+) 30 ♕e7+ ♔g8 31 ♖f6! ♕xd7 32 ♖f8+ wins.

So the queen must go to the back rank.

b) 24...♕a8 allows White to continue with 25 ♖b3! again, when 25...♘c7 26 ♕e7 returns to Kasparov's 24...♘c7 variation. If Black tries 25...♘b4 26 ♖h3 ♕c6, then 27 ♖d6! looks obvious and natural, but there are also considerable hidden depths. After 27...♕e4 28 ♕e8+ ♗f8 29 ♖d1!, it turns White's rook attack was only to push the black queen to a worse square, and now the rook returns. On 29...♕c2 30 ♖f1!! the retreat continues, and after 30...♘c6 31 ♖f3,

one might wonder what is going to be the decisive pawn push three moves later? Play on with 31...♕xa2 32 ♖xf8+ ♔g7, and suddenly the retreated rook is back in the game, as White plays 33 f4! opening the f-file, or if 33...e4 34 f5 g5 (or 34...gxf5 35 ♖8xf5) 35 f6+ ♔h6 36 g4, and mate swiftly follows on the h5-square.

Chess is all about geometry, and a sense of paradox is also useful for tactical ideas.

c) 24...♕b8 is the final try, the queen again going to the back rank, but on the dark squares rather than the light squares.

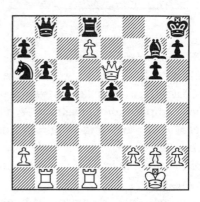

Stohl ends his analysis at 25 ♖b3, with the assumption that White is winning. However, it is not quite so easy, as Black has an important resource in 25...e4!, aiming to set up a queen defence on e5.

Play continues with 26 ♖h3 ♕e5! 27 ♕xg6 h6, and then a exchange sacrifice with 28 ♖xh6+ (not 28 ♖h4? or 28 ♖h5?, both losing to 28...♖xd7!, while if first 28 ♔f1 ♘c7! 29 ♖h4 ♕e6! defends) 28...♗xh6 29 ♕xh6+ ♔g8.

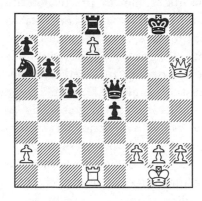

The natural response would be to rush for safety with 30 ♕g6+ ♔f8 31 ♕h6+ ♔f7 32 ♕h7+ ♔f8 and a draw by perpetual check. Black should not be greedy, as 32...♕g7 33 ♕xe4 ♘b8? 34 ♖e1 or 30...♕g7? 31 ♕e8+ ♕f8 32 ♕xe4 ♘b8 33 ♕d5+ and 34 ♖d3 would see White's attack renewed with decisive effect.

There is a possibility White might try for more, though, with 30 ♕h4!? ♖xd7 31 ♕g4+ (but not 31 ♖xd7?? ♕a1+) 31...♖g7 32 ♕c8+ ♔h7 33 ♕xa6. So often in this book we have seen wild sacrificial play by both sides, before a final tactic reaches an endgame with level pawns.

Here the play seems to favour White, the attacker still keeping an edge. His own king is safe, thanks to his three untouched castled pawns, while the black king remains permanently exposed. Black's e4-pawn is also potentially weak, and if that pawn falls, White would have three connected passed pawns, whereas it is difficult for Black to set up a pawn roller on the queenside, the a2-pawn being

awkward to surround.

Possibly Black's safest reply would be 33...♕c3, and after 34 ♕f1, aiming to bring the white rook into play via e1 and e3, to exchange the isolated pawn with 34...e3 35 ♕e2 exf2+ 36 ♕xf2 ♕e5. Black would still have to work to save the game, but one suspects that it should end up as a draw.

Going back, after 25...e4!, White might do better just to take the pawn with 26 ♕xe4!,

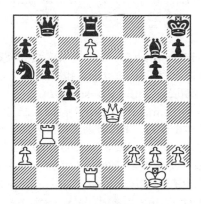

and if 26...♕e5, then 27 ♕a4! followed by 28 ♖e3 is strong. For example, 27...♘c7 28 ♖e3 ♕f6 29 ♖e8+! ♗f8 30 ♖xd8 ♕xd8 31 ♕f4 ♔g7 (or 31...♘e6? 32 ♕f7) 32 ♕xc7! ♕xc7 33 d8♕, and White emerges the exchange ahead. Instead, Black might allow that immediately with 26...♗f6!? 27 ♕c4 ♔g7 (not 27...♗d4? 28 ♖xd4!) 28 ♕xa6, close the d-file with 28...♗d4, and then remove the d7-pawn, but it is debatable whether the defence can hold.

There is still another pawn capture of a minor piece to consider. Stohl took a different path towards holding the position. After 20...♖ad8 21 ♕c4+ ♔h8

22 ♘e5, he examined 22...fxg5 (instead of 22...fxe5) 23 ♘f7+ (not 23 ♕e6? ♘c7!) 23...♖xf7 24 ♕xf7 ♕c6!

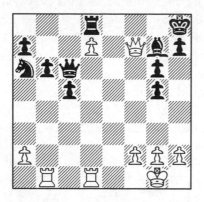

and now 25 ♖e1 ♕xd7 26 ♕xd7 ♖xd7 27 ♖e8+ ♗f8 28 ♖xf8+ ♔g7 is fine for Black with two strong pawns for the exchange. So Stohl gives 25 ♖b3! ♕f6 26 ♕e8+ ♕f8 27 ♖e3! ♘c7 28 ♖de1 ♗f6 29 ♕xf8+ ♖xf8 30 ♖e8 ♔g7 31 ♖c8, and notes that White keeps some degree of an advantage. It is quite possible that this could be substantial, as while the material balance is the same after, for example, 31...♘b5 32 ♖xf8 ♔xf8 33 ♖e8+ ♔f7 34 d8♕ ♗xd8 34 ♖xd8, Black's situation is a lot more difficult without his own rook on the board.

So perhaps Black should set up his defences at once, with 25...♘c7!? 26 ♖e3 h5. Then 27 ♖e7 ♕f6 28 ♖e8+ ♘xe8 29 dxe8♕+ ♖xe8 30 ♕xe8+ ♔h7 has once more netted White the exchange for two pawns, but Black's king is very secure in its little fortress, and he can look for counterplay with his queen and queenside pawns.

But maybe we are moving too far

from the game. In practical terms, it would be more or less impossible for Black to have held. Pribyl did not even come close, and Kasparov did not analyse everything in detail. The perfectionist annotator might wonder whether, at some stage, White could play "better" with a quieter, more positional line. I do not want to go along this path. If a defender has to make ten absolutely precise moves in a wild and complicated variation, and ends up with equality, this is often a far more difficult task than defending patiently over a dozen or more moves under slight pressure.

21 ♕c4+ ♔h8 22 ♘xg5 ♗f6

He needs to cover the queening square. If 22...♘c7?, then simply 23 d8♕ wins, due to the knight fork on f7.

23 ♘e6

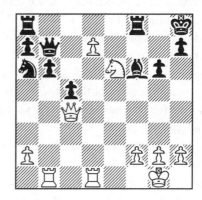

23...♘c7

Pribyl understandably wants to get rid of the white knight, but there is a clever tactic coming up.

The alternative was 23...♘b4!?, when Kasparov, and later Stohl, both chose 24 ♕f4, demonstrating wins after

24...♘c6 25 ♘xf8 ♖xf8 26 d8♕! ♘xd8 27 ♖xd8, or 24...♘d5 25 ♕d6, or 24...♖f7 25 ♘g5.

But there is a fourth, and better, move, 24...♕b8!, the main tactical point being that if now 25 d8♕, it is the other queen that gets taken, with 25...♕xf4!. After 26 ♕xf8+ ♖xf8 27 ♘xf4 ♘xa2, Black would be ahead, with three united passed pawns for the exchange.

25 ♕f3! is more dangerous,

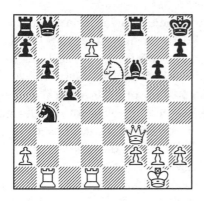

and indeed looks like a straightforward win at first, the two little queen moves seemingly changing nothing. The difference is that Black has managed to defend his f8-rook, and so can block the d-file with 25...♗d4!. Mass simplification then follows 26 ♘xf8 (or 26 ♕e4 ♕d6 27 ♖xd4 cxd4 28 ♖xb4 ♕xd7 29 ♘xf8 ♖xf8 30 ♕xd4+ ♕xd4 31 ♖xd4 ♖f7, and would you like a draw?) 26...♕xf8 27 ♕xf8+ ♖xf8 28 ♖xd4 cxd4 29 ♖xb4 ♖d8 30 ♖xd4, and White's extra pawn on the seventh will soon be recovered, leading to a king and pawn ending after the sequence 30...♔g7 31 f4 ♔f6 32 ♔f2 ♔e6 33 ♔e3 ♖xd7+ 34 ♖xd7 ♔xd7.

Such positions are terrifying, both for players and for analysts. Suppose it's the next move for Black, after the white king advances, should his own king move to c6, d6, or e6? Should he seek the opposition, or seek to defer it? Does it matter? Or would it immediately drop half a point? Quite often the players will have to evaluate whether one of their pawns is threatening to promote before the opponent's, and this might involve ten moves or more of calculation. If you are tired, later on in the game, it is so easy to make a mistake, with a lapse of concentration.

Sometimes catastrophic misjudgements can be made by the strongest of players. Even Fischer once blundered! See the supplementary game 18.1 below.

We add another illustration in Game 18.2 between Ivkov and Mecking, two very strong grandmasters, who reached very close to this position. It would have been the ideal example, except for a couple of errors at the time control.

Returning to the current game, the

question whether White is winning the king and pawn ending or not, while fascinating, is in fact irrelevant, because he has a much stronger line earlier on.

Rather than 24 ♕f4, White can play 24 ♖d6!,

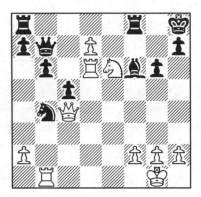

threatening 25 ♘xf8 ♖xf8 26 ♖xf6! and wins. In response, 24...♕b8 25 ♖bd1 is no good for Black, nor is 24...♗e7 25 ♖e1!, as 25...♗xd6 gets mated by 26 ♕c3+. The only move is 24...♘c6, to cover d8, but then 25 ♘xf8 ♖xf8 26 ♖e1 ♔g7 (otherwise 27 ♖xf6! ♖xf6 28 ♖e8+) 27 ♖e8! ♖f7 (or 27...♘e5 28 ♕a4 ♕c7 29 ♖xf6!) 28 ♖xf6! is decisive. Taking the rook with 28...♔xf6 29 ♕c3+ or 28...♖xf6 29 ♖g8+ both lead to mate, which leaves just 28...♕xd7 29 ♖xf7+ ♕xf7 30 ♕e6, and the knight is no match for the rook in this endgame.

24 ♘xf8 ♖xf8

In the current position, Black has bishop and knight for the rook, while the pawns, in numbers at least, are level. Some pawns, though, are more equal than others!

25 ♖d6!

A memorable tactical resource.

Kasparov noted that 25 ♕xc5 is also possible, when 25...♕xg2+! 26 ♔xg2 bxc5 27 ♖b7 ♘e6 28 ♖d6 ♘f4+ 29 ♔f1 ♗d8 30 ♖xa7 offers White a slight edge. He wanted to play for much more. When attacking, a queen exchange often slows things down.

25...♗e7

Probably best. The computer prefers other moves, which keep the material in the short term, but are ultimately hopeless.

25...♕b8 26 ♖bd1 ♕d8 27 ♖c6! leads to a crushing bind, where Black can do virtually nothing. In particular the knight on c7 cannot move due to ♖c8, so all White needs to do is attack it with the queen. Black can prevent the immediate threat of 28 ♕f4, but there's no way he can keep the queen off the diagonal indefinitely. For instance, 27...♗g7 28 ♕e4 followed by ♕e3-g3, or 27...♗g5 28 ♕e4 ♔g8 29 g3 ♖f7 30 ♕e5 wins.

Kasparov also gives 25...♗d8 26 h4 ♕a6 27 ♕c3+ ♔g8 28 ♕c2!, keeping the black queen out of play. It is not immediately obvious why White's position should be strong, even accepting that 28...♗xh4? 29 ♖bd1 ♗d8 30 ♖xg6+! wins, so let us try 28...♔g7 instead. Then after 29 h5 gxh5 (if 29...♗f6 30 h6+!, or 29...♖f6 30 ♕b2!) 30 ♖b3 h4 (or 30...♖f4 31 ♖g3+ ♔g4 32 ♕c3+ ♔g8 33 ♕f6!) 31 ♖e3 ♕b5 32 ♖e4 ♖f7 33 ♕c3+ ♔g8 34 ♖g4+. Simple moves, leading to victory.

26 d8♕!!

Some pawn sacrifices are more valiant than others. The pawn is now in the way, and Kasparov wants the rook on the seventh.

Compare this with the game against Kengis (Game 3), where Kasparov gave up the pawn with 17 d7!! simply to gain time.

26...♗xd8

As Kasparov notes, if 26...♖xd8 27 ♖xd8+ ♗xd8 28 ♕f7 ♕d5 29 ♕xd5 ♘xd5 30 ♖d1 wins.

27 ♕c3+ ♔g8 28 ♖d7 ♗f6 29 ♕c4+ ♔h8 30 ♕f4

Some deft manoeuvring, and he is now attacking the knight while also aiming for mate.

30...♕a6?

Speeding up the loss, by responding to the lesser threat (if White takes the knight, Black would take on a2).

Kasparov gives, as the best chance to hold for a while, 30...♗g7 31 ♕xc7 ♕xc7 32 ♖xc7 ♗d4 33 ♖f1. It is unlikely that Black's position will hold permanently, White's extra kingside pawn being a permanent advantage. As well as picking off any random queenside pawns, White can think about doubling on the seventh, after consolidating with g2-g3, ♔g2, f2-f3 etc. If Black allows the exchange of rooks, White's king will advance to the centre.

31 ♕h6 1-0

Supplementary games

There isn't all that much on the endgame in this book, so let us try to redress the balance. We are looking at ideas around the position arising from the 23...♘b4 24 ♕f4 ♕b8 25 ♕f3 ♗d4 variation in the Kasparov-Pribyl game.

First, a frightening example of how even the strongest players can go terribly wrong in a king and pawn ending.

Game 18.1
R.J.Fischer-R.Letelier Martner
Mar del Plata 1959

A couple of moves back, Fischer exchanged bishop for knight to reach a winning king and pawn endgame.

47 a4??

Seeking to neutralize the queenside majority before pushing his own pawns, but he should have waited for ...a6-a5 before advancing his own a-pawn, as the text lets the win slip away.

Correct was 47 g4! a5 (if 47...♔d6 48 f5 gxf5+ 49 ♔xf5 or 47...♔f6 48 ♔d5 wins easily) 48 a4! b4 (48...bxa4 49 bxa4 ♔d6 50 f5 is trivial) 49 ♔d3 ♔d5, and now 50 g5! ♔e6 51 ♔c4 ♔d6 (or alternatively 51...♔f5 52 ♔xc5 ♔xf4 53 ♔b5 ♔xg5 54 ♔xa5 ♔f4 55 ♔xb4 g5 56 ♔c4! g4 57 ♔d3 ♔f3 58 a5 and the pawn promotes with check) 52 ♔b5 ♔d5 53 ♔xa5 ♔d4 54 f5! c4 55 f6 c3 56 f7 c2 57 f8♕ c1♕ 58 ♕xb4+ with a winning queen endgame.

47...♔d6 48 a5 ♔e6 49 g3

If 49 g4 then 49...♔d6 50 f5 g5! 51 f6 ♔e6 52 f7 ♔xf7 53 ♔d5 c4! 54 bxc4 b4 holds.

49...♔d6 50 f5

And now if 50 g4 ♔e6 51 f5+ gxf5+ 52 gxf5+ ♔d6 53 f6 c4! 54 bxc4 bxc4 55 ♔d4 ♔e6 56 ♔xc4 ♔xf6 57 ♔c5 ♔e5 58 ♔b6 ♔d6 59 ♔xa6 ♔c6 again ends up as a draw.

But Fischer was still hoping for a win.

50...gxf5+ 51 ♔xf5 ♔d5 52 g4 ♔d4!

The only move. White wins after 52...c4? 53 bxc4+ bxc4 54 g5 c3 55 g6 c2 56 g7 c1♕ 57 g8♕+ ♔d4 58 ♕d8+ ♔c3 (or 58...♔e3 59 ♕g5+) 59 ♕c7+ ♔d2 60 ♕xc1+ ♔xc1 61 ♔e5 ♔d2 62 ♔d4! ♔e2 63 ♔c5 ♔d3 64 ♔b6 ♔c4 65 ♔xa6 ♔c5 66 ♔b7.

53 g5 c4 54 bxc4 b4!

55 c5??

A dreadful oversight. Black queens first with check. Instead, 55 g6 still draws.

55...b3 56 c6 b2 57 c7 b1♕+ 58 ♔e6 ♕b7 59 ♔d7 ♔d5 60 g6 ♕c6+ 61 ♔d8 ♕d6+ 0-1

Game 18.2
B.Ivkov-H.Mecking
Kostic Memorial, Vrsac 1971

White to play

Despite the apparently quiet position, there had been plenty of tactics and sacrifices earlier on. Black's king reached d7 only after taking a pawn there, much as in the note to the Kasparov-Pribyl game.

35 ♔d3 ♔d6 36 ♔d4 b5 37 f4 g6 38 g4

This reaches a position from the analysis of 23...♘b4 in Kasparov-Pribyl (after the further moves 35 ♔d4 ♔d6 36 g4 b5), albeit with Black to move here.

When I saw the Ivkov-Mecking game, between two strong grandmasters, and noticed that neither player tried to push hard for the win, I felt reasonably confident that Pribyl could have managed a draw in that line.

38...h6 39 h3

If instead 39 f5 gxf5! 40 gxf5 ♔e7 41 ♔c5 ♔f6 42 ♔xb5 ♔xf6 draws. It takes eight moves for White to promote the a-pawn, by which time Black has his king on g1 and the pawn on h2, for a book draw. 39 h4 h5! 40 gxh5 gxh5 is much the same.

39...a6??

A blunder. 39...h5! was correct, and if 40 f5 hxg4 41 hxg4 gxf5 42 gxf5 ♔e7 43 ♔c5 a6 44 ♔b6 ♔f6 45 ♔xa6 b4! 46 ♔a5 ♔xf5 47 ♔xb4 ♔e6, when the black king makes it across in time to defend.

40 a3??

Ivkov lets the opportunity pass by.

I was hoping to be able to find a good example of precise play between two grandmasters, showing that Pribyl could have drawn. Instead, alas, we have mutual errors, doubtless a result of time trouble. The one thing that White cannot do is to allow the exchange of his a-pawn, as he will need that to stretch Black's defences.

The winning plan is 40 h4! (but not 40 f5 gxf5 41 gxf5 h5 42 h4 b4! with another draw) 40...h5 (or 40...a5 41 f5!) 41 gxh5 gxh5 42 ♔c3, and the white king cannot be prevented from infiltrating, for instance after 42...a5 43 ♔d4 a4 44 ♔c3 ♔c5 45 a3. If Black goes after the kingside pawns with 42...♔e6 43 ♔b4 ♔f5 44 ♔a5 ♔xf4, then 45 ♔xa6 b4 46 ♔a5! wins by a tempo. In the six moves required to promote the white a-pawn this time, Black can only get his king to g1 and pawn to h3, which is not sufficient.

40...a5 41 ♔e4

Now if 41 h4 h5! 42 gxh5 gxh5 43 f5 ♔e7 44 ♔c4 b4! draws, or similarly 41 f5 gxf5 42 gxf5 b4!.

41...♔e6 42 ♔d4 ♔d6 43 ♔e4 ♔e6 44 ♔d4 ♔d6 45 ♔e4 ♔e6 ½-½

So Ivkov was not winning this endgame, not until Mecking gave him a chance, which Ivkov then spurned.

The question is, would Kasparov have won from the same position (38 g4 in Ivkov-Mecking), but with the move. The answer is probably yes. In that case, after 35 ♔d4 ♔d6 36 g4 b5 (returning to the analysis from Kasparov-Pribyl), the fixing advance 37 g5! seems to win, as Black must eventually give way on the queenside. Or if he refuses, then White can achieve a

breakthrough on the kingside.

For example, 37...♔c6 38 ♔e5 a5 39 ♔d4 ♔d6 40 h4 ♔c6 41 f5 gxf5 42 h5 and 43 g6 wins. Alternatively, if 37...a5 (or 37...a6 38 h3) 38 h4 a4 (or 38...b4 39 ♔c4 ♔c6 40 f5) 39 a3 b4 40 axb4 ♔c6 41 ♔c3 ♔b5 42 f5 wins again.

On the other hand, Black has no need to play 36...b5? here. He does much better to hit out with 36...h5!, or else 36...♔e6 37 ♔c4 a6 38 ♔d4 h5!. With White's kingside majority reduced to a doubleton and only a rook's pawn on the other side, Black has no problem in holding a draw.

The next game is hard to understand at first. Kasparov wins a pawn quite quickly, and one would expect that he would consolidate and seek to exploit the material advantage later on. Instead, he sacrifices almost the whole of his queenside, in the hope of an attack on the other wing.

It all seems rather extravagant to the onlooker, but Kasparov's acute sense of the pace of attack and defence allows him to build a strong assault against the opposing king, whereas had he played stereotypical chess, trying to hold the pawn, it would have been difficult to activate his pieces. Kasparov has always preferred the dynamic approach.

Game 19
S.Garcia Martinez-G.Kasparov
Baku 1980
Modern Benoni

---

1 d4 ♘f6 2 c4 c5 3 d5 e6 4 ♘c3 exd5 5 cxd5 d6 6 e4 g6 7 ♗f4 ♗g7 8 ♕a4+ ♗d7 9 ♕b3 ♕c7 10 ♘f3 0-0 11 e5!?

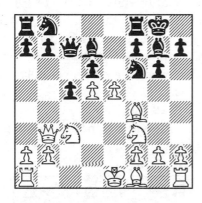

An aggressive way to break open the centre, before White has castled, or has even developed his kingside pieces. There is sharp play in prospect, and Kasparov was happy to accept the challenge.

11 ♗e2 and 11 ♘d2 are the usual choices here; 11 ♗d3 is also reasonable.

11...♖e8!?

A slight, but significant detail of move order, creating extra options for both sides.

The straightforward 11...dxe5 12 ♗xe5 (if 12 ♘xe5 ♘g4! 13 ♘xg6 ♖e8+ 14 ♗e2 ♕a5 gives Black good play for the pawn) 12...♖e8 is level after 13 ♗e2 (transposing to 11...♖e8 12 ♗e2 dxe5 below) or 13 0-0-0 ♕b6 (not 13...♖xe5? 14 d6! and wins), but Black's position lacks dynamism. So Kasparov takes a risk to enliven his game.

12 ♗e2?

And it pays off.

12 0-0-0! was correct, not so much because of any brilliant play by White, but rather because the text was a mistake. Now if 12...dxe5 White can play 13 ♘xe5! with the advantage, as 13...♘g4? loses to 14 d6, attacking f7.

Instead, after 12...♘h5 13 exd6 ♕b6 14 ♗e3 ♕xb3 15 axb3 b6, *Fritz* at first gives it equal, in view of the doubled isolated pawns, but 16 ♘b5!, obvious enough, straightens up the pawns with 16...♘a6 17 ♘c7 ♘xc7 18 dxc7.

White was also better after 13...♕c8 14 ♗g5 ♗f8 15 ♗e7 ♗xe7 16 dxe7 ♖xe7 17 ♗c4 ♖e8 18 ♖he1 in A.Labarthe-T.Dubuisson, St Chely d'Aubrac 2001.

12...♘h5!

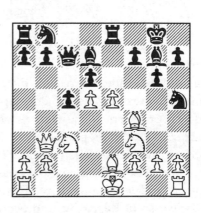

In a game I had long forgotten, I find in *ChessBase* that I drew after 12...dxe5?! 13 ♗xe5 ♕c8 14 0-0 ♗g4 15 ♖fe1 a6 16 h3 ♗xf3 17 ♗xf3 c4 18 ♕b4 ♘bd7, in C.Crouch-G.Lawton, London 1984, but I should probably have made more from this position. As it turned out Black managed later to trade his c-pawn for the advanced d-pawn.

If nothing else, this helps to indicate that Black would not be playing for a win if he had continued 12...dxe5, but one can go further: Kasparov's position was better after 12...♘h5!.

13 ♗e3

Sadly giving away a pawn, as 13 exd6? would lose material after 13...♗xc3+! 14 bxc3 ♖xe2+ 15 ♔xe2 ♘xf4+.

13...dxe5 14 0-0

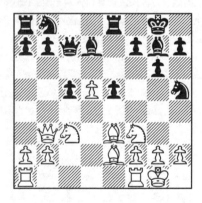

It is not time to resign though. White's pieces are better developed, and can press on in the centre, while Black still has the problem of finding a good way to get his queen's knight into the game. Also, White has that passed d-pawn, and as we have already seen, in the hands of Kasparov, and even of

his opponents, such a pawn can be dangerous.

Play soon became complicated.

14...♕b6 15 ♘d2 ♘f4 16 ♗c4 ♘a6?!

This is probably not the best way of handling the position. A move later, the bishop arrives on f5, a good and natural post. That opens up the d7-square, which could have been useful for the knight. The immediate 16...♗f5! looks more accurate, and if, for example, 17 ♘de4 ♘d7 keeps a slight edge.

17 ♖fc1?!

This, too, seems slightly substandard. As Kasparov notes, in *My Games*, 17 ♘de4! is much better, and indeed is at least fully equal for White. He has lost his pawn, that is true, but his passed pawn is useful, and his minor pieces are solid in the centre, while Black's pieces are not as yet fully coordinated.

17...♗f5 18 ♕d1

18 ♘de4 is still best, according to Kasparov.

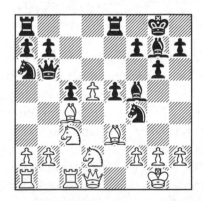

So far, it has to be admitted that the play has not really been at the standard expected from grandmasters. Garcia dropped a pawn at an early stage, Kasparov has developed his knight on an inferior square, and Garcia has unnecessarily delayed his best knight move, ♘de4, which could have kept the game in balance.

The next few moves turn out to be remarkable, and show Kasparov's great sense of the necessary when taking up the initiative. Play through it closely.

18...g5!

As a preliminary, it should be noted that, had Garcia played ♘de4 earlier, this pawn push would not have been possible.

When I first went through this game, via ChessBase and *Fritz*, I was astonished by the seeming recklessness of Black's play, throwing away the whole queenside, in the hope that maybe, possibly, he could attack on the kingside. Black was a pawn up, and at the very least one might expect him just to keep the extra pawn and consolidate, so why would he need to sacrifice?

Naturally there is an opposing point of view. One might argue, and indeed Kasparov would argue, that Black has done well by sacrificing the pawns, the attack being winning, in practice at least. White's kingside is seriously underdefended, and this is what is going to be the problem.

Then one might ask what the alternative is. Black can develop the rooks, through for example 18...♖ac8 19 ♘de4 ♖ed8, but it is not so clear what he will be doing next. Meanwhile, White can start genuine counterplay on the queenside, with 20 a3!, threatening b2-b4. If 20...♕xb2? 21 ♖cb1 traps the queen.

Black could try grabbing the poisoned pawn at once with 18...♕xb2?!, leaving himself two pawns up, but the queen would still be in danger. 19 g4!, not so obvious but effective, looks the best of the competing ideas. After 19...♘h3+ 19 ♔g2 ♘f4+, White does not have to accept the repetition, but can play for more with 21 ♔f1!, when 21...♗d7 22 ♗xa6 bxa6 23 ♖ab1 ♕a3 24 ♘c4 wins the queen again, or if 21...♘d3 22 ♖ab1 ♘xf2 23 ♖xb2 ♘xd1 24 ♘xd1 with excellent prospects.

It is difficult to know how much Kasparov had examined this over the board, but in practice, not even Kasparov, nor Tal, would need to analyse everything to demonstrate that 18...g5 is better than 18...♕xb2. All that is needed is to have a sense of danger over the pawn snatch, and a sense that it was better to go for the attack instead.

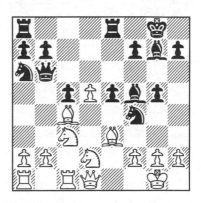

19 ♘b3

Kasparov does not annotate the next few moves, no doubt on the assumption that White has to do what he can on the queenside, but that Black is still much better.

19 ♘de4 might still be considered, but this is a few moves late to be effective, at least as a winning attempt. Black's play is already well underway after 19...♕g6, and then:

a) 20 ♘xc5? runs into piece problems after 20...♘xc5 21 ♗xc5 ♖ec8 22 ♘a4 ♗d7 23 ♗a3 ♕e4 24 f3 ♕e3+ 25 ♔h1 b5.

b) 20 f3 g4 21 ♗xa6 bxa6 22 ♘xc5? allows 22...♘xg2! 23 ♔xg2 gxf3+ 24 ♔f1 ♕g2+ 25 ♔e1 ♗f6 26 ♗f2 ♗g5 and Black wins.

c) 20 ♗xa6 is probably White's best option, when 20...bxa6! 21 ♘xc5 ♖ad8 transposes back to the game. If instead 20...♗xe4 21 ♗xf4 gxf4 (or 21...bxa6 22 ♗e3, or 21...exf4 22 ♗xb7) 22 ♘xe4 bxa6 23 f3 is unclear.

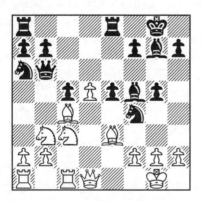

19...♕g6

The consistent follow-up to his previous move. Otherwise he could defend just the c-pawn with 19...♖ac8,

when 20 ♘a4?! ♕d6 21 ♗xa6 bxa6 would leave the white d-pawn hanging.

20 ♗xa6

Not yet 20 ♘xc5?, which transposes to 19 ♘de4 ♕g6 20 ♘xc5? above.

20...bxa6 21 ♘xc5 ♖ad8

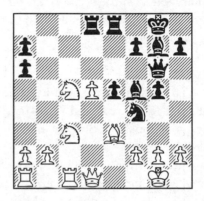

While Garcia has been busy levelling the pawn count, Kasparov has begun his assault on the kingside. Naturally White still has some pressure on the queenside, but there are few concrete threats, except against the abandoned black pawns. He is fighting against thin air.

22 ♕a4?

Which is perhaps why he wants to win a pawn. In his notes at the time Kasparov preferred 22 ♕d2. White refuses to be distracted further on the queenside, and looks to his defences.

In reply, 22...e4! is still strong. For instance, 23 ♗xf4?! gxf4 24 ♕xf4 e3! 25 ♖e1 ♗e5 26 ♕xe3 (not 26 ♕c4? ♗h3 27 ♕f1 exf2+ 28 ♔xf2 ♗d4 and wins) 26...♗xh2+ 27 ♔xh2 ♖xe3 28 ♖xe3 ♕d6+ 29 ♖g3+ ♔f8 is good for Black.

If instead, 23 ♖e1, intending ♗xf4

next move, then 23...♗xc3 24 bxc3 ♖xd5 (24...♘xd5 25 ♘b7 ♖d7 26 ♘c5 is a draw by repetition) 25 ♗d4 ♕c6 26 ♕e3 ♗g6, and Black is slightly better. He might even consider 25...♘xg2!? 26 ♔xg2 ♗g4, with a dangerous attack on the light squares for the sacrificed piece.

22...e4 23 ♕xa6 ♕h5

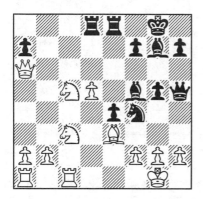

Over the last few moves, Kasparov has abandoned his queenside pawns, but has made much progress with his kingside attack. White has to decide how to respond. On his next move, he has three main choices, an exchange, a withdrawal into the fortress, or counterplay.

24 ♕f1

This is the purely defensive move, which cuts out any sacrifices with ...♘xg2. It does not work out very well, but White probably has no good option in any case. Indeed, Kasparov gives no comment on this position in *My Games*, although White has at least two alternatives.

a) 24 ♕xa7, taking an extra pawn, and gaining connected two passed

pawns, can be ruled out immediately. White's queen is out of play, and it will take too long for the pawns to have any effect on the rest of the board. Simply 24...♘xg2! continues Black's attack, since if 25 ♔xg2? ♗h3+ and Black checkmates.

b) 24 ♘b7 hopes for an unlikely repetition of moves after 24...♖d7 25 ♘c5 ♖dd8 26 ♘b7, but Black can ignore the attack on his rook, and continue again with 24...♘xg2! 25 ♘xd8 ♗e5.

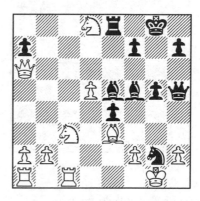

In such positions, when a player is trying for checkmate, what is important is not so much what has been sacrificed, but what pieces remain on the board. Here, queen, two bishops, and knight are enough to try for a win, even if the knight is to be sacrificed or exchanged.

Then 26 ♔f1 is slippery, as the apparently simple checkmate isn't quite there: if 26...♘xe3+ 27 fxe3 ♕f3+ 28 ♔e1 ♕xe3+ 29 ♕e2 defends. However, the calm 26...♖xd8!, taking the knight, while maintaining all the threats, sees Black only the exchange down, and with all his pieces working together against the exposed king, which should be more than enough. 27 ♗xa7 (there is nothing better) 27...♗h3 28 ♘xe4 ♕xg4 29 ♘g3 ♘h4+ 30 ♔e1 ♕b4+ is just one many possible winning lines.

c) 24 ♗xf4 gxf4 is the one remaining try for defence, exchanging bishop against knight before Black can use the ...♘xg2 sacrifice. But the two advanced pawns are now too dangerous:

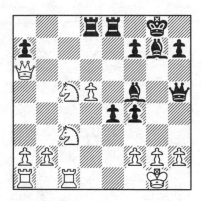

c1) 25 ♕xa7 f3! is easy.

c2) 25 ♖e1 e3! 26 fxe3 (or 26 f3 ♗xc3 27 bxc3 ♖xd5 with a big advantage) 26...fxe3 is very strong, for example 27 ♕a4 ♗e5 28 h3 ♕g5 (threatening ...♕g3 or ....♗xh3) 29 ♘3e4 ♕g7 30 ♔h1 ♗xe4 31 ♘xe4 f5 and wins.

c3) 25 ♘b7 ♗c8! 26 ♕xa7 ♗xb7 27 ♕xb7 is met again by 27...f3! (27...e3 28 fxe3 fxe3 29 ♖e1 is less clear), and after 28 ♕a6 fxg2 29 ♔xg2 (or 29 ♕e2 ♕xe2 30 ♘xe2 ♗xb2) 29...♗e5 30 ♖g1 ♔h8 31 ♔f1 (or 31 ♘xe4 ♕xh2+ 32 ♔f1 ♕h3+ 33 ♔e2 ♗xb2) 32 ♔e2 ♕h3+ 32 ♔e2 ♗xc3 33 bxc3 ♕xc3, the white king is a sitting duck.

24...♗e5?!

With the threat of 25...♘e2+ 26 ♕xe2

♕xh2+ 27 ♔f1 ♕h1 mate, so White's reply is forced, but Black had a much stronger move.

Kasparov expressed his regrets on not having played the spectacular 24...♖d6!

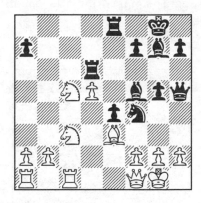

25 ♘5xe4 ♗xe4 26 ♘xe4 ♖xe4 27 ♖c8+ ♗f8 28 ♗c5 ♘e2+ 29 ♔h1 (or 29 ♕xe2 ♕xe2 30 ♗xd6 ♕e1+ 31 ♖xe1 ♖xe1 mate) 29...♕xh2+ 30 ♔xh2 ♖h4 mate. A good line for a brilliancy prize, not least because the checkmating line, although familiar, is unexpected.

White has various alternatives after 24...♖d6!, but none that are ultimately any better. Returning the queen to the queenside with 25 ♕b5 hardly helps, as Black just slides the attacked rook to f8.

Taking on f4 gives Black the dynamic pawn duo after 25 ♗xf4 gxf4, and 26 ♖e1 ♗xc3 27 bxc3 f3 28 g3 ♖h6 29 h4 ♔h8!, threatening 30...♕xh4! is decisive.

If White tries 25 ♕d1, opposing queens, Black sidesteps with 25...♕h4 (25...♗g4 26 ♕a4 ♖e7 is also good) 26 g3 ♕h3 27 ♕f1 (or 27 gxf4? ♖g6! and wins) 27...♕h5, and now 28 ♕d1 fails to

28...♗g4! 29 ♕a4 ♕xh2+! 30 ♔xh2 ♖h6+ 31 ♔g1 ♗f3! 32 ♕ae8+ ♗f8, with mate to follow.

After the game move, White has the chance to put up a defence again.

25 ♗xf4 ♗xf4 26 g3?

Which he fails to take.

He had to try 26 h3!, when 26...♗xc1 27 ♖xc1 g4 28 hxg4 ♕xg4 29 ♖e1 is a great improvement for White on the game, as his light squares are secure.

The critical response is 26...g4 27 ♖e1 gxh3 (or if 27...e3 28 fxe3 ♗xe3+ 29 ♖xe3! ♖xe3 30 ♕f4 ♖de8 31 ♖f1, and White has counterplay) 28 ♘3xe4 ♕g6 29 f3 ♖xd5 30 g4 (but not 30 ♘f6+?! ♕xf6 31 ♖xe8+ ♔g7 32 g4 ♕xb2 33 ♖e2 ♗c2 with a big advantage) 30...♗xe4 31 ♘xe4, and although White is worse, at least he is still in the game.

26...♗xc1 27 ♖xc1 ♖d6

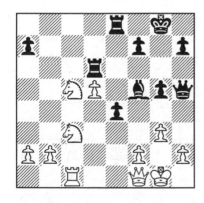

No more fireworks coming up. Black is the exchange for a pawn ahead, and still has his kingside attack. It is noteworthy that White no longer has any threats on the queenside.

28 ♖e1

28 ♕d1, trying to exchange queens, is equally hopeless after 28...♗g4 29 ♕a4 ♖e7 30 ♘3xe4 ♖h6, or 30 ♘e6!? e3! 31 ♘e4 (if 31 fxe3 ♗xe6 32 dxe6 ♖d2) 31...exf2+ 32 ♘xf2 ♗xe6 33 dxe6 ♖xe6.

28...♖h6 29 ♕g2 ♗h3 30 g4

If 30 ♕h1 f5 entombs the queen.

30...♕xg4

30...♗xg4 31 ♖xe4 f5 is also possible, but Kasparov is content to win in the endgame.

31 ♕xg4 ♗xg4 32 ♘5xe4 ♔f8 33 ♖c1

According to Kasparov, 33 ♖e3 would have put up more resistance.

33...♗f3 34 ♘d2 g4 35 ♘xf3?! gxf3 36 ♖d1 ♖e5 0-1

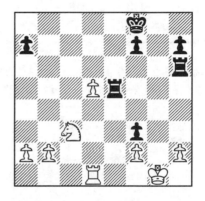

Black follows with 37...♖g5+ 38 ♔f1 (or 38 ♔h1 ♖g2) 38...♖xh2 39 ♔e1 ♖e5+ 40 ♔d2 ♖xf2+ and wins easily.

The remaining games all feature d4-d5 pawn sacrifices, and are just a few examples from numerous others by Kasparov in his younger years. Games 21 and 22, against Najdorf and Gheor-ghiu, and, in the notes, Murey, were essentially crash-bang breakthroughs, catching the king in the centre or, with few protecting pieces, on the kingside.

The first game, against Andersson, is in many ways rather more subtle. Kasparov sacrifices his central pawn, opening up lines as in the other games, but here his attention is to restrict Black's position. Andersson cannot get out in front of his own pawns, and he runs out of active play. The standard response for the defender, perhaps, would be to return the pawn in order to try and activate his pieces, but Andersson is never given the chance.

Game 20
G.Kasparov-U.Andersson
Tilburg 1981
Queen's Indian Defence

---

1 d4 ♘f6 2 c4 e6 3 ♘f3 b6 4 a3 ♗b7 5 ♘c3 ♘e4 6 ♘xe4 ♗xe4 7 ♘d2 ♗g6!?

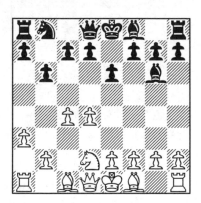

7...♗b7 is simpler, and if 8 e4 then 8...♕f6, aiming to play against or around the extended white centre after 9 e5 or 9 d5. The text has a similar intention, but hopes that the bishop will be better placed on g6.

8 g3!

The point of the unusual bishop retreat is seen if White continues as planned with 8 e4?!. Then 8...♘c6! attacks the d-pawn, and White cannot defend it with the knight as that would leave the e-pawn en prise. So he has to play 9 d5 ♘d4, and Black has solved his opening problems. For example, 10 ♗d3 c6 11 ♘b3 ♘xb3 12 ♕xb3 ♗c5 13 ♕c3 ♕h4 14 0-0 ♗xe4!? 15 ♕xg7 0-0-0 16 ♗g5 ♕g4 17 ♗xe4 ♖hg8 18 ♕e5? ♖xg5 19 ♕g3 ♕xg3 20 hxg3 f5 21 ♗f3 e5 and Black was clearly better in M.Dziuba-K.Chernyshov, Krakow 2004.

So Kasparov holds the e-pawn back, while allowing his light-squared bishop to take up a prime position, unopposed on the long diagonal.

8...♘c6

This may look "fanciful" (Kasparov) or "extravagant" (Stohl), but only after Kasparov's surprising reply. Other players later copied this move, with varying degrees of success, while 8...d5, 8...c5 and 8...♗e7 have also been tried.

9 e3!

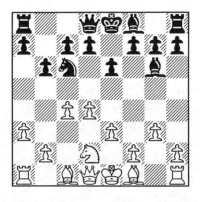

It looks strange at first to play g2-g3 and e2-e3 on successive moves. Has Kasparov failed to make his mind up?

In fact, Kasparov is showing his flexibility. The black knight is on a good square only if it is pressing on the d4-pawn. It is on a bad square if that pawn is securely defended by a pawn on e3. Furthermore, if Black challenges further in the centre with 9...e5, then after 10 d5 the knight must retreat, as d4 is no longer available as an outpost.

In any case, White had no other moves worth considering. 9 ♘f3 would allow the black bishop to return strongly to the long diagonal after 9...♗e4, while 9 d5?! ♘d4 10 e4 is even worse than before.

9...a6?!

Stohl criticizes all of Black's last three moves. Kasparov, writing before the theory on this line had clarified, questions moves 7 and 8, but not this one. Later players, in actual play, have implied that 7...♗g6 and 8...♘c6 are OK, but that the over-quiet 9...a6 is not so good. Something has gone wrong with Andersson's position, but it is not quite clear exactly when the mistake was made.

Andersson's plan, with ...a7-a6 and ...b6-b5, is indeed over-elaborate, and there is a much simpler option with ...e6-e5 and ...a7-a5, nibbling at White's pawn structure.

For example, in A.Rustemov-K.Chernyshov, Russian Championship, Elista 2001, Black started to take over on the dark squares with 9...a5 10 b3 e5

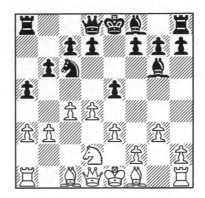

11 d5 ♘b8 (a retreat, but the knight is soon redeployed) 12 h4 h6 13 ♗b2 ♗d6 14 e4 0-0 15 g4 ♘a6 16 ♕f3 ♕e7 17 ♗e2 c6 18 ♘f1 ♗c5 19 ♗e3 ♗d4 20 ♗xd4 exd4 21 ♘d2 ♘c5. White's light-squared pawn phalanx looks impressive, but it does not create any dangerous attacking play, and does not defend on the dark squares.

In a later game, Chernyshov tried instead 9...e5 10 d5 ♘a5!? 11 b4 ♘b7, and again emerged with a good position after 12 ♗b2 ♗d6 13 ♗g2 a5 14 ♗c3 ♕e7 15 0-0 0-0 16 ♕b3 ♗d3 17 ♖fe1 e4 18 ♕b2 f5 19 ♗f1 ♗xf1 20 ♖xf1 c6, in C.Landenbergue-K.Chernyshov, Cappelle la Grande 2006.

So maybe Black equalizes?

What Black cannot do is play 9...d5? 10 ♕a4, with severe embarrassment on the light squares, since if 10...♕d7 11 cxd5! and Black cannot recapture, as 11...exd5 (or 11...♕xd5 12 ♖g1 and 13 ♗g2) 12 ♗b5 just wins. Andersson strives to cover this approach, but his idea is too slow.

10 b4

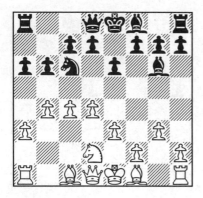 

The natural move, gaining space, although it actively encouraged Andersson's reply. In his notes, Kasparov made it clear he was not too worried about that.

Otherwise 10 b3 was possible, as would be several other moves. In reply, Black's plan would probably be to establish himself in the centre with ...d7-d5, or else ...e6-e5 as in the previous note.

10...b5 11 cxb5

11 ♗b2 would have been the purely positional approach, with White keeping a slight, but stable edge.

Kasparov was more interested in tactical ideas, first putting pressure on b5, and then, once his opponent has been forced to defend the pawn, Kasparov opens up the game.

11...axb5 12 ♗b2

12 ♗xb5? would be a mistake, due to 12...♞xb4! and Black is better if anything. For example, 13 e4 ♛b8 14 a4 c6 15 ♗e2 ♛b6 16 ♗b2 ♞d3+ 17 ♗xd3 ♛xb2 or 16 ♛b3 f5 and Black seizes the initiative.

12...♞a7

Andersson, as is his wont, indulges in slow and grinding manoeuvring. Kasparov tends to favour the quick smash.

Black's play is undoubtedly positionally subtle. He has exchanged his a-pawn for White's more central c-pawn, and aims to set up a strong position in the centre with something like ...d7-d5, ...♞c8, ...♗e7, ...0-0, and either ...♞d6 or ...♞b6. If White plays e3-e4 at some stage, Black can ignore it, as long as his pawn on d5 is secure. But has he got time for all this?

It is difficult for White to equalize strategically, as his dark-squared bishop would be a very poor piece after ...d7-d5. On that basis alone Kasparov's forthcoming pawn sacrifice should come at once under consideration. He has to take the initiative, maybe even sacrifice something, or otherwise break the balance, and try for an advantage!

In a few moves time, it starts to look as though Black has been the one who has played antipositionally, developing too slowly and misplacing his pieces.

13 h4!

Gaining space on the kingside, in preparation for his forthcoming attack. Black has no time yet for 13...d5? due to 14 h5, so he must answer the threat to his bishop.

13...h6

13...h5!? might be a better move. Both Kasparov and Stohl suggest that this would provide more defensive opportunities, albeit without committing themselves to any precise analysis. Stohl notes that if White plays 14 d5, as in the main line, and then 14...exd5 15 ♗g2 c6 16 0-0 f6 17 ♖e1 ♗e7, he now does not have the option of ♕g4.

All the same, and even though Black could try something else at move 16, this seems only a minor improvement. After 18 e4 dxe4 19 ♘xe4, Black still has the problem that if he castles, the h5-pawn will be a target. For instance, 19...0-0 20 ♗f3 regains the pawn, but White can also consider 20 g4!?, and if 20...d5 21 ♘g3 hxg4 22 ♕xg4 ♗h7 23 h5 ♖f7 24 ♘f5 ♗xf5 25 ♕xf5 ♗d6 26 h6!?, continuing to press.

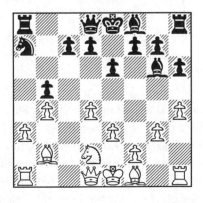

14 d5!

White is trying to open up lines, Black is trying to close them.

Many of the games we are examining here appear, after close analysis, to be "objectively" dubious in their sacrificial variations, gambit play rather than positional play. On this occasion, however, we can say that this is excellent positional play, well thought out, and making it difficult for the opponent to come close to equality, let alone gain the advantage. If I were to select games on the basis of purely positional wins by the young Kasparov, this one would be very close to the top of the list, if not the top.

In terms of his own performance, this tournament was not one of Kasparov's best. He managed only 50%, with losses to Timman, Spassky and Petrosian in rounds 4, 5 and 7. Then in round eight, there was this game. Kasparov's play was on the up again, and showing he could overcome even world-class positional grandmasters in positional chess. The question would arise of how he would fare against Karpov at World Championship level, but as was becoming clearer, this was going to be sooner rather than later.

Back to the game. Imagine what would happen if Kasparov were not to sacrifice the d-pawn. *Fritz* gives the position as equal, in several different lines. Maybe that is fair, but one cannot help feeling that Andersson would be happy playing for slightly more than equality, for as long as it would take for Black to try for a workable edge. Andersson was always a grinder.

On 14 ♘b3, White might be content now after 14...d5 15 ♘c5, but the really crabby move would be 14...c6!?, covering b5 and d5, and keeping the d-pawn back, so that if White tries to press forward with ♘c5, Black still has ...d7-d6. Or he might even throw in 14...♗e4!? first.

Whereas 14 e4, trying to make progress without sacrifice, is easily countered by 14...d5, and White's dark-squared bishop is shut out of the game.

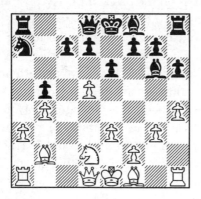

14...exd5 15 ♗g2

White is making excellent use of the bishop pair, a theme of many of these central pawn sacrifices, as for instance in Spassky-Tal (Game 14) and the next two wins by Kasparov.

15...c6 16 0-0

Andersson now has to consider his options. He is a pawn up, and he can expect to remain a pawn up. That is the good news. Everything else is going to be more difficult.

Black's pieces are almost completely undeveloped, and it is hard for him to castle, as 16...♗e7? drops the vital g-pawn after 17 ♗xg7. Moreover, of the two pieces that aren't still on their starting squares, the light-squared bishop is in fact exposed on g6, while the knight is now misplaced on a7. Given time Black might bring the knight into play via ...♘c8 and ...♘d6 or ...♘b6, but it will be difficult to find the time, as White is already preparing to attack with e3-e4.

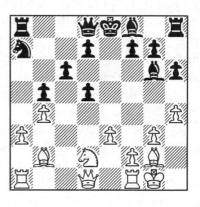

16...f6

According to the theories of the first World Champion, Wilhelm Steinitz, back in the late 19th century, this move would be regarded as poor, an unnecessary advance of his defensive pawns, and creating structural weaknesses. However, Steinitz overplayed this argument, both in theory and in practice, and landed up in some horrendously cramped positions.

Andersson's move is ugly, but at least the dark-squared bishop can now move, while the other one can retreat to f7. Could he have played better by following Steinitzian prescriptions? Most modern players would find this doubtful. The problem is that, while the opposing forces are temporarily in balance, in the sense that neither player is going to win material or give mate immediately, White's pieces will steadily improve, whereas Black's are unlikely to make any real impression on the opponent.

As an example, *Fritz*, clearly an admirer of the ancients, suggests 16...♖g8.

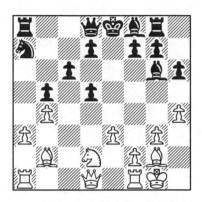

The obvious drawback is that the black king is now stuck in the centre, so that White can build up his position at leisure. Alternatively, he can just go for it straight away with 17 e4 dxe4 18 ♘xe4, and if 18...d5 19 ♘c3 ♗e7 20 ♘xd5! cxd5 21 ♗xd5 smashes through the black centre. Play might continue 21...♖c8 22 ♕f3 ♗f6 (or 22...♕d7 23 h5 ♗f5 24 ♖ad1 ♗d6 25 ♖fe1+ ♔f8 26 ♗xf7!) 23 ♖ad1 ♕c7 24 h5 ♗h7 25 ♖fe1+ ♔f8 26 ♗xf6 gxf6 27 ♕xf6 ♖g7 28 ♖c1 ♕xc1 29 ♕e7+ ♔g8 30 ♖xc1 ♖xc1+ 31 ♔h2 and White wins.

Another possibility is 16...♘c8 17 ♖e1 ♘e7, but after 18 e4 dxe4 19 h5 ♗h7 20 ♘xe4 ♗xe4 21 ♖xe4 d5 22 ♖e3, the problem remains of how Black is to complete his kingside development.

White's sacrifice is of a positional nature, and not a gambit. There is no sense of urgency in having to attack quickly, although of course a direct attack usually helps. The main point is that White is creating so much pressure with his pieces, while Black's forces are so underdeveloped, that it is difficult for Black even to hold onto the pawn (note the problem at g7), and if he ever loses the pawn, Black will be clearly worse.

17 ♖e1!

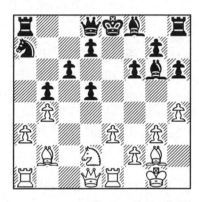

A quiet little move, delaying the pawn break in order to complete his development first.

Even so, White can also play directly 17 e4 dxe4 18 ♕g4!, and if 18...♗f7? 19 ♘xe4 looks even more threatening than the line in the game. For instance, after 19...♗e6?, White has the old idea of a double-check and mate on the e-file, albeit a more novel setting, with 20 ♕g6+ ♗f7 21 ♖fe1! ♗xg6 22 ♘d6 mate. Or if 19...d5 20 ♖fe1! dxe4 21 ♖xe4+ ♗e7 22 ♖ae1 0-0 23 ♖xe7 leaves Black in a hopeless position.

So he should probably prefer

18...♔f7, when 19 h5 ♗h7 20 ♗xe4 ♗xe4 21 ♘xe4 ♗e7 22 ♖fe1! transposes to the game, not that Black has anything to look forward to there either.

17...♗e7

After 17...f5?!, trying to prevent e3-e4, White could play 18 ♘f3 and grind away on the dark squares. Or he could show contempt with 18 e4! dxe4 19 ♘xe4 fxe4 20 ♗xe4 ♗f7 (if 20...♗xe4 21 ♕h5+, with mate to follow) 21 ♗xc6+ ♗e7 22 ♗xa8 ♕xa8 23 ♗xg7 and wins.

Or if 17...♗d6 18 ♕g4 ♔f7 19 h5 ♗h7 20 e4 dxe4 21 ♘xe4 ♗c7 (or 21...♗e7 22 ♖ad1 d5 23 ♘c3 ♖e8 24 ♖xd5!) 22 ♖ad1 d5 23 ♘xf6! gxf6 24 ♕e6+ ♔g7 25 ♗xd5! cxd5 26 ♖xd5, and a win for White. In such lines, the point of the sacrifices is simply to destroy the opponent's pawn structure and bring the king out into the open.

Stohl gives 17...♔f7 as a possible improvement, but after 18 ♕b3!, White threatens e3-e4, as well as building up for another sacrifice on d5. For instance, if 18...f5 19 ♘f3 ♗d6 20 ♘d4 ♖e8, White breaks through with 21 ♗xd5+! cxd5 22 ♕xd5+ ♔e7 23 e4 fxe4 24 ♘f5+ ♗xf5 25 ♕xf5 and the king is caught in the centre. Black can just about survive the mating attack after 25...♕b8 26 ♕xe4+ ♔f7 27 ♕f5+ ♔g8 28 ♖xe8+ ♕xe8 29 ♕d5+, but not the endgame.

18 ♕g4 ♔f7 19 h5 ♗h7 20 e4 dxe4 21 ♗xe4

White is attacking hard on the light squares, which makes it all the more refreshing that his mating sacrifice a few moves later takes place on the dark squares.

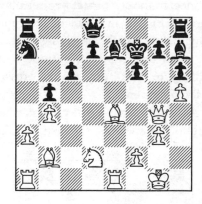

21...♗xe4

After 21...d5 22 ♗xh7 ♖xh7 23 ♕g6+ (23 ♘f3 is also strong) 23...♔g8 24 ♖e6, White wins by purely positional means.

22 ♘xe4 ♘c8

In his notes in *Informator 32*, Kasparov gives a couple of nice variations here: 22...♖f8 23 ♖ad1 d5 24 ♘xf6!, and 22...♖e8 23 ♕g6+ ♔f8 24 g4! intending ♘g3-f5 and wins.

A third option, 22...d5, does not help either. Stohl suggests 23 ♘c5 ♗xc5 24 ♕e6+ ♔f8 25 bxc5 with winning positional pressure.

Alternatively, White can continue as in the game with 23 ♖ad1, and if 23...♖e8 24 ♕g6+ ♔f8, there is another way in with 25 ♘g5! (or the sadistic quiet move 25 ♔g2! first) 25...hxg5 26 h6 gxh6 27 ♕xh6+ ♔f7 28 ♕h7+ ♔f8 29 ♔g2! (but not 29 ♕g6? c5! 30 ♔g2 d4! 31 ♖h1? ♕d5+, when 32...♕g8! turns the tables) 29...c5 (or 29...d4 30 ♖xd4) 30 ♖h1 d4 31 ♕f5, and Black has no defence.

23 ♖ad1

An obvious point to make, perhaps,

and there is no point in repeating it every game, but developing, bringing pieces into action, is absolutely critical for attacking chess. The impact for White, through bringing the second rook into the attack, is far greater than the extra tempo for Black's defence.

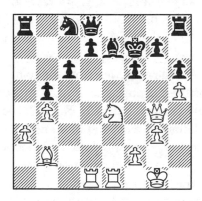

23...♖a7

A difficult decision, and all the more so because, ultimately, Black is already losing. Andersson places his reliance on his rook defence on the second rank, to be uncovered by a later ...d7-d5, and keeps his knight on c8 to defend on e7 and d6.

The other possibility was to try 23...♘b6, covering the pawn on d7 with the knight, and leaving the rook on the back rank. Then the sacrifice 24 ♘xf6? does not work, as after 24...♗xf6 25 ♕g6+ ♔f8 26 ♗xf6 ♕xf6, the e8-square is still covered by the rook, but White has several other ways forward.

24 ♕g6+ ♔g8 25 ♘d6 ♗xd6 26 ♖xd6 ♘d5 27 ♕f5 is one possibility, when White has decisive pressure.

Another option is 24 ♖d6!?, when 24...♗xd6 25 ♕g6+ ♔f8 26 ♘xd6 forces

Black to give up his queen. Note how White is bombarding the dark squares on d6 and f6. If Black tries 24...♔f8 instead, White can show admirable consistency with 25 ♕f5, cracking the queen, rook, bishop and knight against the breaking ice on f6, and if 25...♗xd6 26 ♘xf6! gxf6 27 ♗xf6 is decisive.

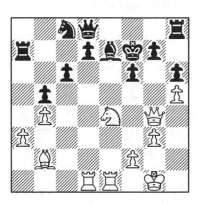

24 ♘xf6!!

This wins. White has placed all his pieces on attacking squares, and now all he needs to do is break open the enemy pawn structure, by means of a sacrifice.

24...gxf6

If 24...♗xf6 25 ♕g6+ ♔f8 26 ♗xf6 gxf6 27 ♖e6, and Black's defence folds.

25 ♕g6+ ♔f8 26 ♗c1 d5

This is the idea behind the earlier ...♖a7, trying to defend along the second rank. For instance, if now 27 ♗xh6+ ♖xh6 28 ♕xh6+ ♔g8 29 ♖d4 ♗f8! 30 ♖g4+ ♖g7 allows Black to hang on.

The only other possibility is 26...♕e8 27 ♗xh6+ ♖xh6 28 ♕xh6+ ♔f7, but it can only be expected that White would find a win somewhere. Stohl gives 29 ♕h7+ ♚f8 30 h6 ♕f7 31 ♕f5 ♘d6 32 ♕f4 ♘e8 33 ♕e3!, and if 33...♖b7 34 ♕xe7+ ♕xe7 35 ♖xe7 ♚xe7 36 h7.

27 ♖d4!

Playing with accuracy. The capture on h6 must wait until the rook trundles in.

27...♘d6 28 ♖g4 ♘f7

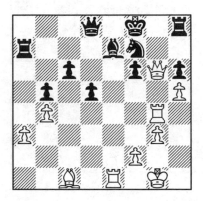

Now Black has an extra defender on h6, but it makes no difference, as White has an extra, and more powerful, attacker.

29 ♗xh6+! ♚e8 30 ♗g7 1-0

If 30...♖g8 then 31 h6 and 32 h7 wins.

A superb blend of positional and tactical chess.

We are leaving a slight gap in the narrative here, rejoining with Kasparov aged 19, a very strong 2640 Grandmaster, and aiming to proceed much further. At Bugojno 1982, he again finished 1½ points clear, as in Banja Luka 1979, and indeed the World Juniors at Dortmund 1980, but he was now playing far stronger opposition. Seven of the participants, including Petrosian, Spassky and Timman, had also played at Tilburg 1981, but Kasparov had learned a lot from his experience the previous year, and went through the tournament without losing a game. In fact, he scored 7½ in the first nine rounds, before easing his way to victory with three quick draws in the final four. (The older Kasparov would have tried to win those games as well.)

All the victories from Bugojno are worth studying, the knight manoeuvres against Lubomir Kavalek being perhaps the most entertaining. For this collection, I wanted to have another look at the central pawn sacrifice.

The win against Najdorf is quick and forceful, and has the wow factor, but is it totally sound? Kasparov revises his earlier opinions, gold dust if one is trying to understand his thought processes, and he was indeed overoptimistic at times. But does pessimism necessarily create better practical results? Najdorf went wrong after the onslaught, and lost quickly.

Game 21
G.Kasparov-M.Najdorf
Bugojno 1982
Queen's Indian Defence

---

1 d4 ♘f6 2 c4 e6 3 ♘f3 b6 4 a3

A loss of a tempo in terms of development, but it can be regarded as useful to prevent any possibility of ...♗b4, putting pressure on the knight on c3.

4...♗b7 5 ♘c3 d5 6 cxd5

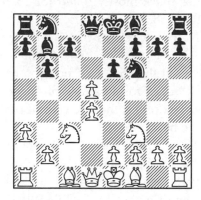

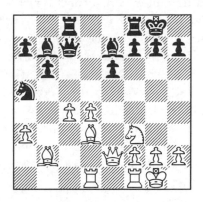

6...♘xd5

Most of Kasparov's opponents in the early years preferred this to 6...exd5. It seems natural to keep the long diagonal open, but Kasparov was thinking up ideas of to utilize the extra pawn in the centre, ideas of an attack. Yes, even a gambit attack, if required.

The 4 a3 variation – the Petrosian System – became extremely popular during Kasparov's advocacy of this line, but soon antidotes were developed, and many others decided that the simple 6...exd5 was also a good way of meeting it.

7 e3

And Kasparov himself was later to switch to 7 ♕c2, as in his win against Gheorghiu a few months later (Game 22), and then to 3 ♘c3, and eventually to 1 e4.

7...♗e7 8 ♗b5+ c6 9 ♗d3 ♘xc3 10 bxc3 c5 11 0-0 ♘c6 12 e4

The following year, against Portisch, Kasparov held back the e-pawn, preferring 12 ♗b2 ♖c8 13 ♕e2 0-0 14 ♖ad1 ♕c7?! and now 15 c4! cxd4 16 exd4 ♘a5,

when Black was again rocked by 17 d5! exd5 18 cxd5 ♗xd5 19 ♗xh7+ ♔xh7 20 ♖xd5 ♔g8, after which Kasparov broke through in a sacrificial attack with 21 ♗xg7!! ♔xg7 22 ♘e5 ♖fd8 23 ♕g4+ ♔f8 24 ♕f5 f6 25 ♘d7+ ♖xd7 26 ♖xd7, and went on to win in G.Kasparov-L.Portisch, Niksic 1983.

It all seems so easy, a pawn breakthrough, then a piece sacrifice in front of the king, then checkmate or win of material. Kasparov had evidently worked hard on this opening, and was rewarded by an excellent victory.

Portisch had earlier traded draws in this line: 15 e4 ♘a5 16 h3 ½-½ L.Portisch-L.Polugaevsky, Moscow 1981, and 16 ♖fe1 ½-½ with reversed colours in L.Polugaevsky-L.Portisch, European Team Championships, Plovdiv 1983. But if he was expecting another quick draw with the black pieces, he was in for a shock. Kasparov was beginning to develop an extraordinarily deep and, for the opponents, frightening opening repertoire.

12...0-0

In the very next round Kasparov

had this line again, against Ivkov, who tried 12...♖c8 13 ♗b2 ♗f6. By now the reader should not be surprised to see 14 d5! exd5 15 exd5 ♕xd5 16 ♖e1+ ♔f8 17 ♕c2 ♘e5 18 ♗e4 ♘xf3+ 19 ♗xf3 ♕d7 20 ♖ad1 ♕c7 21 ♗xb7 ♕xb7, when White had excellent compensation for the pawn, and later won once more in G.Kasparov-B.Ivkov, Bugojno 1982.

13 ♗e3 cxd4 14 cxd4 ♖c8 15 ♕e2 ♘a5 16 ♖fe1

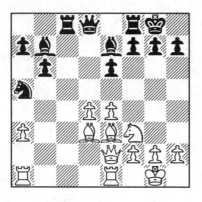

A familiar position, at least since Kasparov started playing it. Theory may suggest that this is equal, and *Fritz* gives over a dozen reasonable lines for Black, but in practical terms White scored an impressive 71% – until 1982, when White, rather surprisingly, stopped playing 16 ♖fe1. Perhaps it was becoming clear that Black had, with accurate play, found more improvements? Or else that it was suddenly a theoretical backwater, as players investigated other ideas earlier on, such as 7...♘d7 and 7...g6 for Black, or 7 ♕c2 and 7 ♗d2 for White.

16...♕d6

One of several attempts. In other games Black mostly opted for 16...♖c3 or 16...♔h8.

Kasparov relates that, while working out his next position, "I managed to exploit the advanced position of the black queen for an attack on the kingside. To do this, the two central pawns had to be sacrificed."

This is definitely the viewpoint of an attacking player. A positional player, such as Petrosian, might take the contrary view that, while White has more space in the centre, his actual advantage is minimal, perhaps even non-existent. White indeed has to be careful over his weaknesses on the queenside, and there is always the danger that the a-pawn could drop, early on or after a later queen exchange.

White, it seems, has either to play very cautiously, or extremely boldly.

17 d5!?

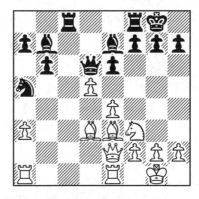

This is the sacrificial idea. Kasparov later suggested that the "routine" 17 h4 would have been better. These were his inverted commas, not mine, unless of course a previous editor had added them.

Whatever the case, this is not quite as routine as it might be to Kasparov. The pawn is not threatening anything, but is rather hoping to threaten, a somewhat slower process, and Black now has the opportunity to develop his counterplay.

There are some interesting lines with 17...♘b3, but it is likely that Najdorf's intention, following ...♕d6, would have been 17...♖c3, attacking the a-pawn. It would seem wise not to allow Black two connected passed pawns, so probably White should try 18 a4, but after 18...♘b3 19 ♖a2 ♖fc8, Black is making the faster progress.

Kasparov's "routine" 17 h4 turns out to be something of a halfway push, as it is neither aggressive attack, nor quiet positional play. Sometimes it is better to go one way or the other. With hindsight, and with the help of *Fritz*, 17 ♗a6! ♗xa6 18 ♕xa6 seems preferable, giving White a small degree of pressure, though even here 18...♖c7! looks pretty equal.

Finally, it is time to consider, if only briefly, 17 e5?! ♕d5. Giving away the d5-square is anti-positional. White gains a small and temporary initiative on the b1-h7 diagonal, but loses control on the more important a8-g1 diagonal. Black is better.

For White to make any effective use of the b2-h7 diagonal, he needs to force Black to block the d5-square with his pawn, and this is the justification for 17 d5!?. It's interesting, but does it work? In the game, yes, though closer analysis gives a different impression.

17...exd5 18 e5!?

With the d5-square now occupied by a black pawn, the timing is right for White to press on with e4-e5. He can then use the d4-square as a stepping stone for the knight, and in some lines the bishop may go there too.

18...♕e6

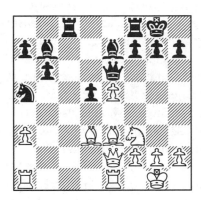

19 ♘d4

There is no possibility of retreat. He has to give up his second pawn, otherwise he would just be a pawn down for nothing.

19...♕xe5 20 ♘f5

White must attack. Having sacrificed two pawns, there is even less point now in doing nothing much, and giving his opponent time to consolidate.

Trying to win the exchange is no great compensation either, when both pawns have gone. 20 ♗f5 ♗d6 21 f4 ♕f6 22 ♗xc8 ♖xc8 23 ♘b5 ♘c4 is just good for Black.

So what has Kasparov gained by his moves? White has no real pawn play to speak of – except perhaps an f2-f4 prod if appropriate. What he is much better able to do is attack with the pieces. His queen, two bishops, a knight and one of the rooks are already on threatening squares, and the other rook is in reserve.

Conversely, Black's forces look scattered. The rook on c8 is on a useful open file, but cannot be said to be dangerous, or even a good defender of the kingside. Black's knight is similarly out of touch. Granted, ...♘c4 might be useful, especially if one of the white bishops would be exchanged, but Black may need a little more than this. His light-squared bishop is also out of play, blocked off by his own pawn on d5, which does not help either.

An even more serious problem is that Black's queen and dark-squared bishop are open to tactical threats. Kasparov uses the threats to these pieces, to organize a quick and thoroughly dangerous attack on Black's underprotected kingside fortress.

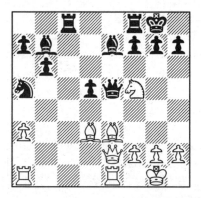

Najdorf was now confronted with a difficult decision. White is attacking, but the natural instinct would be that Black has good defensive possibilities,

and there is certainly no need for his position to collapse. Black might have to calculate extremely accurately, but one would expect that grandmasters should be able to find good moves.

The first essential attributes of good defence are looking for counter-chances and, above all, to avoid falling into traps. In any seriously complicated position, this will mean hard work. It can make all the difference between a quick defeat, or inspired counterplay, and perhaps a rebuffing of a potentially speculative attack.

Black's position should be playable, one might feel, but the nightmare for the defender is the suspicion that there are two seemingly reasonable moves, one of which defends, and one of which leads to a loss. How can you tell which is which?

So, a hint or two for the reader, and how would you deal with Kasparov in aggressive mood, who has chucked in a couple of pawns and is going for mate? This is a question that all Kasparov's opponents would have to confront over the next twenty years, and some managed to answer it better than others.

20...♗f6?!

Najdorf removes the bishop from immediate threats, and increases his defensive options. Sensible play, and Black must hope it will work. Indeed, it should have been good enough, but it was not the best.

First, we should eliminate a couple of tempting but fatal replies, mentioned by Kasparov. 20...g6?? loses at once to 21 ♗d4!, as the knight delivers mate if the black queen moves away. While 20...♗c5?? is refuted by 21 ♕h5!, and the discovered check with the knight will enable White either to checkmate on h7 or win the black queen. Or if 21...♔h8, there is there is another discovery with the bishop, 22 ♗xc5, exposing the rook.

The best option was for Black to bring his knight back into the game with 20...♘c4!,

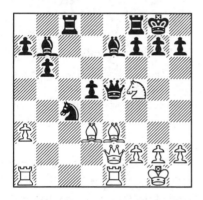

threatening to exchange one of the white bishops, while also usefully defending the queen. The position is tactically complicated, especially over the board, but ultimately it seems to be good for Black.

Kasparov suggested, in his notes at the time, that 21 ♕f1 "!", intending ♗d4, would have given White a clear advantage. But this turns out to be overoptimistic. Indeed, in later comments (in *The Test of Time*), Kasparov described this more strongly as "fairy tales!". 21...♗d6! refutes White's attack, as Black's own threats to h2 gain a vital tempo. Since 22 ♘xd6 ♕xd6 and 22 g3

♘xe3 23 ♖xe3 ♕f6 give White no initiative whatsoever, he has to try 22 f4 ♕f6, but now the hidden point of Black's defence is revealed. If 23 ♗d4, then 23...♗c5! pins the attacking bishop to the king, and White has nothing.

So can Kasparov justify his startling pawn sacrifices? Or is it a case of "interesting but unsound"? Or, as Kasparov himself later suggested, was his play "frivolous"?

Kasparov gave a revised main line, 21 ♕h5 g6 22 ♗d4 gxh5 23 ♘xe7+ ♕xe7 24 ♖xe7 ♘a5 25 ♖ae1 ♘c6 26 ♖xb7 ♘d4 27 ♖xa7, taking the view that White should hold the position, Black's pawns all being isolated. At first this might seem unconvincing, as Black's rook and knight are active, and his passed d-pawn potentially has good support. After 27...♖c3 28 ♗f1, however, the bishop is a good defender, covering any later pawn advances on the b- and d-files, and preventing back row mates, which means that White's rooks have relative freedom.

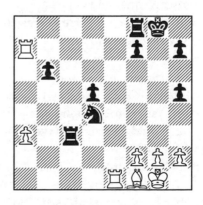

This should be a draw. If 28...♖fc8? 29 ♖d1 ♘c6 30 ♖b7 Black loses a pawn.

Or 28...♘c2 29 ♖b1 ♖xa3 30 ♖xa3 ♘xa3 31 ♖xb6, and White will have no difficulty in holding. Finally, 28...♖d8 29 ♖ee7 ♘c6 30 ♖ad7 ♖xd7 31 ♖xd7 d4 32 a4 also leaves White with a solid position.

Unfortunately, Black can improve on this line too. 22...♕xd4! 23 ♘xd4 gxh5 24 ♖xe7 reaches the same position as after 22...gxh5, but with a white knight on d4, rather than a bishop, so that White's counterplay is less substantial. For example, 24...♘a5 25 ♖ae1 ♖c3! (not possible with a bishop on d4) 26 ♗f1 ♖xa3 27 ♘b5 ♖b3 28 ♘xa7 ♖d8 or 25 ♘f5 ♖c3! 26 ♗f1 ♗c8 27 ♘d6 ♘c4 28 ♘xc8 ♖xc8 28 ♖xa7 b5, and Black is a lot more active than in the comparable position (after 28 ♗f1) in the 22...gxh5 variation.

It should be added that White has several alternatives on moves 21 or 22, including for example 21 ♗d4, or 21 ♗f4, or even 21 ♗xb6. Many of these might be worth investigating, sometimes leading to an opposite-coloured bishop endgame, and a possible draw, though in each case there seems to be at least a degree of doubt.

So the best that might be said, had Najdorf played his strongest line, is that Kasparov's double pawn sacrifice was not necessarily losing for White, but he would certainly have had to suffer for a draw.

But that's with the benefit of home analysis and a strong computer. Over the board, as we shall see, Najdorf failed to find any of the critical lines, not here, nor on the next two moves

either. Perhaps at the age of 72, Najdorf was suffering the same malaise that afflicted Spassky in Game 14, or perhaps it was just an off day. Whatever the reason, Kasparov's hyper-aggressive play was a total success, as Najdorf rapidly capitulated.

21 ♕g4

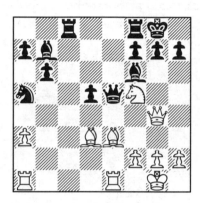

21...♖ce8?

This is a difficult move to understand, given that Black is a strong grandmaster. The rook on the c-file is crucial to any active counterplay, and needs to be preserved, if at all possible. The natural move is 21...♖fe8, again covering the e-file, but leaving the second rook active on c8.

One can only assume that Najdorf was worried about ♘h6+ in some lines, and wanted to keep the f7-square protected, but 21...♖fe8 22 ♘h6+ ♔f8 is good for Black, even if at times complicated. 23 ♗d2 ♕xa1 24 ♖xa1 (or 24 ♗b4+ ♖c5) 24...♗xa1 leaves Black with rook, bishop and two pawns for a queen, a material advantage, and 25 ♘f5 ♖c5 26 ♘d6 ♖e7 sees him in control.

22 ♗d4? is not given by Kasparov, presumably being regarded as too elementary. Indeed, 22...♕xe1+ 23 ♖xe1 ♖xe1+ 24 ♗f1 ♖xf1+! 25 ♔xf1 ♗a6+ 26 ♔e1 ♖c1+ 27 ♔d2 ♘b3+ wins comfortably for Black.

The best line is 22 ♗d2! ♕xa1 23 ♖xa1 ♗xa1, as in the main line of the game, but with the black rooks on much better squares.

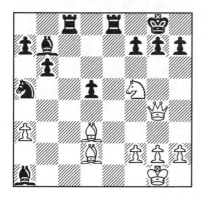

Then if White tries the sacrifice on g7, Black wins after 24 ♘xg7?? ♔xg7 25 ♗h6 ♖c1+! 26 ♗xc1 (or 26 ♗f1 ♖xf1+ 27 ♔xf1 ♗a6+ 28 ♔g1 ♖e1 mate) 26...♖e1+ 27 ♗f1 ♗a6, followed by ...♖xf1+ and ...♖xc1.

White does better with 24 ♘d6 ♖c1+! 25 ♗xc1 ♖e1+ 26 ♗f1 ♗a6 27 g3!, when 27...h5! (not 27...♗xf1?? 28 ♕c8+) 28 ♕xh5 ♖xf1+ 29 ♔g2 ♖c1 30 ♕xf7+ ♔h7 31 ♕h5+ ♔g8 is a draw by perpetual check.

Kasparov instead recommends 24 h4, with an exclamation mark, and given as strong. The advancing of the pawn towards the black monarch is useful, but more important is the escape square for his own king. White

now threatens ♘xg7. These days, the computer forces the analyst to doubt everything, and *Fritz* suggests that Black has several ways to keep an edge, but on closer examination White does seem to have good play.

For example, if 24...♖e6 25 ♘h6+ ♔f8 26 ♗b4+ ♖c5 27 ♘xf7! ♔xf7 28 ♗xc5 bxc5 29 ♕f4+ ♗f6 30 ♕c7+ ♖e7 31 ♕xa5 c4 32 ♗xh7 g6 33 g4! ♗xh4 (or 33...♔g7 34 g5 ♗d4 35 ♕d8) 34 ♕c3 ♗f6 35 ♕c2 frees the bishop with a clear advantage, as Black cannot use his connected passed pawns effectively.

Alternatively, Black might try 24...♖c7 25 ♘h6+,

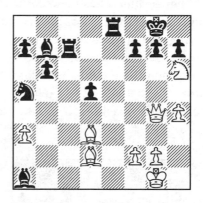

but then 25...♔h8 is met by 26 ♕f4! ♖ce7 27 ♗b4 gxh6 28 ♗xe7 ♖xe7 29 ♕xh6 ♔g8 30 ♗xh7+ ♔h8 31 ♕f8+ ♔xh7 32 ♕xe7, and the queen and kingside pawns are superior to Black's three scattered minor pieces. Or if 25...♔f8 26 ♗b4 ♖c5 27 ♘f5 g6 28 ♘d6 ♖c1+ 29 ♗f1 ♗a6 30 ♕d7! ♖xf1+ 31 ♔h2 ♗e5+ 32 ♔h3! ♖h1+ 33 ♔g4 ♗e2+!? (or 33...h5+ 34 ♔g5) 34 f3 ♗xf3+ 35 gxf3 ♖g1+ 36 ♔h3 ♖g3+ 37 ♔h2 wins, as Black has no good discovered check.

Naturally Black has many other options in these variations, so in order to avoid long pages of analysis, we may say that, while *Fritz* suggests Black is better by about half a pawn, this is misleading, and overstates the material advantage. At the moment Black has two rooks and two extra pawns for the queen. But White's minor pieces coordinate very well with the queen, whereas Black's rooks are relatively ineffective, and his minor pieces are all over the place.

For the annotator, the interesting question is the disjunction between Kasparov's claim that he would have been better after 24 h4, and *Fritz*'s assessment that Black was better. Considering the sample variations given above, I think a fair conclusion would be to suggest that White is at least not worse.

However, Black had another defence in 21...♕c3!,

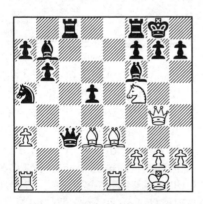

which Kasparov gave as best in *Informator 33*. If nothing else, it is much simpler, 22 ♘e7+ ♔h8 23 ♖ac1 (not 23 ♗f5? ♘b3!, winning) 23...♕xd3 24 ♘xf7+ ♔g8 25 ♘h6+ ♔h8 being a quick draw by perpetual check. Black cannot take the knight because of 24...♖xf7?? 25 ♖xc8+ and mates.

Instead, Kasparov suggested that 22 ♘e7+ ♗xe7 23 ♗d4 ♕xd4 24 ♕xd4 ♗f6 25 ♕g4 ♗xa1 26 ♖xa1 might be slightly better for White, but this seems like more youthful enthusiasm. After 26...g6, for instance, Black is secure with rook, knight and two pawns for the queen, and certainly isn't worse here.

22 ♗d2! ♕xa1?

The final mistake. 22...♕c7? is no better after 23 ♘h6+ ♔h8 24 ♖xe8 ♖xe8 25 ♕f5 ♖e4 26 ♗xe4 dxe4 27 ♖c1 ♘c4 28 ♗g5 and wins, as given by Kasparov.

However, *Fritz* shows that Black can still survive with 22...♕b2!,

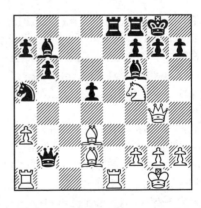

again advancing into the enemy queenside, to keep in contact with a1, d2 and, crucially, f6, so that if 23 ♘h6+ ♔h8 24 ♕f5? g6! thwarts the attack. White obviously has a draw after 24 ♘xf7+ ♔g8 25 ♘h6+, but does he have more than that?

The critical line would seem to be 24 ♕h5! ♖e4 25 ♗b4 g6 26 ♕f3 ♖xb4 (if 26...♖fe8?! 27 ♗xe4 dxe4 28 ♖ab1 e3 29 ♖xb2 ♗xf3 30 ♘xf7+ ♔g8 31 ♘d6 ♗xb2 32 ♘xe8 with a clear advantage) 27 axb4 ♘c6 28 b5 ♘a5 29 ♖ab1 ♕d4 30 ♖bd1, when White may well be better, but at least Black is still in the game, with two pawns for the exchange.

23 ♖xa1 ♗xa1

If the rooks were on c8 and e8, this would still have been an absorbing struggle. As it is, Black's game collapses.

24 ♘xg7!

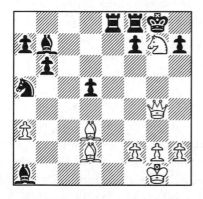

24...♗xg7

If 24...♗c8 then 25 ♘e6+! ♔h8 26 ♕f5 with mate to follow. Or 24...f5 25 ♘xf5+ ♔h8 26 ♕h5 and White wins again.

25 ♗h6 1-0

We end this book with the Moscow Interzonal which, in 1982, kicked off Kasparov's first challenge for the World Championship.

A few readers may be disappointed that some of Kasparov's most extraor-

dinary games are not included in this collection of attacking and combinative play. And perhaps this final game is too ordinary to be regarded as a brilliancy, but we must still remember that Kasparov beat a strong grandmaster in great style, playing utterly convincing chess.

We need some of these clear technical attacking games as something of a correction to the brilliant, but slightly unsound games, such as the one we have just examined.

Game 22
G.Kasparov-F.Gheorghiu
Moscow Interzonal 1982
Queen's Indian Defence

---

1 d4 ♘f6 2 c4 e6 3 ♘f3 b6 4 a3

Another outing for the 4 a3 variation. Before long Kasparov had turned to other systems, a loss to Korchnoi in the first game of their 1983 Candidates match putting something of a question mark on Kasparov's strategic plan. Naturally, he worked on developing his ideas, but by that time, his opponents had also improved their understanding of the line, and the surprise element had gone. Kasparov moved on.

In the unfinished 1984-85 World Championship match against Karpov, for example, Kasparov switched to 4 g3, albeit without much success. He did try the a2-a3 system a couple of times, and indeed won a game, but this was now his second string. And in their second match, Kasparov opted instead for 3 ♘c3, allowing the Nimzo-Indian after 3...♗b4.

4...♗b7 5 ♘c3 d5 6 cxd5 ♘xd5 7 ♕c2

Despite the victories with 7 e3 at Bugojno in May, Kasparov had spent the summer working on new ideas, and brought out 7 ♕c2, then rarely played, at the Interzonal in September. As we shall shortly see, he won a couple of games quickly with his new move. But as easy equalizing methods were worked out for Black, this line, too, became less appealing for Kasparov.

7...c5 8 e4 ♘xc3 9 bxc3

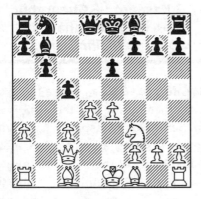

9...♗e7?!

If such a natural developing move is weak, what hope is there for Black? And particularly against an opponent like Kasparov? Black can in fact hold the balance, if he is careful later on, but there are simpler options:

a) 9...♘d7! 10 ♗d3 ♕c7 soon proved difficult to crack. If White allows 11...cxd4 12 cxd4 ♕xc2 13 ♗xc2, he has no hope of an advantage. But to keep the queens on, with 11 ♕b1, say, costs White a tempo, so that Black has no

difficulties there either.

Kasparov gives this as equal in *The Test of Time* (1986), and players with the white pieces were soon trying out 10 ♗f4, preventing ...♕c7. Nevertheless, it is doubtful that White gains much after 10...cxd4 11 cxd4 ♖c8.

b) 9...♘c6 10 ♗b2 ♖c8 (10...♗e7 is more solid) 11 ♖d1 cxd4 12 cxd4,

and now 12...a6 13 ♕d2! ♘a5 14 d5! soon gave White a crushing position in G.Kasparov-J.Murey, Moscow Interzonal 1982 (nine rounds before the win against Gheorghiu). Black's position soon collapsed after 14...exd5 15 exd5 ♗d6? (but if 15...♕e7+ 16 ♗e2 ♘c4 17 d6! ♘xd6 18 0-0 ♘e4 19 ♕f4 with a clear advantage) 16 ♗xg7 ♕e7+ 17 ♗e2 ♖g8 18 ♕h6! f5 19 ♗f6 ♕f8 20 ♕xh7 ♕f7 21 ♕xf5 ♖g6 22 ♕e4+ ♔f8 23 ♘g5 ♖xg5 24 ♗xg5 ♖e8 25 ♗h6+ ♔g8 26 ♕g4+ 1-0.

In the late 80s, Joel Lautier tried 12...♗d6!?, and was rewarded with good wins against IM Sarno, and GMs Miles and Petursson, showing that close attention to Kasparov's opponents' moves can sometimes be highly productive. Since this is the last game in the book, I add no supplementary material. But the reader will enjoy these games, which can be found in the databases, and then to go through the spectacular White reply in I.Naumkin-A.Adorjan, Kusabasi 1990. Treat this as a training exercise!

10 ♗b5+ ♗c6 11 ♗d3

By now a familiar Kasparov motif, a bishop check on b5 to create an obstruction on c6, then the bishop withdraws.

11...♘d7 12 0-0

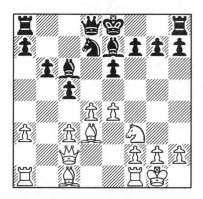

12...h6?!

You do not want to make unnecessary rook-pawn moves.

Gheorghiu would have been worried about dropping his h-pawn after 12...0-0 13 d5 exd5 14 cxd5 ♗xd5 15 ♗xh7+ ♔h8, but while the king is slightly exposed, it is not going to be under serious mating threats, for example after 16 ♗e4 ♗xe4 17 ♕xe4 ♔g8!. And the pawn structure would tend, if anything, to favour Black as we approach the endgame.

Black can also consider disentan-

gling his pieces on the queenside, if not by 12...♖c8? 13 ♗a6, which is extremely unproductive. In A.Yusupov-J.Campos Moreno, Lucerne Olympiad 1982, Black declined the humiliation of a retreat with 13...♖a8, preferring to resign the exchange down a few moves later.

However, 12...♕c7, with the follow-up of ...♗b7, is fully acceptable, and maybe also 12...♗b7 first. For example, a draw soon resulted in P.Cramling-B.Spassky, Veterans vs Women, Copenhagen 1997, after 12...♕c7 13 ♖e1 ♗b7 14 ♕e2 0-0 15 ♗d2 ♖ac8 16 a4 e5 17 d5 c4, though White could perhaps have tried harder.

The general impression is that White has only a slender edge. The only chance of a quick substantial advantage seems to be if Black is inadequately prepared. Back in 1982, this might have worked, when Kasparov had the advantage of trying out new ideas in an under-researched opening, but players soon wised up. Apart, that is, from the occasional mishap (see the note to 25 c4 at the end of the game).

13 ♖d1!

With Black having squandered a tempo on ...h7-h6, White is happy to postpone his attack slightly, and continue his development.

Kasparov says that 13 d5 immediately was also possible, and then 13...exd5 14 exd5 ♗xd5 15 ♖d1, but as Stohl later noted, after 15...♗xf3! 16 gxf3 a6 17 ♗f5 ♖a7, Black's defence is holding and he keeps his pawn advantage, even if White still has a lot of play for it.

Kasparov mentions 13 a4 as well, but White could only hope for a slight advantage here.

When one reads through Kasparov's earlier notes, one often gains the impression that, every time he played a good move, his trainers had advised him that he must also consider all other promising moves, to try to find something even better, or at least to find out why other moves are not quite so good.

Sometimes, though, the natural move does not require explanation. If it is clearly the best, why bother with alternatives?

13...♕c7?!

Gheorghiu's plan of defence is heavily based on preventing d4-d5, and in consequence he avoids the natural 13...0-0, in view of 14 d5 exd5 15 exd5 ♗xd5?? 16 ♗h7+, while after 15...♗b7 16 c4, White has a dangerous and well-protected passed pawn, and his pieces remain active. White is better, but Black can struggle on.

If instead 13...cxd4, Kasparov points out that 14 ♘xd4! ♕c7 15 ♘xc6 ♕xc6 16

♕e2, followed by ♗b5, makes it difficult for Black to complete his development.

14 d5!

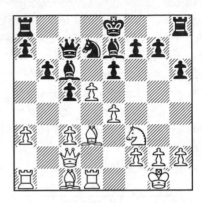

So often in chess, the more that a player tries to prevent something, the greater the thunderclap when it finally takes place.

Gheorghiu declined castling, worried about a later ♗h7+ after d4-d5, and as a result landed in much worse trouble. White plays d4-d5 anyway, but this time the black king is caught in the centre, precisely because he did not castle.

14...exd5 15 exd5 ♗xd5 16 ♗b5

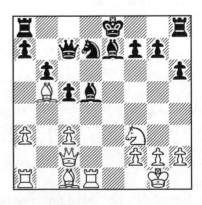

16...a6

Kasparov gives the line 16...♗c6 17 ♗f4 ♕b7 18 ♗xc6 ♕xc6 19 ♖e1, when the black king is stuck in the centre, and the bishop pinned. On the attempt to untangle the position by 19...♔f8 20 ♖ad1 ♖e8, he proposes 21 ♕f5 ♘f6 22 ♘e5 ♕c8 23 ♘d7+! ♘xd7 24 ♕xd7 ♕xd7 25 ♖xd7 g6 26 ♖dxe7, winning a piece after 26...♖xe7 27 ♗d6. A further tactic is seen after 23...♔g8? 24 ♖xe7! ♖xe7 25 ♘xf6+, but Black can avoid that one by playing 22...♕a4!, when there is nothing clearly decisive for White.

Instead, *Fritz* prefers 21 ♕e2!, when 21...♘f6 22 ♕c4 b5 23 ♕xf7+! ♔xf7 24 ♘e5+ and 25 ♘xc6 sees Black in a terrible mess. 21...♕c8 22 ♕d3! ♘f6 23 ♖xe7! ♖xe7 24 ♗d6 ♘e8 25 ♗xe7+ ♔xe7 26 ♕d5! followed by 27 ♘e5 is no better for Black, despite him still having the extra pawn. Finally, if 21...g6, at the very least White has 22 ♗d6!, netting the exchange and a probable win.

Kasparov does not mention 16...♗e6, presumably because it leaves the a8-h1 diagonal open, but White's advantage still has to be proven: 17 ♕e4! ♖d8 18 ♗f4 ♕c8 19 ♘e5 piles pressure on the pinned bishop, and if 19...0-0 20 ♘xd7 ♗xd7 21 ♗d3! enables White to take the other one.

Black has no solution to his problems. 19...a6 is met by 20 ♘xd7! axb5 (if 20...♗xd7 21 ♖e1 0-0 22 ♗d3 again, or 20...♖xd7 21 ♖xd7 ♗xd7 22 ♖e1 0-0 23 ♗xd7) 21 ♘xb6 ♗f5 (or 21...♕a6 22 ♕c6+ ♔f8 23 ♖xd8+ ♗xd8 24 ♘d7+) 22 ♘xc8 ♗xe4 23 ♘xe7 ♔xe7 24 ♖e1 f5 25

f3 wins a piece. And here 19...♔f8 runs into 20 ♘g6+! fxg6 (or 20...♔e8 21 ♖xd7!) 21 ♕xe6, threatening ♗c4 and mates, while if 21...♘f6 22 ♖xd8+ ♕xd8 23 ♖e1 and the threat is renewed.

17 ♗f4!

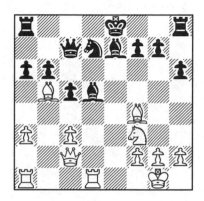

The one slightly difficult point in the rest of the game. After this, everything goes smoothly. White had to avoid 17 ♗xd7+? ♕xd7 18 c4 ♗e4!, and Black escapes.

17...♕xf4

On 17...♕b7, Kasparov gives 18 ♗xd7+ ♕xd7 19 c4 ♕g4 20 ♖xd5 ♕xf4 21 ♖e1 ♖a7 22 ♘e5 (threatening ♘c6) 22...♖c7 23 ♘g6! fxg6 24 ♕xg6+ ♕f7 25 ♖d8+!, with another winning position, based yet again on the pin on the e-file.

18 ♗xd7+ ♔xd7 19 ♖xd5+ ♔c7?!

Not the best defence, though the reason is not immediately obvious: that it allows White to capture on f7 with check.

Then again, 19...♔c8 is not inspiring either. After 20 ♖f5 ♕c4 21 ♖e1 ♗d6 22 ♖e4 ♕b5 24 ♖xf7, Black's position is slightly better than in the game, but he is still losing. Or if he tries 21...♗f6?, then 22 ♖xf6! gxf6 23 ♕f5+ ♔b8 24 ♕xf6 is curtains.

20 ♖e1 ♗d6

Now if 20...♗f6 21 ♖e4 traps the queen, while 20...♖he8 21 ♖de5 ♕f6 22 ♕e4 wins the bishop.

21 ♖f5 ♕c4 22 ♖e4

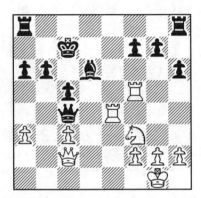

Showing the domination of White's major pieces. This is no accident. As we have seen, Black was behind in development throughout, and neither of his rooks have as yet moved at all.

22...♕b5

It's lucky there is a move, but it's not a good move.

23 ♖xf7+ ♔b8 24 ♖e6 ♖d8 25 c4

A later game concluded 25 ♕e4 ♗c7 26 g3 1-0 Y.Yakovich-R.Akesson, Stockholm 1999. One of the greatest embarrassments in chess is losing a game which has been played before. The winner remembers the opening, the opponent forgets, and everything is over all so quickly.

25...♕c6

Kasparov mentions one final tactic: if 25...♕a5 26 ♕e4 ♖a7 27 ♖xd6! wins.

26 ♘e5 ♕c8 27 ♕b1 1-0

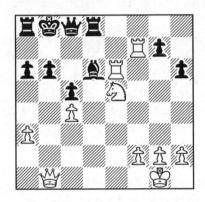

Postscript

We have now gone through a couple of dozen epic chess struggles, dating from the 1970s and the early 1980s. In some ways it might be regarded as an unusual selection from that time, with no wins by Fischer, and very little from either Karpov or Korchnoi. However, what we have been doing is examining a strand of chess development, not the whole picture. The players we have been considering are, or rather were, players who adored complexity, and searched hard over the board for ways to attack, rather than keeping the game solid. It was the Alekhine style of chess, as opposed to than the Capablanca style, and it was highly invigorating.

Karpov was still the World Champion for most of this period. Even in Tal's miracle event in Montreal 1979, he was in fact first equal with Karpov. It was becoming clear, though, that Kasparov was soon going to make a serious challenge to Karpov's supremacy. With the benefit of hindsight, it is easy to suggest that Kasparov was "inevitably" going to succeed him, but history does not always work like that. Karpov had the chance to dent Kasparov's ambitions in the 1984/85 endless match, and who knows what might have happened if Karpov, four points up after nine games, had taken the initiative? The 1980s matches between Kasparov and Karpov, between attack and defence, between tactical play and positional play, will be examined closely for decades to come.

Kasparov dominated through much of the 1990s, but less so as the 2000s progressed. This was not due to any decline of his own play, but rather because of younger challengers, such as Kramnik and Anand, coming through. In 2000, in the London BGN World Championship match, Kramnik paid enormous attention to eliminating Kasparov's plans of attack, winning two games, drawing thirteen, and no losses. Chess continues, and the standard of play improves.

Players at different levels will use the computer to improve their chess. That is inevitable and fully understandable, and the game will become increasingly tougher. However, players will never be able to analyse everything in advance, and while they may understand the basic ideas of attack and defence in various positions, with the help of computer analysis, ultimately it is still player versus player, with no electronic help, and long may this be true. At some stage, in almost every game, everyone has to think for themselves, uncertainty will kick in, and attacker and defender will have to try and find the correct moves over the board.

Index of Openings

Index of Players

Bold type indicates that a player had the black pieces.